the flash of capital

Asia-Pacific

Culture, Politics, and Society

Editors: Rey Chow, H. D. Harootunian,

and Masao Miyoshi

ERIC CAZDYN

the flash of capital

Film and Geopolitics in Japan

Duke University Press   Durham & London 2002

Printed in the United States of America on acid-free paper ⊗
Designed by Rebecca Giménez   Typeset in Trump Medieval by
Tseng Information Systems   Library of Congress Cataloging-in-
Publication Data appear on the last printed page of this book.

contents

illustrations

acknowledgments

I would never have dreamed of this book without Masao Miyoshi. I thank him for his critical infectiousness; his sharp-eyed and tireless intellect; his fearlessness to think about unfamiliar things; and the deadly seriousness with which he takes his job as a professor, critic, and teacher—while being quick to laugh at the profession and himself. To his intellectual mentorship and personal friendship I owe so much.

While researching in Japan I had the opportunity to work with Karatani Kojin, whose own ideas, especially about cultural and historical transformation, have influenced me tremendously. I also thank Fredric Jameson, who read drafts of some of these chapters and whose seminars and numerous books have generated many of the intellectual problems with which I have grappled over the years. Rosaura Sanchez and Don Wayne were indispensable in provoking many of the ideas at the inception of this work, and thanks also to Jean-Pierre Gorin and Haneda Sumiko, whose films have taught me more about cinema than the countless books that line my shelves. The students in my Film, Literature, and Globalization courses at the University of Toronto and the University of Oregon have given me much, especially the challenge of explaining why ideas matter and what we are doing at the university. I also thank the two anonymous readers at Duke University Press (as well as Reynolds Smith, Sharon Torian, and Shelley Wunder Smith) for their support and eminently useful responses to this project.

In Toronto I have been tremendously lucky to cross paths with Peter Fitting. The warmth he has shown me, along with his supreme hospitality and friendship has made life much more agreeable and captivating. Thanks must also go to my remarkable set of colleagues and friends. Invaluable among them are Leo Ching, Josh Goldstein, Andre Schmidt, John Zilcosky, Ian Balfour, Mitsuhiro Yoshimoto, Margherita Long, Jeff Hanes, Chris Hill, Rick Guisso, Sue Ehrlich, Mike Fishlin, Imre Szeman, Andrew Johnson, Graham Sanders, Christina Turner, Jim Fujii, Eric Gower, Karen Riley, Elaine Stavro, David Galbraith, Mari Paz Balibrea Enriquez, David Kersh, Abigail Pugh. Thanks, finally, to Norman and Suzanne Cohen for their endless support over the years.

introduction

Like every medium, film exceeds itself. It bleeds into the meanings of education and public policy, into the landscapes we see when looking out a train window and on the urban streets we walk when killing time. Likewise, Japan—the nation—exceeds itself. It bleeds into all that which is not Japan; into the workings and meanings of the world system; into our imaginations, whether we live there or not, whether we know it or not, whether we like it or not. The task of this work is to theorize a cultural history based on these excesses—to spotlight the spaces in which film and the nation fly away from their fixed borders, in which aesthetics and geopolitics meet—in order better to explain historical change and transformation in modern Japan and beyond.

There are countless ways to organize such a history, from the encyclopedic to the stylistic, from a way based on famous individuals to one based on the prosaic lives of the rest of us. This history is organized around a relation: the transforming relation between the history of Japanese film and the history of Japanese capitalism. Unlike in the West, where capitalism proper is about two hundred years old and the history of film is only half that long, in Japan the two histories share about the same span of time — one hundred years. This chronological correspondence does not make the relation between the two histories any easier to analyze; it does, however, generate a set of very rich theoretical problems that turn on the old conceptual saw of mediation (or, in this case, how aesthetic categories dynamically relate with political-economic ones). To say that I want to study the relation between culture and capitalism, that I want to tie an unlikely knot between film aesthetics and geopolitics, does not necessarily mean that my interest hinges on the profits and losses incurred by the film industry in Japan. The focus, instead, is on the aesthetic just as much as it is on the political-economic, on the text just as much as on the context. I am interested in how films relate to political-economic problems, problems that seem worlds away from the very immediate plot concerns of a film's narrative (for instance, how a melodrama about two sisters relates to the Japanese colonial project or a twelfth-century story of a famous bandit relates to the immediate postwar debate over subjectivity). By theorizing these relations and producing these connections (by pushing together into the same idea two elements that seem to have nothing to do with each other), Japanese modernity is approached from a rather unorthodox direction, one that hopes to offer a fresh perspective of the various functions film (and our reading of film) plays in shaping individual consciousness, thinking, and everyday life in Japan.

The relation between the history of Japanese film and the history of Japanese capitalism holds within it four problems: Japan, film, capitalism, and history. As for what is commonly held to be "Japan," the problem lies in how we might be able to think of it as being simultaneously the same as and different from the "West." Japan as a modern nation (that is, as a historical formation and idea that solidified in the Meiji period, from 1868 to 1912, and that may well be eroding with the rise of globalization) occupies a different history from that of the nations of the West, but at the same time it shares the same world situation. Japanese capitalism is different from capitalisms in the West, but the same fundamental rules of capital apply to both. Japanese film is different from Western film, but both use the same materials. To walk the tightrope between outright difference and outright identity will be one of the underlying risks of this work. It seems a risk well worth taking, however, because so much depends on what we understand Japan to mean and how we understand it to mean. For example, I have always found it strange that many people understand film as a Western invention that, despite being deftly adapted by the Japanese, still leaves traces of the West on every print that is made. Is there not a similar logic in saying that the invention of the Western printing press marks every Japanese *shosetsu* (prose narrative) as Western? It is not too provocative to argue that without Johannes Gutenberg or Thomas Edison, the shosetsu and Japanese film still would have emerged (indeed, were emerging). Film may well be contingent on modernization, and modernization may well have happened in the West first, but modernization is part of a world structure that seems infinitely more productive to understand as having no firsts, only dependencies.

Another example has to do with the raging debate over whether Japanese capitalism works in the same way as capitalism in the West. This fight over identity and difference seems to reveal less about the nature of Japanese capitalism than about how a particular individual ideologically invests in capitalism as an adequate system to provide for the welfare of human beings. For many who understand Japanese capitalism as having very little in common with Western capitalism (or very little in common with capitalism, for that matter), and therefore as rendering irrelevant neo-classical and Marxist categories of analysis, the idea of a planned market economy that can, as one scholar puts it, square the circle of a managed economy without the disasters that befell the socialist states stands in for the hope that the logic of capitalism is not fundamentally to blame for the problems and inequalities that have been, and continue to be, registered on its watch. During the 1980s, for example, emphasizing difference provided a way to come to terms with the problems of capitalism by shifting blame to the architects of older-style capitalisms (U.S., U.K.) for their orthodoxy or by reproaching the architects of newer capitalisms (Japan, the "Asian Dragons") for not playing fair. Since the onset of the Asian economic crisis in the second half of the 1990s, however, the emphasis on difference to legitimate capitalist logic has remained, but the terms have been inverted. The leaders of the Asian economies are now criticized for financial irresponsibility and rigidity, while those in the

United States are praised for their flexibility and leadership. Those who draw an identity between Japanese capitalism and Western capitalisms, however, seem to come to terms with the problems of capitalism—from ecological destruction to low pay and poor working conditions for many of the world's citizens and the perpetual exportation of problems to the Third World—by viewing them as not structurally contingent and waiting faithfully for natural market mechanisms to solve the difficulties on their own. The point in translating this debate into the philosophical terms of identity and difference is to reveal that by attempting to think about Japan and Japanese capitalism as simultaneously *same and other* vis-à-vis the West and Western capitalism might help us to (1) forestall a discourse of firsts, hierarchies, and absolute difference or identity; (2) draw attention to what may be the ideological stakes and historical limitations motivating various positions regarding Japanese film and capitalist history; and (3) bring us closer to the notion that Japan and the world—however different or the same they may be—are constitutively related.

Film faces the same problem as Japan: The task is to see it as the same as and different from other cultural forms all at once. This was the aim that several Japanese film theorists writing before and after World War II (such as Imamura Taihei, Iijima Tadashi, and Iwasaki Akira) attempted to reach when they argued that film should be considered an art form that is as rich as literature, music, or drama while, at the same time, arguing for the unique possibilities and limitations that film possesses.[1] Today, the first part of this fight has been won: Very few dispute Japanese film's inclusion as an art form, especially when the canon of Ozu, Mizoguchi, and Kurosawa is routinely brandished as representing a high point in Japanese culture, often placed on the same pedestal as Basho, Zeami, and Hokusai. The problem of film's difference from the other arts, however, remains to be worked out. In addition to constructing a cultural theory in this work, I will also construct a film theory, one of whose tasks will be to demonstrate the particularities of film's relation to capitalism and where that relation differs from capitalism's relation to literature, drama, and other cultural forms.

History, finally, is the crucible of this work. Mentioning the histories of film and capitalism in the same sentence might evoke unfriendly ghosts of past, such as reflectionism, economism, or any number of heavy-handed interpretive methods that relegate culture to the status of a wholly instrumental tool of capitalist reproduction—or, even worse, to that of an utterly insignificant byproduct of capital. The most important risk taken here is to push film and capitalism into the same idea without reducing the complexity of either the aesthetic or political economy. To do this, I will focus on form—or, more specifically, on the formal relations between cinematic categories (such as acting, film adaptation, film historiography, canon formation, aesthetic representation, and pornography) and capitalist categories (such as accumulation methods, social agency, nationalist discourse, money, political representation, and crisis). I zoom in on those critical moments of Japanese modern history during which the forms of both cinematic and capitalist categories mutate. My project is to map and theorize these mutations in order to make sense of how film—for good or ill—has shaped and has been shaped by the Japanese modern nation and, ultimately, how it affects the lives of those who live through it.

To make sense of these formal relations and their transformations, I produce the concept of "problem cinema." Problem cinema refers to the historically dominant problem with which all cinematic production must (in however unconscious or indirect a way) come to terms. The three problems I identify are coterminous—they do not begin and end on a linear timeline but exist simultaneously—and, at the same time, correspond to three moments of Japanese modernity: (1) between being colonized and being a colonizer nation of the pre–World War II moment; (2) between the individual and collective of the postwar moment; and (3) between the national and the transnational of the contemporary moment.

The first problem is well known. By the end of the nineteenth century, more than three-fourths of the planet had been colonized by a handful of Western powers; Japan's Asian neighbors were being swallowed up one by one; and it was clear that the capitalist development of a nation-state was inextricably tied to the availability of markets abroad and the capacity to compete over these markets with other colonial metropoles. In short, Japan could either promote its own colonial project or become politically enfeebled and next in line to be colonized. It could either manage the economic crisis of the 1920s by violently breaking open new markets abroad or become economically crippled and defeated. This problem informed everyday life in Japan; it wafted through every artist's studio, every dance hall, every home. It may not have been found in the direct content of films or in the conversations of families, but it was there nonetheless, and the task is not to expose bald determinations but to make subtle connections between this paradox of colonialism and the film aeŝthetics of the day.

The second problem—of the individual—overlaps with that of colonialism but emerged in the post–World War II moment as dominant. Contrary to some accounts, Japan was far from annihilated following the war; in fact, it was poised for recovery and actually encouraged by the U.S. Occupation Forces to continue many of its prewar institutions, from its tightly integrated and micromanaged economic and political structure to the highly influential ideological structure of the emperor system. Nevertheless, Japan was in disrepair and miserable shape when those somber Japanese statesmen signed the surrender document on the U.S. battleship *Missouri* (on September 2, 1945) in Tokyo Bay. Ten years of wealth production (equivalent to that gained between 1935 and 1945) had been snuffed out by indiscriminate Allied bombings and attacks.[2] Homelessness was rampant; the built environment blasted. Like the very moment that one wakes from a dream, it was time to question all that people had believed and trusted over the past fifteen years. People asked, "What happened?" "How could political representation so radically fail?" "What could I have done?" "What is an 'I'? What is a 'We'?" "How do I (an individual subject), and how do We (a collective nation), prevent something like this from ever happening again?" The discourse of the day turned on individual subjectivity (in the form of the *shutaisei* [subjectivity] debate): The individual must be rethought, fleshed out, constructed, fostered so as to prevent a future breakdown in civil society and lack of popular accountability. A sense of self—of one's capacity and legitimacy to act as an individual and to intervene against the state and collective opinion—was crucial to keep the nation from ever being hijacked again. At the same time, an emphasis on the collective and the nation (not too dissimilar in logic to the discourse promoted during the war) threatened to trump the individual. The individual must be sacrificed, must give himself or herself over to the collective and to the nation, to rebuild the country. One must submit to the occupation and the reconstruction project. Perseverance and the suppression of one's desires was the order of the day. Japan lost the war, and the citizens had to pay by mortgaging their individuality. But how can one be free to act on one's own, to resist a militaristic oligarchy, if from the other side of the state's mouth comes the order radically to sacrifice one's individuality? (And on top of all this, the categories of subject, individual, and agency are riddled with so many philosophical cracks that it is impossible to think through them without backing up and questioning their own production and possibility.) Indeed, like the paradox of colonialism in which the very logic of the problem short-circuits a solution, this paradox of the individual provided no solution. People were forced to exist at the dead center of contradiction.

The third problem is that of globalization. Again, the logic of the problem is similar to that of the first two problems. "Globalization" is the god term of the new millennium: From global culture and corporations to global poverty and politics, there seems to be no way to escape the term's endless reach. But has culture not always been trafficked? Have trade and exchange not always exceeded local borders? Why is globalization any different from an older form of internationalization that has marked modernity ever since nations needed to justify colonial expansion? Or, why is globalization any different from Nakasone Yasuhiro's discourse of internationalization (*kokusai-ka*) in the mid-1980s, which reflected little more than a desire to placate U.S. complaints about Japan's huge trade surplus? Throughout this work, I will use the term "globalization" not as a gratuitous code word for the international but as a historical category that refers to the prodigious leap in the world system that has occurred over the past few decades. Fired by cybernetic technology, flexible accumulation networks, the rise of transnational institutions (corporations and trade organizations), new immigration and cultural flows, new speeds and scales, "globalization" first and foremost marks a transformation in the operations of the nation-state. Globalization is still capitalism. And capitalism is still based on the profit motive and a specific relationship between capital and labor; capitalism is still a system structured in dominance and still one of the most productive places to go to understand how power works in the world today. But there is a difference: Capitalism turns differently on the nation-state compared to how it did in the past.

This transformed configuration of the world system, in which the balance of power is shifting away from the nation-state, dramatically affects the operations of representational democracy and nation-state–based economies. Transnational institutions (such as corporations, regulating boards, and banks), as well as the emerging transnational capitalist class (composed of high-level bureaucrats, executives, politicians, and academics), appropriate the role of the nation-state while preserving the latter's ideological usefulness.[3] In other words, at the precise moment in which the decision-making power of the nation-state is declining, nationalist ideologies and identities are as strong as ever. In Japan, one need look only as far as the re-energized Flag and Anthem movements.[4] There are two immediate explanations for this. First, a proper global ideology has yet to emerge to work alongside the global political-economic realities.[5] Second, transnational corporatism can consolidate its power more effectively by hiding behind the flag of the nation-state. In short, national narratives and identities are some of the most profitable commodities transnational corporations sell.

One of the common confusions in globalization discourse is the assumption that its political-economic and cultural-ideological dimensions move at the same speed. For this reason, many political and cultural theorists expect to find the rise of global cultural movements and global working-class movements on par with the rise of global corporations. Whereas no one is surprised to learn that chief executives of transnational corporations may have more power than local or national politicians in congresses and parliaments around the world, faith is still strong in the idea of national identities and ideologies—the primary units by which people locate themselves in the world. We still root for our own teams in the Olympics and our own armies in war while the political-economic stakeholders—who have no nostalgia—focus on the bottom line. National debates and divisions over television content or local control over the movie industry noisily make the front pages of our national newspapers while the business pages quietly tell a story of political-economic consolidation and transnational cooperation.

This contradiction between the *national* and the *transnational* (Japan and the world) has produced a post-miracle malaise in Japan that, despite some important inroads that have been made toward social change by various local groups, seems to be at an all-time high.[6] In the face of huge government scandals as well as the unraveling of the Japanese financial system, political pronouncements of reform and other tinkering around the institutional edges are shrugged off by most of the populace as just so many expedient defenses of a thoroughly flawed system. At the same time, pointing to the economic "miracle" as a way to delegitimate criticism (the sure-fire strategy from the postwar period until the bursting of the bubble in the early 1990s) no longer seems to work for those who are as weary of U.S.-style global capitalism as they are of their own neo-national blowhards. Along with this skepticism and relative stasis come some very difficult questions. How does one live in a world in which national tropes are being appealed to every day on the level of ideology while, on the levels of production, consumption, and distribution, the decision-making power of the nation-state is declining? How are national ideologies and identities refigured within the emerging space of transnationalism? How does one resist certain globalizing trends without inadvertently embracing a Japanese exceptionalism? Is this last question (when understood more broadly) not the fundamental issue faced by the eclectic medley of activists who have come together at the World Trade Organization (WTO) gathering (Seattle, 1999), International Monetary Fund (IMF) and World Bank meeting (Washington, D.C., 2000), Group of Eight (G-8) Summit (Okinawa, 2000), and other events in Prague, Durban, Quebec City, Genoa, and elsewhere? That is, how does one criticize current trends of globalization without simultaneously speaking the same language as the xenophobes, ultra-nationalists, and Luddites of one's own national situation? At the present moment, there seems to be no available language to solve this problem; the situation is something like an eyeless needle that can be threaded only by radical transformations in the social situation. In other words, only after globalization processes come into greater relief, only after national identities weaken even more, will an effective language emerge with which to solve these historically particular contradictions (which, of course, means that different contradictions will emerge that will be equally unspeakable). This offers one frame through which to examine the current paradox of globalization. But (and this explains why I have gone on longer about this third problem) it also offers a frame through which to view the other problems mentioned thus far. We must live in the center of the contradiction until the movement of history—a movement shaped by individual choices and collective action just as much as by the structural logic of the historical moment itself—reconfigures the situation.[7]

And then there is the aesthetic. It is here that a close reading of cinema enters the picture, for it is formal inventions on the level of the film aesthetic that figure a way out of these impossible situations before a grammar becomes available to make sense of them. In other words, what is unrepresentable in everyday discourse (from a back-alley chat to a political stump speech) is flashed on the level of the aesthetic. Whether they are utopias in acting (experiments in representing the body, of framing the actor in the mise-en-scène, of positioning the actor in relation to the structure of the film narrative or the director); in writing film history (writing to reach a predetermined goal or writing to break open new possibilities that cannot yet be thought); in documentary filmmaking (attending to how the act of documenting an event necessarily transforms the event itself); or in thematics (post-human cyborgs, nationless cities), these formal inventions figure the struggle to solve a problem for which there is no immediate solution. By paying close attention to the details of cinematic texts, I read the works of Japanese film history as so many symptoms of the most pressing social problems of Japanese modernity. These symptoms allegorize the dreams and nightmares of modernity—dreams and nightmares that necessarily will be absent from the economic ledgers and historical fact books that crowd our libraries.[8]

It is crucial to resist the temptation to view these problems of modernity as separate and neatly corresponding to this or that stretch of time. Rather, they overlap and crisscross; they persist and mutate from one historical moment to the next. Still, in spite of their coexistence, I have situated them in relation to three moments in Japan's modernity. One way to underscore the significance of this historiographical complexity is to refer to the other great (perhaps the greatest) transformation to occur in Japanese modernity—namely, the transformation to modernity itself in the latter part of the nineteenth century. In chapter 1, the discussion turns to the emergence of modern subjectivities in relation to new technology (railways), fiscal and monetary policies (taxation and money), social spaces (modern cities), and other forms introduced by the Meiji government. Perception—the way of imaging the world and thus the way of making sense of everyday life and relating to others—transforms with modernity. But certainly, people did not wake up one day in 1868 to find themselves modern, no longer connected with the feudal ways that had dominated the country for the previous two hundred and fifty years. The corrosion of the pre-modern with the development of mercantile capitalism that triggered the restructuring known as the Meiji *Ishin* (restoration) did not replace or cancel the persistence of pre-modern modes of subjectivity (if this term can be used anachronistically for a moment). Rather, the post-Meiji engagement with modern forms of subjectivity required a negotiation with pre-modern cultural forms. Likewise, the pre-modern engagement with cultural forms involved a negotiation with emerging modern forms.[9] And on top of all this, different subjects (based on gender, class, and ethnic identities, for example) came to terms differently with these transformations. The same can be said for the way in which the earlier problems of colonialism and the individual persist at the contemporary moment, just as the current problem of globalization existed in nascent form throughout the twentieth century.

Still, the stake in retaining a diachronic impulse (together with a synchronic logic of discontinuity) in charting the dominance of these problems has much to do with the stake in retaining the narrative of Japanese capitalism. That is, I find it indispensable to recognize Japanese capitalism's unity as a system that, although continually expanding and at critical moments mutating into different incarnations, holds recognizable continuities through the course of its existence. There are certain rules of capitalism, in other words, that have less to do with the mode's self-destruction after saturating the globe than with the concepts of surplus value, commodity fetishism, and crisis. These generalities, whose realities in Japanese everyday life are special to the capitalist mode of production, have remained continuous—although forever changing—from early mercantile capitalism following the Meiji Restoration, to its monopoly stage before and after World War II, up to its present transnational embodiment.

The object of study, then, is the whole one hundred years of film and capitalism in Japan, with a focus on the relations between these two registers at particular moments of transformation. Rather than dedicate each chapter to a different historical moment or problem of modernity, I move (in each chapter) from problem to problem and moment to moment using certain cinematic categories as the pivot. This produces a dialectical repetition and a certain scholarly accumulation that intends to reach a critical mass in dealing with the more difficult theoretical problems circulating through the work, such as mediation (the relation between various levels within the social formation), periodization (continuity and discontinuity in both film and capitalist history), aesthetic allegory (a movement to represent the unrepresentable), and directorial and spectatorial agency (individual control and lack thereof over the production and consumption of both aesthetic and political meaning).

One of the underlying arguments is that the method of telling the story of Japanese film directly influences the type of story that ends up being told. Some stories place Japanese film's golden age in the 1930s; others place it in the '50s. Some tell a story of decline, others of progress. Some focus on directors, others on audiences. The point is that the chosen historiographical method is crucial in shaping the kinds of questions asked (and not asked), interpretive claims made, and, ultimately, positions taken. By organizing my own history around the transforming relation between the film aesthetic and political economy, and by examining how cinema necessarily exceeds itself and gestures to the sociological problems of its day, the story of Japanese film that ends up being told is one that is not often heard. It foregrounds directors (such as Kamei Fumio, Hani Susumu, Imamura Shohei, Shindo Kaneto, Ogawa Shinsuke, Haneda Sumiko, and Hara Kazuo) and problems (film's relation to the prose narrative, film historiography, pornography, canon formation, and acting) that are usually relegated to footnotes in canonical histories. My own historiographical impulse, moreover, underscores Japanese film's critical role in shaping social relations while always containing within its very logic the possibility for producing meaningful disruption and social change.

Yet, as I will argue in chapter 2, it is not only the historiographical method that shapes the story that is told but also the moment in history in which the story is being told. And this moment of globalization, when the nation-state and national cultures are transforming (however unevenly), demands a rethinking of what it means to write a national film history. Cable-television stations that broadcast "foreign films" day and night, local video stores that carry new and classic foreign titles for easy rental, the emergence of multiplexes that reserve one screen for the most recent foreign film, and the recent boom in international film festivals have brought with them a new industry of international film scholarship and criticism. International film compendiums, director and actor profiles, film Web sites, and reviews are legion. What is notable about this new industry, both in and out of academic film studies, is how similar its forms and methods are to older methods of history, theory, and criticism. I do not mean to suggest that there is no value in employing older methods that are not fashionable and different. Rather, the argument is that the formulation of one's methods and theories must always be in movement and in historic restructuring along with their objects of study (in this case, the globalization of film and capitalism).

This leads to a related problem that has surfaced recently in the field of Japanese studies: whether Western theory or Japanese theory should be applied to Japanese objects of study. Is it imperialistic to subject Japan to Western theory, to use it as just another case to test the universality of a theory? Would it be less Orientalist and less presumptuous to search out native theories and apply them to Japanese objects? Given what I have just written regarding the movement of theory and the necessary relation between the thought mode in question and the freshness of the issue at hand, we should already begin to detect the false problem in this concern. Not only is there the question of how to categorize the work of Japanese living abroad, non-Japanese living in Japan, or the work of Japanese who themselves are immersed in Western theory, but those invested in this debate appear to take theory as a template into which Japan-related content can be placed. It is crucial that the assumptions of this debate be rethought, especially since "theory" has recently attained scholarly legitimacy in the Japan field. The theories that we set off with, Western or Japanese, are only points of departure that are then shaped by, just as they shape, the objects of study into which they bump. To put this another way: Theories change with every subsequent theorization. My own theorization of Japanese film history intends to feed off of the vigor and restructurings of the contemporary world system, with the hope of generating its own dynamic analysis of the past one hundred years of Japanese film and capitalism.

I. relation

Film, Capital, Transformation

There is a story about Ichikawa Danjuro IX, the renowned *kabuki* actor who "starred" in the oldest remaining Japanese film, titled *Momijigari* (Maple viewing) made in 1899 (figs. 1 and 2). Using seventy feet of film and a stationary camera temporarily set up two hundred feet behind the Tokyo *Kabuki-za* (Kabuki theater), Danjuro and Kikugoro Onoe V performed a single scene from *Momijigari*.[1] In fact, Danjuro had to be persuaded by the director of the Kabuki-za, Inoue Takejiro, to do the performance and did not view the film until the following year, when a screening was held at his private residence. A newspaper at the time reported that during the screening Danjuro exclaimed, "It is terribly strange (*fushigi*) to be able to see my own dance."[2] At that time, Danjuro also made it clear that the film should never be screened during his lifetime. What did Danjuro find so strange? And, more important, why did he find it so strange?

1. Ichikawa Danjuro IX in *Momijigari* (Maple viewing).

Danjuro's story is usually interpreted to mean that he was disturbed by the filmic representation of his dance and that he recoiled from the distortion produced by the "popular" and "fledgling" medium of film against the "high" and "traditional" art of kabuki (of course, kabuki as "high" culture had itself recently been refigured from its more popular roots). The story becomes more illuminating, however, if we think about it in terms of the rise of Japanese modernity and the role that film and visuality played in its formation. The phrasing of Danjuro's statement is important: "It is terribly strange to be able to see my own dance." It is not strange, in other words, to watch *Momijigari*, and it may not even be strange to watch film for the first time. What is terribly strange is seeing oneself in this new technological medium.

Danjuro's experience speaks to the emergence of modern subjectivity, in which the strangeness or shock of seeing oneself in film for the first time produces an *awareness* of being—at the same time—spectator and spectacle, subject and object, seer and seen. For the first time, Danjuro understood what it meant to be himself in the modern world; as spectator of himself, he obtained self-consciousness of that famous kabuki actor called Ichikawa Danjuro. Of course, not every Japanese filmgoer at the turn of the twentieth century was able to see his or her own image projected back. But as was the case during Japan's first public film screening held in Osaka in 1897 (when Louis and Auguste Lumière screened twenty films depicting New York, France, England, Italy, and Russia) the image of non-Japan can be just as significant in producing the awareness of that new thing called the modern Japanese nation.[3]

Rey Chow, in a different context, calls this the "menace of visuality," by which she means that the shock of the visual medium in the non-West produces (1) the realization of individual and national existence as a spectacle; and (2) the realization of a powerful new medium that threatens the role enjoyed by the more traditional art forms.[4] Simultaneous with this menace, however, is what might be called a liberation of visuality, a utopian dimension of recognition and self-consciousness; a realization of hitherto nonexistent possibilities. In other words, the shock represents—at one and the same time—the liberation from older forms of visuality and older systemic constraints as well as the crucial menacing element in reenforcing a whole new system of control. It is this dual process of menace and liberation that was set in motion at the precise moment in which Japan was transforming from an early modern society to a modern one, from a culture dominated by the oral and written to one dominated by the visual. It was this process, moreover, that broke open a whole new pack of possible modern subjects and modern nations that were realizable in Meiji Japan.

But the emergence of the modern subject and nation cannot be separated from the emergence of Japanese capitalism. Capitalism demands a certain way of coming to terms with time and space, with work, with consumption, with abstraction, with the contract—in short, with the concrete over and above the transcendental, with the part over and above the whole. Capital-

2. Ichikawa Danjuro IX.

ism requires the type of "modern self" that film was instrumental in making possible. To underscore this point, we can return to Danjuro's film experience. In the summer of 1903, four years after the filming of *Momijigari*, Danjuro was contracted to perform in Osaka. Because of a sudden illness (which led to his death later in the year), Danjuro could not make the journey, and he was forced to cancel the performance. It was at this point that Danjuro went back on his word never to screen *Momijigari* publicly in his lifetime and had the print immediately sent to Osaka to compensate for his absence. Here the cinematic reproduction of Danjuro's performance was recognized as a more satisfactory substitute than a performance by another troupe. Wildly successful, the print remained in Osaka for more than four weeks of screenings, despite the original one-week plan.[5] Film, like the transformation of consciousness that it helped enable, was more conducive to capitalism than the theater. The die was cast.

Like modern visuality, capitalism in Japan also came equipped with its own menacing/dystopian and liberating/utopian possibilities. My point here is to relate the emergence of film with the first moment of capitalist development in which a new individualism was required to meet the needs of Japanese consumer society (a domestic market) and service an ever specializing division of labor; at the same time, limits were placed on this individualism by the new categories of capitalist production, such as commodity exchange, labor–management relations, the extraction of surplus value, and the modern contract. For example, as commodity production became dominant, the new form of money as an "abstract thing"—itself a contradiction insofar as money is immutable, exchangeable, and perfectly replaceable (abstract) at the same time that it is concrete, material and destructible (a thing) —corresponded to a new form of thinking, a form of thinking that experienced different possibilities and limitations in its quest to make sense of everyday life.[6] Or there are labor–management relations: The contract Danjuro signed with the Osaka Kabuki-za obliged the screening of *Momijigari*, forcing Danjuro to break his promise with the theater's management and enter into unfamiliar relations. Moreover, forms of distribution and consumption enabled by the reproducible film negative itself were transformed, thus reconfiguring the way Danjuro's performance produced value. Repetition, reproducibility, exchangeability, ubiquity, simultaneity, circulation,

3. Promotional flyer for Haneda Sumiko's
Kataoka Nizaemon: Kabuki Actor.

distribution, mass production—these were the new categories of film and
capitalism.

Let us jump ahead almost one hundred years to an event in which another
famous kabuki actor watched himself on screen. In 1994, Kataoka Nizaemon
was helped onto the stage after a screening of all five parts of Haneda Sumiko's eight-hour documentary about Nizaemon's life, *Kabuki yakusha:
Kataoka Nizaemon* (Kabuki actor: Kataoka Nizaemon). Ninety-one years old
and blind, Nizaemon remarked after extended applause from the audience:
"Although I could not see the screen, because I could hear the film, I was
still able to see it" (figs. 3 and 4).[7] Whereas Danjuro could see but not hear the
silent *Momijigari,* Nizaemon could hear but not see Haneda's film. I will use
this inversion as a way to think about the first great transformation of visual
representation and reception that occurred in modern Japanese history.

Nizaemon was born in the same year that Danjuro died (1903). Although
he had been on stage from the age of two and led a very confined life within
the kabuki world, Nizaemon lived during the age of film, during the age of
the mechanical image. One of the most powerful scenes in Haneda's film
comes when Nizaemon, now fully blind, is shown riding the Tokyo subway
by himself. Nizaemon navigates the huge staircases, the train cars, the ticket
machines, and the throngs of people with the greatest precision and ease.
Since childhood, Nizaemon explains, he has adored the trains and has rid-
den them so many times that to do so without seeing is no feat at all. But, of

4. Kataoka Nizaemon on the cover of promotional booklet for Haneda's *Kataoka Nizaemon: Kabuki Actor.*

course, Nizaemon is not alone: Haneda and her cameraman follow (or direct) his every move. What is stunning about this scene is how similar Nizaemon's movement through space is to the film's. For example, there is a close-up of a ticket dispenser, then a medium shot of the crowd, followed by a quick cut to a close-up of the ticket gate. The spatial and temporal categories that govern the scene in Haneda's film and the perceptual ones that the film anticipates of the viewer—forms of memory, attention span, imagination, spatial and temporal mapping—seem to be employed by Nizaemon. The shots selected by Nizaemon are organized to construct continuous movement in a thoroughly discontinuous spatial reality. In other words, Nizaemon, notwithstanding his blindness, apprehends the reality of the train station with what might be thought of as an interior camera of his own so that he can "see" and "direct" his way through the station. Nizaemon is not only the subject of Haneda's film; he is film itself.[8]

This is to say that Nizaemon's ability to see through his blindness occurs not only because he knows his life and craft so well, but also because he has internalized the conventions of film so well: The moving image becomes his own thought, just as thought becomes the moving image. Like the shock that Danjuro experienced, this cinematic visuality contains both utopian and dystopian dimensions. Unable to throw the on–off switch to suspend dominant visuality—with no chance, in other words, to leave the theater of our historical situation and turn off the film that is our individual lives—a very dark side emerges, one that is inextricably connected to all new means of circulating mass ideology and, thus, connected to the horrors of the twentieth century. But to be able to see even when one does not see produces new possibilities for change and social collectivization, an imagined community vis-à-vis the image. Indeed, the dynamic play of utopian and dystopian events throughout Japanese modernity—militarism, fascism, social welfare, large-scale collective movements—seems to attest to this dual dimension.

Nizaemon's experience can be used to mark off the second great moment in the transformation of visuality and image culture in Japan: the first being when a spectator gains self-consciousness at the strangeness of seeing images projected onto a screen, and the second when one sees even when one does not see. The first moment gestures to the relation between technologized images and visuality and the formation of the modern nation and modern subjects, and the second gestures to the transformation of modern subjects that have been born into an existing situation of technologized visuality. This second moment, moreover, relates to the first significant transformation of the capitalist system (which occurred in the late 1920s and '30s) in coordination with Japan's colonial project, during which there was a radical consolidation of industry and banking organized around the strengthening of the *zaibatsu* (privately owned industrial empires) system. Before incorporating difference and the dialectic into the moments that these two stories represent, and before elaborating on the historiographical problem of transformation and on the very knotty relation between culture and capitalism, there is a third moment to be delineated: the contemporary moment of globalization, a moment in which one sees but does not see.

The 1995 release of sarin gas on a Tokyo subway by members of the Aum Shinrikyo cult serves as a striking example of this third moment.[9] After the incident, the Japanese police commenced a full-scale hunt for seven Aum fugitives. No matter where one went in Japan—from urban side streets to village telephone booths—it was impossible not to run into leaflets, flyers, posters, placards, billboards, lanterns, full-body replicas, and other types of visual advertisements of these seven fugitives (figs. 5, 6, and 7). And at home, one could not escape the barrage of the fugitives' images on the television. In 1996, the advertisements were still ubiquitous, but everyone in the coun-

5. Aum placards in Takadanobaba, Tokyo. Photo by Eric Cazdyn.

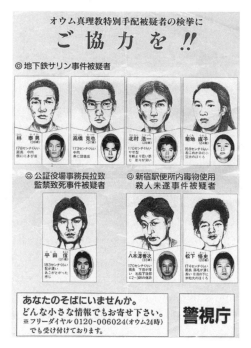

6. Aum police flyer; the first line of text in the
bottom paragraph reads: "Are they near you?"

7. Full-body of Aum fugitives displayed in Shibuya Station. Photo by Eric Cazdyn.

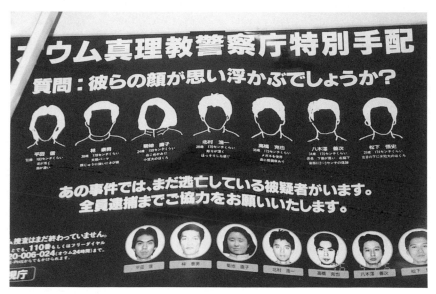

8. Poster of Aum fugitives displayed on a Tokyo subway car; the text above the silhouettes reads: "What do their faces remind you of?" Photo by Eric Cazdyn.

try was so familiar with the seven faces that the police altered their strategy. One advertisement, for example, no longer showed the fugitives' faces; instead only the outlines of their faces remained, with their individual features cut out (fig. 8). The advertisement read: "Do these shapes remind you of anyone?" The police assumed that, without seeing the faces of the Aum fugitives, everyone should still be able to see. They were relying on the logic that accounted for why the blind Nizaemon could still see Haneda's film: The installation of visuality was so complete that, when the images were finally shut off, they would doubtless persist, still organizing the lives of those who lived through them—not unlike the way in which a recent amputee might still feel and live with his or her severed limb. It is a logic to which any advertising executive can attest: The more images of a product that abound, the more a potential consumer—at the point of purchase—will remember. Apparently not. In December 1996, one of the Aum fugitives walked into a neighborhood station in downtown Tokyo. No one recognized him until, after patiently waiting his turn, he identified himself. Information circulated by way of the technologized image, but reception to these images and their effects have been transformed. Unlike Danjuro's seeing but not hearing and Nizaemon's not seeing but seeing, in contemporary life, people are saturated with images and tend to see but do not see.[10]

To not see what one sees suggests a certain degree of collective unconsciousness, a sort of automatonization by which awareness and sensitivity to one's everyday surroundings and life are severely weakened. But, as usual, things are more complicated than this. There is another dimension in which not seeing what one sees turns out *not* to be an altogether regrettable situation. In fact, wrapped up in this non-recognition is the possibility of recognizing something else, something that does not yet exist, something that can exist in the future. Or to come at this from the other direction: This non-recognition might be a symptom of a different way of seeing, of different subjectivities. Perhaps the sheer abundance of images might shape a symptomological subject, one (however split) that sees something other than what she or he is looking at. But what else is there to see in the mug shot of an Aum fugitive?

Triggered by the global capitalist crises of the 1970s, capitalism has been reconfigured—marked by the greater flexibility of accumulation methods, information technology, supranational institutions, and the emergence of

cybernetic currency markets that absorb and expand idle capital without re-
sorting to the usual fixes provided by what used to be called the welfare state
and the Third World. Compared with earlier moments of capitalist global
relations, this reconfiguration betrays different circuits and flows, different
temporalities and spaces, different dynamics of cause and effect. These dynamics appear unthinkable at present; they currently exceed the possibilities to properly map them. In other words, the dynamics produce a train station that is no longer navigable.[11]

The point is to stress the relation between these transformed capitalist
categories and the forms by which the Aum fugitives' images are organized
and perceived. It is true that there is a long history of non-recognition of
images of wanted people, but my point is that there is a qualitative difference
between how the Aum advertising campaigns occurred and how older campaigns were conducted. This is also why I have chosen a non-filmic example
to signify this third moment. Like the way film shaped literature in the early
twentieth century (for example, the way serial descriptions of a cluttered
Tokyo street by the wandering *flaneur* in Kawabata Yasunari's prose fiction
Asakusa Kuranaiden [1929–30] are clearly influenced by the tracking shot
in cinema), today new-media production and delivery systems undeniably
shape contemporary cinema.[12] Information technology now makes possible
a heightened diffusion of imagery. Not only are the images themselves digitally generated, producing different graphic possibilities—such as one Aum
poster in which the fugitives' features are mixed and matched with different
hair styles and even genders (fig. 9), but the advertisements also compete in
a transformed built environment and work in relation to transformed habits
of perceptions and consciousness. In short, transformations in accumulation
methods dynamically relate to transformations in aesthetic forms and the
reception to these forms. Or to put this still another way: Social categories
formally correspond to (are constituted by and constitute) categories of individual thought and the body.

The Aum anecdote stands in for a moment in which meanings and effects
of capitalist accumulation and images are transforming, ratcheted up to a
different level of abstraction, and the way people experience them (albeit
variously) has also transformed. What needs to be stressed is that I have not
worked through these stories in order to argue that perception is structurally
determined and that everyone, without struggle and without intersecting

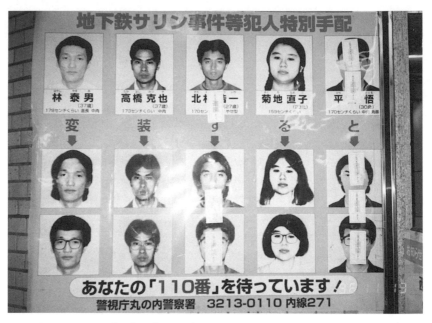

9. Large Aum poster displayed in a subway station with the face of each fugitive digitally remastered. Photo by Eric Cazdyn.

pluralities, makes meaning in the same way. And I have not delineated the various issues within cognitive science, such as the neurobiological dimension of our categories of perception. Rather, my point is to use these three stories as a point of departure in order to argue for the formal and dynamic relation between how we produce meaning and how we produce wealth (the relation between cultural value and economic value), and to track this relation as it changes from one historical moment to the next throughout Japanese modernity. Pushing these seemingly disparate categories of culture and capital into the same idea allows different questions to be asked, such as how and why the meanings and effects of film and perception transformed in Japan, how these transformations dialectically relate to one another and to the history of Japanese capitalism, how these transformations are lived differently by different subjects, and how certain filmmakers coordinate(d) their work so as to flash these transformations, to anticipate and call forth alternative and unthinkable formations, and to intervene with the most crucial sociological work that film performs.

Danjuro's shock when watching *Momijigari* marks a problem in Japan that, although it existed in nascent form in the 1890s, would come to dominate the first part of the twentieth century. As mentioned in the introduction, this is the problem between being colonized and a colonizing nation. This problem is fixed to the structure of capitalism, which, at least during this earlier moment, requires spatial expansion (the breaking open of new markets and new places of production and distribution that exceed the nation) as one of its methods of crisis management.[13] The year 1900 is the one in which Danjuro screens *Momijigari*; it is also the year that splits the Sino-Japanese (1894–95) and Russo-Japanese (1904–05) wars, marking a transition from a more cooperative relation among Western colonial powers (including Japan) in Asia to a more conflictual one. Danjuro's shock at seeing his image projected back to him prepares consciousness for the shocks of capitalism. Film and Capitalism. Shock and Crisis. Capitalism shapes the coming-into-being of film; film shapes the conditions of perception of capitalism's crises. In one way or another, the films of the first stage of Japanese film history are making sense of—*and making the senses for*—this new structure called capitalism. And it is the problem of colonialism that is positioned squarely at the center of film production during this first stage of Japanese cinema.

But when we reach the immediate postwar moment, the dominant problem of Japanese modernity transforms: It now can be framed between the individual and the collective, between the need to differentiate individual wants and desires (to appeal to the ideals of democracy as well as cultivate a domestic consumer market) while restricting these needs and desires to the requirements of the collective (in order to idealize sacrifice and legitimate exploitation). To put it another way, it can be framed between the need to venerate the collective (all citizens working together to rebuild the shattered nation and construct a modern one) while protecting against the dangers of uncritical collectivization. Of course, this is one of the fundamental contradictions of all capitalist situations: a collective organized on the basis of individual profit. But it is at this second stage of capitalist development that this problem becomes dominant. Given Japan's particular national situation, this problem plays itself out differently there from other countries; nevertheless, all Japanese films of this second moment face this problem. These films could not help but speak to the individual–collective contradiction, for it is wrapped up inside each film's formal struggle; most notably, it is depicted in the struggle between the (individual) director and the (collective) film industry. Indeed, these are the films that Nizaemon grew up with, the films that trained him to navigate the train station.

By the Aum moment, however, the dominant problem in organizing Japan's modernity had once again transformed: The problem was now—and still is—between the national and the global. How do national categories (the autonomy of the nation-state, national industry, national ideologies) relate to global ones (transnational production, distribution, and consumption; transnational military campaigns; transnational class identities)? How can the nation perform its task of providing for all its citizens when it must act more and more like a corporation, which by its very logic and requirement to meet the bottom line has a different commitment and responsibility to the nation and national citizenry? Can we still speak of national film history? Of national directors? This is another impossible problem—one for which, at least at the present moment, there seems to be no answer.

Film becomes the place to examine these problems and their dynamic transformations. Film not only reflects and explains but, more important, actively participates in the construction of these very transformations. Film also becomes the place to examine the *concept* of transformation—a gnarled concept, indeed, and one that seems particularly crucial to re-examine at this moment in which the global system is economically and culturally transforming. With globalization discourse split between those mouthing pious slogans about how the new world order will eliminate the horrors of labor and disseminate a democratic global culture, and others dismissing the nation-state altogether and touting the draconian measures taken by transnational corporations as they emerge as the only true superpower after the Cold War, the concept of transformation moves to the foreground as one crucial key to help make sense of contemporary Japan and the world. Japanese film's relation to the present global situation (if the category of Japanese film—or national film history, for that matter—still means anything) is best understood in relation to earlier moments of transformation and to a theory of transformation itself.

The remainder of this chapter works through this issue of transformation. After delineating short histories of both Japanese film and capitalism, I foreground continuity, discontinuity, and crisis as the key concepts to make sense of each history's transformations. Then, to elaborate the issue

of perception and how economic forms insinuate themselves in consciousness and the body, the three stories with which this chapter began (Danjuro,
Nizaemon, Aum) are linked to the transformations of the money form over
the past hundred years.

Two Histories Let us begin with a thumbnail sketch of Japanese capitalist
history. After a considerable Ur-history stretching back into the Edo period
(1603–1868), the national stage of capitalist development emerged at the end
of the nineteenth century with the reorganization of the land-ownership and
taxation systems.[14] By moving from a capricious rice tax paid in kind to a uniform monetary tax in which a taxpayer was the legal owner of the land, the
new Meiji government established the private-property system. These fiscal
reforms were combined with monetary ones that, in 1889, standardized currency and established the Bank of Japan as the sole note-issuing institution.
At the same time, the Tokaido railway line, linking Tokyo and Kobe, was
completed; steamships were modernized, lowering the cost of national and
international transportation; and an advanced network of communications
(including postal and telegraphic services) laid the groundwork for the first
economic miracle to occur over the next thirty years.[15] Emphasis was placed
on the labor-intensive production of consumer goods (such as textiles, which
reached a 46 percent share of industrial production in 1926) combined with a
low-wage system (depending disproportionately on female workers from the
countryside) that was under constant pressure to avoid demand-side problems by exporting what the domestic market could not absorb.

The economy was not cranked up to "miracle" status, however, until
World War I—a war in which Japan did not directly fight but from which
it sweetly profited (not unlike in the Korean, Vietnam, and Cold wars that
followed). As Western colonial countries deserted their Asian markets to
participate in the war, Japan quickly filled the void by supplying manufactured goods to its neighbors, thus fueling its own heavy industries.[16] When
the Western countries returned to their Asian markets following the war,
Japan's boom in export surpluses quickly reversed. Severe recession ensued.
Over the next ten years, until 1931, the Japanese economy ran a significant
trade deficit.[17]

The Great Kanto Earthquake of 1923 further exacerbated Japan's economic woes, and by 1927, stemmed by a depression in the agricultural in-

dustry, the Japanese economy was experiencing serious crisis a few years before similar effects were felt in the West. Amid crisis, General Tanaka Giichi wedged himself into power and soon sent troops to China (Qingdao) to secure business contracts in order to stimulate the flagging economy. In September 1931, after the Manchurian Incident, Japan's imperial drive to take over the whole of China was unleashed as the second phase of monopoly capitalism emerged. This second stage was symbolized by a shift to capital-intensive industries, such as ammunitions, shipbuilding, chemicals, and steel, in which these heavy producer goods were assured markets by Japanese capital itself under the aegis of the zaibatsu system. Under this system, each of six separate cartels (Mitsubishi, Sumitomo, and Mitsui, for example) was composed of a diverse group of businesses that shared directors, stockholders, key lending institutions, and sales outlets, thus ensuring the cooperation of banking, industrial, and commercial capital.

After World War II, the decolonization of Asian countries, from Manchuria to Indonesia; the U.S. occupation; the "Korean War boom," which generated a program of war-related procurements that were indispensable to economic growth; the Vietnam War; and the student and labor movements of the 1960s and early '70s, this second phase of capitalist development hit its peak of corporate/state rigidity by the mid-1970s. At this moment, Tokyo became one of the leading industrial capitals of the world. The oil crises of the 1970s severely affected the importation of raw materials used to make heavy producer goods, creating a redoubled effort to return to consumer goods such as automobiles and electronics. This was the moment of the second Japanese "miracle." The circle of high production and low wages was once again squared (for the time being) by relying on healthy export markets, managed labor unions, and a large pool of rural farmers who, unable to cover their own costs, were forced to moonlight by selling their labor on a temporary basis to firms that did not need to worry about proper compensation or worker welfare. Of course, indispensable to this rapid growth was a global environment wrapped up in a Cold War logic, which emphasized military–industrial national policies such as those produced by the Pentagon and the Kremlin, as opposed to (or that produced the possibility for) commercial–industrial national policies such as the one generated by the Ministry of International Trade and Industry (MITI) in Japan.

The severe revaluing of the yen in 1985 (which caused the yen's value to rise from 240 to 155 yen against the dollar within a year), however, cut into Japan's export markets, then expressed the perennially feared crisis at home. This finally put an end to the era of unprecedentedly high rates of growth, in which the average level of real gross national product (GNP) rose a little more than 10 percent each year from 1955 to 1970. The oil-crisis recession also abruptly ended the upward trend in real wages, marked by the defeat of organized labor's 1975 "spring offensive" calling for modest wage increases. Trade disputes and the heating up of U.S.-Japanese relations severely strained both the existing export markets and the immature domestic market; this was further aggravated by foreign companies' crying foul at being excluded from the internal Japanese market. Out of this national and global situation, the Japanese economy angled into the third stage of capitalist development, a transnational stage that is symbolized by the flexible accumulation of capital (for example, the *keiretsu* [the organization of each industry by conglomerates] system is exported abroad so that non-Japanese companies are now gradually being integrated into the networks); cybernetic technology (space practically disappears as a barrier as communications advance and electronic currency markets and speculation thrive); a global division of labor (production is shifted in greater degrees to the developing countries); direct foreign investment by Japanese corporations (with the intention of sidestepping national protectionist policies, which are becoming less and less meaningful and enforceable); and the weakening of the nation-state's decision-making power (as corporations begin to divorce themselves from the imperatives of the nation [infrastructure, environmental concerns, quality of life] and wed themselves more tightly to transnational objectives). This brings us to the more recent economic crisis that first appeared in Thailand in 1997, then hit Indonesia and Malaysia and ripped through South Korea and shook Japan. Whether this phenomenon is an Asian "flu," a product of "crony capitalism," or a symptom of structural needs of the global economy will be discussed later. For now, however, what is clear is that the various bailouts and austerity plans, not to mention steady diets of national deregulation and transnational regulation (in Mexico, South Korea, and Indonesia, for example) by the IMF, World Bank, WTO, and Organization for Economic Cooperation and Development (OECD), serve to consolidate the world system further, thus reconfiguring the meanings and effects—the sovereignty and decision-making power—of the nation-state.

Before entering this narrative and examining what some of the method-ological objections to it might be, let us move to an equally condensed nar-rative of Japanese film history. After the Lumière brothers came to Osaka to premiere their films and to introduce the new cinematic technologies (the Kinetoscope, the Vitascope, and the Cinematograph) in 1896–97, they filmed various shorts throughout the country—street scenes, trains, ports, family dinners, geisha, Ainu (early inhabitants of Hokkaido), religious ceremonies, Shinto processions, dance, theater and music performances, sword fighting, the Imperial Palace, and rice fields.[18] Constant Girel and Gabriel Veyre oper-ated the camera for most of these shorts, but Shibata Tsunekichi also had his turn using the cinematograph (filming Tokyo street scenes in 1898), thus becoming one of the very first Japanese filmmakers.[19] However, it was not until the outbreak of the war with Russia in 1904 that film gained a more widespread popularity in Japan. Not only were authentic war films made by the likes of Shibata who traveled to actual locations in Asia, but also what may be called "docu-dramas" (fake documentaries about the war) were made at home.[20] The first studios were built in 1908, followed by the birth of the Nihon Katsudoshashin Company (Nikkatsu) in 1912, which immediately be-came the largest film trust in Japan after consolidating four existing produc-tion companies. During this time film production was largely split between *kyuha* (old-school; generally samurai and historical films) and *shimpa* (new-school; generally films about contemporary issues). Fueled by the foundation of the modern Taikatsu, Shochiku, and Kokkatsu studios, in the late teens a more focused effort emerged to westernize the Japanese cinema. Taking the form of rapid editing, mobile camera work, interior acting, a star sys-tem, realistic set design, narrative autonomy, and the phasing out of the *on-nagata* (men playing women's roles) and *benshi* (commentator), these new experiments were more generally installed (not only in the new *gendai-geki* [modern dramas] but also by Ito Daisuke's *jidai-geki* [period dramas]) after the Great Kanto Earthquake of 1923 radically reorganized the industry.

We can otherwise designate the first period (1890s to 1930s) as beginning when the cinematic technology arrived in Japan during the 1890s and run-ning through the rise of the benshi in the first three decades of the twentieth century to their demise in the 1930s.[21] The emergence of cinema should be situated next to reforms in drama (such as the trend of kabuki actors using more colloquial language and applying powder to their faces) and literature (such as *genbun itchi*, literally the unification of spoken and written language).[22] According to Karatani Kojin these two reforms, coming in the third decade of the Meiji period (1890) at a time by which a great inversion (*tento*) of perception was occurring, hinged on a new experience of interiority and the emergence of the modern subject. Early Japanese cinema, as expressed by Danjuro's visual experience, was essential in contributing to this inversion of perception.

The colonial project, however, revealed the critical limitations within film and brought with it the need for newsreels and war films that *spoke* from authority (such as the disembodied talkie), not from the very particularistic (usually leftist) position of the very much embodied benshi.[23] Japan's Film Law, which had been in place during most of the thirties before its formal implementation in 1939, consolidated the film industry, leaving very little room for experimentation and resistance.[24] Out of this second period (1930s to 1970s) emerged not only a studio system modeled on Hollywood, but an impressive number of great auteurs, including the more classic ones (such as Itami Mansaku, Mizoguchi Kenji, Ozu Yasujiro, and Kurosawa Akira) all the way to the more avant-garde ones of the 1960s and '70s (including Yoshida Yoshishige, Shinoda Masahiro, Oshima Nagisa, and Imamura Shohei) working both in the established studios and (in the case of Hani Susumu and Teshigahara Hiroshi) working independently.[25] Their work emphasized elaborate codes and consequently the new demands placed on spectators to interpret them, for example, Ozu's challenging formal compositions, Kurosawa's intricate plots, and Imamura's nonlinear temporalities. Along with the wider use of color and widescreen technologies by the late 1950s, this was also the period in which television (which had its golden age from 1955 to 1965) emerged as one of the very few spaces available for experimentation by young filmmakers before it was sealed off by government officials and film industry executives who could no longer ignore the new medium's crucial ideological and market potential. This is the moment of Nizaemon, when film is most dominant, when the novelty has worn off and film is no longer only something to do with one's leisure time, but the dominant cultural apparatus shaping ways of acting, thinking, and behaving.

With the fragmentation of the Japanese left following the ratification of the 1970 U.S.–Japan Security Pact, and with the arrival of a heightened state of commodification that brought to a head the perennial relationship between art and business, the dominant forms of expression and perception were again in need of deep reorganization. Japan's major film corporations experienced severe decline with Daiei going bankrupt, Nikkatsu recouping losses by concentrating on soft-core pornography (*roman poruno*), and the three other major studies turning to genre film (horror, disaster, yakuza, and so on), the number of theaters throughout the country dropped significantly, and by the mid–1980s, video production and the preponderance of neighborhood video stores marked a significant transformation in the way film was made and experienced. Since Japanese film celebrated its one-hundredth anniversary in 1995, new questions have emerged regarding the so-called decline of Japanese cinema, its relation to the so-called emergence of the national cinemas of Asia (China, Hong Kong, the Philippines, Indonesia, and Iran, to name just a few), the deterritorialization of Hollywood, the rise of the Internet and new media, the explosion of *anime* (Japanese animation) and associated fan clubs worldwide, and the consolidation of a global film industry.

One way to enter these roughshod narratives is to examine what some of the methodological objections to them might be. As for the representation of Japanese capitalism, some might argue that it is too continuous. The appeal to crisis, for example, suggests that crisis is a necessary repetition within capitalism as opposed to a mere response to aberrant causes. Others might argue that this narrative is too dependent on capitalism as a global category without paying heed to the fundamental distinctions offered by the Japanese model.[26] Still others might object to my naming the third stage "capitalism" at all, because we are no longer speaking of capitalism but of a post- or beyond-capitalism that is as different from capitalism as capitalism was from feudalism (thus making wholly anachronistic all of the usual capitalist categories that have been pressed into analytical service since the Industrial Revolution).[27] However, some might argue that the narrative is too discontinuous. My emphasis, for example, on distinguishing a third stage (globalization) from the monopoly stage might not appreciate the similarities between what exists now and what has existed for at least the past sixty years in Japan. In other words, both the utopian and dystopian labeling of a new informatic mode of production or a post-capitalist global market is really symptomatic of a refusal to appreciate that, despite surface changes, in the long run things operate in a way that is remarkably similar to the way they have always operated under capitalism.

These objections are reminiscent of how the Japanese economist Nagasu Kazuji once described the pre-war Marxist debate between the *koza-ha* (the faction that remained loyal to the Japanese Communist Party and the Comintern) and *rono-ha* (the faction that split from the Japanese Communist Party in 1927 and argued that a bourgeois revolution had been achieved with the Meiji Restoration). The central point of controversy, as Nagasu saw it, was whether the object of study was the development of *Japanese* capitalism or the development of Japanese *capitalism*. Now we might add a third option: the development *out* of Japanese capitalism.[28] This also serves as a convenient way to pose the problem of writing Japanese film history. For example, those who want to stress the development of *Japanese* film usually emphasize Japanese film's continuity to earlier cultural forms. For example, the benshi are no longer connected to ways of coming to terms with silent film that all national cinemas faced; they are seen as directly connected to the role of the *joruri* (narrator) in *bunraku* (puppet theater) or other traditional roles in which a commentator is integrated into the work.[29] Or there is the case in which Kurosawa is seen not as the most "Western" Japanese filmmaker but as bound tightly with Japanese cultural traditions such as *sumie* (ink paintings) and *noh*.[30] Then there are those who stress the development of Japanese *film* and how the film medium itself is markedly discontinuous from earlier cultural forms, arguing that any similarities or continuities therefore should be regarded as simply trivial surface appearances. For example, to draw a connection between, say, *emakimono* (narrative handscrolls) and the role of its text commenting on the pictorial narrative is less a basis for the benshi than the fact that the benshi needed work as modernization eliminated their usual employment in the theater. In other words, Japanese film could have progressed just as well without the benshi had film not emerged at a time of such radical vocational instability. And finally, there are those who may want to argue that the dominance of television, advertising, and digital video and the computer (not to mention transnational production and distribution networks) have so revolutionized film that any film produced within such a situation must be regarded as wholly distinct from what has usually been called film, just as film was seen as distinct from the shadow play or theater.

Continuity, Discontinuity, Crisis   Each of these objections about how to narrate Japanese film history and capitalism is at one and the same time an argument about history. This is not to suggest that these arguments offer narratives about—and interpretations of—historical events. Rather, these positions propose genuine philosophies of history: They theorize (however unconsciously) the movement and logic of historical transformation and the abstraction called *History*. For example, the historiographical trope of discontinuity (such as the discontinuity between Japanese capitalism/Western capitalism or Japanese global capitalism/Japanese monopoly capitalism, as well as between Japanese film/Western film or Japanese post-war film/Japanese pre-war film) signifies fundamental geographical and historical breaks over which we cannot cross. Any desire to have it otherwise, to make commensurate again the now and the then, the here and the there, is blind to the magnitude of the differences.

What this invocation of discontinuity makes immediately evident is how its language—of breaks, differences, and incommensurabilities—relates to some of the most significant advances in critical theory over the past forty years. Here I am referring to structuralism and its progeny: methods that emphasize the synchronic and relational space of structures over the temporal transformations from one structure to another. Consistent with its methods, structuralism's emphasis on the synchronic came about negatively and as a radical assault on diachronic forms of analysis: forms of analysis privileging historical continuities and persistances over discontinuities and mutations. Structuralism's intervention (from its linguistic genesis to its Marxist and poststructuralist inflections) was—and still is—crucial. This is primarily due to structuralism's principal stance: to redirect analysis from a metaphysical search for ontological and universal meaning (What does it mean?) to the more political exploration of function and logic (How does it work? What are its effects?). Oddly enough this de-emphasis on historical continuity is precisely an attempt to return history to the discussion. One must always historicize because even though two elements at two different moments or in two different places might look the same (film styles, subjectivities, financial crises), the different geo-historical situations in which they dwell position their meanings and effects in radically different ways.

In response to the thinkers of radical discontinuity are those thinkers who invoke what may be called *radical continuity*. That is, things are not significantly changed and if one moves from surface appearances to deeper logic, one is quickly disabused of such melodramatic notions. If the former illustrates a reductive synchronic analysis (we cannot compare what happened before the 1970s with what happened after) or what we may call a reductive syntopic analysis (we cannot compare what happened in Japan with what happened in the West), then the latter illustrates a reductive diachronic or diatopic analysis (when comparing, all we see are straight continuities across time and space). Of course, we can nuance these positions by recognizing the qualitative differences of different historical moments and geographical places while retaining the similarities they share.

This is the historiographical path I take when making sense of the transformations of the two histories presented in this chapter—a path not unlike the one we may take when walking down a Tokyo street. The finance capital of transnational banks is within walking distance of a merchant economy not far from older industrial factories. We can also see noncapitalist modes of production if we keep an eye out for the underground barter economy, which itself might be in shouting distance from a virtual slave trade, either in the form of sex workers who must pay off huge sums of money in order to liberate themselves from bogus contracts, or garment workers locked up in prison-like factories. Out of one eye we view the three modes existing simultaneously (with each new configuration producing mutations in the three stages so that each is refunctionalized), while out of the other eye we see each mode emerging consecutively. This double optic views the continuities and discontinuities at the same time.

Yet this visual trick does not untie the knot of historiography. One must emphasize (however strategically and contingently) one over the other. It is impossible to be even-sighted when negotiating the problem of continuity and discontinuity. While the moment of structuralism in the 1960s and 1970s provoked a needed emphasis on discontinuities, the present is a moment to reemphasize and rethink continuities. But of course we do this only after learning the lessons of structuralism and acknowledging the enduring significance of a synchronic analysis.

Another way to make sense of all of these objections is to take a closer look at the concept of crisis.[31] Crisis is about emergency and emergence, destruction and reconstruction, disorganization and reorganization, change and repetition, and contingency and necessity. But crisis, in contrast to these universal characteristics, also has a historical coming-into-being in relation to Japanese capitalism and film and thus a particular context from which it must be examined. Here the concept of crisis can be historicized so we are not tempted to resort to it as that faithful ahistorical prop that can be pulled out of the bag when all of the usual explanations fail. Indeed, how thinkers come to terms with the concept of crisis will usually determine where they line up regarding the histories of both Japanese capitalism and Japanese film.

The concept of crisis in economics, in either its neoclassical form of market cycles or its Marxian forms of overproduction or underconsumption, is quite dominant in contemporary thought. Very few today take issue with the view that the boom-and-bust cycle is somehow connected to the workings of the capitalist system itself. What is open to debate, however, is how a thinker accounts for a crisis in which everything from the mismanagement by individual policymakers and the overextension of credit to natural disasters and wars are offered as reliable causes. For example, the cause of the Japanese economic crises in the early 1970s is regularly explained by pointing to the quadrupling of oil prices by the OPEC nations. The Asian economic crisis of the late 1990s, which hit Southeast Asia and Korea the hardest, is usually thrown at the feet of a few irresponsible, ignorant, and greedy Asian bankers and bureaucrats. But these are only expressions of crisis, not the causes. Instead, the causes will necessarily be linked to capitalism's need constantly to expand production without regard to market limits; the market is not the only variable to determine production, but the need (the structural requirement) to expand and make profit is equally crucial.[32] This "need" is the essential rule of all capitalist situations in which the production of goods, ideas, entertainment, and information is subordinated to the production of surplus value. The tendency toward crisis is thus caused by this fundamental rule, a rule whose effects—despite calls that "the rules have changed"—are abundantly documented daily in the pages of the world's leading newspapers.[33] In the end, it is the perpetual production and realization of surplus value that transcends borders and cannot be sidestepped, even with the most muscular public-sector involvement by MITI, the Japanese Ministry of Finance, or the wTO. It can, however, be recouped after the fact by sustained reorganization of accumulation methods. It is at this point that the particularities of the various national capitalisms, such as those in Japan after the crises in the late 1920s and the early 1970s, make the greatest difference.

Crisis, therefore, is not contingent on any type of anomaly. Rather, it is wrapped up in the very logic of capitalist and cinematic development. This then shifts the concept of crisis from a secondary concern to a primary one in the attempt to account for change on both the capitalist and filmic levels. What happens after these crises—how they are recuperated and whether they can be linked to revolutionary (both cultural and political) movements—is not inherent in this logic itself. It is contingent on social praxis and a particular historical conjuncture. In a very general sense, a similar logic can be detected within the history of commercial film forms. This is not to say that capitalist crises will immediately be reflected in crises of film forms; rather, film forms must always be expanding, however little this expansion may coordinate with the film forms' own market needs (such as particular historical events in need of narrativization). Technology, spectators, directors, and even studio executives do not have the final say about the production of new film forms; the rule within the aesthetic economy requires film forms to expand or shut down. The history of wide-screen cinema in the West is a case in point. Wide-screen technology existed as far back as the 1890s and was reintroduced in the 1920s, most notably with the three-camera system used by Abel Gance in his 1927 film *Napoleon*. However, wide-screen technology did not stick during this time, partly because of its competition with the even more radical transformations to sound. Wide-screen film would have to wait until the 1950s before reaching a critical mass. The reasons for this are overdetermined, but one crucial element, as John Belton explains, was the redefinition of the motion picture experience at a time that disposable income and leisure time were increasing.[34] In addition to these non-technological explanations of why wide-screen film "worked" in the 1950s and not the 1920s is that perception habits were in crisis and historically ready for, and desiring, different forms of narration.

This logic of crisis is built into film production and consumption. It is a logic to which film may be particularly susceptible, given its own mode of production, which, in its social relations and organization, resembles more than most other cultural forms that of the capitalist mode of production in that it has experienced its own local, monopoly, and transnational moments. One might recall Oshima Nagisa's famous comment that Japanese cinema ended in 1970 because, at that moment, an older mode of filmmaking was replaced by a corporate division of labor that had more in common with the dispersions of multinational capitalism than with the collective spirit that had marked Japanese film up to that point.[35]

Of course, this logic can be coordinated with market needs or particular ideological demands, but, just as in the capitalist economy, film forms must be in a state of perpetual expansion in which their overproduction will produce a crisis (in perception) that will then require recuperation. This suggests that another term can be added to the film–spectator diad: history. Spectators experience film in relation to actual social possibilities and limitations, to the cultural practices of looking of any given time and place.[36] One way to illustrate this is to track the changes in what is considered "realistic." A certain type of technology (synchronized sound, for example) or narrative strategy (flashback) might be considered "realistic" at a particular moment. But after repeated viewing of such modes, the "realistic effect" wanes. Then different kinds of technology (Dolby sound) or narrative strategies (real-time representation) emerge and appear more real until they, in turn, are exhausted. This is to say that there is no inherently realistic mode, no inherent form that hits maximum verisimilitude; rather, the realistic effect is wholly dependent on viewers' perception habits as well as on cultural, institutional, and social constraints, not to mention the great ambiguities of what is meant by realism.[37] The transformation from the benshi to the full-fledged talkie, for example, was caused not only by ideological necessities of the colonial project (to mass-produce an ideological statement to be simultaneously and identically screened throughout the nation without benshi interference). It was also caused by the need to estrange spectators' perceptual habits at a moment in which the same story—told in the same way—was quickly losing its force. The talkie, therefore, turned out to be just as much the effect of crisis as the cause. What is at stake here is a dialectical transformation of perception that shares a historical relationship with the dialectical transformations in Japanese capitalism.

The Meiji Perceptual Revolution   It has often been remarked that the Meiji Ishin was a restoration from above that involved very little participation by the masses. Whether the Meiji Restoration represented a bourgeois revolution was one of the primary issues that divided the two Marxist schools of thought in the 1920s. For the koza-ha, the miserable conditions of the tenant farmers and the immaturity of the domestic market made it clear that a two-step revolution was required: first, bourgeois, during which the emperor system and the feudal remnants would be stamped out; then a second, properly socialist revolution. The rono-ha interpreted the Meiji Restoration as a bourgeois revolution, and it stressed the similarities between Japanese capitalism and the European and American varieties. Rono-ha thinkers pointed to the various changes going on all around them as proof that capitalism was more dynamic and developed than the koza-ha had thought.

Revolution or restoration? Bourgeois or not? On whichever side of this debate we might fall, it should not prevent us from recognizing that a cultural revolution accompanied the Meiji Restoration. Crucial to this revolution was a transformation in perception. Here it is useful to return to Karatani's discussion of the emergence of genbun itchi and his argument that this new system is what made possible the interiority, the "discovery of the self," in the last decade of the nineteenth century. For Karatani, the genbun itchi movement, which originated in Maejima Hisoka's will to abolish Chinese characters in favor of a phonetic writing system that would be more conducive to universal education (not to mention capitalist development) in Japan, incorporates not only fiction but also drama and poetry. But as Karatani makes clear, it was not the actual abandonment of *kanji* (Chinese ideograms) that was at stake for the movement but, rather, "a profound undermining of the privileged status of writing (as kanji), which was accomplished through advocating an ideology of phonetic speech."[38] This new ideology gave priority to speech so that, in the end, it did not matter whether kanji was scrapped because the damage would be done at the precise moment in which kanji no longer evoked figural and transcendental meanings (such as when the character for tree evoked not the concept of tree but its silent reading and concrete image). The unification of writing and speech generated by the genbun ichi system thus produced the possibility for an "inner" world of the subject to emerge, with meaning and "individual expression" tied to the word (the inner voice).

Although genbun itchi is usually related only to literature and the emergence of the *shi-shosetsu* ("I" prose narrative), Karatani argues that the reform movement in drama (*engeki kairyo undo*), which began in 1888, could also be considered part of the system. It was the same Ichikawa Danjuro who was so shocked to see his own image projected back to him in 1900 who most importantly represented the drama reforms. Danjuro promoted innovative techniques such as speaking in a more ordinary fashion, relinquishing the exaggerated kabuki acting techniques, attempting to evoke a more self-possessed and psychological expression (known as *hara-gei*), and no longer applying makeup to his face. The painted face of kabuki and the grandiose movements emerged from kabuki's attempt to imitate the puppets of *bunraku*. The painted face of the kabuki actor, like the puppet's face and even the noh mask, represented the "face as concept" in which looking at a face meant looking at the transcendental concept of face, not at an individual, concrete face (similar to kanji, as discussed earlier). What is important is that, before the inversion of perception (this perceptual revolution), the painted face came closer to a spectator's *sense of reality* than did the naked face. "It was only through such an inversion," Karatani writes, "that the naked face—the naked face as a kind of landscape—took on meaning in and of itself and what had been insignificant became profoundly significant."[39]

The key to Karatani's notion that genbun itchi marked an inversion of perception is that, once the inversion takes place, its origins are repressed from memory. In other words, the psychological expression of the kabuki actor will appear as if it has always existed, as if it has always been perceived. The same can be said of film. Although a new cultural experience, the way to perceive film—despite its radical newness—may not have appeared new to a spectator at the time. In other words, the way to perceive film may have seemed just as old as the way to perceive other traditional cultural forms. This is not, however, to agree with the view that early Japanese film is a continuation of older cultural forms. Instead, I want to argue these older forms are not in fact "older." Rather, when considered from the standpoint of a different mode of perception, they are just as new as film. Kabuki, noh, bunraku—even haiku and *hanga* (prints)—were all vulnerable to this transformation of perception. It was not only film that was fresh at the time. All culture was, because a more general transformation of perception was under way.

But if we add film to Karatani's broadened system of genbun itchi and stress how all cultural forms are affected by modern perception, then we must at the same time draw attention to film's difference from the other forms in this system. A return to Danjuro's first film experience will be useful to underscore this. It was not the *looking* at film that was so strange; it was Danjuro's looking at his *own* dance being technologically projected back to him that produced the shock of self-consciousness. In other words, the inversion of perception that occurred during Danjuro's day was not something of which he could have been consciously aware. Still, there was a shock—one that he would not have experienced with any of the more traditional art forms.[40]

This is the ground zero of a certain concretization in Japan—in culture and capital. But just as a perceptual revolution followed the Meiji Restoration, so, too, were there transformations during the next one hundred years of Japanese modernity. They were perhaps not as radical, but they were equally significant. This returns us to the question of how to account for this transformation in perception from Danjuro at the end of the nineteenth century to Nizaemon in the greater part of the twentieth century to Aum at the turn of the twenty-first century. Danjuro was shocked by his own image staring back at him, whereas contemporary viewers did not seem to recognize the imagery of the Aum fugitives. It seems all too simplistic to argue for a continual process of desensitization, a spectatorial habituation that makes viewers increasingly unaware of their image environments. What troubles me about this approach is that it cannot help but denigrate contemporary image culture and pine for some mythical moment before the flood of mechanical imagery. It also assumes a nondynamic and ahistorical subject whose sensorium is governed by a transcendental logic: "We have become less perceptive over the last one hundred years" or "We have become more discerning over time" would be typical refrains of such a logic. But I do not see the issue as being "more" or "less" anything; rather, the issue is one of difference. We perceive differently. We discern differently. We represent differently. And to complicate matters further, this "we" is shot through with difference so that we not only perceive differently, but we also differently perceive. The question then becomes how to account for differences in perception and representation at different historical moments and among different subjects. The following chapters all attempt to get at this question by examining the inextricable relationship between dominant forms of cinematic production and dominant forms of capitalist accumulation. The intention is not to draw a straight line from level to level but to highlight the way form jumps the space between the levels. To illustrate this, given the present problem of perception, the task is to place the Danjuro–Nizaemon–Aum trajectory in relation to the money form and argue that forms of perception and their transformations over the past hundred years inextricably relate to the money form and its transformations.

Money   In 1899, Danjuro experienced shock at his own image staring back at him; in the same year, the Meiji government consolidated the Japanese monetary system, fixing paper currency to gold and setting convertible banknotes from the Bank of Japan as the sole currency. Thus, the government guaranteed and stabilized the value of money for the first time since money had superceded rice as the primary medium of exchange at the end of the seventeenth century. (Of course, coin and paper money have existed since the fifth and fifteenth centuries, respectively.) At that time, the value of money was too arbitrary to be recognized as a general equivalent, because loans could be waived on a whim or the bottom could drop out of one currency due to the competitive rise of another. It was not until the beginning of the twentieth century, finally, that the Japanese banking, credit, and monetary systems were consolidated.

Tetsuo Najita explains that, at the beginning of the nineteenth century, thinkers associated with the merchant academies of Osaka, such as Kusama Naokata, theorized the need for a stable monetary system to cultivate trust, virtue, and morality in the national citizenry.[41] In other words, they saw that money has not just an economic function but also an ideological one: If people trust in the monetary system, they will be more likely to trust one another. Non-arbitrary monetary exchange, in other words, is crucial in cultivating the individual virtues of a modern nation. Najita goes on to explain, however, that Kusama's theory was dismissed during his own day, only to be employed by the new Meiji government following the restoration. What I will suggest here is that money not only influences moral behavior, as Kusama argued, but that it is also instrumental in shaping thought and perception itself—indeed, the form of money, the form of thought, and the form of film share a similar abstract structure.[42]

The Meiji government had implemented land reforms and a new tax system; the centralization of the monetary system was the final piece of the puzzle needed to ensure the transition to a commodity mode of production—that is, to capitalism. Within capitalism, money functions as a general equivalent, a form in which the value of commodities appears as pure exchange value. Money quantifies qualitatively different commodities. Of course, this has radical implications for social relations. When a commodity is considered not in relation to its process of production but only in terms of its relation to other commodities, then the act of buying and selling becomes impersonal to the extent that a whole network of social relations is congealed. This is the classic definition of what is called "commodity fetishism": Value seems inherent in the commodity itself, thus mystifying the commodity's historical coming-into-being and the labor and power relations that went into producing it.

According to Alfred Sohn-Rethel, every time a person purchases a commodity, the form of abstraction wrapped up in the exchange becomes more firmly set in his or her consciousness. Sohn-Rethel's thesis is that the act of exchange itself necessarily occupies consciousness, so that the abstraction to the social goes unrecognized. Money is an abstract thing. It is the thing that enables one to purchase a commodity, the thing that is exchanged for something else. But it is also the abstraction that stands in for the social totality, for the structure of social relations that gives the particular exchange act its meaning. But each time we perform an exchange act, we necessarily misrecognize this situation as one between two individuals instead of one that ricochets throughout the social totality. For Sohn-Rethel, then, the daily act of exchange inscribes itself into our very conceptual categories.[43] I find this thesis compelling, but there are two aspects that Sohn-Rethel leaves underdeveloped: first, the historical transformations that both money and the conceptual categories undergo; and second, the distinguishing factors that different national situations might present (such as Japanese modernity, a situation that emerges from a late-Tokugawa [pre-Meiji government] status system in which the mercantile class inhabited the second-lowest rung on the social ladder, even though their wealth exceeded that of the aristocracy).

The Japanese economic crisis of the late 1920s was expressed as a series of bumper crops that lowered rice prices, thus exacerbating problems in other industries. This generated an immense campaign of government-sponsored exports that, assisted by a rapid depreciation of the yen, sanctioned the great cartels and sent a flood of Japanese goods into foreign markets. By 1936, exports had almost doubled, stemming the crisis and convincing Japan's political leaders that economic expansion abroad for markets and raw materials was absolutely essential to a healthy economy at home. And, of course, they were right. But Japan's interest in northern China, Manchuria, and Korea, which was crucial to manage the structural needs of Japanese capitalism, also served its political function. Expansion abroad was about forming an empire and standing up to the Western colonial powers, which were sent abroad looking for markets because of their own structural demands. Militarism in Japan then grew, with rightist groups plotting assassinations and coups, thus snuffing out any openness that might have emerged in the 1910s and '20s. At the heart of this restructuring of the Japanese economy was a policy of monetary expansion in the form of deficit spending. The development of the credit system, assisted by the Bank Law of 1928, promoted the integration of financial and industrial capital, enabling the export of money capital throughout Asia. This integration, combined with the consolidation of the zaibatsu system, marked the Japanese economic system's mutation from merchant capitalism to monopoly capitalism.

Money was moved abroad as home industries searched feverishly for new markets outside Japan. It was at this point that the focus shifted from commodities as such to money itself, so that the circuit of value production began with money and ended with the increase of money. This, of course, is the classic inversion from C–M–C (commodity–money–different commodity) to M–C–M (money–commodity–more money), in which money is used to buy commodities in order to sell them at a profit—that is, in which money is converted into capital. Money no longer functions to attain concrete commodities; it functions only to expand into more money. But as the Marxist economist Uno Kozo points out, M–C–M exists at earlier moments of merchant capitalism (when a merchant buys from one community and sells to another at a higher price) as well as at moments of money-lending capital. Uno writes, "Capital, therefore, cannot secure a firm foundation for its value augmenting activity unless it goes a step further than mere resale business and produces the commodity that it sells by means of the commodities that it purchases."[44] This "step further" for Uno comes with industrial capitalism and when the commodity form of labor power exists. Uno continues, "Hence the development of the form of industrial capital requires, in addition to the accumulation of monetary wealth, the formation in great numbers of the modern, propertyless workers, free in Marx's double sense: this is to say, free from feudal bondage and also free from the means of production necessary for the realization of their own labor."[45] It is at this point that capital becomes self-expanding and the subject (*shutai*) of the self-repeating motion—generating surplus value by the logic of its own circuit.[46]

It is this transformation and the dominance of money that I see as linked to the transformation in perception from Danjuro to Nizaemon. Danjuro was shocked at the concretization of his own image. In the first stage of Japanese film (from *Momijigari* to the end of the benshi system in the early 1930s), film's concrete quality was stressed. Donald Richie is fond of explaining how, during some of the first screenings, the projector was placed on the left side of the stage and the screen on the right: The science of projecting light into images was more fascinating for maiden Japanese audiences than the narrative of the film itself.[47] Moreover, benshi would often comment on production processes, explaining how the film stock had been produced or a particular scene contrived. During the first stage of Japanese film, to view a film was still to view a concrete artifact that was unique, that would be different from one presented in another location or at another time (despite the reproducibility of the film negative).

The abstraction of film, therefore, in which a viewer in Tokyo could imagine a viewer in Osaka experiencing the same series of images at the same time only spread when the talkie emerged and the benshi were displaced. In a certain sense benshi were not unlike merchant capitalists. The merchant capitalist negotiated the barter from one commodity to another; only with the onset of industrial capital, as Uno reminds us, does money become self-generating so that the merchant is no longer needed to produce value. (Rather, surplus value is extracted by the very circuit of M--C--M itself.) Film's value production also becomes self-generating in the sense that the mediator (the benshi) is no longer required. The interest in objects (the film technology in the case of film and the commodity in the case of circulation) is no longer foregrounded as the more abstract qualities of money and the filmic narrative (fictional or nonfictional) become dominant and seemingly autonomous.

With the second moment of film, the grammar is internalized. Although it seems to be autonomous (a private relation between the spectator and the images projected on the screen), the experience exceeds itself each time one sees a film. This concerns the social as much as it does the individual, the public as much as it does the private. It is ideological. In fact, just as Sohn-Rethel argued that the very exchange act crowds out the possibility of thinking the various relations of money within the social totality, the very act of viewing film crowds out the possibility of tracking how the grammar affects everyday perception and behavior. When Nizaemon navigates the train station, he does so without seeing. If money and film during Danjuro's moment intensified the relation to the concrete (by way of the new attention monetary equivalence provoked in the property of commodities and the new attention the benshi provoked in the materiality of film), then money and film during Nizaemon's moment intensified forms of abstraction. As capital has shifted to more profitable forms and places of production in Asia, and as film has shifted to more profitable forms of production in the talkie and Hollywood grammar, the deterritorialization of production from consumption has intensified. If Danjuro's moment represents a semiotic inversion in which a wholly different relation to the concrete emerged (concrete ground zero), then Nizaemon's moment represents another inversion in which a turn to the abstract is heightened.

When we reach the present moment of the Aum imagery, there seems to be another transformation in money and perception. Since 1987, the amount of money that crosses the wires connecting the world's major banks has doubled, reaching a total of $1.25 trillion (168 trillion yen) a day.[48] Foreign-exchange transactions have ballooned more than seventy times since 1977.[49] The currency markets, moreover, turned over almost $1.5 trillion in March 1998, an amount that exceeds a month's worth of world product and that is greater than the total amount of foreign-currency reserves around the world.[50] What all this money does is speculate on exchange rates to increase its initial investment. Speculation is basically the process by which someone buys a financial asset in the hope of selling it at a higher price in the future. This speculation is a symptom of the new requirements of the global economy. The older forms of value production—investing in domestic production or in production facilities abroad—are no longer as dominant in attending to the capitalist logic of expansion and profit. Speculation, goaded by ever increasing financial innovations (such as high-yield bonds, foreign-currency futures and options, currency swaps, derivatives, and dozens more such instruments invented every month), is the emerging form of choice for managing this new situation. High-risk investments that enable one to undertake large transactions with a smaller amount of capital threaten to bust not only corporations and banks, but also whole nations and governments.

One glaring example of this new situation is the East Asian financial crisis. In July 1997, the Thai government abandoned its efforts to retain a fixed exchange rate for its currency, the baht. The baht immediately lost 20 percent of its value, and the currency crisis quickly spread to Malaysia, Indonesia, the Philippines, and Japan. Paul Krugman writes, "What forced Thailand to devalue its currency was massive speculation against the baht, speculation that over a few months had consumed most of what initially seemed an awesomely large warchest of foreign exchange. And why were speculators betting against Thailand? Because they expected the baht to be devalued, of course."[51] This self-fulfilling logic, in which speculators' concerns about whether the Thai government would deflate its currency to re-inflate its economy, fed on itself to such an extent that it produced the crisis that was the very matter of concern in the first place. Of course, this psychological dimension has always been a part of economics; the likelihood of runs and the significance of investor confidence is nothing new. But the recent prodigious leap in speculation in the global economy does seem to have cranked the meanings and effects of money up to a qualitatively different level. Moreover, with the growth of cybernetic technology that allows the instantaneous movement of capital all over the globe (which, of course, includes the all-new cyberspaces), temporal and spatial boundaries have been reconfigured so that the meaning of the "short term" and "neighboring countries"—not to mention the "nation-state" and the "region"—are radically transformed. Fredric Jameson makes sense of this new situation this way:

> For it rather implies a new ontological and free-floating state, one in which the content (to revert to Hegelian language) has definitively been suppressed in favor of the form, in which the inherent nature of the product becomes insignificant, a mere marketing pretext, while the goal of production no longer lies in any specific market, any specific set of consumers or social and individual needs, but rather in its transformations into that element which by definition has no context or territory, and indeed no use value as such, namely, money.[52]

Mentioning that the "content . . . has definitively been suppressed in favor of the form" seems to offer one explanation of how film and image culture operate in Japan today—not to mention of how the Aum fugitive could go unrecognized after such a sustained and extensive advertising campaign. The images of the Aum fugitives usually consisted of mug shots, a frame totally occupied by face. The faces were everywhere, hauntingly staring back at the nation. The images took on an abstract quality that was wholly separated from the fugitives themselves. The images represented the pure form of the criminal, the criminal as abstraction that exists only in the collective consciousness. If the films that Nizaemon grew up with still had a connection to everyday life, to the spatial configuration of a train station (and if money during this moment of monopoly capitalism still had a connection to national and international production), then the connection that links the Aum images to contemporary Japanese life has been severed (just as global money has been detached from its usual spaces of value production).

If there is indeed a transformed situation in which money and images produce value, then what does this mean for social activism and change? As mentioned earlier, to not see what one sees, as in the case of the Aum example, suggests a certain degree of collective unconsciousness, a sort of automatonization by which awareness and sensitivity to one's everyday surroundings and life are severely weakened. When the content is separated from its form, when the Aum images no longer connect to living human beings, concerns about accountability surface. I also mentioned that the situation is invariably more complicated. Another dimension is wrapped up in this non-recognition, in this separation: the utopian possibility of recognizing something else, something that does not yet exist, something that can exist in the future. Perhaps the sheer abundance of images and the way they seem cut off from their content (the way the content has been suppressed by the form) might produce symptomological subjects—subjects that see something other than what they are looking at. I can now repeat the question posed near the beginning of this chapter: What else is there to see in the mug shot of an Aum fugitive?

Perhaps one can see the structural relations between everyday life in Japan and the fact that, at the beginning of the twenty-first century, a handful of transnational corporations control one-third of private productive-sector assets; that more than 850 million workers are working at or below subsistence level; that nearly 40 million people are living with HIV; or that in the 1980s and '90s alone, the gap between the rich and poor in Latin America, Africa, and Asia doubled. Or to put this another way, perhaps one can see the gap between the spectacle of advertising and the banality of global capitalism; between the new cybernetic spaces of value production and the existing earthly spaces of labor production and exploitation; between the content and its form. This is to long not for the rejoining of the Aum mug shots with the "real" fugitives but for the rejoining of the mug shots with the real situation: that of global capitalism and the everyday realities that this situation produces. Perhaps with the dystopian elements of social fragmentation and hitherto unknown inequality of global wealth and power that accompanies the qualitatively different meanings and effects of money and cultural reception might also come the utopian elements of producing different ways of perceiving the world and different ways of changing it.

II. historiography

Nation, Narrative, Capital

Form and Japanese Film Histories   The writing of any national film history is inextricably tied to the larger history of the nation itself. There is nothing unusual about this statement, especially when one remembers that, in the case of Japan, the history of film and the history of the modern nation share approximately the same span of time, both emerging in the 1890s out of a long Ur-history that included photography, bunraku, and emakimono for film, and merchant academies, philosophy and political economy for the nation. To mention the benshi, then, is at once to invoke Taisho democracy and to bring up Oshima Nagisa or Ogawa Shinsuke is at once to imply the struggles over the revision of the U.S.–Japan Security Treaty. It comes as no surprise, therefore, that almost every history of Japanese film has used the history of the nation to chart its course. But there is another relation between historiography and the nation that I want to explore in this chapter.

This is the relation that is not directly referred to in the content of the histories themselves but is (1) figured in their respective forms (their historiographical methods); and (2) integrally tied to the historical situation out of which each history is produced.

The most significant histories of Japanese film have been produced at times that the idea of the nation has been critically destabilized. It is precisely at these moments in which nationalist discourse is disrupted—disruptions that are themselves related to crises in the Japanese and world capitalist systems (post-Meiji, 1930s, 1970s)—that the various historiographies under examination here, in however indirect (or even unconscious) a way, emerge as acts of crisis management. In other words, film histories do not only analyze their acknowledged objects of study, such as plots, directors, audiences, actors, profits and losses incurred by the film corporations, and so on; they also, at the same time, symbolically intervene with the most critical transformations of the nation-state and, perhaps more important, with the politically charged ways in which these transformations are thought.

In this chapter, I conduct a formal analysis of six histories of Japanese film, two of which are themselves films: *Eiga to shihon-shugi* (Film and capitalism, 1931) by Iwasaki Akira; *Nihon eiga-shi* (Japanese film history, 1941) by the Shinko Film Corporation and Ministry of Foreign Affairs; *Nihon eiga hattatsu-shi* (A history of the developments of Japanese film, 1957) by Tanaka Junichiro; *The Japanese Film* (1959) by Donald Richie and Joseph Anderson; *Nihon eiga hyaku-nen* (100 years of Japanese cinema, 1995) by Oshima Nagisa for the British Film Institute (BFI); and the four-volume opus *Nihon eiga-shi* (A history of Japanese film, 1995) by Sato Tadao.[1] Each history works out in narrative form what Fredric Jameson (in another context) calls an "ideological determinant"—a real social contradiction of modern Japan that each work comes to terms with or "resolves."[2] This resolution of a social contradiction cannot be *directly* addressed by the historiographical text itself, thus taking the form of what Jameson calls the "antinomy":

What can in the former [social contradiction] be resolved only through the intervention of praxis here comes before the purely contemplative mind as logical scandal or double bind, the unthinkable and the conceptually paradoxical, that which cannot be unknotted by the operation of pure thought, and which must therefore generate a whole more properly narrative apparatus—the text itself—to square its circles and to dispel, through narrative movement, its intolerable closure.[3]

The key here is that these social contradictions—these ideological determinants of post-Meiji Japan—that cannot be engaged head-on but only through form and narrative development *shift* throughout the course of modern Japanese history. For what at one moment is unknottable at another moment is freely unraveled in the face of newly unsolvable but very real problems. Regarding the first two histories, made in 1931 and 1941, respectively, this ideological determinant is in the opposition between *colonized* and *colonizer*. Of course, the Fifteen Year War (as many in Japan still call World War II) began in 1931 with the Japanese invasion of Manchuria and did not end until Japan's surrender in August 1945. Questions still being asked are whether Japan had to colonize Asia and construct the East Asian Co-prosperity Sphere in order to stave off colonization by Europe or the United States; was Japanese colonization different from the Western type to which it was responding; was there a third way by which Japan could resist Western colonialism while at the same time engage in a colonial project without imitating Western colonial practices? It was precisely this "third way" that the two histories of the first wave of film historiography under consideration here were trying to carve out. They were doing so, however, in a way that is not evident when studying each history's content. It is evident but only when one analyzes their narrative structures—structures that are teleological.

The second moment of significant historiographical production occurred in the late 1950s and early 1960s. The social contradiction addressed by Richie and Anderson's work, as well as by Tanaka's shifts to that between *individualism* and *collectivism*. Here, individualism must be tapped to meet the new requirements of postwar Japanese consumer society—a domestic market demanding individuated consumers who can locate their personal desires in the purchase of commodities—while collectivism is appealed to in order to reinvent a work ethic that subordinates the individual to the nation. The detailed and additive chronological forms that the authors employ, with thick description, a filled-in linear timeline, and an attempt at inclusivity, seek to transcend the contradiction between the individual (the director) and the collective (the film industry) by positing a third term (in this case, the "genius") that breaks out of the rigid structure and trumps the other two terms. These two works engage the real social problem of individual agency in the face of huge social structures by building their chronological narratives with a trapdoor, one that allows a select few to escape without razing the structure altogether.

By the third wave of film histories (in the 1990s, in coordination with the one-hundred anniversary of Japanese film), the ideological determinant can once again be relocated. At this point, the unanswerable question is one that involves thinking the *national* and the *transnational* (Japan and the world) at the same time. How does one identify with the nation and obey its codes when the process of globalization seems to call many of these codes into question? Or, to locate this contradiction in relation to the more specific task at hand: How does one write a national film history within a fully integrated global economy? At the present moment, there are no answers to these questions, and this, I think, partly explains why both Oshima's and Sato's histories take the forms they do—forms that I will call nostalgic neo-chronological. These forms, although similar to the histories of the second stage, produce different meanings and effects within the different historical moment of global capitalism.

This chapter is the story of how these "unsquarable circles"—colonized–colonizer, individual–collective, national–transnational—transform at particular historical moments, and how being attentive to them may offer new insights into the meanings and effects of the most dominant histories of Japanese cinema. But what is the relation between the *histories* of Japanese film and the *films* of Japanese history? Can a rereading of film history change the films themselves? Why would it matter to analyze the forms by which other writers have written about this history? I certainly do not mean to suggest that film histories can somehow miraculously invent new content or retroactively delete earlier content. But I do want to argue that the writing of film history does not just record, clarify, or comment on past directors, films, and events. Rather, it actively participates in producing these very objects of study. In other words, by presenting the past in a way that hinges on the present and is crucial in shaping the possibilities of the future, film histories are not only constituted by the film community and society at large. They are integral in constituting these contexts, as well.

Left Telos, Right Telos: The Logic of Colonialism   In 1956, Iwasaki Akira, the well-known leftist critic; editor of the day's leading film journal, *Eiga hyoron*; and author and translator of more than twenty books at the time, published a short and passionate work titled *Eiga no riron* (Film theory).[4] Iwasaki worried that, as film was becoming dominant and as the critical distance that viewers brought to it was quickly disappearing, a subsequent relegation—if not denigration—of theory might emerge. Unlike earlier Japanese audiences, the film audience of 1956 had so successfully internalized a dominant cinematic grammar that questions such as "What is going on?" and "What does that mean?" were no longer being raised when watching a film. With a theoretically engaged spectator, as Iwasaki envisioned it, the why, how, and what of a film's meaning would return, and this new critical situation would turn back on the filmmakers themselves and compel them to refine their work and crank it up to a level of sophistication that both domestic and foreign critics were just then beginning to confer on Japanese cinema.[5]

Iwasaki's stake in theory emerged from his earlier involvement in the Proletarian Filmmaker's League (Prokino), which furnished him with the ideal opportunity to think through the relation between theory and practice (and aesthetics and politics) that later motivated him to produce *Film Theory* and its main thesis: that theory and practice needed to be worked on and expanded together, for one without the other spells the inevitable decline of both. Prokino was a diverse group of critics, activists, filmmakers, and students who from the late 1920s would film events such as demonstrations, strikes, and sit-ins. Then they would screen their work—often illegally—throughout the country (fig. 10), along with experiments in animation and *rensageki* (linked film and drama). Despite the movement's rapid growth, most of its members found themselves behind bars by 1935 as government officials successfully snuffed out the last traces of Prokino's operations.

Iwasaki was the house theorist at Prokino. Not only did he help edit and consistently contribute to one of the movement's journals, *Shinko eiga* (New film); he also published independently. His first work, *Eiga geijutsu-shi* (History of film art), was a companion piece to the more important and substantial *Film and Capitalism*.[6] As Iwasaki states in the preface of his second book, dated 1931, "This theoretical activity runs alongside the practical activities promoted by the soldiers of the proletarian film movement."[7] Again,

10. Prokino members participating in May Day demonstration. From Iwasaki Akira's *Eiga ga wakakatta toki* (When cinema was young) (Tokyo: Heibonsha, 1980).

one can see Iwasaki's stake in theory and his desire to stress its inextricable connection to practice. A glance at the drawing on the page before his preface presents us with a fitting image to think about this project (fig. 11). The drawing shows three people looking at a screen projecting the book's title and author's name. This picture presages Iwasaki's polemic: that the role of the critic is no epiphenomenon to the practical activity of making film. In other words, the critic does not come after to clarify the meanings and make judgments about the worth of a product; instead, the critic's voice is inscribed on the very screen, into the very form and content of the film, just as the film finds its way into the ideas and narrative structures of the critic. This could, of course, be understood as an expedient extolling of the critic on Iwasaki's part, but then again it could just as easily be understood as a fierce criticism of the critic, who is now fully implicated in the production of inferior film.

Based on this understanding of theory and practice, Iwasaki set himself the task in *Film and Capitalism* to carve open the space to theorize and produce proletarian film. To this end, he stated the absolute necessity of analyzing mainstream Western film history. The first section of *Film and Capitalism* is a periodization of the first thirty years of film in the United States and Germany. Iwasaki divides this history into three parts: from the first

11. Cover of Iwasaki Akira's *Eiga to shihon-shugi* (Film and
capitalism). The larger characters on the screen signify the
title of Iwasaki's book (Eiga to shihon-shugi), and the smaller
characters below them indicate his name (Iwasaki Akira).

permanent movie theaters to World War I (1900–13); from the end of the war
to the beginning of the talkie (1914–25); and from the talkie to the present
(1926–30). Iwasaki traces the rise of film corporations and the effects they
had on the content/form (*naiyo/keishiki*) of each period's films. Written in
the political fervor of the early 1930s, when proletarian culture in general,
from theater to literature, was thriving, *Film and Capitalism* was intended
for all those who were connected to the movement and for those who were
interested in proletarian culture in general.

From the early 1930s to the early 1940s, one sees a move from Iwasaki's
leftist version of Japanese film history (one that, at bottom, is committed to
revolution not only in Japanese film but also in Japanese society at large) to a
rightist version that is coordinated with the Japanese colonial project itself.
It is during this period that the first history ever made on film, *Japanese Film
History*, appears.[8] The film is composed of three parts, the third of which
has now disappeared, and was released in 1941 by the Greater Japan Film
Association (*Dai-nihon eiga kyokai*), a newly formed ideological arm of the
government, in cooperation with the Shochiku film company. *Japanese Film
History* was produced to commemorate the 1939 Film Law, whose censor-
ing strategies, to name just a few, streamlined the film industry by requiring

licensing for various film tasks, such as projection; imposed limits on the number of times a foreign film could be screened; set age limits for theater access; and required that a short "culture film" (*bunka eiga*) be included with all screenings of dramatic films.[9] *Japanese Film History*, one of these culture films, is an anthology of foreign and domestic film clips, newspaper headlines, newsreel footage, and photographs, with voiceover narration piecing the fragments together. Each part begins with the same paragraph of text explaining that the 1923 Great Kanto Earthquake destroyed many old film resources and that this film would attempt to reconstruct the history by organizing the remaining fragments in a coherent fashion.

Part 1 of *Japanese Film History* begins with Eadweard Muybridge's famous galloping horses, then moves to a still shot of Edison and a shot of the vitascope. Next one sees an advertisement for one of the first screenings in Japan of the moving pictures (*katsudo shashin*), then a quick cut to two of the first Japanese films made, *Momijigari* (1899) and *Nio no ukisu* (The grebe's floating nest, 1899). Following this are extended clips from such Western films as *Antony and Cleopatra* (1913) and *Attila* (1918) each with benshi commentary that, by highlighting the most famous benshi of the day (such as Matsuda Shunsui) commenting on crucial scenes, celebrates the transformative role of this Japanese complement to early film. Part 2 begins with more clips of silent foreign films, such as *The Cabinet of Dr. Caligari* (1919). Newsreel footage of a 1922 film conference sponsored by the Ministry of Education is interspersed, with the objective of choosing films that are the most pedagogically suitable for the classroom. This is followed by a clip of a government-sponsored film taken only weeks after the 1923 earthquake, in which Tokyo's homeless are depicted as harmoniously cooperating and organizing as they take on the task of reconstruction.[10] After a few more scenes from silent foreign films, the talkie enters with an extended clip of Gosho Heinosuke's 1931 *Madamu to nyobo* (The neighbor's wife and mine), a film that ushered in many of the new Hollywood codes later to be perfected as well as a new narrative style that would no longer depend on the benshi to suture discontinuities. From this point on, *Japanese Film History* focuses on the growth and success of Japanese film and Japanese film corporations. The next shot is a magnificent overhead panorama of the Shochiku Film Studio (the company that coproduced the film) taken in 1933, with a fitting shot of a lone worker entering the studio late at night—a possible allusion to the well-known Lumière brothers' 1895 film *Sortie d'usine*, in which workers were filmed leaving the famous Lyon studio.[11] After clips from such films as Nikkatsu studio's *Tsuchi* (Earth) and Shinko studio's *Ajia no musume* (Daughters of Asia), part 2 concludes with an extended scene from the financially and technologically successful melodrama *Aizen katsura* (The compassionate Buddha tree), made by Nomura Hiromasa in 1938, which marks a point of arrival for Japanese film.

It is certainly unfortunate that part 3 is not available to analyze, but given what we know about the first two parts, it seems safe to say that part 3 was roughly fifteen minutes long and composed primarily of clips from the more popular films of the day. Neither does it seem much of a risk to extrapolate on the form—all of the film's moments were meaningful insofar as they pointed to a final moment, a final scene from a film that not only represented success but, more important, represented the fulcrum on which the earlier moments turned. For example, the inclusion at the end of part 2 of the domestic film *Aizen katsura*, which was held up by government officials as a shining example of the quality that could be produced under the new Film Law, can be understood to stand in for the independence of the Japanese film industry from the West, its mastery of the technology, and, ultimately, its capability to lead Asia. All of this is to say that a teleological history is one that begins with the desire to celebrate a present moment (or to celebrate a present moment by acknowledging its evolutionary indispensability to a future teleological moment) by organizing the prior moments in such a way that they make each successive moment wholly fundamental to the existence of the privileged object. But if each moment is fundamental to the next, and ultimately to a present or final moment, then—and here we begin to detect the great violence wrapped up in this form of organizing history—this provides each moment's tautological justification. In other words, an earlier moment can get away with murder (or, at least, the crimes can be de-emphasized), because at bottom it represents the only progressive link to moments before and after it. The logic of this low-flying Darwinism precludes a sustained critique of any one of the preceding moments, for such a critique would immediately place in jeopardy the final moment's privileged status as the high point of progress. But even more crucial is that those moments that are left out of the history are to be understood as insignificant in the overall evolutionary progress of the history at hand.

I cannot leave this issue without some mention of how a teleological historiography hooks up with the logic of colonialism. The most striking element of *Japanese Film History* is the date that it was produced, 1941. Commencing with production in the late 1930s, this will to make a history out of cinematic culture and its relation to the colonial project in general suggests comparisons to the history of literature. In Great Britain, a literary canon was not formed until the end of the eighteenth century, and literature as a discipline was not instituted until the mid-nineteenth century.[12] The creation of a literary canon and literature as a discipline became the most significant cultural justification for conquest as the role of religion diminished. The same can be said—and has been said by Masao Miyoshi—about the construction of a Japanese literary canon and the establishment of the Department of National Literature at the Imperial University of Tokyo in the mid-1880s.[13] This association between a teleological history and colonialism is not to say that *Japanese Film History* was exported to Korea, Manchuria, or any of the other Japanese-occupied territories, or that the film's content revealed any direct reference to Japanese colonialism. Instead, it is to suggest that the teleological form of historiography is bound up with the construction of the nation-state. The desire to tell a story about the film's past, to place its elements on a linear track that then could be heralded as a story of success, progress, and natural—if not divine—development, is consistent with the ideological story of the nation, and it certainly befits both the British and Japanese situations. For *Japanese Film History*, the telos—not only the point to which everything points, but also the point from which everything is set in motion—is Japan as the colonial center of Asia. What seems particularly interesting about these teleological characteristics for my purposes is that they are embodied not only by *Japanese Film History* but also by Iwasaki's 1931 *Film and Capitalism*.

At the beginning of *Film and Capitalism*, Iwasaki clearly states the three problematics that will organize his work: "(1) The cinema's social role in reproducing class relations in capitalist society; (2) the process of corporate film development as part of the same moment of large totalizing forces of capitalist development; and (3) the influence over film form and film content by the economic corporate requirements of the capitalist mode of production."[14] Iwasaki's Marxist language might strike us as vulgar today, and indeed, his movement from the economic to the cultural is one-dimensional, with no hint of how the cultural might affect the economic, how spectatorship might vary according to such categories as gender or even class, or how the periods themselves might dialectically relate to one another. But the problem does not lie in the problematics themselves. The three concerns remain rich points of departure for any attempt to theorize culture. The problem, instead, lies in the way Iwasaki works through the problematics, which ultimately betrays (the dialectical implications of) his work's title and resembles a teleological history more than a relational one, with the telos being the birth of proletarian film or even a later moment of actually existing socialism.

In both works, the utopian gesture of transcending the colonized–colonizer paradox is tied to the ideological limitations of a teleological historiography. In both cases, the teleological form cannot deal properly with difference. H. D. Harootunian has written about how Walter Benjamin, in his "Theses on the Philosophy of History" (1940), exposed similar trends occurring in Europe at approximately the same time. In the European context, a vulgar Marxist rendering of history, in which the present was reduced to a mere transition, mirrored the formal historiographical structure of its ideological enemy: right-wing historicism.[15] Harootunian writes, "For both bourgeois historicism and Marxist historiography shared what he [Benjamin] described as an irresistible 'conformism,' an aspiration for a 'universal history,' a deadening resignation to the evolutionary story of the 'same,' which historical practice, whether Marxian or not, obediently documented. Moreover, both historical practices were bonded to the same conception of 'homogeneous empty time.' "[16]

For Benjamin, this story of the "same" could be blasted apart by employing the strategy of montage, the artistic form most conducive to his project of historical materialism. Montage, according to Benjamin, "had special, perhaps even total rights as a progressive form because it interrupts the context into which it is inserted and thus counteracts illusion."[17] Some might argue that *Japanese Film History*, with its piecing together of various fragments of the first forty years of film, is itself montage. But as Susan Buck-Morss makes clear, it is not the montage form as such that is crucial, "but whether the construction makes visible the gap between sign and referent, or fuses them in a deceptive totality so that the caption merely duplicates the semiotic content of the image instead of setting it into question."[18] Indeed, in both *Japanese*

12. Kamei Fumio on location in Shanghai. From Kamei Fumio's *Fighting Film* (Tokyo: Iwanami Shincho, 1989).

Film History and *Film and Capitalism* there is no room for any content that might suggest alternative paths or interrupt the one-dimensional demands of the telos.

There is at least one place, however, where montage was being developed in Japan: in the film work of the documentarist Kamei Fumio. An art student, Kamei went to the Soviet Union in 1928 with the idea of studying painting. After being impressed with the aesthetic and political possibilities of film (documentary film in particular), Kamei moved to Leningrad, where he enrolled in the Leningrad School of Film Art. Influenced by Sergei Eisenstein and Dziga Vertov, Kamei writes, "I came to think of film montage not merely as a technique, but as a method of philosophical expression . . . with revolutionary potential."[19] After participating in several film groups and on various film sets in Leningrad, Kamei returned to Japan in 1931 and began working in the documentary department of the Photo Chemical Laboratories (PCL). In the mid-1930s, newspapers and newsreels were filled with information about Shanghai, yet, as Kamei explains, the majority of images were of soldiers shouting "*Banzai! Banzai!*" beneath the Japanese flag.[20] The idea was then suggested to Kamei to make a film about Shanghai and the various colonial powers (Japan included) that had descended on the city (fig. 12).[21]

Shanghai is a melodic meditation on the banal (faces, buildings, daily chores, schoolchildren) in the midst of the spectacle of colonialism. With financing also provided by the Japanese government, the film was supposed to be a war document that firmly supported the Japanese presence in China. Even though on the level of content there is very little in *Shanghai* that can be interpreted as anti-Japanese, Kamei was still punished for his antiwar sentiments—for even the Japanese censors were impressed by the montage form that so elegantly con-fuses the Japanese presence with the presence of the British and other foreign powers in the city, thus delicately pointing its viewers to the logic of colonialism in general as opposed to the "good" (Japanese) and "bad" (Western) versions of it. When commenting on the general mode of filmmaking in both Japan and the West (especially the United States) and his own strategies, Kamei writes:

> The form [of mainstream film] is constructed so that a viewer can only start thinking about the film after it is finished; during a film, however, the viewers are not allowed to develop any creative ideas on their own. . . . If with shot A an idea arises then the director explains that idea with shot B. This type of art is contrary to that of haiku . . . and I think documentary film *must* be like haiku. If the viewer observes something with shot A, then shot B must produce the space for the viewers to freely develop their own creative possibilities. Shot B, therefore, demands a new observation by the viewer [as opposed to the ones that are usually supplied for them]. Shot B is what I call the *ma* of documentary film.[22]

In Japanese aesthetics, *ma* usually refers to the absences, gaps, silences, or negative spaces that, when not filled in (on a canvas, in a musical composition, in a poem), draw attention to the essential lack in the presences or positive spaces. *Ma*, in other words, exposes that which is experienced as incomplete and as meaningful only in relation to something else, something not positively provided.

Eisenstein is usually credited with recognizing the dialectical and cinematic potential of haiku and Japanese aesthetics.[23] But it was Kamei who seriously pursued the connections.[24] Just as haiku depends on the reader to transform (to rise from[25]) the combination of intellectually abstract concepts into emotional and concrete qualities, so, too, did Kamei want the viewer of his films to transform the flat images of a broken bugle, an abandoned military helmet, and a Japanese flag into a moment of recognition that might shatter (*pace* Benjamin) the "myth of progress," or the one-way street of rational connections that, by the late 1930s, was surely headed for destruction. Kamei was struggling with a form in which Shot B would not heavy-handedly push the viewer into a single direction but provide the space for new possibilities to be produced, possibilities that were not locked into a predetermined course.[26]

Indeed, both *Japanese Film History* and *Film and Capitalism* were locked into a predetermined course, and along with their utopian gestures of transcendence (revolution, Asian liberation) were reactionary ones as well. Nevertheless, this teleological form was dominant at this time, and the challenges made by Kamei were marginal, at best. It must be remembered, however, that although Kamei may have been producing a philosophy of history through his documentaries, he was not producing a history of film. This simple fact leads me to expand on the first thesis of this chapter—that historiographical forms face historical limits and emerge in relation to the more general social contradictions of a particular moment—by developing a second thesis in the form of a question: Do certain moments in the life span of a history necessitate certain historiographical forms?

Limits of Chronology and Chronology of Limits   The first thesis is about the larger history in which film is but one element. Is there something about Iwasaki's historical moment in 1931—a moment in which production is being successfully transformed into a military economy; in which the Manchurian Incident brightly flashes the Japanese colonial project; in which Japanese intellectual culture, on the heels of one of the most progressive decades in Japanese thought, is being squeezed into a censored hole—that limited him to writing a teleological history? This is to ask what happens when we place the writing of Japanese film history onto the larger narrative of history. The second thesis focuses more on a particular history and the limitations and possibilities that are produced by its stages of development. For example, does the earlier the moment in the course of a cultural history—say, thirty years from its birth in the case of *Japanese Film History* and Iwasaki's *Film and Capitalism*—lend itself to, if not relegate itself to, a teleological form of historiography?

The questions can be dealt with best by shifting the narrative analysis to

13. Cover of Tanaka Junichiro's *Nihon eiga hattatsu-shi* (A history of the developments of Japanese film), volume 1.

14. Cover of Donald Richie and Joseph Anderson's *The Japanese Film.*

two chronological histories: Tanaka's *History of the Developments of Japanese Film* (1957) and Richie and Anderson's *The Japanese Film* (1959) (figs. 13 and 14). One question to be asked is why these two works, film histories that have had such remarkable and enduring influence and that remain the classic texts of the genre, were made within only two years of each other and employ similar historiographical forms. Sato Tadao notes that Tanaka's work set the standard for Japanese film history and that nothing to this point is comparable in depth or breadth. Sato writes, "Because very few resources remain from the earlier days it will be hard to surpass this work. Whoever sets off to write a history about Japanese film history will have to rely on this work."[27] In fact, Sato set off to do precisely this, collecting many of the articles he has written over the past twenty years to produce his four-volume *History of Japanese Film* (1995), a work that will also be analyzed here.

The influence of Richie and Anderson's *The Japanese Film* may be even greater. I cannot imagine many contemporary film critics writing in English about Japanese film who would not in some way make use of Richie and Anderson's work. One might recall Noel Burch's statement in the first paragraph of *To the Distant Observer:* "It is hoped that the reader will be familiar with the several writings of Donald Richie and in particular *The Japanese*

Film, written in collaboration with Joseph Anderson and drawing much data from Tanaka."[28] Or as Richie and Anderson put it themselves in the 1982 Foreword to their work, "It is not often that authors have the opportunity to expand their material and review their ideas twenty-three years after the original publication of their work. It is also unusual that a film history this old should be thought worth republication. While we are happy about both events, we also feel that the primary reason is that no subsequent work has superseded ours."[29]

As to why both of these enormously influential Japanese film histories were produced within a period of only a few years, the argument to be made here can be previewed by mentioning that I do not think the two Americans wrote their book on the back of Tanaka's labor. In fact, Richie and Anderson quote Tanaka's work only once, and the wealth of primary sources to which they refer, as well as the many years they spent writing for Japanese film journals, establishing contacts, and, in Richie's case, even directing film in Japan, seems to make the case that they could just as well have produced their work had Tanaka's not existed. What seems more plausible, and what links up with the theoretical question posed earlier, is that the moment in the history of Japanese film was uniquely suited to the writing of such a film history. This moment came immediately after all of the classic directors could be identified (Ito, Mizoguchi, Ozu, Naruse Mikio, Kurosawa, to name just the most famous) and when Japanese film had "made it" in the West. It was a moment of recovery from two major traumas: first, the war and the requirements that wartime ideology placed on the film industry; and second, the U.S. occupation and requirements that Supreme Commander for the Allied Powers (SCAP) officials placed on the industry. Finally, it was a moment that immediately preceded the emergence of the New Wave as a disruptive force within the industry and when that other great disruptive force, television, would hit a critical mass. But what is it about a chronological history that would make it conducive to such a transitional moment? Of course, the answer is overdetermined by a whole series of possible reasons. There is the subjectivity and agency of the authors that positioned them to write such histories; there are all of the geopolitical reasons that Japanese film became popular in the West at this time; there is the issue of accessibility of resources, or even something as trivial as the whim of a publisher. This is to say that the reason cannot be pinned down. Yet, at the same time, this should not keep us from locating a certain historical conjuncture that produced the possibility for writing such works.

But we should be clear on what a chronological history is. First, a chronological history abides by a forward-moving timeline. In other words, it will not examine a director who produced in the 1960s before one who produced in the 1930s has been analyzed. Second, it is inclusive. It attempts to serve as a database that will contain even the smallest amount of information regarding any possible topic or person. Third, it uses the larger history as a ballast instead of as an explanatory device: For example, beginnings or endings of chapters will reference the larger history as little more than markers of the course of the particular history being worked on. Fourth, it is bottom-heavy. In contrast to the top-heavy teleological history (in which the top elements, the present or future moments), fashion the bottom elements (or earlier moments), a chronological history's earlier moments organize the thinking about any later moment. Making sense of a later moment in a history, then, necessarily requires a continuous return, a type of meticulous retracing of steps, to the logic of the origin. Fifth, and connected to this, a chronological history is unconsciously diachronic. That is, it does not concern itself with the way discontinuities, or breaks in history, might shape the meanings of seemingly similar cultural products, not to mention epistemologies or phenomenological relationships, that exist on either side of one of these breaks. What is de-emphasized is the way in which culture undergoes dialectical transformations from one historical moment to another. In other words, a chronological history groups products together by their stylistic or generic similarities. Thus, if a film under consideration is about children, it is labeled a "child film," regardless of when it was produced. But the possibility also exists that a so-called child film made in the 1930s shares more similarities with a film in a different style, or genre, of a later period than with a child film from this later period.[30]

Tanaka's preface to his first volume presents an accurate account of what his work sets out to do (and the first part of this account applies equally well to Richie's and Anderson's work): "This work . . . begins from the point of wanting to connect the history of film's mechanical, corporate, and aesthetic development. On top of all this, the recent developments in the film business relating to mass communications and the large effect this has on society must also be considered. It is for this purpose and from this position that this work has been composed."[31] This desire to connect the mechanical, corporate, and aesthetic triangle is indeed a tremendous task, and the fact that both works attempt to do so by accumulating an enormous quantity of facts and figures regarding each of these points accounts for why chronological histories tend to be so thick. As for how and why these three points might connect to, or interact with, one another, or how their relations are figured in everyday life or in the film narratives themselves, is simply not on the agenda of these two projects. The rigor, in other words, is in the accumulation of facts, not in the thinking through of relations. But this is not to suggest that the works are mere chronicles of Japanese film history and do not offer critical judgments, criticize political positions, or even propose, often unintentionally, methods for explaining the relationship among the mechanical, corporate, and aesthetic elements. They do, sometimes in a stunningly heavy-handed fashion.

Tanaka published the first three volumes of *A History of the Developments of Japanese Film* in 1957 (volume four was not published until 1967, and volume five was not published until 1980).[32] The five volumes comprise more than 2,500 pages, referencing more than 3,000 names and 2,500 films. Indeed, the work is a staple for even the smallest library and, since it was published in paperback (*bunko-bon*), has become not only the dominant historical narrative but also the essential reference guide on Japanese film for the general user. What strikes me about this work is how Tanaka uses foreign films to organize his narrative. At the end of almost every chapter one finds ten to fifteen pages of notes on the foreign films that were available in Japan during the period Tanaka is analyzing. Titles, names of director and actors, and sometimes brief plot descriptions are given for each film, and the inclusion of this material is without doubt the principal controlling device of the work. Of course, foreign films have much to do with the development of Japanese film, so the inclusion of these works is not surprising. But the way in which these pages are left suspended at the end of each chapter, almost in note form, illustrates how chronological histories use *other* histories as a timeline, or as a ballast, without delving into what the relations between the histories might be. In other words, despite the gesture to its outside, the chronological film history, in the end, remains thoroughly autonomous.

For Richie and Anderson, however, it is not foreign films that organize their narrative but political and social historical events themselves. For example, at the beginning of chapter 2, they write, "Japan as a modern nation was swiftly maturing and, despite its comparative youth, was beginning to be treated as a responsible adult in the family of nations."[33] At the beginning of chapter 7, they say: "The war with China was not unexpected. The Japanese, long looking toward the continent and seeking a weak, disunited China, had seen the chance to force its leadership of the new Asia upon the larger country."[34] In these examples, and in many others strewn throughout the work, this other history functions as a reference point that, after serving its navigational purpose, is stored away, only to be wheeled back out at the next plot point. This technique may well be inherent in the very logic of a chronological history, in which an immense volume of material is being manipulated. In a certain sense, then, given that both *A History of the Developments of Japanese Film* and *The Japanese Film* are indispensible works in their respective languages, they do seem to rise above any formal criticism. The fact is that we needed (and still need) these histories, and the amount of scholarship that they have generated, assisted, or simply enabled is remarkable. Indeed, my own study of Japanese film historiography is indebted to their labor. And certainly all three authors have modified their work over the years and should not be handcuffed to these early works (works that represent only a portion of their respective oeuvres). But as should be clear from the underlying aim of my examination, I am less interested in criticizing individual historians than in analyzing how their dominant historiographical structures relate to the most pressing social problems of their moment. Despite the similar historiographical structures of these classic works, however, two great differences position them quite differently in terms of subsequent scholarship. The first is that Richie and Anderson's work is relied on as the fundamental resource of Japanese film history by those who cannot read Japanese.[35] By contrast, Tanaka's work is consistently replenished by new scholarship for Japanese readers. This has produced a trickle-down effect on contemporary Japanese film scholarship that is worth mentioning here.

In Richie and Anderson's *The Japanese Film* one gets a work that is not only well researched and inclusive, but also one that is impulsively quick to criticize any political project, a work that is routinely—and at times fiercely —anticommunist in a way that discloses uninterrogated political reflexes more than it does responsible thinking through of the relation between aesthetics and politics. It is also curiously driven to denounce Japanese critics. On Kamei Fumio, mentioned earlier, for example, Richie and Anderson write, "[He] revealed competence in direction but too often got lost in polemic."[36] On the overtly political message in the films of Imai Tadashi, they write: "[Imai's message] is far removed from the simple faith of Kurosawa's humanism; it is resolutely political and continues to indicate the limitations of the director."[37] And on Japanese film critics' appreciation of Imai, they write, "Perhaps they like him because he is Communist and all Japanese film critics (one might say almost any Japanese of any intellectual pretensions) still find it very chic to affect a leftist orientation."[38]

The simple assumptions at work here regarding the relation between aesthetics and politics—that is, the need to disregard the constitutive relationship between the two terms so as to fail to recognize that any work cannot help but be "resolutely political," not to mention the resolutely political nature of Richie and Anderson's comment itself—seem almost fruitless to question. And today, many readers (and perhaps even Richie and Anderson themselves), I suspect, simply avert their eyes from such demagogic remarks and focus solely on the rich factual information. Still, no matter how strategic one may be in using Richie and Anderson's work, certain inevitable effects do seem to be borne by such dependence. This becomes clear if we move to the second great difference between *A History of the Developments of Japanese Film* and *The Japanese Film*, which has to do with how critical judgments are made. For example, Tanaka dedicates about two pages to explaining when the Prokino movement was established, why it was formed, and who its founding members were; he also provides the names of some of the films that it produced, a bit about *Shinko eiga* (one of the movement's companion journals), and how the movement was crushed as a result of government tightening after the Manchurian Incident.[39] As is true in most of *A History of the Developments of Japanese Film*, Tanaka does not make an overt critical judgment of Prokino's films or objectives. Instead, he presents the movement as one more component in the evolution of Japanese film history.

Richie and Anderson's work contains only one paragraph about Prokino. The two writers place its activities on the "Left Extreme" of the tendency movement (*Keiko Eiga*) and explain that Prokino was formed "specifically to make documents of the Communist movement in Japan."[40] They go on

to write, "Despite the extremely low quality of its products, this organization . . . was kept active filming demonstrations, slums, and May Days."[41]
The point is not to favor Tanaka's more encyclopedic account of Prokino.
Nor is it to criticize Richie and Anderson for not including more on Prokino or for not being more imaginative and seeing how the "quality" of Prokino's films might be better judged by using criteria other than those used to
judge the output of major studios' films. Instead, the point is to suggest that
it is this type of inclusivity of data, followed by the trivialization of certain
topics that Richie and Anderson find politically distasteful, that represents
the real force of *The Japanese Film* and its particular strand of chronological
historiography.[42]

My interest is in how a chronological history shields its own political
interventions from sustained critique. This is done not so much by particular strategies of writing by the authors as by the historiographical form itself.
A chronological history is authoritative and especially so when the object
of study is as foreign to a reader as Japanese film is to most non-Japanese
speakers. Critical acclaim of such histories only strengthens their power:
"The definitive study," "The indispensable history for anyone interested in
Japanese film," "The classic for years to come"—it is hard to imagine these
labels being applied to a history that is, say, more concerned with theoretical
issues than with the accumulation of data. (Although in the case of literature, Karatani Kojin's *Nihon kindai bungaku no kigen* [Origins of Modern
Japanese Literature] does seem to have achieved this status.)[43] Rather than
rethink the form by which a history is organized, Richie and Anderson, as
well as Tanaka, need only add more material to their databases (a new volume in the case of Tanaka, and a new edition with a few additional essays in
the case of Richie and Anderson). The form stands unaltered and is always
ready to absorb new information. In the end, rather than die or fade away,
chronological histories from this second stage of historiography just get peri-
odically updated.

The argument here is not that chronological film histories are limited to
the 1950s and '60s. Rather, it is to stress that at this particular moment, the
chronological form became dominant for two reasons. First, by the late '50s
there was finally enough film history (sixty years' worth) to produce such a
comprehensive form. Second, and more important, the form was an attempt
to work out in narrative form one of the most difficult problems of post-

war Japanese modernity: the antinomy between the individual and the collective. Both histories were produced during years of spectacular economic growth: Between 1953 and 1960, the economy grew at an average rate of 9.5 percent a year. Further, although there were gestures to individual rights and democratic freedoms, such as the right to strike and to establish trade unions, after 1945, SCAP officials, with active participation by Japanese officials, soon scrapped these ideals for the larger geopolitical imperatives of the day. Whatever antimonopoly measures taken immediately following the war had been revised by 1952, spurring the realignment of firms along former zaibatsu lines. Although discourses of individual rights and "Western" notions of freedom abounded, most people seemed to believe in the end that the individual was most free when the national polity and economy was most "successful," and not the other way around.

It is in relation to this contradiction between individualistic ideologies and political-economic realities that the chronological histories of this second wave of historiography can be located. The way in which Richie and Anderson manage this contradiction is encapsulated in their inscription on page one of *The Japanese Film:* "Dedicated to that little band of men who have tried to make the Japanese film industry what every film industry should be: a directors' cinema."[44] Echoed in Kurosawa's foreword to the book, this "great man theory," as it gets worked out in the pages of Richie and Anderson's narrative, turns out to mean that an individual can rise up and produce greatness within—if not transcend—any structure.

In *The Japanese Film*, we see this determinant being played out on the battleground between the director (individualism) and the film industry (collectivism). Imai Tadashi (communism) represents the synthesis of collectivism and non-individualism. Richie and Anderson write, "If Imai were interested only in moral propaganda, if he were interested, let us say, in revolt for its own sweet sake, then what he says would be worth listening to. But the propaganda is never that personal and therefore never that valid."[45] Big, unbridled business represents the resolution between non-collectivism and nonindividualism because it is bound to destroy the industry itself (as it embraces TV), therefore leaving no room for the individual director to produce. The resolution between individualism and non-collectivism is the total outsider (which in Japan has never had to be that far) who will go his or her own way alone (perhaps a Wakamatsu Koji or a Terayama Shuji). Finally, we have

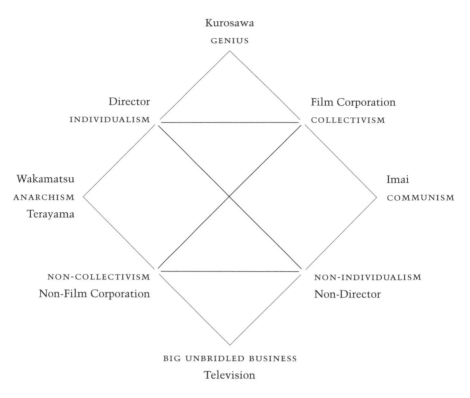

Kurosawa
GENIUS

Director
INDIVIDUALISM

Film Corporation
COLLECTIVISM

Wakamatsu
ANARCHISM
Terayama

Imai
COMMUNISM

NON-COLLECTIVISM
Non-Film Corporation

NON-INDIVIDUALISM
Non-Director

BIG UNBRIDLED BUSINESS
Television

15. Diagram of the narrative structure of Richie and Anderson's *The Japanese Film.*

the formal resolution of the real contradiction between the individual and the collective, which takes the form of Kurosawa (the genius)—that person who can be an individual *and* stand in for the collective, therefore replacing the need for the ugliness of unions, strikes, peasants, workers, or, in short, revolution. This is akin to one of the more notorious strains of modern skepticism in which the system is criticized while, at the same time, any commitment or attempt to achieve collective action is seen as equally impossible, if not sinister. This type of *resentiment* leaves individual genius or greatness as the only logical path of resistance. Here is what Richie and Anderson write about Kurosawa: "Perhaps it is for this reason that the films of Akira Kurosawa have taken so experimental and so original a form: The thought behind them, and the personality of the director, are so completely original that a new form had to be created to hold them."[46]

74 The Flash of Capital

Figure 15 diagrams this narrative analysis of Richie and Anderson's text. It is precisely the construction of such a rigid chronological narrative, one that allows for transgression in a way that does not confront the dirty realities that inevitably accompany real structural change, that contains the underlying impulse of Richie and Anderson's text and the dominant histories of the second wave of Japanese film historiography.

Interlude: The Historiographical Unconscious

So far I have presented two moments in this narrative of the writing of Japanese film history. The first begins in the 1930s, with the film *Japanese Film History* and Iwasaki's second book *Film and Capitalism*, and continues to the late 1950s, with Tanaka's *A History of the Developments of Japanese Film* and Richie and Anderson's *The Japanese Film*. The first two histories were shown to represent a teleological historiographical form, while the latter two represent a chronological one. This brings us to a third moment that, although not quite formed, recently has been fueled by the one-hundredth anniversary of film celebrated in Japan and in many countries throughout the world. The two histories I have chosen to consider are Sato Tadao's *History of Japanese Film* (1995), a more than 2,000-page compilation of more than twenty years of Sato's research, and Oshima Nagisa's *100 Years of Japanese Cinema*, a fifty-two-minute documentary produced for the BFI.

But before working through these histories, a few remarks are in order about my selection process and my narrativization of the works included here. One of the leading resources on film materials, *Eiga no tosho* (Film publications), contains more than one hundred citations under the heading "Japanese Film History."[47] So why have I selected the four histories already discussed and the two to follow? To complicate matters further, works that do not announce themselves as "histories" of Japanese film may very well be proposing methods for thinking about the history of Japanese film or for doing history itself. A book that turns on a single genre or a single period, for example, usually offers historiographical methods for thinking about other genres or periods. This then opens the floodgates, perhaps too wide, to what can be considered a history of Japanese film: Such a history could now be almost anything written about the subject, because wrapped up in any work's methodology are the writer's assumptions made about historical research (how to make sense of textualized versions of past events), methods of historical representation (how to express the past), and, finally, narrativization (how to organize one's story about the past).

The works that I have chosen all announce themselves as "histories" and are all diachronic, freely moving from decade to decade until reaching their respective presents. And my own story of Japanese film histories has also been diachronic, marking three moments in the course of the one-hundred-year history—beginning in the 1930s, stopping off in the late 1950s and early '60s, and working up to the 1990s. Without this narrative (and its relation to the narrative of capitalism), my work would look entirely different, inevitably venturing off into atomistic textual readings (this or that particular film or genre), isolated contextual readings (this or that particular historical event or period and its relation to film), or removed theoretical readings (this or that problematic regarding film).

This is not to suggest that these projects could not be rich in social knowledge, especially if we consider the many absences that need to be engaged regarding Japanese film scholarship in English and Japanese. For example, works in English such as David Desser's *Eros Plus Massacre,* about the Japanese New Wave of the 1960s, and Darrell William Davis's *Picturing Japaneseness,* about a group of pre-World War II films that the author labels "monumental,"[48] are two examples of this type of welcome scholarship. In Japanese, *Nihon eiga to modanizumu* (Japanese film and modernism), edited by Iwamoto Kenji and about the modernization of the 1920s and 1930s, and Komatsu Hiroshi's *Kigen no eiga* (Cinema of origins) are two more examples of recent scholarship that represent important advances in previously under-researched topics.[49] In a certain sense, one might view these works as "histories" of Japanese film that, in however unintentional a way, present their own historiographical methods.

Desser and Davis argue that they are breaking with an older form of Western Japanese film scholarship. Both writers zero in on a short historical period—ten years for Desser, and less than five years for Davis—and go to great pains to move back and forth between the historical context and the films under consideration. This method is intended to contrast those that recognize Japanese film "as an outgrowth of a preexistent, relatively unchanging essence,"[50] as Davis puts it, and one that "denies integrity to the possibility of deliberate, active, conscious change,"[51] according to Desser. Neither writer wants to see his objects of study collapsed into a reductive historiography that resorts to essentializing Japanese character and its historical manifestations. For Davis, this would deny the importance of historically specific spectator reception as well as the significance of Japan's militarization and the "monumental style" that it called forth—a style that evokes a traditional Japanese heritage for ideological purposes in the late 1930s and early 1940s. For Desser, this type of reductive history denies the agency employed by the New Wave directors, who were not merely a new, angrier version of the older, golden-age directors, but quite distinct and discontinuous from them. And for both writers, the leading purveyors of such retrograde methods are Richie and Anderson (in *The Japanese Film*) and Noel Burch (in *To the Distant Observer*).

Can one call Desser's and Davis's works "synchronic," meaning that they are more concerned with the space of a period and its own relationships than with its temporal transformations? Perhaps, but Davis seems to fumble in his last chapter when he attempts to show what happens to monumental style when it reached the 1980s and '90s. When analyzing Kurosawa's *Ran* (1986) or Teshigahara's *Rikyu* (1990), Davis searches for the monumental characteristics that he identified in the late 1930s, from a celebration and appropriation of Japanese tradition and aesthetics to epic narrativization and an exaltation of feudal hierarchies. But if Davis was more faithful to a synchronic history—or, at least, more faithful to his opening salvos at continuous historiography—he would have de-emphasized how contemporary texts "attenuate" the monumental style. Instead, he would have focused on what happens to the *concept* of style—and its relation to genre—at two very different moments in history, as well as on the stylistic and generic formations, if any, into which monumental style mutated. (This, of course, implies that these new formations might not look anything like the older ones on the level of style or content but might be linked by a shared ideological function.)

Apparently more conscious of his methodology, Desser pauses to consider what is at stake in the type of period critiques that are employed by Richie and Anderson, Burch, and Audie Bock's *Japanese Film Directors*.[52] Desser criticizes these writers' older, "linear" periodizations and substitutes the word "paradigms" for "periods" in order to allow for the coexistence of different paradigms during the same moment. For example, Desser worries that periodizing will cause a filmmaker such as Kurosawa to be grouped with one as paradigmatically different as Oshima because of the many years that overlap in the course of their careers. Desser's use of paradigms, symbolized by Ozu (classical), Kurosawa (modern), and Oshima (modernist), "should not prevent us from understanding that one mode does not necessarily replace another."[53] Paradigms, for Desser, can coexist: "Thus the notion of paradigms allows for continuity and simultaneity and it allows for the kind of deliberate rebellion that characterizes the New Wave."[54] Here Desser makes an important intervention that seems to offer a way to see "residual" and "emergent" aesthetic paradigms (*pace* Raymond Williams) as operating within the dominant paradigms of the day. Not only is this a needed critique of how many periodizations, such as Iwasaki's in *Film and Capitalism*, envision cultural production as a unified and passive reflection of the economic base, it also appears to suit Desser's need to carve out a space for artistic agency.

But as Mitsuhiro Yoshimoto perceptively notes, "A mere substitution of the word 'paradigm' for 'period' does not solve a problem of periodization and the problematic of writing history in general. . . . The question is how these paradigms of Japanese cinema can explain historical change or transformation."[55] Desser cannot explain historical change in *Eros Plus Massacre* because what remains after his theoretical tinkering is a theory of paradigms detached from a larger theory of history. According to Desser, paradigms, which reveal themselves in narrative form, change because *individuals* acquire different objectives. For example, Desser explains the change from one paradigm to another as follows: "In the shift from the classical to the modern paradigm, we find a shift in the attitude toward the status quo. From the acceptance of Life's problems we find the emergence of the individual who fights against his circumstances; we find, in short, the emergence of bourgeois individualism."[56] But this shift in attitude and its narrativization still needs explanation. For instance, we might ask, How do dominant cinematic paradigms and cinematic reception relate to dominant socioeconomic paradigms? And how might this opening—or closing—of paradigmatic possibilities work? Of course, these questions, which hinge on the concept of mediation (or how various levels within a social formation dynamically relate) are beyond the scope of Desser's project, and I do not mean to criticize his work for not being more rigorous on this score. In my own work, however, the mediation among film, historiography, and capitalism is a running theme.

Chronology out of Time   At this point, it is important to remember that the preceding section grew out of the earlier discussion of how I am employing a diachronic form to chart the course of Japanese film histories. I mentioned that this history might have its own moments of development, with each moment represented by a dominant form—the first, teleological, and the second, chronological. (To this we might now add those histories that exhibit a hostility toward diachronic histories, such as the work of Desser and Davis.[57]) I also suggested that, without relying on a narrative of Japanese capitalism, it would be difficult to make sense of the changes from one dominant historiographical form to another—not to mention of the limitations that film historians face.

What needs to be stressed now is that this periodization of Japanese film history does not need to be linear, rigid, or determining in the way that many end up being. For example, this periodization, as per Desser, recognizes the coexistence of different historiographical forms within a period in which a dominant form exists. But this seems to fall short of explaining how the different paradigms interact with one another. That is, not only do older paradigms not get replaced by newer ones, but older paradigms become refunctionalized within the dominant paradigm, thus transforming their effects and meanings. One way to illustrate this palimpsestic process, this simultaneous process of persistence and mutation, is to examine the last two Japanese film histories on our agenda. These histories, by Sato and Oshima, both use a chronological form, but we can now ask: Were the effects I described earlier, when discussing the chronological histories of the late 1950s, unchanged forty years later and after a transformation into a different moment of Japanese capitalism (figs. 16 and 17)?

In the essay "Nekkyo no jidai" (Age of enthusiasm), published in the same book that contains the scenario of *100 Years of Japanese Cinema*, Oshima writes, "Even though the request [from the BFI] was totally open and provided me with the flexibility to make a film using my own vision and methods, in the end I decided on an orthodox and objective documentary. I chose various clips and stills from the different periods' most representative films and commented over them with my own narration."[58] Choosing what can be categorized as an expository mode (direct address to the viewer, rhetorical continuity, impression of objectivity), Oshima's work begins at the be-

16. Cover of Oshima Nagisa's *Sengo 50 nen, Eiga 100 nen* (Fifty years after the war, one hundred years of film).

17. Cover of Sato Tadao's *Nihon eiga-shi* (A history of Japanese film), volume 1.

ginning and ends at the end, as any properly chronological history should.[59] Oshima's documentary thus turns out to be one of the more "orthodox" films made for the BFI's Century of Cinema series, which contracted a number of renowned filmmakers to produce works about their own countries' film history. The other directors in the series (Stanley Kwan, Martin Scorsese, Wim Wenders, to name just a few) each depart in varying degrees from standard chronological and expository historiography.[60]

In "Age of Enthusiasm," Oshima goes on to note the coincidence of the one-hundred-year anniversary of film falling on the same year as the fifty-year anniversary of the end of World War II. "But," he continues, "this, in fact, represents more than just a mere coincidence."[61] Oshima employs the war in his documentary as the single event that shoots through each moment of the hundred-year history of Japanese film. He moves from the films made before the war that point toward it, to the films made during the war under the Film Law, to the films made right after the war (under SCAP command), and then to the response to these films (New Wave), to films representing new symptoms of postwar contradictions (*Yakuza, Roman-Poruno, Tora-san*), to his own war film in the early 1980s (*Senjo no merii kurisumasu* [Merry Christmas Mr. Lawrence], 1982), to the final film mentioned in the history, Sai Yoichi's *Tsuki wa dotchi ni deteiru* (Everything under the moon,

1994). From the last film, about the problems of the *zainichi* (foreign permanent or long-term residents in Japan), Oshima chooses to show a clip of the two protagonists (Tadao, a Korean, and Connie, a Filipina) sitting at a booth in a family restaurant as Tadao explains that he had come to Japan for a better life after his father was killed by the Japanese army. By organizing the history from a median moment, as opposed to a beginning or final one, it appears as if Oshima's film departs from the earlier criteria I described for chronological form. But Oshima explains in his essay that World War II and Japanese film both flow from the onset of industrial capitalism, whose logic is the primary cause of both the war and the direction film has taken. This appeal to the logic of capitalism seems to account for why Oshima's film history foregrounds the larger historical situation in a way that reveals how it limits the possibilities available to any individual director and how it has structured the types of films that he has made in the course of his own career.

Although Oshima's historiography is similar to that of Tanaka's and Richie and Anderson's on a formal level, the ideological determinant shifts, reconfiguring the stakes quite dramatically. At the present moment, for Oshima, the unsolvable antinomy, or the real social contradiction, that is being worked out in his documentary is that between the *national* and the *transnational*. Over the past thirty years, a shift has occurred in the global capitalist system from what has been called Fordism to post-Fordism, flexible accumulation, disorganized capitalism, transnational capitalism, late capitalism, or what recently, and with striking and suspicious unanimity, has been labeled "globalization." Fordism, which is symbolically based on Henry Ford's organizational technological innovations, began sometime— at least, in the West—at the end of the nineteenth century. Fordism is based on mass-production and consumption of homogeneous goods, uniformity and standardization, single-task performance by workers, a high degree of job specialization, strong regulation and centralization, and, most characteristically, intense rigidity. This type of economic organization took force in Japan during the 1920s and 1930s and then was crushed, but not totally destroyed, by Japan's defeat at the hands of the Allied powers in World War II. Tapping into the markets opened by the Korean and Vietnam wars—not to mention the benefits received during the United States' Cold War drive to secure markets and police the world—Japan was able to centralize its economy and assume a highly successful Fordism within twenty-five years. By the early 1970s, as triggered by the oil shocks that set off quakes in the capitalist world, the rigidity of Fordism could no longer contain the inherent contradictions of capitalism. The capitalist system could recuperate only by radically changing its mode of organization; hence, the shift from Fordism to post-Fordism or globalization.[62]

The political economist Ito Makoto has written extensively about Japan's transition from Fordism to post-Fordism.[63] Arguing against a "Japanese exceptionalism" that understands Japanese capitalism to be unique, so that it does not merit such general capitalist labels as "Fordism" and "post-Fordism," Ito writes that based on such factors as flexibility and the globalization of labor processes, labor markets, products, and patterns of consumption, Japan in fact exemplifies the transition.[64] It is precisely this transition that raises the following questions: If the nation-state is restructuring, is a new global imaginary being produced? What is the network of production and consumption that shapes this new transnational imaginary? What will happen to older national identities and ideologies and to those who still have much invested in the nation as a site of resistance?

In the narrative of *100 Years of Japanese Cinema*, it is Oshima's presence itself that attempts to resolve the social contradictions that are contained in these questions. More recently, Oshima can be seen wearing kimono and affecting a traditional role on late-night talk and quiz shows. In an interview given before the Japanese broadcast of *100 Years of Japanese Cinema*, Oshima's interviewer, the writer Hisae Sawachi, is wearing a kimono as the two sit in a "traditional" set complete with Japanese-style benches and a stylized tree trunk. During the film, we hear Oshima's voice, which represents the unseen narrator that marks the orthodox form. The figure of Oshima is the national *and* the transnational, Japan *and* the world, without having to resort to what Oshima recognizes as dangerous extremes: a total loss of the nation (its traditions, culture, rituals) and wholesale globalization on the one hand, or a pro-Japan, anti-world agenda symbolized by emperor worship and the Japanese right wing on the other. An example of this can be found in an interesting comment Oshima makes in *100 Years of Japanese Cinema* about one of his earlier films, *Max Mon Amour* (1986), a film he directed with French financing, French actors, and an old Buñuel story about the French bourgeoisie. Oshima says, "This is an Oshima film, but whether it is a Japanese film is not entirely clear. I'm not sure if questions regarding nationality really mean anything anymore when we are dealing with film."[65] In this case, Oshima's presence represents both the national (which can no longer be talked about as a collective, as "Japan"; it can be talked about only as an individual who stands in for the national, like Oshima and his Japanese affectation) and the transnational (which can no longer be talked about as a single unifying force; it can be talked about only as a more benign differentiating force that can allow for individuality). Although on the narrative level the chronological history looks like the histories made forty years earlier, its effects and meanings are quite different because of a different historical situation. This is most notable in how Oshima and his film relate to global culture and the global economy. But the new "transnational individualism" suggested by Oshima does seem to open itself to a number of questions about politics at the present moment. It is precisely this skepticism and presumed unrealizability of a collective project that links Oshima's later work to the earlier work of Anderson and Richie.

This may also account for why a critic such as Masao Miyoshi feels a great sense of dissatisfaction with Oshima's later work, primarily from *Merry Christmas, Mr. Lawrence* on, than with his earlier films. What Miyoshi exposes is a shift in Oshima's work from such early films as *Koshikei* (Death by hanging, 1968), in which the Other is examined in a way that depicts the Japanese from the standpoint of the victims of racism. In *Merry Christmas, Mr. Lawrence,* however, Oshima represents the Japanese from the viewpoint of the white prisoners of war (Lawrence, Van Der Post, Celliers). In this later film, for Miyoshi, Oshima ends up "accepting the hegemonic and hierarchic view that would rank nations and races on a scale of progress and development."[66] In *Death by Hanging,* Oshima is working from a different ideological determinant (individualism–collectivism), and his earlier work is powerful precisely in how it reveals the Japanese construction and use of the Korean Other, as in the last scene, when the body of R (the Korean who is hanged) vanishes, leaving only an empty noose, signifying that the Other lives in ideology that cannot be killed; it can only be overcome. It is collective social praxis that inevitably involves everyone, including the politicians, bureaucrats, police, students, Koreans, Japanese, filmmakers, film viewers, and others, that is required to transform the Japanese nation (which is one way to interpret the prophetic call by Oshima himself at the end of the film: "*Anata mo, anata mo, anata mo . . .*").[67]

It was always this ideal—to delineate Japan's national situation and recognize the Japanese state as the primary site of resistance—that, it seems to me, provides the reason that Oshima disdained the generic "New Wave" label that was often ascribed to the younger Japanese directors of the 1960s.[68] When Oshima attempts to depict the Japanese from the standpoint of the Other within a transformed contradictory space of the national and the transnational (starting from about the mid-1970s), however, his work forfeits the political use of the nation for any collective project and ends up wedding itself to the objectives of a transnational cultural movement (a type of transnational vanguard). Indeed, this might speak more to the difficulty of resistance at this particular moment, and to the strength of the contradiction between the national and the transnational as the world system reconfigures, than to Oshima's individual failings.

In order to push some of these themes, a shift is in order to the work of Sato Tadao. One of the very few organic intellectuals in Japan, Sato has written more than a hundred books and a tremendous number of articles and collaborative works; he has also made several television appearances. He grew up in a working-class family in Niigata, and after failing the high-school entrance examination for forgetting to bow while a poem to the emperor was being read, he became a naval air cadet.[69] Following the war, Sato returned to his hometown and began working for Japan National Railways, then Nippon Telegraph and Telephone. At this time, Sato began to write his own film criticism and later contributed to such journals as *Eiga hyoron*, of which he eventually became an editor. From popular culture to film theory to Asian and Western cinema, Sato's work ranges over a remarkably wide field of study. Then there are his several books on education, which place him somewhere near an Ivan Ilich or a Paulo Friere; in those books, Sato argues for an overhaul of the entire educational system, which, by organizing manual and intellectual labor by age, would produce the space for more "organic intellectuals" like himself to emerge. Few non-academic film critics writing in the West today resemble Sato in depth, breadth, endurance, and theoretical instincts.

For those familiar with Sato's writings, what is most interesting in *A History of Japanese Film* is how he decides to edit and organize the work. What is included, where is it included, and how much of it is included turns out to be very significant because almost every one of the sentences has been published somewhere else.[70] Indeed, Sato's narrative does not depart much from Richie and Anderson's, or from Tanaka's. In fact, as Sato explains in the preface to his four-volume work, just before Tanaka's death in 1989 he was asked to organize the enormous quantity of materials, including pictures, clippings, and many original resources collected for the 1959 publication of Tanaka's *History of the Development in Japanese Film*. Sato then took the liberty of including some of these materials in his own history. Sato's deference to Tanaka could be one reason that he waited so long to publish his multivolume history of Japanese film. Of course, another reason lies in the fact that the marketing of the one-hundredth anniversary of film produced a particularly propitious moment for such a publication. Whatever the reason may be, the question at hand is, How did a similarly chronological history published in 1995 differ from one published in the late 1950s?

Sato's *A History of Japanese Film* is a chronological history insofar as it uses thick description, a forward-moving timeline, inclusivity, and other chronological techniques. At the same time, it departs from this form. Sato's history is not only vertical; it also spreads out horizontally and ultimately is a national film history that exceeds the borders of Japan. For example, Sato's history dedicates several sections to Japanese film in Taiwan, Korea, China, Manchuria, Indonesia, and the Philippines.[71] Sato also writes about Japanese film audiences throughout Asia and the reception of Japanese film in the United States.[72] The final volume, moreover, contains only one chapter (excluding the extensive index and chronology), titled "From a Different Direction" (*Kotonatta shiten kara*), in which Sato deals in detail with questions of genre and such topics as the emperor system, the police, the Japanese Communist Party, sexuality, and Japanese cities. This "different direction" is a two-way street: One way heads from the world to Japan, and the other leads from Japan to the world. It is such lateral moves away from the core of the chronological national film history that hint at the chronological form's ultimate instability at the present moment. Moreover, in several places in the four volumes, the very three words of the title—"Japanese," "Film," and "History"—fail to contain the work and seem to confirm that Japanese film history cannot be only about Japan, about film, or about history when linearly configured. Sato attempts to square the circle of the national and the transnational, therefore, by widening the scope of the work's content not simply historically, but also geographically.

Sato's work, in other words, seems to open new opportunities to pursue various local film histories (such as Japanese colonial film, feminist film, documentary, and others), not to mention film's relation with philosophy, cognitive science, literature, and other disciplines. *A History of Japanese Film*, which will surely be the last great single history of Japanese film to be written for quite some time, is at the same time a multiplicity of local histories that mark the end of the "great history" once and for all. Sato keeps these multiple histories from flying off into their separate and autonomous orbits by unifying them in the pages of his colossal work.

But all of these strengths are also the weakness of *A History of Japanese Film*. The common complaint about Sato's history is that it gives short shrift to particular movements and issues in which various people (usually the complainants themselves) are invested. To be sure, much more could be included. I have my own wish list to add to the chorus of complaints: more on Ogawa Shinsuke and the documentary inventions pursued by Ogawa Productions; more on the remarkable work of Haneda Sumiko, the documentarist whose political commitments over the past four decades of filmmaking are matched only by her subtle sensitivity to the aesthetic; more on the history and recent rise of experimental film and video culture; and more on the genealogy leading to the recent boom of gay and lesbian film.

To be sure, the incorporation of previously underresearched and underpublished content into dominant histories is almost always cause for celebration. Ideally, this incorporation process will generate more scholarship, with the potential to turn back on and transform the representation and understanding of history itself. But then there is another, if not more realistic, possibility: that the inclusion of the new content will be marginal, at best elevating one of the dominant history's footnotes to a single page or extending a small section to a whole chapter. Instead of undermining the dominant history, including the hitherto underrepresented material may serve only to reinforce the dominant history's authority. For example, just as political calls for pluralism tend to disguise and legitimate the power of a small minority (say, the way in which a marginalized group such as the impoverished is sometimes raised up as a shining, albeit ironic, example of social diversity), so too might content-based calls for historical pluralism tend to disguise and legitimate the power of a dominant historiographical form. Despite the incorporation process, therefore, the assumptions of writing and organizing history are usually left unchanged and are legitimated.

One implication of the argument that chosen historiographical forms are inextricably linked to large-scale social problems is that it is on the level of form where the inclusion of hitherto marginalized content can most significantly be incorporated into film history. Failing to inquire into the methods of writing history and the social situation out of which the underrepresentation of certain content emerged in the first place risks merely filling in the absences in the existing dominant histories and participating in the self-marginalization of its own content. In other words, the assumption held by many who criticize *A History of Japanese Film* is that their own work needs to be included because Sato has either found it unworthy or misrepresented it. One problem with this approach, of course, is that it reproduces the very historiographical methods that it presumably wants to criticize.

It seems infinitely more important to take Sato's history for its strengths rather than for its weaknesses. The work has fulfilled its historical mission, and now, with the passing of the hundredth anniversary of Japanese film, the due respect granted to Tanaka and Sato, as well as the daily consolidation of the global system, the fading of the star (nation-state) to which film history has traditionally linked its chariot, and the inseparable relationship between Hollywood and Japanese film, Sato's history represents the long overdue funeral of the national film history. The six tombstones depicted by the histories analyzed in this chapter have cleared the way for film histories that need not be either enormous tomes of encyclopedic data nor microanalyses of highly specific content. They can be histories that speak about film and any number of seemingly unrelated topics at the same time, such as other cultural forms, philosophical concepts, economic policy, the international division of wealth and labor, aesthetic theory. As the global system reconfigures and the contradiction between the national and the transnational comes into greater relief, connections between Japanese film and the world will appear less as esoteric deviations than as the passkeys that allow entrance to a whole new series of productive questions and problems.

III. adaptation

Origin, Nation, Aesthetic

Cinematizing the Shosetsu   The Japanese term *eiga-ka* (meaning "to make into film" or "to cinematize") refers to the process generally called *film adaptation* in English. Of course, the most famous example of eiga-ka is the more than one hundred films made from the story of *Chushingura* (The loyal forty-seven ronin). Then there is the *shosetsu* (prose narrative). Almost every work in the canon of modern Japanese prose fiction has been made into film, usually more than once. The Izu dancer has parted with her new lover at that same Shimoda harbor six times. Sasuke has thrust pins into his eyes in order to enter Shunkin's world five times. There have been four Naomis and two conflagrations at Kinkakuji. Sensei has killed himself twice. Naruse adored Hayashi Fumiko's hard-headed women; Imamura sent Nosaka Aki-yuki's pornographer out to sea; Oshima caught Oe's prisoner of war. Tera-yama Shuji has implored us, in book and film, to throw away our books and storm the streets. Kurosawa's Akutagawa has become (how many times?) the West's Kurosawa, and even that beloved cat with no name has starred in its own film.[1] This is truly only the tip of the iceberg. Any comprehensive list of eiga-ka would need to contain hundreds and hundreds of titles.[2]

In two works that track the eiga-ka of Kawabata and Tanizaki, Nishikawa Tatsuki's *Izu no odoriko monogatari* (The tale of the Izu dancer, 1994) and Chiba Nobuo's *Eiga to tanizaki* (Film and Tanizaki, 1990), both authors depart from the shosetsu to see what has been done to it over the many decades of remakes.[3] There is much to be gained by tracking how a particular scene has transformed over seventy years, as each version, made at a different moment, will necessarily spread its historical concerns over the representation of the narrative.[4] One problem with this approach, however, is that although changes in particular eiga-ka are tracked, the very concept of eiga-ka and how it has transformed over time is usually left unexamined. Thus, the stability of the concept of eiga-ka and the stability of the shosetsu from which the eiga-ka departs remains unquestioned.

For example, what grounds the work of Nishikawa and Chiba is an ontological privileging of the word over the image, the shosetsu over the film, and, most important for the task at hand, the original over the adaptation. If these issues are not rethought in relation to film adaptation, then each adaptation of literature serves only to recanonize the shosetsu and delegitimate the film. Perhaps more important, the refusal to question textual origins theoretically is almost sure to lock out of the discussion any extended analysis of how cultural origins dynamically relate to ideologies of national, political, and racial origins. Rather than examining the transformations of particular eiga-ka over time, therefore, this chapter will examine the transformations of the more general category of eiga-ka. I will distinguish three dominant modes of eiga-ka that occur at three moments of modernization — the 1930s, the late 1960s–early 1970s, and the 1990s — and show how each mode's conception of "origins" (in relation to an original literary text) differs from the others and how each relates to dominant ways in which the nation is being thought at its particular historical moment.

In the second half of the 1910s, the contours began to appear of the *jun-eigageki undo* (pure film movement), which was bent on modernizing the Japanese film industry. Kaeriyama Norimasa and Emasa Yoshiro of Tenkatsu; Tanizaki and Kurihara Thomas (Kisaburo) at Taikatsu; Osanai Kaoru at Shochiku Research Lab; and Tanaka Eizo at Nikkatsu led the movement. Inspired by *shingeki* (new theater) and Western film, and intent on bringing Japanese film in line with Western developments, the movement was fiercely opposed to the onnagata, benshi, and acting styles that reflected the highly stylized movements of kabuki and noh. The force of the movement had slowed by 1924, the same year that Japanese film experienced a huge spurt in production and for the first time surpassed the number of imported foreign films.[5] The movement was short-lived, but its effects were broad.

The movement's effects can be seen in the first important eiga-ka movement to emerge in the mid-1930s.[6] With the "Fifteen Year War" already under way, censorship became tighter by the day. One way for directors and the studios to circumvent censoring practices was to base films on already proven "pure" literature (*jun-bungaku*). Gosho Heinosuke's eiga-ka of Kawabata's *Izu no odoriko* (The Izu Dancer, 1933) and Toyoda Shiro's eiga-ka of Ishizaka Yojiro's *Wakai hito* (Young People, 1937) are typical examples of this movement. An exemplary example is an eiga-ka of Tanizaki's *Shunkinsho* by Shimazu Yasujiro (*O-Koto to sasuke*, 1935). This first important eiga-ka movement corresponded to the most significant ideological return to "origins" that modern Japan had yet to experience. Whether it was the origins of the Japanese people (in which a single identity or "spirit" is traced back to its origins without being racially sullied) or the origins of economic production (in which Japanese capitalism, with its "unique" origins based in Japanese industriousness, wondrously avoids the usual effects of labor exploitation, extraction of surplus value, and class divisions) or cultural origins (in which cultural canons are installed with convenient touchstones of genius that neatly move forward while burying in their tracks the history of cultural contestation), the early 1930s marked the moment in which film would need to straighten itself out and become an equal partner in advancing the war effort.

Thus, the first important moment of eiga-ka occurred in the early to mid-1930s with the movement following a fidelity line of eiga-ka—one in which the story of the shosetsu is linearly traced by the film, and the plot is literally (and cinematically) granted center stage, or center frame. The second important moment can be located in the mid-1960s and early 1970s, with some of the eiga-ka connected to the Art Theater Guild's (ATG) productions of canonical shosetsu, usually the same works that the first group used. The ATG was (and still is) composed of young film and theater directors, actors, activists, and other cultural producers searching for an alternative space free from the rigid hierarchies for which the Japanese film corporations are traditionally known. Works within this second moment commonly exceed the original text either by focusing on a particular section or adding content to the narrative. Shindo Kaneto's 1973 production of *Kokoro*, for example, focuses on only the third letter (*Sensei to isho*) of Soseki's famous shosetsu.

The dominant aesthetic of eiga-ka during these two stages interestingly connect to the dominant national discourse of their respective historical moments. In the 1930s, the Japanese imperialist project was being ideologically justified at home. Both the Japanese left and right attacked the West by rewriting Western history and recanonizing native texts. The highest philosophical defense for nationalist-based aggression came from a certain strand of thinkers of the Kyoto school, who, in building on Nishida Kitaro's search for metaphysical certainty, theorized Japan's optimal position to lead Asia. During the 1960s and 1970s, the West was still a target of mass social movements but came second to the criticism lodged against the Japanese state itself. It is within this situation that various eiga-ka make noticeable departures from the original literary texts. Despite the differences between the two movements, they are united in their comparable dependence on the identity and integrity of the original shosetsu. The same can be said about the nation. Whether the nation is frenetically defended or ferociously attacked, what remains is the integrity of the nation as such: It provides leverage, a center, a point with or against which to coordinate. The comparison that is being drawn here is between the stability of the national form during two different moments of political upheaval and the stability of the shosetsu form at two moments of eiga-ka.

Then there is the emergence of a third moment, both in the meanings and effects of the nation and in the meanings and effects of eiga-ka. This moment is best represented on the level of political economy by the decline in the decision-making power of the nation-state and the rise of transnational corporatism in which identities, needs, desires—indeed, subjectivities (not to mention the very concept of identity itself)—are being re-formed. On the cinematic level, I see this moment represented by films (most notably, a particular strain of documentary) that find markedly different ways of relating to the identity of an original literary text.

In the history of Western film theory, there are generally two interrelated topics when examining film adaptation. The first concerns the mode by which literature is adapted (the degree to which the adaptation relates to the original), and the second concerns the relation between the different semiotic registers of the linguistic and the visual. Dudley Andrew develops a tripartite schema by which the film relates to the original text that includes (1) borrowing, which mines (reverently if not loosely) the prestigious material of an archetypal text (here one might think of a film that employs *King Lear*'s focus on inheritance and all of its aesthetic, political, and economic implications without referencing Shakespeare); (2) intersection, which hews most closely to the original text in the way André Bazin claimed that the "film is the novel as seen by cinema" (or, in architecture, one might be reminded of Teshigahara Hiroshi's delicate film about Antonio Gaudi's work in which Gaudi's signature structures of Barcelona themselves dominate); and (3) transformation, which brings us to the somewhat tired tropes of "fidelity" and "freedom" (or how close to the "letter" or "spirit" of the original text the adaptation comes).[7]

It is this last category, transformation, that most intricately crosses into the problem of comparative semiotics, or the very possibility of comparing two different systems of signification. Clearly, literary languages work qualitatively differently from cinematic ones. The Japanese language includes (among many other elements) ideograms, grammatical conventions, and sentences, while film includes lighting, cutting, camera angles, and gestures. Here one may be reminded of George Bluestone's classic statement that "what is peculiarly filmic and what is peculiarly novelistic cannot be converted without destroying an integral part of each,"[8] or Jean Mitry's account that film can neither proceed in the same fashion nor signify the same thing as literature.[9] But the qualitative differences between the two forms should not deter us from recognizing the rock-bottom similarity—namely, an addresser's communication of information within time and space to an addressee. It is this recognition that has inspired some of the impressive reworking of linguistic semiotics into a semiotics of the cinema, such as Christien Metz's work on Saussure and Gilles Deleuze's on Peirce. Here, a process of transcoding occurs (to use Yuri Lotman's term) in which there is the "recoding of one type of communication act, issued by an addresser according to certain codes and systems of expression, into a second type of communication act with its own unique codes and systems."[10] Examples are the way a single sentence of a literary text might be recoded as a shot in a film or a paragraph as a scene, or the way an icon is expressed by resemblance in a literary text (the egg with furrowed brow) while expressed by a face in a film.

I will be working through these concepts (in relation to eiga-ka and to literary translation) throughout this chapter. At the same time, I will be exceeding them by incorporating two dimensions that are invariably lacking in adaptation theory: the political and the historical. Like Chiba's and Nishikawa's works mentioned earlier, Western film theories of adaptation consistently rehearse and extend the same issues but almost always within the contained field of aesthetics. The move to be made here is to ask how transcoding might occur not only between two different aesthetic texts or communication acts, but between "two different structural levels of reality"?[11] For example, how might it occur between the cinematic and the political, or between the mode of literary adaptation and the mode of nationalist discourse? On top of all this, I will ask how a chosen adaptation mode (and the very theoretical debate about adaptation) might relate to the conceptual possibilities of the historical moment during which it is produced.

To work through this transforming relation between aesthetic discourses and national discourses, I will begin by examining the concept of eiga-ka and how it can be illuminated when understood in terms of literary translation and the various theoretical debates that have occurred around this issue. An important tract on translation written by Tanizaki Junichiro in 1938, "Genji monogatari no gendai goyaku ni tsuite" (On the modern translation of *The Tale of Genji*), will be considered.[12] I argue that Tanizaki is influenced by a capitalist logic that, by enforcing strict copyright laws at the time, is invested in indelibly marking an original text from its adaptations. The task then will be to translate the issue of translation into the issue of eiga-ka and to show how the usual debate over the best method of eiga-ka (fidelity to the text versus freedom from the text) can be rethought. Then I will move on to an analysis of Tanizaki's *Shunkinsho* and two eiga-ka of it (one by Shimazu Yasujiro in 1935, and the other by Shindo Kaneto in 1972), and an examination of how these two works illustrate different conceptions of eiga-ka as they occur at different historical moments. Finally, I will discuss Hara Kazuo's

1994 film *Zenshin shosetsu-ka,* a documentary about the prose fiction writer Inoue Mitsuharu that offers new ways to envision the transformations and processes of eiga-ka within the different situation of capitalism.

In sketching out these three moments and assigning a dominant form of adaptation to them, I do not want to suggest that diverse modes of adaptation have not occurred throughout the one hundred years of Japanese film history. Even though I detect an emerging form of "fidelity"-based adaptation in the mid-1930s this does not exclude the existence of radically alternative forms. Ten years earlier, in 1926, for example, Kurihara's film *Sanjigoto* adapted D. W. Griffith's 1911 *Enoch Arden,* itself an adaptation of the 1864 Tennyson poem by the same name. Kurihara whimsically transformed a rather staid morality tale into a Chaplinesque farce about greed and self-indulgence. Another example is Ozu's *Tokyo no yado* (An inn in Tokyo, 1935). This film portrays itself as an adaptation of an original story by a writer Winthat Monnet, but this is a fanciful move on Ozu's part, because "Winthat Monnet" is nothing but a sly parody of "Without Money." Or there are a number of contemporary nostalgic adaptations of canonical literature (such as *The Tale of Genji* and *Botchan*) in animated form (intended as learning tools) that do anything but question the identity of the original text. This is all to say that there are adaptations made at the moments under examination here that depart from the fidelity trend set in the mid-1930s or the new experiments of the current moment. Setting up these three modes of adaptation that occur at three moments of Japanese modernity, then, does not obliterate the heterogeneity of production during each moment. In fact, it does the exact opposite: It draws attention to the coexistence of other modes whose meanings and effects can be more significantly registered when examined in relation to the dominant. Fredric Jameson calls such a dominant mode a force field "in which very different kinds of cultural impulses must make their way." He goes on to write, "If we do not achieve some general sense of a cultural dominant, then we fall back into a view of present history as sheer heterogeneity, random difference, a coexistence of a host of distinct forces whose effectivity is undecidable."[13] Only by marking off these three moments of adaptation is it possible to reflect on their political meanings and speculate on how film not only is shaped by the most profound problems of Japanese modernity but also, at the same time, significantly shapes these problems and the Japanese nation.

The Problem of the Translator: Tanizaki's Theories Like the debate over film adaptation, the debate over literary translation usually centers on the issues of fidelity and freedom. The former designates a strategy that sticks as closely as possible to the text being translated, while the latter departs from the text as the translator sees fit. The objective of both, as is usually the case, is to transmit the meaning of the original text in a different language. In "The Task of the Translator," Walter Benjamin dismantles this debate and questions the priority placed on the transmission of meaning as the sine qua non of all translation.[14] By focusing on syntax and a word-for-word translation that is not concerned with comprehensibility, fluency, or "saying the same thing" in a different language, Benjamin envisions the task of the translator as something completely different: as representing the hidden kinship among languages. The task of the translator is not to get as close as possible to the original text but to release or liberate the pre-Babelian "pure language" (*die reine sprache*) that is imprisoned in the original as well as (and this is crucial) in the language of the translation. This pure language is not the original in its pristine state that is then defiled by the translation; rather, it is a negative category that cannot be attained by any single language. It can only be hinted at by the totality of intentions (of both the original and the translation) supplementing each other. For Benjamin, then, the act of translating is a longing, a promise, a messianic hope for linguistic complementarity. Or to put this another way: The deadly serious task of the translator lies in the importance placed in the concept of utopia as such—in utopia as a critical category in its most tactically disabused and reflexive form.

To speak of utopia in such terms is thus to suggest not the actual possibility of achieving it, but the significance in the strategy (no matter how doomed it may be from the very outset) of working toward it.[15] The promise of touching the untouchable pure language is what marks the thoroughly dialectical character of Benjamin's preface: to be fully aware of the limitations of translation and of the structural impossibilities of language, while at the same time aware that these limitations are not static and thus occupy within their very logic the possibility of transformation. This pure language is not a destination or even an ultimate beginning, but it is what inspires the task of the translator. By strategically sacralizing such a notion as pure language, Benjamin is able to desacralize the original text.

Now I will make the move to Japan to see how translation figures within this different national and linguistic situation. In the middle of his 1938 essay "*Genji* monogatari goyaku ni tsuite," Tanizaki delivers his own theory of translation:

> The principle of translation is to produce a literary translation in which the translation can be read on its own as literature; thus the evocations (*kankyo*) the reader receives when reading the translation are like the evocations a past reader received when reading the original—this is the crucial point. But this is not to imply that the translation can freely move away from the original; rather, the objective is to conform to the original as much as possible. I try not to produce parts in which the translation does not follow the characters and phrases (*jiku*) of the original. Although sometimes this cannot be helped, it should be avoided as much as possible. Thus, it is not fruitless to read by way of a meticulous movement back and forth between the original and the translation (*genbun to taishou shite yomu no ni mo yaku tatanaku wa nai*). I translated [*Genji*] with this intention.[16]

It is precisely Benjamin's notion of "pure language"—this utopia, this no-place—that seems to be implied by Tanizaki's term *kankyo*.[17] Just as the linking of *intentions* is projected by Benjamin as a task that is impossible to realize in any single language and can only be "pointed to" by the (failed) act of translation, so too can we understand Tanizaki's kankyo in similar fashion. Tanizaki's kankyo does not posit a transcendental subject with a homogeneous sensibility that will be possible to reconcile over hundreds of years. Rather, for Tanizaki, the task to unite kankyo among readers is impossible yet meaningful nevertheless to perform. Tanizaki and Benjamin also resemble each other in sharing the crucial assumption of being able to read both the original and translation at the same time. For Benjamin, the reader should be able to read the language of the original as well as the translation. Translation is not simply for those who do not have access to the original or for those who are unable to read the original; it is a distinct mode by which one reads the original and translation together—side by side, as it were—so that the promise of something larger than both texts is sought. For Benjamin, one would learn a foreign language not (only) to read all of those works that are not available in the native language, but also to reread in the language of the translation all of those works that one has already read in the native language.[18]

Likewise, Tanizaki (notwithstanding his remarks regarding how the translation should be read on its own as literature) assumed that anyone who would read his translation of *Genji* could also read the classical Japanese of the original. It is this assumption that allows for the possibility of the "meticulous back-and-forth movement" expressed in his 1938 comments on translation. It is precisely this assumption by Tanizaki that interestingly connects to his own participation with Japan's military government and seemingly contradicts his prefatory comments to the first *Genji* translation. Tanizaki completed three translations of *Genji*, the first one at the height of World War II, the second one in 1954, and the third in the year of his death, 1965. The fact that Tanizaki retreated to the fragmentary and dispersed monogatari form (with *Genji*, *Sasame yuki*, and *Ashikari*, for example), not to mention his anthropological work *In Praise of Shadows*, was certainly one way to manage the military demands placed on all Japanese intellectuals from the Manchurian Incident in 1931 to the dropping of the atomic bombs in 1945. Masao Miyoshi argues that, although Tanizaki's work during this period might seem escapist and collaborationist, his stories and relative reticence at times of such nationalist fervor are indeed a remarkably bold attempt at resistance.[19]

What is to be made, then, of Tanizaki's expurgation of key passages in his first translation of *Genji* as a way apparently to satisfy the military government and right-wing critics such as Yamada Yoshio? Tanizaki cut all reference to Genji's great longing for—and incestuous affair with—Fujitsubo. Of course, Tanizaki anticipated the censorship and dissatisfaction that would certainly flow if his translation hinted at any "unseemliness" regarding the imperial throne. But how does this square with his 1938 essay on translation, in which he stresses that the translator should stay as close as possible to the characters and phrases of the original text?

The first place to go might be to his preface in the 1941 translation. The opening paragraph begins with the following: "Since the primary aim of this work is for it to be appreciated as a single independent work, I was not bound to an inquiry of individual characters and phrases. I wanted, as much as possible, for it to be read by a contemporary person in an unconstrained manner as if it were an ordinary modern work."[20] Here there is no mention of reading with the original in hand, and there is less concern about departing from the original text. The preface suggests the classic "freedom from the original text" line of translation. But, as usual, historical considerations are crucial. Tanizaki no doubt feared that he would not be able to publish the translation over which he had so diligently and persistently labored. By deleting the incestuous elements of the story, therefore, he secured its publication. This does not need to be understood only as concession and collaboration (which certainly is part of the story), however. Rather, Tanizaki was surely mindful of the most significant effect of censorship—that it usually foregrounds and highlights precisely what it wishes to expel and bury. In other words, even though Tanizaki's first translation makes no mention of the ascension to the throne by the son born to Genji and his mother, this element (no doubt one that the playful and taboo-transcending Tanizaki would normally seize and exploit) cannot help but pervade the translation despite—or because of—its expurgation.

Although Tanizaki writes in the preface that his translation can be appreciated independently (*Kono ho wa dokuritsu shita ikko no sakuhin toshite ajiwatte morau no ga*), this does not need to be understood as the translation's no longer being inextricably connected to the original. When Tanizaki finished his second modern translation, what happened to the first translation? What role did the first translation, with its expedient excisions, play in the production of the second translation? What role did the first translation play in transforming the original eleventh-century text that then affected the second translation that was based on this transformed original? Can there be a translation of a translation, or must every subsequent translation return blindly to the original? These questions—which are dizzying— lead to the crucial relationship between the original and the translation, to the heart of debates over eiga-ka, and, ultimately, to the much wider aesthetic and political issues of representation and interpretation in general.

What we find in both Benjamin and Tanizaki is the construction of a third category to go along with the first two, "original" and "translation." For Benjamin the third category is "pure language," and for Tanizaki it is "kankyo." Because the task of the translator is to aim for this third category instead of faithfully reproducing the content of the idealized original, the original is destabilized. But both writers still insist on holding on to the identity of the original and to the distinction between original and translation. Benjamin writes, "Translations . . . prove to be untranslatable not because of any inherent difficulty, but because of the looseness with which meaning attaches to them."[21] In other words, because the translation is not concerned with meaning, it will itself be meaningless to translate. Tanizaki writes in the preface to the second translation that at first he wanted to supplement and revise the skeletal structure of the first translation, but then he realized that this process would not allow him to overcome the difficulties of the first translation (here, he is referring to the long and complicated sentences that, for many, made the translation even more difficult than the original). Tanizaki then goes on to ask, "Without pressing close against the original (nikuhatsu suru), would not the attempt at a new translation be meaningless?"[22]

Of course, although they wrote within decades of each other, Benjamin and Tanizaki were writing from very different national situations. Still, their theories of translation can be read with an eye to a shared capitalist logic that was at work in both countries. For example, the significance of transformations in copyright law and new requirements to differentiate the original from a copy must be integrated into both Tanizaki's and Benjamin's translation theories. Regarding Benjamin's argument that a translation cannot be translated, Jacques Derrida takes him to task for holding fast to the distinction between original and translation. By privileging the original over the translation, Benjamin repeats the transcendental law that sees "expression" as more authentic than the "expressed," or "speech" as more authentic than "writing." It is not a coincidence for Derrida that Benjamin's writing resembles the language of legal treatises that consider the translation of the translation as necessarily derived from the original. If this distinction is not maintained, there will be no way to maintain the intellectual property rights of the original author (let alone determine who the original author is in the first place). Thus, the very foundation of copyright law will collapse.[23]

By quickly reviewing the history of modern copyright law in Japan, one can perform a similar analysis of Tanizaki's translation theories. Copyright law was first introduced in Japan in 1899 and recognized as an important element of the Meiji Restoration and modernization. Although Japan did participate in the Berne Convention for the Protection of Literary and Artistic Works in 1886, the formation of a modern conception of authorship came much later than it did in the West. Modern authorship, in which individual creators produce—with their own intellectual labor—original works for which they are entitled to profit, needed to be installed within a situation in which the economic categories (intellectual labor, profit, entitlement) and the cultural categories (original creation, individual authorship, modern subjectivity) possessed a short history. The decision to return to the original, therefore, is based not only on aesthetic choice (what renders a more fluid or concise translation) but on other historical concerns, which, in Tanizaki's day, related to the most important ideologies of the nation.

Another way to illustrate this is by turning to film culture at the time. As mentioned in chapter 1, one of the most interesting elements of the early benshi system is how the identity and integrity of an original text is severely undermined. For example, because early films were usually less than an hour long, and maiden Japanese film audiences were accustomed to three- to four-hour theater experiences (as was regularly the case in noh and kabuki), theater owners might employ four benshi to comment on the same series of images. In this way, the same film could be transformed, depending on the proclivity of a particular benshi, from a melodrama, to an action adventure, to a period piece, even to a documentary about the Russo-Japanese War. Komatsu Hiroshi has written that the benshi Takamatsu Toyojiro would travel around the country and walk into any theater showing any film and always transform the film's narrative in order to speak about labor issues.[24] With the benshi able to compensate for the incoherence that the film might not be able to manage visually, directors would be less concerned with producing continuous narratives. In this way early films were left "incomplete," always anticipating a subsequent transformational/translation process.

The openness of the benshi system suffered attacks from both the political right and the cultural left. Beginning in the early 1920s, the deregulation of the benshi system was streamlined by the Japanese police, who began a benshi licensing system. And in 1926, bureaucrats within the Ministry of Education held seminars to teach "proper" film commentary techniques and distribute written materials that outlined step-by-step rules. Indeed, one effect of this pedagogy was to privilege the original film over and above its transformation or adaptation by the benshi. Then there were those on the cultural left who attacked the benshi system for inhibiting progress and development of Japanese film. With the benshi more famous than both directors and actors, audiences were becoming dependent on having commentary and explanation provided for them. Moreover, the high-culture pretensions of some artists were interrupted by the bustle and noisy atmosphere of the theaters that the benshi provoked. For example, Osanai Kaoru was impressed by how Western theater audiences sat still and quiet during performances and how this type of spectatorial focus was more conducive to transmitting political, social, and aesthetic agendas. Osanai, along with Tanizaki himself, believed that only by producing films that stood on their own, without the interference of the benshi (or too much dialogue or too many titles, for that matter), could a more artistic and modern film culture prosper in Japan. A. A. Gerow argues that an important paradigm shift occurred during the life span of the benshi system. This shift is marked by a change in terminology from benshi to *setsumei-sha* (explainer). The former term suggests more freedom from the film being screened (such as incorporating personal commentary, historical background, performative dialogue), whereas the latter suggests a more constricted role in which the accompaniment transmitted only established meaning.[25] With the shift, finally, came the strengthened identity of the original text as the benshi took on the role of the passive translator.[26]

The privileging of the original in both literary translation and the benshi system occurred at a time in which nationalist discourse in Japan itself was transforming. The global economic crises of the interwar years abruptly shattered any hope of an integrated world economy. By 1913, ideals of free trade had been discarded and capitalist economies were moving precipitously toward state-managed models. Supported and guided by the government, the Japanese economy was no exception. The result: a reformulated nationalism and a retrenched nation-state. On the global situation, Eric Hobsbawm writes, "As the economic blizzard swept across the global economy, world capitalism retreated into the igloos of its nation-state economies and their associated empires."[27] Of course, Japan differed considerably from its Western counterparts, but it remained part of, and was influenced by, the world system. As occurred in the economy, so, too, happened with culture. Any hope during the Taisho democracy period of a hybrid culture—one not limited by the strictures of Japanese tradition—was dashed. Just as took place with Tanizaki's translation theories and with the benshi commentary, many cultural forms saw their progressive possibilities snuffed out by nationalist ideologies that, on the level of the aesthetic, held tight to the absolute separability of an original and its translation or adaptation. Indeed, from Taisho to early Showa, Japan returned to its national and aesthetic origins (however much invented in the present) with a vengeance. And this intersection of aesthetic and national imperatives comes into sharp focus precisely at the site of eiga-ka.

Formal Utopias: Shosetsu, Nation, Eiga-ka (Part I)

In 1935, Tanizaki wrote an article for a local film magazine about his recent impressions of film and the 1935 eiga-ka of his shosetsu titled *Shunkinsho* (A portrait of Shunkin, 1933).[28] The essay is both a sour critique of film currents in Japan and a harsh discouragement against ever being able successfully to adapt his shosetsu to film. These are not, however, the impressions of a writer who resents the popularity of the new medium and rejoices in bashing film's inferior status while privileging the more important work of literature. Tanizaki, in fact, was one of the most important spokespeople for the great potential that film offered. Only twelve years earlier, he had written several articles explaining film techniques and terminology ("Eiga no tekunikku") and his excitement about Robert Weine's *The Cabinet of Dr. Caligari* ("Karigari hakushi wo miru," 1919).[29] His "Katsudo shashin no genzai to shorai" (The present and the future of the moving pictures, 1918) was a well-informed paean that celebrated the new medium and prepared Tanizaki's own entrance into film production the following year for the newly developed Taikatsu film corporation.[30] Of course, after the Great Tokyo Earthquake in 1923, Tanizaki moved to Osaka and began experimenting with more traditional content, as exemplified in his *Genji* translations as well as in the shosetsu he produced in the 1930s (such as *Momoku monogatari* [A blind man's tale, 1931], *Bushu ko hiwa* [The secret history of the Lord of Musashi, 1931], and, of course, *Shunkinsho* [1933]). But traditional content does not require the use of traditional form. And it is on the level of form, just as in his translations of *Genji,* that Tanizaki made his most significant interventions during this period. Tanizaki's critique of the eiga-ka of *Shunkinsho,* therefore, was not a reactionary attack against film. It was an attack on how the eiga-ka of the 1930s obliterated what was most radical of the shosetsu: its formal strategies.

Shunkinsho begins with a writer (the "I" of the shosetsu) visiting the graves of a famous blind musician (Shunkin) and her assistant, disciple, and lover (Sasuke).[31] The writer, who is narrating in the present, the early 1930s, attempts to piece together the fascinating story of the young lovers' lives by reading an official tract on the couple (*Mozuya shunkin-den* [The legend of Mozuya Shunkin]), speaking with a woman who worked for them (Shigizawa Teru), reading newspaper articles (from the *Asahi Shinbun*), and so on. We ascertain (however unreliably) from these shreds that Shunkin, born into a well-to-do merchant family in 1828, was blinded at the age of eight. In the same year, 1836, Sasuke begins working for Shunkin's father's pharmaceutical business and soon becomes the daughter's most favored assistant. Appreciating Sasuke's reticence and humility, Shunkin calls on him to accompany her to a daily music lesson. Sasuke, with great earnestness and pleasure, waits and listens while the precocious Shunkin practices the *samisen* and *koto*.

Sasuke soon purchases his own samisen and begins to teach himself, until he is discovered and reprimanded by Shunkin's parents. But Shunkin is intrigued. After hearing how much Sasuke has been able to teach himself, the young Shunkin, only thirteen now, takes him on as her student. Shunkin is a harsh teacher and often scolds Sasuke to the point of tears; nevertheless, Sasuke is enraptured to be so close to his secret love. It becomes obvious to everyone that the two are in love, and after Shunkin becomes pregnant, there is no one else to suspect but Sasuke. Still, the two deny their love. After Shunkin's teacher dies and she attains her own coterie of pupils, she moves to a new home and takes Sasuke along as her servant and assistant music teacher. Known as a relentless teacher who often beats and yells at her students, Shunkin is soon visited by catastrophe. Asleep one evening, an intruder sneaks into her room and pours boiling water over her face, leaving ghastly burns. On the day before the bandages are to be removed, Sasuke thrusts a knitting needle into his eyes to escape ever having to see Shunkin's scars. In ecstasy, Sasuke and Shunkin are now able to enter a higher plane of artistry, communication, and love.

Tanizaki leaves the various details of the shosetsu ambiguous. The first ambiguity lies in the truth or falsehood of the legend itself. At one point, when the narrator is commenting on how Osaka people differ from those in Tokyo, the shosetsu refers to an actual series of Tanizaki's essays about Osaka (titled "Watashi no mita osaka oyobi osakajin" [The Osaka and Osakians I saw]) published in *Chuo Koron* between February and April of 1932, the same journal in which *Shunkinsho* would be published in June of the following year.[32] Not only does this question the fictionality of *Shunkinsho*, but it further complicates the already unstable relation between the "I" in any shosetsu and the author himself or herself. Moreover the authorship of the "Legend" (the shunkin-den), is also in question. There is no official mark of identification, and the narrator can only guess that the writer is Sasuke, based on how whitewashed the representation of Shunkin is. These principal ambiguities, then, serve to direct suspicion toward other details in the narrative, such as how Shunkin was originally blinded (by purulent ophthalmia or by a jealous sibling?), who impregnated Shunkin (was it Sasuke or a fellow student of Shunkin's mentor?), who snuck into the house and purposely spilled boiling water on Shunkin's face (was it a resentful student, a fellow musician, or Sasuke himself?), and whether Sasuke had really seen the awful burns on Shunkin's face on the day she was attacked. These questions are left unanswered. Yet even if they were answered, doubt about their reliability would remain, given the uncertainty of the sources. As in most of his work, Tanizaki is able to foreground problems of representation and pull apart the usually seamless threads of a narration, while—at one and the same time—weaving a delicate story that delivers aesthetic compensation for its reader's hermeneutic trials. It is this form of simultaneously providing a positive and negative hermeneutic that, I will argue, is the most profound feature of Tanizaki's work produced during the war years.

My own reading of *Shunkinsho*, therefore, has less to do with chalking it up as one more brilliant element of Tanizaki's oeuvre than with locating it historically in terms of 1930s nationalist ideology. Tanizaki wrote *Shunkinsho* at a moment in which film's stock was rising and the shosetsu's stock was on the decline. At one point near the beginning of the shosetsu, the narrator explains that he has discovered a photograph of Shunkin. The photograph, however, which was taken immediately after the Meiji Restoration, does not represent Shunkin's beauty and intrigue, and the narrator remarks that his own narrative will do a much better job of representing her. No doubt, this is a jab at the insufficient nature of the image compared with the richer form of the prose narrative. But Tanizaki is critiquing the image as a form that is not a priori degraded but only insufficient in its nascent stage of photography. This statement, therefore, could very well be understood less as a critique of the reproducible image than as an appreciation of its possibili-

18. Shimazu Yasujiro's *O-Koto to sasuke*. Shochiku, 1935.

ties—that is, once the technology advances, perhaps into film itself, then the image might gain the capacity to convey more than just superficial content.

To underscore this point, let us return to the end of the 1933 essay, in which Tanizaki discussed how he would go about producing an eiga-ka of *Shunkinsho*: "If I were to produce an eiga-ka, I would eloquently paint Shunkin's fantasy world, from the point when Sasuke is blinded, and combine this with the real world. In fact, I'm not sure whether this could be done, but if it succeeded I really think it would produce a tremendously interesting work."[33] This plan is certainly far afield from what Shimazu Yasujiro produced in his 1935 eiga-ka of *Shunkinsho*.

Shimazu's eiga-ka, titled *O-Koto to sasuke*, is one of the most significant works of the *bungei eiga* movement (films based on literary masterpieces) that was emerging as tendency films and nonsense comedies died out (fig. 18). The aim of the movement was to produce eiga-ka from recognized literary works in order to (1) legitimate the artistic qualities of film; (2) sidestep the growing censorship at the time (that coalesced in the 1939 Film Law); and (3) further instantiate Hollywood codes, thus further marginalizing the role of the benshi. When we look at the data on film production between the years 1924 and 1945 (as provided by Inoue Mitsuaki's *Nihon eiga koryuki no sakuhin mokuroku* [A film-by-film record of the periodic rise in Japanese cinema]) what is most striking is the rapid increase in the number of films based on literary texts. For example, in 1924 only 17 percent of the films produced by Nikkatsu, one of the larger corporations at the time, were based on an original literary text. That proportion grew to 44 percent in 1930, 48 percent in 1935, and 58 percent in 1941.[34] One way to explain this dramatic increase is to place it in relation to the parallel increases in censorship: Choosing texts that were already approved allowed film projects to jump through the first hoop of legitimation. When one looks at the most successful eiga-ka of the 1930s (by Gosho and Toyoda, for example, as well as by Yoshimura Kimisaburo and Shibuya Minoru), one locates a dominant form that (1) presents a temporality that traces the story linearly; (2) focuses primarily on dialogue to advance the plot; (3) centers on characters in the frame and overall narrative; (4) de-emphasizes narrative complexity; (5) contains little non-diegetic sound; and (6) refrains from adding to, or cutting elements from, the original text that might distort its dominant canonical reading. These characteristics, as analyzed in Shimazu's film later, will represent a "fidelity"-based adaptation.

Starring Tanaka Kinuyo, one of the best-known actresses of the time, *O-Koto to sasuke* is as "faithful" to Tanizaki's shosetsu as a film could have been at the time. (One should remember that the talkie was less than five years old, and women had been acting in film for less than fifteen). The multiple levels of narration (from the shunkin-den to the Teru character), as well as the "I" of the shosetsu, are eliminated; thus, the problematic of representation that is so central to Tanizaki's work also disappears. Whereas the shosetsu cuts up time by referring to the various sources, Shimazu's film establishes a simple chronological ordering of events. Time is subordinated to the cause–effect chain by, as David Bordwell and Christen Thompson note about the classical Hollywood cinema, "omitting significant durations in order to show only events of causal importance."[35] Shimazu employs another classical Hollywood technique with the hard close, leaving no loose ends that, when picked up and pushed, might undo the narrative itself. Finally, the centering of narrative events and the cause–effect chain is matched by a compositional centering of the characters in the frame. Without the narrative sophistication and meta-text on textuality itself, the action generates from individual characters as causal agents. Because it was stripped of all the shosetsu's idiosyncrasies, and nothing was "added" to it, as Tanizaki argues, as the most interesting possible eiga-ka, *O-Koto to sasuke* was bound to disappoint Tanizaki.

But Tanizaki admits that he never saw the film. He writes:

Shimazu Yasujiro sent the script to me, but I'm really embarrassed to say that I never read it. Speaking about film scripts: Because film and literature are really two separate things, to make *Shunkinsho* into a sufficiently cinematic film would require one to freely deconstruct it and then reconstruct it again. Since this is the best way to proceed, there is sure to be difficulty if the person in charge of the script cannot be trusted.[36]

Tanizaki adds, "I have no hope for the film. . . . But this is not simply a comment about *Shunkinsho*. I have been unhappy with all of the previous films made from my work."[37]

When Tanizaki's work is reduced to mere narrative content, as it was in Shimazu's eiga-ka of *Shunkinsho* (and as was the underlying quality of the bungei eiga movement), all that remains are the most reactionary and conservative elements. But, as Tanizaki makes clear, if the film exceeded the shosetsu by "eloquently paint[ing] Shunkin's fantasy world, from the point when Sasuke is blinded, and combin[ing] this with the real world," then something extraordinary might result. Like his priority of linking evocations (kankyo) among eleventh-century readers of the *Tale of Genji* and the twentieth-century readers, Tanizaki's hope was that the eiga-ka of *Shunkinsho* could evoke similar reactions in its viewers as the shosetsu could in its readers. Only by moving beyond the shosetsu—without leaving it—could there be the possibility of such a project. But when Tanizaki writes, "In fact, I'm not sure whether this could be done," it seems interesting to speculate on whether he is referring to the technical or the historical possibility. In other words, is it that he personally would not be capable of producing such a work, or that film technology was not capable of producing such a work, or that the historical situation itself prevented the very possibility of producing such a work?

Whatever Tanizaki may have intended, the historical limitations are what interest me. The temptation is always present to represent Tanizaki's career as a move from an obsession with the West to one with the East, from an obsession with the progressive to one with the traditional, from an obsession with Tokyo to one with the *Kansai* area (Osaka–Kyoto–Kobe), and so on. Now we can add from an early obsession with film to a renewed one with the prose narrative. But this trajectory reduces the subtlety of Tanizaki's work, as well as the complexity of the different historical moments out of which he is producing. For instance, the fantasy eiga-ka that Tanizaki dreams of making, as well as the fantasy translation that he is struggling to produce during the wartime years, has less to do with solving the aesthetic riddle of how to make a film from a shosetsu or modern translation from a classical text than with articulating an imaginary solution to the growing paradoxical situation of the Japanese nation in the years leading up to World War II. To push this relationship between the aesthetic and the national even further, Tanizaki's dream eiga-ka and dream translation could be read as a dream nation in which Japan could reach utopian heights only by moving beyond the West without leaving it. By constructing a formal utopia on the level of aesthetics, Tanizaki negotiates the most crucial social contradiction of the 1930s: that between being colonized and being a colonizer nation.

But by the early 1970s, both the technical and historical limitations of film had transformed, and Tanizaki's dream film would in fact be made by Shindo Kaneto (*Sanka* [1972]).[38] Yet with a transformed historical situation in which both the nation (discursively and operationally) and the world system function differently, the meaning of Tanizaki's dream film is not entirely clear. At precisely the moment in which the film can be made, the very social contradiction (colonized–colonizer) that produced the need for its formal solution slides into something else. To put this another way: Just as Japan finally was able to thread the needle between East and West (via what came suspiciously to be called the Japanese "economic miracle," synthesizing "Western" capitalist practices and "Eastern" spiritual ones—for example, "Japan, Inc.," "Zen Capitalism"), the very problem of East–West was no longer the most pressing social issue of the day.

Formal Utopias: Shosetsu, Nation, Eiga-ka (Part II)

Shindo's eiga-ka begins with a fish-eye view of a cemetery caretaker thinking about a question that was asked right before the opening shot (fig. 19). He remarks that the Mozuya family plots are up the hill, and that he will show the way. At the plots, the I/narrator/author/Tanizaki character of the film, who is in the scene and is actually the director of the film (more on this later), asks whether the tombstone of the Mozuya daughter, Shunkin, is nearby. The caretaker answers "Yes," then leads the way. In requesting more information about the plots, the author learns about Teru, the servant who was closest to Shunkin and Sasuke after they moved into their own house. Pressed, the caretaker explains that Teru visits the grave a few times a year. Of course, the author wants to meet Teru and asks about her whereabouts. Throughout the scene, the caretaker's manner is one of detached deference, until the end, when he

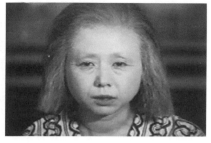

19. Shindo Kaneto's *Sanka*. Kindai Eiga Kyokai, 1972.

20. Otowa Nobuko in Shindo Kaneto's *Sanka*. Kindai Eiga Kyokai, 1972.

suggests a slight degree of cunning (for example, he smirks right before a jump cut to another fish-eye shot of his face and bald head). Already, Shindo, in the spirit of Tanizaki, is undermining his own sources.

Next, we see the author walking into the old folks' home, where he is to meet Teru (fig. 20). Sitting across a table from her, the author explains that he has come to inquire into the legend of Shunkin. Teru, played by Otowa Nobuko (who was married to Shindo), appears to want nothing to do with her inquisitor. "I have nothing to say" and "I don't know a thing" are all she says. When Teru stands up to leave, the author pleads with her to stay and reminds her that he has reserved the whole morning, so she might as well relax. Teru begrudgingly agrees but not before lending doubt to her own motivations for—and, thus, credibility of—the narrative she will tell.

Subverting the credibility of the various sources is crucial to Shindo's film. By moving back and forth between the author and Teru's conversation in the present and the events between Shunkin and Sasuke in the past, Shindo pushes the relationship between the author and Teru into a more central role. At different moments during their conversation, Teru's mood dramatically transforms. Sometimes she coldly and abruptly demands a cigarette, and at other times she exhibits her own fascination with the legend. Her credibility is also questioned within the story she tells of the two lovers. For example, Teru comments about two men who, in the same afternoon, separately asked whether they could spend the night with her. She dispassionately agrees to both, and when one suitor comes to Teru's room, he is shocked to find the other hiding under the futon. Both men scurry out of the room while Teru appears utterly unaffected, if not a little amused. Scenes

Origin, Nation, Aesthetic **109**

such as this develop Teru's character by granting her agency and the where-withal to toy with the random—and, to her, annoying—author. Thus, another key source of Sasuke and Shunkin's legend is called into question.

Then there is the author character himself. The film is fraught with shot–reverse-shot sequences of the author speaking with Teru. These are always shot frontally, with the camera on the center line, so that the entire face of each character occupies the frame. This technique is most conspicuous when the narrative returns to the old folks' home and there is an abrupt cut to the author's face in which his eyes are blankly staring forward and a stream of blood is slowly running out of his mouth (fig. 21). The shot (at three different moments in the course of the film) is held for a few seconds before cutting to Teru's face, then back again to the author's, but this time without the blood and with a slightly more reflective expression. These scenes are always positioned after long excursions, approximately fifteen minutes in cinematic time, back into the narrative of Shunkin and Sasuke. Right at the moment that the author (or the viewer) is gaining uncritical interest in the legend, the stills of the author's bloody face ingeniously shake us out of our reverie and back into the problems of representation.[39]

The fact that the author is played by Shindo himself is important. Of course, in the shosetsu there are countless moments in which the "I" character and Tanizaki overlap. For example, there is "I" 's (like Tanizaki's) fascination with Osaka and how Osaka and Tokyo differ. The same connections exist between Shindo and the "I" of his film: Shindo is the director as well as the "I"; Shindo is from Tokyo (and uses his own Tokyo dialect in the film) and Otowa Nobuko (Teru) is from Osaka and naturally affects the Osaka dialect. In fact, there are stories of Shindo's infatuation with Otowa's Kansai origins when she began to act in his early films that oddly match Tanizaki's well-known obsession with Matsuko, his third wife. Indeed, Shindo's ties to Tanizaki, and the other formal ties between *Shunkinsho* and *Sanka*, are uncanny.

But on the level of narrative content, *Sanka* and *Shunkinsho* differ quite significantly. Many of the scenes that are merely suggested by Tanizaki are filled in and embellished by Shindo, such as when Sasuke helps Shunkin to the toilet. Tanizaki only mentions that Sasuke would wash Shunkin's hands, because she would not be expected to do such chores. But the film has Sasuke actually accompany Shunkin to the toilet. There is an extravagant overhead

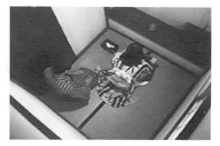

21. Shindo Kaneto's *Sanka*; Shindo himself with blood dripping from his mouth. Kindai Eiga Kyokai, 1972.

22. Shindo Kaneto's *Sanka*. Kindai Eiga Kyokai, 1972.

shot of Sasuke patiently sitting off to the side in an elegant two-mat room while Shunkin squats over the toilet as her unfastened kimono covers her body and the tatami (fig. 22). At Shunkin's cue, Sasuke takes a tissue and places his hand underneath Shunkin's kimono and proceeds to clean her. The scene ends with Sasuke almost lovingly collecting Shunkin's stool on a black lacquer tray, then digging a hole in which to bury it. There is also the scene of Shunkin's pregnancy. The shosetsu only mentions that Shunkin was sent to Arima hot spring to have her baby. The film, however, dedicates an extended scene to her difficult delivery at which Teru and a midwife help as Shunkin screams in excruciating pain for almost an entire minute of film time. And then there is the sex. Tanizaki writes in his shosetsu, "Sexual relations are infinite in their variety. Sasuke, for example, knew Shunkin's body in the most exhaustive detail: He was bound up with her in an intimacy beyond dreams of any ordinary husband and wife or pair of lovers."[40] In the film, however, as Shindo has Teru spy on the two having intercourse, we see Shunkin fully naked and in the throes of ecstasy while Sasuke, with knitted brow and still wearing his cotton kimono, is wholly focused on pleasing her.

It is precisely these excesses that obligated the film critic Matsumoto Kenichi, in a 1973 article in the journal *Eiga hihyou*, to pan the film.[41] In the article, titled "Kindai shugiteki meishi no kansei" (The pitfalls of modernist transparency), Matsumoto essentially attacks *Sanka* for shining too bright a light on the dim beauty of Tanizaki's imaginary. He argues that Shindo makes a fatal methodological error by constructing the Teru character as a seer, thus providing more detail than necessary. Matsumoto writes, "To be able to see right through the misty beauty of Shunkin and Sasuke's world is the hubris of rationalism, or rather of the rationalism that is part of modernism."[42] Matsumoto concludes his polemic by writing, "By shining the light on the details one is unable to see what is unseeable."[43]

With this last line, Matsumoto implies that Tanizaki's shadows and lack of detail render the unseeable seeable.[44] What Matsumoto fails to see, however, is how the accuracy of what Teru sees is itself undermined in Shindo's film. More important, Matsumoto's assumptions about Tanizaki's shosetsu, and his assumptions about the aesthetic in general, need to be questioned. As I argued earlier, Tanizaki's aesthetic choices were not only connected to the closed world of the literary text; they were also inextricably related to the most crucial issues facing the Japanese nation in the 1930s. Like a tapestry that can offer aesthetic pleasure precisely *because* of the exposure of its knots and threads, Tanizaki weaves an eloquent story—with its devices exposed—to which a reader can still cathect. During this period, when political options are being fatally reduced to that between Western colonialism and Japanese colonialism, Tanizaki's response is to construct an aesthetic that offers both a negative and a positive hermeneutic. On the one hand, there is the will to demystify how cultural artifacts (and this clearly relates to national ideologies) tease the desires of the receiver, conceal their own means of production, and serve ideological purposes. On the other hand, Tanizaki offers a positive, or utopian, dimension by providing the story itself, a story still filled with all of the elegance, beauty, shadows, and other aesthetic elements that many are loath to abandon. I view this as an allegory of Tanizaki's own ideal ways of managing national politics: to critique mass political movements that exhibit fascist overtones while holding fast to the utopian possibilities of collective unity. Whether Tanizaki is successful at actually living this ideal is, of course, another issue. It should not be forgotten that Tanizaki's participation in the militarist project, however marginal, is a fact and certainly deserves criticism. Unlike in *Shunkinsho*, in which he successfully strikes a balance between a positive and negative hermeneutic, Tanizaki's positive support for the collective dimension of the Japanese militarist project outweighed any negative critique of imperial conquest and destruction.

Yet by the late 1960s, Japanese aesthetics and politics had been significantly reconfigured. When Matsumoto compared Shindo's film to Tanizaki's shosetsu, however, he did not account for the fact that the cultural and political-economic situations had transformed. It is precisely these situations that must be accounted for before a more subtle analysis can be conducted of the aesthetic meanings and effects of Shindo's *Sanka*. By the late 1960s, the ATG had formed. A young director would usually have to wait some ten years before directing his or her first film. Directors such as Hani Susumu, Oshima Nagisa, Yoshida Yoshishige, Okamoto Kihachi, and Shindo pooled resources to construct an alternative space for the production of everything from films (including features, shorts, documentaries, and eight- and sixteen-millimeter films) to experiments in theater and dance. It was out of this movement that Shindo's *Sanka* emerged. But this is not to suggest that no eiga-ka were made between Shimazu's 1935 film and Shindo's in the 1970s. Indeed, there has been a consistent spate of eiga-ka throughout the one-hundred-year history of Japanese film. But in the early 1960s, there appears to be a break in which more "experiments" were being conducted with the films.

One of the more conservative experiments is the 1963 eiga-ka of Kawabata's celebrated *Izu no odoriko* (The Izu dancer, 1926). The story is about a high-school boy, from Tokyo's elite Number One High School, who takes a solitary trip to the Izu Peninsula. He sees, then becomes obsessed with, a beautiful young dancer who is part of a family of troubadours who move from town to town looking for venues. In the end, due to class and other differences (the family might have a connection to an outcast [*burakumin*] group), the two young lovers must endure a painful separation at Shimoda Harbor. Directed by Nishikawa Tatsumi, the film begins in the present, in black and white, during a university lecture in which an old professor is droning on about democracy. Hundreds of uninterested students are relieved when the professor, himself bored and tired, stops the lecture. Outside on the streets of Tokyo, a student with a request hails the professor. The male student wants to get married but needs the professor's approval to placate his concerned parents. When the professor asks whether the girl is a high-school student, the student explains that she is a dancer. After granting permission, the professor mutters to himself, "a dancer," then thinks back to a distant memory. At this point, the film changes to color, and the story of the Izu dancer is told. Immediately after the two young lovers separate at Shimoda Harbor, the film returns to Tokyo—and to black and white—where the student interrupts the professor's reverie by thanking him for consenting to the proposed marriage. The final scene shows the young couple, holding hands and elated, dancing down a crowded Tokyo street, to the professor's amusement and delight.

In this eiga-ka, information from the present is added to the original narrative, but only on the edges, leaving the integrity of the original shosetsu unchallenged. In short, the present represents a moment of progress from the past. But what about the present in the film? It is 1963, and student, farmer, and worker movements are rocking the nation. This student, however, dreams of marrying and opening a dance studio with his new bride. In other words, for Nishikawa, a return to the past (by the professor) is required in order to make the correct decision in the present (for the student)—a process that, in the end, is determined to stabilize the past and present during a period of considerable social upheaval. The film—and this strain of eiga-ka, in particular—performs a task of crisis management by de-emphasizing the importance of contemporary social problems. In *Sanka*, however, new material is not simply added to the original shosetsu. The whole work is re-configured.

Somewhere between Shindo's and Nishikawa's approaches lies the work of Ichikawa Kon. Ichikawa is renowned for adapting almost 70 percent of his more than seventy feature films.[45] Ichikawa is also renowned for changing the endings of some of the most important original texts. For example, in Ooka Shohei's *Nobi* (Fires on the plain, 1959), after Private Tamura discovers unbridled cannibalism among the Japanese soldiers in the Philippines, he blanks out, only to find himself in a Japanese mental hospital. But Tamura is already too far gone, and Ooka thus resigns him to chronic suffering as his post-traumatic life collapses and the inadequate psychiatrists look on. Ichikawa, by contrast, ends the film by adding a scene in which, instead of blanking out, Tamura is shot and killed. By radically altering the ending, Ichikawa explained in an interview, he was able to grant Tamura his salvation and declare his (Ichikawa's) "total negation of war"—Ichikawa effectively allowed Tamura to "rest peacefully in the world of death."[46] Or there is the classic reworking of *Kagi* (Odd obsession, 1959) in which Ichikawa, in the final scene, has the maid poison and kill off the three remaining maddening characters; Tanizaki, in a less "humanistic" move, had allowed them to live. Once again, Ichikawa takes liberties with the content to stake out his own positions and historical relationships to the primary texts.

I want to read these experiments as political allegories in the context of the rise and fall of social activism in the 1950s and '60s, such as the student movement and the rapid growth experienced by the Japanese economy from 1960 to 1975. Of course, the U.S.–Japan Security Treaty, the threat of nuclear weapons, the opening of the Korean War, the signing of the San Francisco Treaty, and the Vietnam War mobilized the students to think about the role of the Japanese nation-state. The movement began to wither, however, after the ratification of the U.S.–Japan Security Treaty in 1960 and when Prime Minister Ikeda Hayato and his cabinet presented a new paradigm of growth for the Japanese economy. Ikeda's plan was to work toward 8 percent growth in the GNP for each of the next ten years in order to double the GNP by 1970. There were immediate results, as investment in capital facilities by private enterprises showed a 38.8 percent increase in 1960 compared with the previous year. In 1964, the Olympic Games were held in Tokyo; bullet train services had commenced on the New Tokaido Line; and the Meishin Expressway had been completed, connecting the eastern and western parts of the country. Japan was finally considered one of the advanced capitalist nations of the world. The growth in the economy intensified even more, with the average annual GNP growth rate exceeding 13 percent between 1967 and 1969. By 1969, the GNP had reached 60 trillion yen—twice the GNP only four years earlier.

These strong economic indicators made anticapitalist politics difficult to sustain. For example, dissent would often be met by an appeal to the visible growth in living standards and impressive additions to the built environment. The demise of the left in Japan was further exacerbated during the 1970 revision of the U.S.–Japan Security Treaty and the hijacking by the Sekigun (Japanese Red Army) of a Japan Airlines flight to North Korea in the same year. The hijacking marked a time in which public sentiment became highly critical of the student movement in general, and of its militancy in particular. At bottom, 1970 marked the end of a certain utopianism in Japan. Not only was there a "de-Marxification" in the universities and public discourse that was no less profound than that in France after 1968, but there was also a redoubled acquiescence to the rhetoric of the Japanese "economic miracle."

During these years, whether one was criticizing the nation or defending it, the nation as the central organizing unit was essential. This leads back to the second strand of eiga-ka that is being marked off here. Whether it took a conservative approach toward the original shosetsu or a radical one, the shosetsu, like the nation, remained the central organizing unit. Thus far, I have presented two stages of eiga-ka and how each relates to national discourse. The first moment of eiga-ka in the 1930s, represented by Shimazu's eiga-ka of Tanizaki's *Shunkinsho* and other bungei eiga works, was dominated by a "faithful" allegiance to the original shosetsu in a way that was not unlike the "faithful" allegiance to the mythic origins of the Japanese nation held by most citizens during the wartime years. The second phase was dominated by a "freer" connection to the original shosetsu (represented by Shindo's *Sanka*, Nishikawa's *The Izu Dancer*, and the eiga-ka of Ichikawa Kon) and its reconfiguration of the original shosetsu so as to engage the different social problems of the present.

In fact, Shindo, one of the more politically active Japanese film directors, has hinted that his film can be read as a response to the social movements of the day.[47] It was an attempt to criticize the Japanese nation and the continuities it shared with the prewar era. At the same time, it did not want to give up on the possibility that the nation could still be used in an effective and just way. Shindo, and many involved in the social movements of the 1960s and '70s, attacked the Japanese nation, *but only on the level of content*—which is to say that they attacked officials, laws, security treaties, and so on. The *form* of the nation, however, was spared—and, indeed, strengthened by being placed at the center of debate. These categories of form and content, which are usually reserved for aesthetic analyses, can indeed be employed to think through how Shindo and this second wave of eiga-ka engaged original literary texts. Shindo criticizes the content of Tanizaki's shosetsu (by adding more to it, or by shining a light on what is already there), but the form is respected and brandished as what is most valuable about the work. No matter how critical the political and cultural movements were toward the nation or toward older cultural forms, at bottom they remained securely anchored in them.

Transformative Eiga-ka: Toward a Third Moment of the Transnational and the Aesthetic This leads to the third phase of eiga-ka, which has been emerging over the past decade or so, a phase marked by a different relation to the original literary text. This different conceptualization centers on the following problem: All film, as it adapts an original text, invariably transforms the original text itself. This problematic, one that I will call "transformative adaptation" (or better yet, "transformative eiga-ka") seeks to delink and deterritorialize the adaptation from the original. At stake is a disruption of the usual temporalization ascribed to the original–adaptation trajectory. The following example, for instance, represents the usual way in which the trajectory is understood. First comes the writing of the original shosetsu, followed by public and critical recognition. An adaptation will then follow, only to be followed in turn by alternative adaptations that may criticize the first adaptation and attempt to catch the original in an even more faithful or experimental way. Each adaptation organizes the elements of the original literary text in a certain way in order to wrap it up with meaning and anchor it to the past. Yet transformative eiga-ka implies that the original is not only what it is, but also that it exceeds itself. In the earlier example, for instance, the original is part of a dialectical process in which it is at once part of the past, present, and future. When does the original shosetsu end? After the author writes the last word? After the last adaptation? After the most faithful or free adaptation? If we view the original and the adaptation as happening in the present tense—every reorganization of the original's elements as changing the meaning of the original itself—then we will be right in the thick of a method that stresses the through-and-through dynamic and political nature of adaptation.

Quite a lot is at stake here, because in Japan and the world, the inequality of wealth and power is a result of centuries of past events, and many of us justify our concerns and make daily life choices depending on how we explain this past to ourselves. To say that the past has not ended (and for our present purposes, to say this about an original shosetsu) is to set this past (or shosetsu) in a space of real vulnerability. But this vulnerability is marked not only with danger but also with possibility. Pulling up the anchor of the past not only risks obscuring a historical explanation of the present moment; it also enlivens the past and stresses how the past is not only past but part of the present and thus integral in shaping the future. Transformative eiga-ka is a concept that draws attention to this process. Although this process *is always in motion*—even during the bungei eiga movement of the 1930s or the new adaptation impulse of the 1960s and '70s—it seems to become dominant when discourses of "origins" are at their weakest. It is for this reason that the emerging phase of transformative eiga-ka in Japan is occurring at the precise moment in which the nation-state is experiencing an important transformation.

As argued in the preceding chapters, since the mid-1970s, the Japanese economy has been angling into a third moment of capitalist development, symbolized by the flexible accumulation of capital, cybernetic technology, a global division of labor, transnationalization of business practices, and the weakened decision-making power of the nation-state. To be sure, the nation-state and Japanese nationalism (on both the discursive and operational levels) is still alive and well, as cultural-ideological and political-economic developments are moving at different speeds.[48] One can confirm this by taking only a cursory glance at recent Ministry of Education policies, which require schools to raise the national flag (*hi no maru*) and listen to the national anthem (*kimi ga yo*) (the Flag and Anthem movements). But even this seems to be transforming. As transnational consumer culture gains more and more access and power, new identities (for those who can afford to participate in the global market) will certainly challenge (or mutate) older national ones in the future.

It is precisely at this transforming moment that an interesting strain of eiga-ka is emerging. The documentary films of Hara Kazuo seem to represent this strain best. Hara, who has made four films since his first, *Sayonara CP* (Goodbye, cerebral palsy, 1972), received quite a bit of notoriety following his 1987 film *Yukiyukite shingun* (The emperor's naked army marches on) and has no qualms about engaging the most consequential taboos of Japanese society—such as the emperor system, the medical establishment, the marginalization of unconventional women, and the treatment of the disabled.[49] Hara's two more recent works, *Naked Army* and *Zenshin shosetsu-ka*, are particularly good examples of the emerging form of transformative eiga-ka.

Naked Army narrates Okuzaki Kenzo's relentless and violent search to find and publicize the truth of a murder that occurred in New Guinea on August 23, 1945. Okuzaki, an enlisted man in the Japanese Imperial Army's Thirty-sixth Regiment, was one of the few survivors of the regiment to return home. At stake for Okuzaki, so many years after the war, is the cannibalization of two enlisted men who were officially labeled deserters. Although it is widely known that acts of cannibalism occurred during World War II, Okuzaki wants to publicize the fact that Japanese troops ate not only enemy soldiers, but Japanese soldiers, as well. After returning from the war, Okuzaki becomes involved with organized crime and spends thirteen years and nine months in prison for murdering a real-estate broker (in 1956), distributing pornographic leaflets emblazoned with pictures of Emperor Hirohito (in 1976), and firing four pachinko pellets, using a homemade slingshot, at the emperor (in 1969). (The last incident makes him a household name in Japan.) In prison, Okuzaki experiences a type of spiritual revelation and becomes fiercely determined to expose the corruption that has occurred, and that still occurs, in Japan. "I repented for my crimes; I took responsibility. Why doesn't the emperor repent for his?" Okuzaki chants with the faith and frequency of a mantra.

Hara follows Okuzaki around as he attempts to locate those who gave the orders to cannibalize the two soldiers. There are visits to officers' homes, to a hospital where a former officer is recovering from surgery, to the restaurant of a former medic, to the grave of one of the cannibalized soldiers, to the prison where Okuzaki served time, and to relatives of the victims. Okuzaki wants confessions, apologies, and remorse from those he interrogates; when he does not get them, there is violence. It does not matter that the other person is sick or his wife and grandchildren are in the room. Okuzaki leaps up and begins to wrestle with those with whom he finds fault. As the narrative progresses, Okuzaki and Hara's team go to New Guinea to continue the search for details. We learn, however, that Indonesian government officials confiscated more than forty-nine rolls of footage shot in New Guinea.

On returning to Japan, Okuzaki concentrates his mission. Following the sound of a sudden gunshot, then a black frame, we learn that he has attempted to murder the son of one of the former officers with whom he (we) met earlier in the film. We do not see the murder attempt itself; we only read about it in the newspaper clippings that fill the screen. "Criminal at large for wounding his superior officer's son," reads one of the headlines. Another quotes Okuzaki as stating, "His son will do." Next, we find ourselves outside Hiroshima prison as Okuzaki's wife, Shizumi, approaches the camera. Shizumi explains that her husband is fine and that "he eats better now than

23. Hara Kazuo's *Yukiyukite shingun* (The emperor's naked army marches on);
Okuzaki Kenzo and Okuzaki Shizumi. Shisso Productions, 1987.
24. Hara Kazuo's *The Emperor's Naked Army Marches On*. Garage shutter of battery
shop in which Okuzaki lived and worked; the large text reads," A Proclamation to
Kill Tanaka Kakuei." Shisso Productions, 1987.

when he was living at home." "He's satisfied," she adds. The film ends by
noting that Shizumi has died and Okuzaki will serve twelve years of hard
labor in the Hiroshima prison (fig. 23).

Hara was introduced to Okuzaki by the veteran filmmaker Imamura Shohei. Although Imamura had wanted to include Okuzaki in a film for some
time, he bowed to threats from the right-wing (threats that are still common
when critiques of the emperor system, such as Okuzaki's, are made). Instead,
Imamura introduced Okuzaki to Hara. Imamura began by sending Hara the
book that Okuzaki had written and self-published. Titled *Tanaka Kakue wo
korosu tame ni shirusu* (Proclamation to murder Tanaka Kakue).[50] Okuzaki
distributed the thick book to Japan's intelligentsia and advertised it by painting its title and other slogans on the garage shutter of his used-battery shop
in Kobe (fig. 24). When Hara met Okuzaki for the first time, Okuzaki realized
that a film about his book would be priceless advertising—and this is how
Hara sold the film to Okuzaki. Indeed, *The Emperor's Naked Army Marches
On* is a sort of eiga-ka of Okuzaki's work. Or, rather, it is the first step toward
developing a film practice that might be called transformative eiga-ka.

For example, by following Okuzaki on his mission to locate and destroy
the officers of his former military regiment, it becomes deadly clear to Hara
—and to the viewers—that he is (or we are) becoming more and more of an
accomplice to a future murder: It is the presence of the camera and Oku-

zaki's acute awareness of our desire to see that animates his actions. In other words, Hara, in the process of adapting Okuzaki's book/story, not only interprets Okuzaki's actions; he changes them, as well. This concept of transformative eiga-ka (and the consequences it might have for the contemporary shosetsu) becomes even more apparent in Hara's next film *Zenshin shosetsu-ka* (A dedicated life or more literally, The whole body of a prose narrative writer, 1994).

A Dedicated Life is about the life and work of Inoue Mitsuharu, an important writer in postwar Japan. After reading a number of Inoue's shosetsu and attending one of his fiery lectures, Hara was inspired to make a film.[51] Not knowing what type of film to make, Hara suggested to Inoue that he should write the script. This way, Hara reasoned, Inoue could act the character of himself. This plan was up-ended, however, once Inoue discovered that he had stomach cancer in 1990. Hara immediately shifted gears and decided to make a film about Inoue's struggle with cancer and his various professional appointments. By filming New Year ceremonies at Inoue's house and Inoue's writing seminars and lectures; interviewing his writing circle (including the famous proletarian writer Haniya Yutaka); and filming the cancer surgery, in which Inoue's body is cut open and part of his stomach is removed (hence the significance of the Japanese title), Hara confronts a delicate task of wanting to learn more about Inoue without igniting the pyrotechnics that are the staple of his other films and rudely disturbing a dying man.

Through all these different fragments, Hara carefully narrates Inoue's biography. We learn about Inoue's childhood and the time he spent in China before he was traumatically separated from his mother. We learn about a Korean girl with whom he fell in love as a young boy and who radicalized him about certain racial and gender issues. We learn about the school entrance exams that Inoue aced. Sometimes Inoue explains this to groups of students and sometimes directly to Hara. There are also narrative switches to a dramatic form in which young actors perform the relationship of Inoue and the Korean girl. These "facts" of Inoue's life are well known to most viewers who are also readers of his shosetsu, because Inoue commonly incorporates them into his fiction. But a new narrative line develops when Hara finds discrepancies in the biography Inoue has been telling and the pieces of his life that others have been providing. After doing some detective work at the local government office, and with more focused questions directed to Inoue's relatives, the discrepancies are corroborated, and Hara comes to realize that Inoue has fabricated much of his life story.

This realization, however, does not undermine Inoue's or Hara's project. Instead, it strengthens an objective that they share: to make a cultural artifact in the present that necessarily refigures past ones. For example, Inoue's original shosetsu have transformed insofar that their characters must now be interpreted through an entirely different relationship to the author. Even though Hara touches on many of Inoue's shosetsu instead of focusing on only one, and he dedicates most of the film to Inoue's life in the present, I will still locate Hara's work as eiga-ka. In this phase of eiga-ka, however, the very identity of Inoue's shosetsu is destabilized and is made as transformable and mutable as Inoue's life itself. Indeed, the opening image of the film, showing Inoue's handwritten texts crammed with crossouts and arrows pointing in all directions, powerfully represents the utopian possibility to rewrite our own lives (fig. 25). And the final still image, of Inoue writing at his desk (after he has died of cancer), once again confirms this continually transforming process (fig. 26).

This is not to suggest, however, that people are unfettered when reconstructing their own identities or that cultural producers are able freely to reconstruct past artifacts. Rather, these transformations are always conducted within the limitations of a particular historical situation. For Shimazu's eiga-ka of Tanizaki's *Shunkinsho* in 1935, the limitations were forcibly produced by imperial demands. For Shindo's *Sanka*, the situation was limited by the pressing social issues of the day (such as the U.S.–Japan Security Treaty, issues of urban and rural development, and the Vietnam War). For Hara, and the emerging third phase of transformative eiga-ka, the deterritorialization of capital that is now based less on industrial and manufacturing investments within and outside the nation than on the speculation of capital in cyberspace (money markets, bond and stock markets), is bringing new limits on—and new possibilities for—producing different and significant cultural forms.

For example, the form of the original shosetsu, which was so crucial during the first two stages of eiga-ka in modern Japan, is no longer the fundamental organizing unit. Eiga-ka—at least, as demonstrated by Hara—no

25. Hara Kazuo's film *Zenshin shosetsu-ka* (A dedicated life); the large vertical characters are the film's title over Inoue's handwritten text. Shisso Productions, 1994.

26. Inoue Mitsuharu sits at his desk after his death. From Hara Kazuo's film *Zenshin shosetsu-ka* (Tokyo: Kinema Jumpa-sha, 1994).

longer seems to "need" the shosetsu as it once did; rather, the film turns back on the shosetsu and reveals its instability and fragmentary relation to the film. Or to take this a step further: The film adaptation produces the shosetsu. This is to say that the shosetsu is no longer whole and autonomous; it exists only in incomplete relation to the life of its author, to its readers, and to its adaptations.

It is this reconfigured world and national situation, in which Hara (and others) are producing today, that seems to hamper both Tanizaki's and

Shindo's use of the beautiful. Of course, the negative dimension demonstrated by Tanizaki and Shindo (problematizing representation and contextualizing the impulses to produce the beautiful) still exists, but the positive dimension of their work (the beautiful story itself, the long and complex but still elegant sentences of Tanizaki's prose in which a single sentence might contain six or seven negations; the lush colors; the precious flute soundtrack against the intense foregrounded music of Shunkin's samisen and koto; the disruptive frontal shot–reverse-shot compositions against the seamless transitions of Shindo's editing) is transforming during the contemporary moment. It is precisely a new positive dimension to place in relation to the well-honed negative one that this third phase of eiga-ka is struggling to represent, one that not only will affect the very concept of eiga-ka but may have radical consequences for the shosetsu, as well.

It is interesting to speculate whether the films that Hara and others connected to his experimental documentary circle are making might not present a new possibility for the shosetsu. In fact, at a conference that Hara also attended during the early 1990s, Karatani Kojin mentioned that he thought Hara's films were *shi-shosetsu* (I-prose narratives). The reason is that Hara is the cameraman for his films and acts as a critical character in the development of the narrative. I am not sure whether I agree with Karatani's analogy, but the more extroverted, interrogative, and social dimensions of Hara's films—as opposed to the introverted and individual dimensions that are the hallmark of the shosetsu since its birth in the 1880s—may very well represent one way for the shosetsu to regain its audience and its position as one of the more significant cultural forms in contemporary Japan.

Finally, I will compare Hara's work to another work that can be situated within this third moment of eiga-ka; Okuyama Kazuyoshi's 1995 film *The Mystery of Rampo*. In this blockbuster, Okuyama combines the life of Edogawa Rampo, the great horror- and detective-fiction writer (1894–1965), with a series of Rampo's stories. The film, which takes place in early Showa (late 1920s–early 1930s), contains a recently finished work titled *The Appearance of Osei*. Osei is a beautiful young woman with an invalid husband. One day, after Osei has left home, neighborhood children ask her husband to play hide-and-seek. He obliges and secretly ducks into a hope chest (*naga-mochi*). The kids seek far and wide, then become bored and give up. But when the husband attempts to reveal himself, he is terrified to learn that he is trapped in the self-locking chest. Osei returns to the faint sounds of her husband trying to escape. She opens the chest, then, without hesitation, closes it and murders her husband. Because the story has been censored, and because Rampo has burned the original handwritten copy, he is astonished to read a current newspaper article recounting the event. Rampo tracks down the woman, falls immediately in love, and realizes that he must continue writing fiction in order to shape the real world.

After some documentary film footage (ranging from Tokyo street scenes and wartime battles to aristocratic balls), the film moves to Rampo's study, where books by Sigmund Freud and Sir Arthur Conan Doyle—and, of course, Edgar Allan Poe—fill the shelves (Edogawa Rampo, the nom de plume of Hirai Tare, sounds like Edgar Allan Poe when pronounced rapidly in Japanese). There is then a shot of the *The Appearance of Osei*'s handwritten manuscript pages before it is represented in animation form. At the conclusion of the scene, there is a jump-cut to the film's present and a stern bureaucrat thrusting down the "censored" stamp on the manuscript. From here on out, the film cuts among Rampo writing in his study, walking the city streets, and living (through his alter ego Detective Akechi) the fantastic scenes of his fiction.

The theme of the film intersects with the theme of many of Rampo's stories: the construction of the perfect crime, the elegantly assembled murder that cannot be pinned on the perpetrator. In another work, *The Red Chamber*, Rampo writes about a man who is so bored that he must entertain himself by dreaming and committing perfect murders. For instance, as an old woman crosses a busy street, he shouts, "Look out, old woman!" She becomes flustered and is consequently struck by a streetcar. Rampo's main character states:

> Yes, in such a case the man who sounds the warning actually become a murderer! Who, however, would suspect him of murderous intent? Who could possibly imagine that he had deliberately killed a complete stranger merely to satisfy his lust to kill? Could his action be interpreted in any way other than that of a kindly man bent only on keeping a fellow human being from being run over? There is no ground to suppose even that he would be reproached by the dead! Rather, I should imagine that the old

27. Okuyama Kazuyoshi's *The Mystery of Rampo;* Rampo (right) and his editor, Yokomizu Masashi, viewing an eiga-ka of Rampo's *The Phantom with Twenty Faces.* Shochiku, 1994.

woman would have died with a word of thanks on her lips . . . despite her having been murdered.[52]

Here the perfect crime within Rampo's literary universe relates to the perfect crime of the Japanese state during the prewar moment. The state requires men to go off to war (to die) and most others to bear inhuman sacrifices in the name of the emperor. The state, however, is not suspected of murderous intent. Rather, the citizens obey "with a word of thanks" on their lips. But the perfect crime is always imperfect; it always contains the possibility of being undone, of releasing its essential surplus, of being exposed by the tenacious and implicated detective. For Rampo, this logic is birthed by way of the imagination—an imagination that must be honed (in both writer and reader) to crack open a seemingly closed totality. Like that of other great political detective-fiction writers (Paco Ignacio Taibo, Manuel Vázquez Montalbán, Dashiell Hammett, Raymond Chandler), the work contains a pedagogical aspect that trains a popular readership to make connections, to move back and forth from the particular (the individual clue) to the universal (the larger crime), from their own lives to the larger social structure.[53]

During the film, there is a screening of an eiga-ka made from one of Rampo's most commercially successful stories, "The Phantom with Twenty Faces." Rampo and his editor (Yokomizu Masashi) watch a few minutes of the film (composed of amateur framing and editing, silly secret hideouts, and childish histrionics) before abruptly walking out of the screening room (fig. 27). Rampo is simply uninterested, not unlike the way Tanizaki was uninterested in Shimazu's eiga-ka of *Shunkinsho.* As with any aesthetic device that is self-reflexive, the film-within-the-film punctuates Okuyama's own thoughts on adaptation. In other words, by lampooning the one-dimensional eiga-ka within the film, he elevates the presumed complexity and cleverness of the techniques he is employing in his eiga-ka, such as the movement back and forth between Rampo's writing and the cinematic representations of what he is writing.

In a number of scenes, a character inside the fiction hangs on a single word that Rampo himself hangs on with pen in hand. After cutting back to Rampo's writerly struggles, the author finds the next sentence, thus animating the character's next move. What we see then is an *illustration* of transformative eiga-ka, a cinematic demonstration of how film transforms the original text. Indeed, film and literature are dynamically related; neither comes before the other. But unlike in Hara's film, which *performs* this function by practically rewriting Inoue's shosetsu, Okuyama merely gestures to it without risking much. Instead of calling attention to the transformative operations one text can have on another, and therefore to what this might mean for rethinking the canonization of Japanese literature, *The Mystery of Rampo* effectively reanchors Edogawa Rampo to the past, wiping out any radical dimension existing within the original works themselves. It may very well be the case that experimental documentary, such as the kind produced by Hara Kazuo, lends itself—more than the standard feature film—to exploiting the possibilities of transformative eiga-ka.

What is truly interesting is that Rampo seemed to understand the stakes in adaptation. In the English translation of ten of his stories, translator James B. Harris explains the following:

Edogawa Rampo, while fully capable of reading and understanding English, lacks the ability to write or speak it. On the other hand, the translator, a Eurasian of English–Japanese parentage, while completely fluent in spoken Japanese, is quite unable to read or write the language, as he was educated solely in English schools. Hence, for each line translated, the two collaborators, meeting once a week for a period of five years, were forced to overcome manifold difficulties in getting every line just right, the author reading each line in Japanese several times and painstakingly explaining the correct meaning and nuance, and the translator sweating over his typewriter having to experiment with sentence after sentence until the author was fully satisfied with what had been set down in English.[54]

Instead of employing a fully bilingual translator, Rampo risks the mysterious two-way street that opens new directions for his work. Perhaps Rampo anticipated the current moment in which a new relationship to origins is emerging, one that has everything to do with the reconfigurations of aesthetic and national discourses within the age of globalization.

iv. acting

Structure, Agent, Amateur

The Amateur   On May 27, 1997, Hase Jun, an eleven-year-old boy, was found dead in Kobe. His head, severed from his body, was discovered at the entrance of the junior high school that Hase's fourteen-year-old killer attended. Inside his mouth was a note from the killer: *"Saa, geemu no hajimari desu"* (Well, let's begin the game); "Stop me if you can, police officers"; "It is a delight for me to murder"; "This is bloody judgment for years of personal bitterness." On the evening that the note was discovered, and more than a month before the identity of the young killer was uncovered, a number of news broadcasts asked criminologists what they made of it. Not a few of them mentioned that the killer's note resembled challenges that can often be found in *manga* (graphic novels) as well as in a number of U.S. mystery novels that have been translated and are popular in Japan.[1] One commentator expressed confusion that the words of the killer were marked by a profound contradiction: On the one hand, they celebrated the thrill kill, killing for sheer delight, while on the other hand, they expressed real discontent and bitterness at Japanese society.[2] These two motivations are rarely found in the same person; thus, the commentator concluded, the murderer must be an amateur.

This issue raises the old question of the relation between fictional acting within popular culture and real social acting. And, as would be expected, it has been linked to the case of Miyazaki Tsutomu, who in 1989 was also playing a game with the media when, before being found out, he took on the persona of a female manga character to explain that he had killed adolescent girls out of the frustration that he could not bear children. After Miyazaki was captured, police not only discovered that he was a man. They also found thousands of videocassettes of animation, children's programming, and manga crammed into his small, six-mat room. No doubt, cultural imitation is a difficult problem that is often obscured by simplistic and ahistorical notions of the aesthetic, the subject, and the social.[3] The issue itself, however—and the moral debate over mass-culture representations that inevitably accompanies it—is a red herring: It serves to crowd out the less obvious but, to my mind, much more significant issue of the status of the social agent itself and the possibilities and limitations for resistance in contemporary Japan.

The comment that caught my attention in the Hase Jun murder was the one about the killer's being an amateur. (It should be noted that the comment was made before the killer was revealed to be a boy and when many thought the leading suspect was a man in his forties.) In this case, "amateur" seems to contrast with "professional"—say, the yakuza or even the killer who is a more intentional actor with a less conflicted subjectivity. It is certainly odd usage. But the more one thinks about this notion of the amateur, the more one might see that it has served as one of the most important tropes in the history of both Japanese film acting and Japanese social acting. When Japanese capitalism experiences significant restructurings, the concept of the amateur (in both film and social action) has been invoked. The untrained amateur, as opposed to the overly trained professional, represents the utopian element that can break through the rigid film structure and bring about needed change. In the political arena, "amateur" has been used to refer to the proletariat, housewives, farmers, female textile workers, students, burakumin, homeless people, consumers, and other individuals or groups who pose an institutional threat. The amateur is embarrassing, unskilled, unpredictable, uncontracted, go-for-broke, rule-breaking, spontaneous, and dangerous. The amateur, in other words, sets the smooth workings of a system in a state of potential peril. It is no surprise, therefore, that the amateur is invoked at times of systemic crisis and instability. But the concept of the amateur is not always utopian; it also has a dystopian dimension in which it is connected to an unavailing anarchism or is used to supplement the superiority of the professional and reinforce systemic hierarchy and thus systemic coherence itself.

Although the amateur appears to be a transhistorical category, I will argue that it is a thoroughly modern invention. Of course, amateurs—or those who are untrained in a certain action—have existed throughout Japanese history. But the "amateur" as we conceive it today did not exist prior to the emergence of Japanese capitalism's reorganization of society following the Meiji Restoration. Following the formation of capitalism, a heightened discourse on the amateur always seems to be refigured and refunctionalized in dialectical relation to significant restructurings in the Japanese capitalist system. In this chapter, I historicize this category of the amateur actor, in both Japanese film and modern social history, in order to speculate on the meanings, effects, and possibilities of film actors and political actors throughout modern Japanese history. In other words, instead of investigating how real actors reflect or mimic fictional actors and get locked into that tortuous hunt on which the Japanese police found themselves during the summer of 1997 (relentlessly searching films, novels, manga, the Internet, video-rental receipts, and other popular-culture artifacts for the golden lead that would reveal the Kobe killer's identity), I will pursue another course: that of examining how the dominant forms of film and political acting relate to the historical situation in which they dwell, then to ask what type of new acting forms are emerging within the contemporary situation of global capitalism.

The Mistake The notion of the amateur was an important subject of debate within shingeki (new theater) in the first part of the twentieth century. To break through the acting constraints of kabuki and noh, many asked whether the professional actor should be trained to be an amateur or whether the amateur should be trained to be a new type of actor (*Yakusha wo shiroto ni suru koto* or *shiroto wo yakusha ni suru koto*).[4] Osanai Kaoru and Tanizaki

Junichiro were both instrumental in transferring this debate to film in the late 1910s. For Osanai and Tanizaki, film could not develop into its own if it simply remained on the level of filmed theater. A less stylized and more seemingly "natural" form of acting emerged in films such as *Rojo no reikon* (Souls on the road, 1921), directed by Murata Minoru, produced by Osanai, and starring Murata and Osanai themselves, and Tanizaki's first film, *Amachua kurabu* (Amateur club), made in 1920 for the newly established Taikatsu film company.[5]

Before discussing these two films and the move to what might be called acting "realism," I will return to an even earlier moment of film acting—the first moment, in fact. This came, as I mentioned in chapter 1, when the famous kabuki actor Ichikawa Danjuro IX acted in a film version of *Momijigari* in 1899. As noted, Danjuro, who was not particularly thrilled with being filmed, had to be persuaded by others to lend his talents to the project. Moreover, on the day of the shoot, an intense wind caused Danjuro accidentally to drop his fan.[6] There was neither enough time nor film stock to retake the scene, so the "mistake"—"the failure"—remains in the film. This mistake may also account in part for Danjuro's shock when the film was being screened the following year at his residence. In other words, when he dropped the fan, he was Danjuro—an individual actor traumatized by this new medium—not the great star who represented nine generations of kabuki.

This is all to say that it was the formation of this new cinematic structure that refigured Danjuro's acting and produced the possibility for his mistake. But this is not to suggest that mistakes were not committed on the kabuki stage; rather, it is to stress that what constituted a mistake—and, perhaps more important, the very conceptualization of a mistake—had changed. For example, an actor's mistake in kabuki could be seamlessly incorporated into the performance and corrected in a following performance. The transitory nature of a kabuki mistake, therefore, made it not a failure as such, because the way in which the mistake was managed determined its value. With film, the mistake became reproducible and indelibly inscribed on the print; it was frozen in time, taking on a permanently negative value. It was precisely this new situation of the mistake that was then repressed for the next twenty years. At bottom, fear of the mistake drove the first stage of Japanese film production.

28. Osanai Kaoru. From Chiba Nobuo's
Film and Tanizaki (Tokyo: Seiabo, 1989).

For example, as editing skills progressed, a director could conceal the mistake by easily cutting away from Danjuro (perhaps to a closeup of Kikugoro) at the precise moment that he dropped the fan. Or a benshi could incorporate the mistake into the narrative to refigure its meaning. Or the simplest solution might be to retake the shot at a later moment, when the wind had died down. These techniques were employed to control the film's structure and eliminate the possibility of the recurrence of such a mistake. Or to put it another way, these techniques were employed to elevate the power of the film structure over that of the individual actor. It was not until the early 1920s (with films such as *Souls on the Road* and *Amateur Club*) that film structures and actors began to transform. This opened the possibility to make what had been a mistake at an earlier moment into the centerpiece of a whole new acting style.

Osanai was the foremost theorist of theater and acting in Japan at the time. Known as the father of shingeki, Osanai incorporated Western realist forms into an entirely different type of unstylized drama in Japan (fig. 28). After graduating from Tokyo Imperial University in 1906 with a degree in English literature, Osanai began translating modern Western dramas before establishing the shingeki movement in 1907.[7] Five years later, he traveled to Europe to view as many plays as possible (by Ibsen, Shaw, Archer, and others), all the while collecting postcards, photographs, and other documents that would be useful in teaching movement and characterization when he returned to Japan.[8] Then it was off to Russia, where Osanai was immediately attracted to Vsevolod Meyerhold's biomechanics, as well as to Konstantin Stanislavsky's Moscow Art Theater, in which the actor attempts to merge emotionally with the part being played so that the role grows from within the actor himself or herself.[9] Of course, for Stanislavsky and those influenced by his theories, this new method of acting (or "method acting," as it would later be known) was a response to the mechanical acting of nineteenth-century Europe, the type of generic acting characterized by the shoulder shrug (bewilderment), the hand over the heart (compassion), and the tearing of hair (anxiety). Unlike those in Europe and the Soviet Union, however, Osanai confronted a different theatrical history—one dominated by noh and kabuki.

When Osanai returned to Japan, the Shochiku Film Company, newly set up in Kamata in the south of Tokyo, sent for his services. With the Japanese success of D. W. Griffith's *Intolerance* in 1919, the company heads sensed the potential of a modern cinema and granted Osanai carte blanche to establish an actors' studio in the new style. Although he focused on the theater for most of his student and professional career, Osanai remained curious about the cinema. As a child, he took extensive notes while viewing films, and years later, when granted private access to view *Intolerance*, Osanai destroyed the print after countless close viewings.[10] In 1921, Osanai oversaw the production of three films (*Sansai ruru* [Details of a mountain fortress], *Rojo no reikon* [Souls on the road], and *Kimi yo shirazu ya* [Don't ya know?]). Only *Souls on the Road* has survived.[11]

Souls on the Road departs from Maxim Gorki's *Lower Depths* and is recognized, along with Kinugasa's *Kurutta ippeiji* (Page of madness, 1926), as one of the great experiments of prewar Japanese cinema. The film juggles four narrative lines that, directly and indirectly, bounce off each other vis-à-vis a subtle employment of montage, cross-cutting, and flashback techniques.[12] Noel Burch views the simultaneous use of alternate and parallel montage as exceeding anything produced by Griffith at the time and anticipating the great work to come out of the Soviet Union in the late 1920s and early 1930s, most notably Eisenstein's *Strike* and *October*.[13] But it is not so much the narrative structure that interests me here as the acting and how it responded to Japanese theatrical traditions as well as to the emergence of the modern subject.

Griffith and Lillian Gish, both enormously influential in Japan during the 1910s and '20s, were instrumental in bringing about the birth of modern film acting. The older type of theater acting was seen at a distance, always as a medium shot in which the bodies of the actors remained in their totality. This is proscenium acting. Griffith recognized and pursued cinema's capability to fracture the body—a body that could be shown in its details to delay and strengthen the tempo and drama of the narrative. For Griffith (and it took the incomparable talents of Gish and cameraman Billy Bitzer to complete his project), the parts of the body—the hands, fingers, and face—all function at different speeds. It is the closeup, refined by Griffith, that foregrounded these details. For example, wildly gesticulating while hiding in a closet in *Broken Blossoms* (1919), Gish's body is virtually cut up as she nervously awaits a force (her deranged father) that will come and destroy her.[14] For Eisenstein, it was this representation of acting, with the various body parts shot in closeup, that "create[d] a new quality of the whole from a juxtaposition of the separate parts."[15] The brilliance of the Griffith–Gish machine for Eisenstein was that the actor worked in a dialectical relation with the director. In Japan, however, noh and kabuki (not to mention bunraku) were already about a fractured body. There was something essentially cinematic in these forms before the invention of the cinema.

Eisenstein recognized this when he wrote about kabuki acting in the 1929 essay "The Cinematographic Principle and the Ideogram."[16] On kabuki, he wrote, "There is a pure cinematographic element—its basic nerve, montage."[17] Eisenstein then listed three characteristics of kabuki acting that are perfectly cinematic. The first is "acting without transitions." Eisenstein offers the example of Sadanji's transforming from a drunk into a madman in the play *Narukami.* Instead of having the actor work from one emotion to the next, as in European acting, an assistant (*kurogo*) would conceal the actor from the spectator until the actor appeared in new make-up. This is nothing other than the cinematic cut—a jump-cut from the face of a madman to one of a drunk. The second is "disintegrated" acting—acting that is cut up into pieces, creating the "role of the leg, the role of the arm, the role of the head." This is Gish in the closet during *Broken Blossom.* The third is the slow tempo of kabuki (or, more appropriately, noh), in which a single action—say, a suicide—is based on a slowing down of all movement that can take hours to perform. This is slow-motion in the cinema. Yet, whereas Eisenstein looked to Japanese traditional culture for his model of modern cinema, Osanai looked to the new naturalism of the Western theater for his model.

It was precisely this looking to the West by Japanese filmmakers that disturbed Eisenstein. It is not clear whether Eisenstein saw *Souls on the Road,* but the following comment explicitly expresses his views about Osanai's project:

> Instead of learning how to extract the principles and technique of their remarkable acting from the traditional feudal forms of their materials, the most progressive leaders of the Japanese theater throw their energies into an adaptation of the spongy shapelessness of our own "inner" naturalism. The results are tearful and saddening. In its cinema Japan similarly pursues imitations of the most revolting examples of American and European entries in the international commercial film race.[18]

Eisenstein concluded with this provocation: "To understand and apply her cultural peculiarities to the cinema, this is the task of Japan! Colleagues of Japan, are you really going to leave this for us to do?"[19]

One problem with Eisenstein's criticism is that Japanese film in the 1920s was fighting not against Western traditions but against Japanese ones. If Eisenstein's project was to create "a new quality of the whole from a juxtaposition of the separate parts," then Osanai's and Murata's was to create a new quality of the separate parts from a juxtaposition of the whole. But here, the part and the whole refer to the individual, to the formation of the modern subject that developed later in Japan than in the West. In the new Soviet Union it was crucial to show how the various parts related to the whole, how a worker existed in dialectical relation to a bourgeois, or how each part was instrumental in producing the whole—the whole of society. In Japan, it was not so much the totality of society that needed to be revealed as the totality of the individual—the individual as an agent. Japanese were only too aware of the whole, of the hierarchical cosmic order advanced by the Tokugawa *bakufu* (shogunate)—an order so predictable that it precluded the very concept of the individual human actor from being thought. There was a need to emphasize the materiality of the body, not its ideality—its sensuous qualities rather than its abstract ones. This Japanese modern subject, which was crucial to both spurring and resisting capitalist development, needed to be reassembled (no matter how impossible a project of unified subject formation might be); it must be seen again in its totality in contrast to its fractured state as fashioned by a hyper-formalized aesthetic.

No doubt Eisenstein would have admired the inventive cross-cutting and storytelling of *Souls on the Road*, but he would not have been able to see the acting as anything more than a miserable imitation of already flawed Western realist acting. But here it seems important to stress an understanding of realism as not a content-based, but a formal, response to an earlier aesthetic. In other words, realism cannot be defined simply as acting that seems "real" or acting that is unstylized and reflective of everyday life. Rather, realism in this context is that which defamiliarizes—or makes strange—a spectator to the dominant.[20] Thus, what is realist in one context (geographically or historically) might look quite different in another, and, as stated in chapter 1 by noting Roman Jakobson's classic essay on realism, the employment of the category itself is usually marked by great ambiguity and confused assumptions. It is for this reason that we must distinguish Eisenstein's use of realism as it relates to Soviet film or the fractured body of Lilian Gish from the very different Japanese context. For Osanai and Murata, the fractured body of kabuki and noh must now be represented as a total body in the new Japanese cinema of the 1920s.

Both systems have as an underlying goal the shaping of the modern human agent, but they must get there in different ways because of their different aesthetic histories of performance and reception. For instance, *Souls on the Road* is dominated by mid-range shots that catch the entire body in motion. During the first scene, two men are chopping down trees in the forest as the falling trees punctuate the rhythmic motion of their entire bodies (fig. 29). There are also several shots of Osanai's character pacing in a state of distraught decision-making (fig. 30). Walking back and forth inside his modest farmhouse, he broods over what to do about the return of his prodigal son. Pacing is a thoroughly modern act. It is literally about thinking on one's feet, about weighing choices regarding a social decision. Does Osanai accept his son back into the family or not? He is not an abstraction that obeys fixed laws of Tokugawa social relations; he is now a human agent who must decide

29. Murata Minoru's *Rojo no Reikon* (Souls on the road); two bodies shot in totality. Shochiku, 1921.

30. Murata Minoru's *Souls on the Road*; Osanai Kaoru pacing. Shochiku, 1921.

on his own, and he must use his entire body in the otherwise purposeless act of endlessly criss-crossing a room to stimulate an answer that only he can provide. But, of course, the modernity of the act is not the decision at which Osanai's character finally arrives, but the form by which he arrives at it. And it is this shot of Osanai moving to all four regions of the film frame— side to side and up and down—that most powerfully represents the modern Japanese subject.

But for all Osanai's theorization about acting, his own acting—stiff and overwrought—leaves something to be desired. The director Murata Minoru, who plays the lumberyard boy in the household of Osanai's character, Sugino Yasushi, emerges as the actor of the day. He is seen chopping wood, running errands to the train station, and even displaying some affection for the frivolous daughter who lives next door. Midway through the film, Murata's character is shot gathering kindling. He reaches for the door, then a few of the sticks drop (fig. 31). He reaches down for the sticks while managing to open the door. What Osanai tries to achieve in his pacing—indeed, what Osanai tries to achieve in much of his theorization about acting—Murata captures in this single act. He acts without hesitating to pick up the accidentally dropped sticks. Instead of cutting away from the mistake or reshooting it, the shot remains and does so as one of the most important scenes in the film. From Danjuro's dropped fan to Murata's dropped sticks, film acting comes of age in Japan. The mistake is now something to be provoked rather than repressed, something to remain intact rather than corrected, something revered rather than averted.

31. Murata Minoru's *Souls on the Road*;
Murata dropping sticks. Shochiku, 1921.

Professionally trained actors could not have realized the acting of Murata;
only the amateur untrained in the traditional theater could move in such a
way. This is precisely what Tanizaki and Kurihara tried to exploit in *Amateur Club*.[21] *Amateur Club* is a slapstick comedy about amateur actors who
perform a mock kabuki play on Yuigahama beach in Kamakura. Tanizaki
hired real amateurs to play the characters because he believed that traditional actors would not be able to unlearn their training, to unlearn the disciplining of their bodies (fig. 32). In this acting, each body is differentiated.
In works made during the first twenty years of Japanese film, the individual
bodies of characters were structured by their roles (so that, for example, all
of the lord's retainers moved in the same way, and, for that matter, all of
the lords moved in the same way). Tanizaki's and Osanai's intervention was
to introduce what might be called more self-determination, in which actors
would be able to act for themselves, as opposed to being restricted by traditional theatrical movement (the *kata* of noh and kabuki) and by the benshi
(who was castigated by Tanizaki and Osanai for impeding the expression of
the individual actors). Moreover, both used intertitles to preempt the role of
the benshi. Perhaps the most important restriction that Osanai and Tanizaki
transgressed was the presence of the onnagata.

The two films represent the introduction of female actor playing female
roles. In *Souls on the Road*, the squire's daughter, played by Hanabusa Yuriko, is seen shooting the hat off an old man with a rifle, frolicking about
as she prepares to throw a big Christmas bash, and trying to wrestle down a
huge pine tree with her bare hands. While dancing, laughing, and being quite
eccentric, Hanabusa's acting is wrapped up in her body in a way that departs

32. Kurihara Kosaburo's *Amateur Club;* Tanizaki sits below the tripod.

considerably from the onnagata's introverted representation of female characters. *Souls on the Road* gave Hanabusa, who had had very little shingeki
training, her first film role after going to Shochiku earlier in the year. She immediately caught Osanai's eye: He saw in Hanabusa a Japanese Lilian Gish.[22]
By showing the untrained Hanabusa pictures of both Lilian and Dorothy
Gish, Osanai attempted to form the young actress into his image of a Western
woman.[23] Soon, Hanabusa became one of the most famous actresses representing the Western style.

   The links to political agency within the Taisho democracy movements,
such as the 1918 rice rebellions, are important. Here there are many disfran-
chised people, differentiated by gender, occupation, and education, struggling to change unpopular policy, overthrow government officials, and represent themselves in the political process. When rice prices doubled from
January 1917 to the summer of 1918, riots hit all the major Japanese cities,
with more than 700,000 people participating.[24] There was a considerable universal suffrage movement between 1919 and 1920 (though it did not bring
about the vote until 1927); female textile workers began to organize unions
in the 1920s; and after burakumin suffered harsh penalties for participating
in the rice riots in the late 1910s, they formed their own activist groups to demand compensation. Tenants struggling against rural landlords were some

of the most militant groups. What was distinct about the tenant uprisings, and what was part of all the uprisings, is that they were directed against individuals as opposed to the government as a whole. To know oneself as an individual, as a political actor who differs not only from an adversary but also from those fighting at one's side, emerges most powerfully when defining oneself against someone whom one is not—truth by way of the Other. In this case, the Other serves to flesh out the modern subject when it is embodied in an individual landlord, government official, or factory boss.

Of course, the history of the modern Japanese subject dates back earlier than the 1920s. H. D. Harootunian locates an important transformation in the mid-nineteenth century, when various discourses—Mito/loyalism, nativism, new religions, and the discussion of wealth and power—turned on issues of difference and marginality, thus producing new subjectivities.[25] These new forms of human consciousness searched for ways to "harness the body for productive work, master a history that they themselves now made through their own activity. This disciplining of the body resulted in reuniting mental and manual, head and hand, even thought and action, to eliminate the baneful effects of the division of labor that had shaped Tokugawa rule since its inauguration."[26] Tetsuo Najita goes back to the eighteenth century, where he locates the emergence of the modern subject in the birth of economic epistemologies in merchant practices.[27] It was not until the rice riots, however, that this new conceptualization of human agency expressed itself most profoundly.

By the 1920s, the benshi, when representing the film actors, had been linked to professional politicians or intellectuals who heavy-handedly represented political agents and thereby impeded their ability to act individually.[28] This is to say, the benshi was to the government politician as the new political agent (the peasant, female factory worker, burakumin, consumer) was to the new film actor. The onnagata, moreover, was linked to the very suppression of the female actor from even entering the political arena. For rural women (who were powerless over whom they were to marry and over claims to family property) or for the female textile workers (reproached by many when striking for better working conditions), the chance to act on one's own and for oneself was crucial. The same went for film actresses.

The fact that the discourses of the film world related so significantly to those within the social should come as no surprise. Both liberals and

Marxists of the 1910s and '20s were, in one form or another, theorizing new forms of the individual in relation to the emerging structure of modern Japanese society. For example, liberal democrats such as Yoshino Sakuzo argued for a people-centered democracy (*minponshugi*) in which citizens would be active political actors as opposed to passive subjects.[29] Or the somewhat unorthodox Marxisms of thinkers such as Kawakami Hajime and Miki Kiyoshi tried to theorize a space for the human actor within the structural logic of the capitalist mode of production. As the Taisho democracy movements waned and new repressions rose, the film community became a sort of safe house for those who wanted to study and practice radical politics. Iwasaki Akira explains that, when choosing groups in which to participate, many intellectuals joined film clubs because they were some of the only spaces where members could read Marx's *Capital* without suffering the usual consequences, ranging from censorship to imprisonment. Because film clubs were viewed as insignificant and puerile, government officials did not think to scout them as a place where radical politics might be housed.

But this utopian space was soon discovered. The group that suffered most at the time was Prokino (the Proletarian Filmmakers League), an organization in which the cinematic and political merged most profoundly. In 1929, the newly established Prokino screened a number of short films at the *Tsukiji ko gekijo* (Little tsukiji theater). The films were documentaries of May Day demonstrations and labor strikes that Prokino made with 9.5 millimeter cameras. When the projector inevitably broke halfway through a screening, members in the audience would spontaneously take to the streets and march through Tokyo.[30] Indeed, Prokino marked the possibility for both a socialist film culture and a socialist nation. But by 1933, most of Prokino's members were behind bars, and government officials had successfully closed down the last traces of Prokino's operations. Prokino is one of the most direct examples of the relation between actors in a film and the social actors who view these films. The Prokino filmmakers, even more than Osanai and Tanizaki, realized that new historical agents would emerge only when the structure in which they acted had been wholly transformed and transcended. But they also realized that the structure (Japanese society, the Japanese film industry) would be transformed and transcended only by new historical agents. Thus, film practice had to merge directly with political practice (not in a separate register of cultural politics, as it did with Osanai and Tanizaki). It was this radicalism in the face of an ensuing fascism that hastened Prokino's ultimate demise.[31]

Osanai and Tanizaki never suffered the suppression that those involved in Prokino experienced. This was true not only because they refused to embrace radical politics, but also because their respective radicalisms were contained most significantly in formal invention. But for all Osanai's and Tanizaki's utopian gestures, there was also what might be called a dystopian dimension. In the debate over the amateur within shingeki, the term *shiroto* (in Chinese characters) means "simple, naked, beginning" and "person." But in the title of Tanizaki's film, the word *amachua* (in *katakana*, the syllabary reserved for foreign loan words) is used. In contrast to shiroto, which points to degree of skill or training, the new word amachua brings with it the modern concepts of contract and wage labor. We know that the real actors in Tanizaki's film were wage workers, whereas the characters in the film (those happy-go-lucky youths playing by the seaside) certainly did not earn wages. In this sense, the characters in the film are both shiroto and amachua—acting outside the acting economy—while the actors who portray these characters, although shiroto (untrained), are contracted and thus not amachua but professionals. Although Tanizaki and Osanai invoke the amateur to criticize the older system of acting (and Japanese feudalism itself), its invocation also functions to conceal the systemic inequalities spawned by the newly emerging relations of production within the profit-driven film industry.

Once again, the link to the various Taisho democracy movements is important. Although many were calling for freedom of expression, citizens' rights, and the removal of elected politicians and appointed officials, very few questioned the system itself—or, say, the right of the zaibatsu families to own property or the emperor to rule through his cabinet. Indeed, the peasants linked their chariot to the star of the emperor and the possibility of national socialism, not to mention imperialist expansion. In other words, the amateur actor (on the cinematic and social terrains) represented both the liberation from older forms of acting and older systemic constraints and the crucial element in re-enforcing a whole new system of control.

First Interlude: The Structure–Agent Problematic To work through the relation between film actors and political actors, it will be useful to turn, if only briefly, to what I think is the most symptomatic theoretical issue of the modern moment: the structure–agent problematic, or how individuals are shaped by social structures while, at the same time, they shape these structures. Engaging this problematic always means walking the tightrope between outright structural control and outright agent autonomy. In Japanese modern history, the structure–agent problematic takes its most familiar form in the *shutaisei* (subjectivity) debate that has stretched from the prewar period (over issues such as liberalism, revolution, and proletarian literature) to the postwar period (over debates surrounding modernity and parliamentary democracy) to the present (over concerns such as the decline of the nation-state, emergence of global capitalist structures, and the breakdown of the subject).[32] Here I want to think about the structure–agent problematic (which will be raised in more detail in chapter 6) in terms of film structures and film actors and to see how these terms relate to those in the shutaisei debate. Mindful of recent debates over the problems of structure, totality, intentional actors, unified subjects, and other issues that have come to define the philosophical terrain of the current moment, I will argue that the transformations in the structure–agent problematic (socially and cinematically) relate to transformations within the Japanese and global capitalist system. This will then prepare the way to think about political resistance—and the meanings and effects of cultural practices as they aid and obstruct political resistance—within contemporary Japan.

But even to name the issue at hand the "structure–agent problematic" tells us something about its nature. A "problematic" suggests that there is no a priori solution to it that stands outside of history. There is no static answer, because (1) the relation between the terms themselves are in constant flux (at times, structural constraints are high and agency low, and vice-versa); and (2) the very forms of the individual categories—"structures" and "agents"—are themselves historical and thus in constant flux and (re)formation. The attempt, therefore, to square the circle of the mechanical reproduction of societies (which is usually thrown on the doorstep of "orthodox" Marxism—the Japanese Communist Party, for example) and the ability of individual actors to control their destinies to their own liking (which can be found in any number of bourgeois notions of individualism) must be in a state of constant retheorization in relation to the historical situation at hand.

The historical situation at hand for more than one hundred years in Japan has been that of capitalism. Capitalism requires the type of individuated "modern actors" who can promote consumerism while fulfilling their particular roles within the complex division of labor. But this is not to suggest that all agents share desires or styles of acting; rather, it is to say that they share an objective situation in which a range of varied responses is possible but always lies within the situation's structural limits.[33] Or to put this in its most classic (and unfortunately gendered) form: "Men make their own history, but they do not make it just as they please; they do not make it under circumstances chosen by themselves, but under circumstances directly encountered, given and transmitted from the past."[34] At moments of significant capitalist restructuring in which there are changes in the possible forms of accumulation, the possible forms of agency are also restructured. What we see with the formation of capitalism in Japan following the Meiji Restoration, for example, is the concomitant opening of new possibilities and limitations for political and social actors. The structural transformations that occurred with the move to heavy industries generated by the colonial project, and that continued through and after the war, were tied to new limitations and possibilities in political and cinematic acting. This is most interestingly expressed in a new conceptualization of the amateur actor—an amateur that refers less to the individual than to the collective.

The Collective as Amateur
This takes us to the 1950s and the work of Hani Susumu and the resistance movements of the time. Hani, who graduated from the famous *jiyu gakuen* (free school) that his grandmother, Hani Motoko, founded, not only influenced the New Wave and its departure from the Japanese film corporations. He was also at the heart of a new documentary movement that would see its flowerings in the work of Ogawa Shinsuke, Tsuchimoto Noriake, and Haneda Sumiko—all of whom, like Hani, started out in Iwanami film productions[35]—all the way to the current work of Hara Kazuo and Sento Naomi. It was Hani's fifth film, *Kyoshitsu no kodomotachi* (Children of the classroom, 1954), that shocked many who saw it. In that documentary, Hani goes to Sumida public elementary school in Tokyo, forms a close relationship with the students and teachers, and shoots everyday scenes of the school's activities.[36] Critics did not understand how Hani could represent the kids acting so naturally, and many wrote that he must have used a hidden camera.[37] The film took both the education and film communities by storm. It is not the usual scientific documentary, culture film,

or public-relations film, which would be burdened with a heavy overnarration (the voice of god) as it methodically plotted out the day in the life of an elementary-school student. But it is also not a feature film, in which the drama of the situation is prepared and staged. Rather, Hani carved out a third type of film—one that would forever change the shape of Japanese documentary and feature-film production.

For Hani, the key was in drawing attention to the camera and to himself as director while including himself as a member of the group to be filmed. Hani and his crew stayed at Sumida for more than a month and were able to talk to the students about the very act of making a film. In the documentary, kids run and jump around, make faces, and pick their noses. One second-grader, who was aware neither of the camera nor of his own imitative actions, is shown inhaling from a pencil as if it were a cigarette (fig. 33). The kids are shown in art and music classes, serving one another food at lunchtime, or running wildly on the playground. At times, Hani focuses on a child who is left out of the activities and speculates about her rejected situation. But in the end there is little analysis in the twenty-eight minute film, which was sponsored by the Ministry of Education and received rave reviews from the left-wing Teachers Union. Most important, *Children of the Classroom* marked a new mode of representation—a mode that (1) opened the possibility for subjects to act on their own (in which the director did not heavy-handedly determine the behavior of the actor); and (2) opened the possibility to express the political power of collectives that hitherto were powerless, such as students and adolescents.

As for acting, one need only to look at another film that portrays an elementary-school scene to see Hari's profound departure. In 1939, Kamei Fumio made the culture film *Shanghai*. Commissioned by the Japanese Ministry of Foreign Affairs, Kamei was sent to China to make a pro-war film that condemned Western colonialism while legitimating Japan's colonial project. As explained in chapter 2, the film was a great disappointment to Japanese government officials and managed to land Kamei in quite a fix.[38] Kamei, a Marxist who was experimenting with dialectical film practice picked up during his studies in the Soviet Union, was in fact one of the great architects of documentary film in Japan, a figure to whom Hani and everyone at Iwanami film productions in the early 1950s looked for inspiration. Still, the historical moments of *Shanghai* and *Children of the Classroom* were quite different,

33. Hani Susumu's *Kyoshitsu no kodomatachi* (Children of the classroom). Iwanami Film, 1954.

34. Kamei Fumio's *Shanghai*; schoolchildren bowing in front of military guard.

and a comparison of the two films points to some of the transformations in film and political acting that I want to explore.

Like Hani's film, Kamei's segment about elementary-school children in *Shanghai* begins with the students walking to school on the early morning Chinese streets. But unlike the romp and play of the kids in Hani's film, the neatly dressed students in Kamei's film walk in uniform groups and bow deeply when passing Japanese military personnel (fig. 34). Inside their old and decrepit classroom, the kids in *Shanghai* are orderly, mature, and serious. They read poems about the war effort and express how diligently they must study for country and emperor. They listen attentively to the day's lesson from the stern but respectful teacher, then, at the end of the day, they crowd around the teacher to listen and answer questions about the dangers of living in Shanghai. Throughout the short segment, many of the students stare directly into the camera, rapt and curious about the process of filming. It is scenes such as this that turn out to be most significant in Kamei's film.

For Hani, the goal is *not* to have the students pretend that the camera is not there; for them *not* to be consumed with its presence. Rather, he wants the students to be comfortable enough with the filmmaking process that they act no more or less "real" than they would if the camera was not there. But Kamei does not have the luxury to spend a month with the students in Shanghai. To draw attention to this constraint, Kamei to his credit, does include shots in which the students are looking straight into the lens. Then there is the framing. Most of Kamei's shots are of the whole classroom in which all the students are included in the frame as they hunch over their

Structure, Agent, Amateur   **147**

textbooks. But in Hani's documentary, when the students are in the classroom, they are almost all shot in closeup. It is through the combination of closeups, Hani explains, "that I can catch not only the individual children but the collective unit called the classroom."[39] *Children of the Classroom* is about the emergence of a collective unit that is greater than its individual parts. But it is about the collective as *amateur*—collectives that were not previously thought of as such. We might say that what Eisenstein theorized in the 1920s for Soviet film, regarding organizing the parts to flash the whole, found its moment in 1950s Japan. Finally, Hani believed that a new category of the amateur could emerge only when the films themselves, documentary and dramatic (and Hani made both), were independently produced, outside the dominant cinematic mode of production. One of Hani's greatest legacies is to have trailblazed many of the innovations of independent Japanese film that exist to this day.[40]

But no other filmmaker was as important in breaking open a space for independent film production and for theorizing the collective as amateur, in his writing and in the very act of making film, than Ogawa Shinsuke. Ogawa, who made seven of his Sanrizuka films over a period of nine years (1968–77), recorded the farmers' rebellion at Narita over the construction of the new international airport. With his small crew, Ogawa became part of the movement itself, and the films, which were screened all over the country (usually in makeshift theaters), were instrumental in disseminating information about the struggle. But the films are noteworthy not simply because they document one of the most important struggles to occur in the past one hundred years in Japan. If this alone accounted for their significance, then nothing would distinguish them from so many reels of documentary news footage. Rather, the Sanrizuka films are crucial for what they do formally, for inventing a way of documenting the anti-airport struggle that was as radical as the struggle itself.

Born in 1936, Ogawa made more than seventeen films before his untimely death in 1992.[41] He is one of the very few directors in the history of cinema to have become simultaneously a filmmaker's filmmaker and a people's filmmaker.[42] From the work of the New Wave to any documentary made in the past fifty years to the most current feature films produced by emerging filmmakers such as Suwa Nobuhiro and Aoyama Shinji, Ogawa's influence is tremendous.[43] Taking on almost cult-like status, Ogawa ranks with Imamura

Shohei, Haneda Sumiko, and Kurosawa Akira as one of the most important postwar filmmakers. And having sparked the establishment of the Yamagata International Film Festival in 1989, Ogawa made a mark on world documentary that is as profound as that made by Robert Flaherty or John Grierson. Ogawa's first film, *Seinen no kai* (The sea of youth), made in 1966 about the Ministry of Education's policy to abandon university correspondence learning for part-time students, turns on four part-time students who are mobilizing a resistance movement at Hosei University. Struggling for the value of an "open university," these working-class students collide with both the conservative government and apathetic students. In this first film, Ogawa's signature style of long takes, sparse editing, and casual overnarration was already apparent.[44] In particular, the real-time filming of organizing meetings in *The Sea of Youth* can be seen throughout the Sanrizuka series.

The Sanrizuka movement had already begun by 1966. After groups protested plans for constructing the new airport in Tomisato, the government—without any discussion or participation from the villagers—shifted plans to the Sanrizuka–Shibayama site. A year later, various *Zengakuren* (National Federation of Student Self-Governing Associations) sects joined the movement, and these little villages came to represent a much larger struggle against the Japanese state, U.S. imperialism, and foreign involvement in the Vietnam War—at bottom, the violent and destructive path of unbridled modernization on which Japan and the world were firmly set. In the late 1960s and throughout the '70s, saying "Sanrizuka" immediately invoked the most pressing social issues of the day. When the officials failed in their quest to frame the conflict as one in which an insignificant number of stubborn farmers would not give up their land for the greater good, "Sanrizuka" (especially after the renewal of the 1970 U.S.–Japan Security Treaty) became a rallying cry for general protest and discontent. Those in the movement were almost always open to outside participation (except by the Japanese Communist Party, which ignited heated debates within the farmers' meetings), a tactic that became crucial in waging its violent resistance.[45]

But Ogawa did not simply film the movement; he was part of it. He lived in a communal house for seven years in Sanrizuka, and those in the struggle quickly came to entrust him. And most agree that the Sanrizuka films, distributed throughout the country by an energetic band of supporters, changed the very nature of the movement.[46] Whether filming the farmers building underground tunnels (*Nihon kaiho sensen: Sanrizuka no natsu,* 1970); constructing a sixty-meter tower to interfere with the runway (*Sanrizuka: Iwayama ni tetto ga dekita,* 1972); chaining themselves to trees (*Sanrizuka: Daini toride no hitobito,* 1971); violently clashing with riot police (*Sanrizuka: Satsuki no sora sato no kayoiji,* 1977); or explaining village rituals and history (*Sanrizuka—Heta buraku,* 1973), Ogawa and cameraman Tamura Masaki never forgot the importance of the aesthetic.[47] At the center of these aesthetic concerns is the problematic of representation. How can Ogawa represent the activities of the farmers without exercising the type of dominance and control over them that they are so committed to overthrowing? Ogawa had to ask himself, in other words, how to represent people who were so desperately struggling to represent themselves. What for *hantai domei* (the anti-airport movement) was an all-out struggle on the level of politics became for Ogawa and his crew an equally intense struggle on the level of cinematic form. And this, of course, was itself shot through with politics.

Despite a delay from its master plan, the airport was built and seems to be in a perpetual state of expansion.[48] Yet the utopia of both the movement and the films never were contained simply in their possible fulfillment; they were contained in the processes and methods by which they strove for such fulfillment. And this touches on one of the most consequential and complex elements of utopian politics: that one must act as if the outcome for which one is struggling is the ultimate goal, even though the ultimate goal will always be the experience one gains along the way. This reality—that, in other words, the ultimate goal is not in fact the ultimate goal—must always be repressed, for if it is not, then the needed commitment to continue the struggle will be hard to muster. This acting *as if* is not unlike the logic being worked out in Pascal's wager, the famous "bet on God" in which Pascal's imaginary partner in dialogue persuades him to act as if he already believes in God, because only then will the belief come true. This type of "belief before belief" is what the farmers are doing throughout their struggle.[49] This is all to say that the real utopia of the anti-airport movement was the inclusivity by which the farmers conducted their actions. It was a way to transcend (however temporarily) the more conservative dimension of the farmers' modern existence in Japan—an existence that was marked by parochialism, emperor worship, and exclusivity. Moreover, unlike the peasants of the 1920s and '30s, the peasants of Narita were generally opposed to the emperor and emperor system. It was this crucial difference that led the postwar peasants to self-representation.[50]

Again, the utopia of the farmers' movement was wrapped up in its form, not only in its content. The movement's significance was not solely about what actually happened (whether the airport was built) but about how it happened (the way the farmers mobilized and acted in resistance to the state). For Ogawa, it was not only what was being filmed, but how it was being filmed. All of Ogawa's films were produced outside the dominant mode of production: They were distributed outside the large film companies and financed by private donations, not-for-profit agencies, and screening sales. Even more important, like Hani but to an even greater degree, Ogawa spent long periods living with his subjects. Of course, the Sanrizuka films are a prime example. But this was also true of two films made in the mid-1970s, one about a community of day laborers in Yokohama (*Dokkoi! Ningenbushi* [Song of the bottom, 1975]) and the other about trash collectors in Yamagata Prefecture (*Kurin senta homonki* [Interview at a trash dump, 1975]). In Yokohama, Ogawa moved into the dormitory in which the laborers lived, going to their work sites, the pubs where they drank and socialized, and even to their funerals. Most notably, in 1973 Ogawa and his crew moved to Magino village in Yamagata Prefecture, where they spent the next decade and a half learning how to cultivate rice fields all at the same time making two remarkable films: *Nippon koku: Furuyashiki-mura* (A Japanese village: Furuyashiki mura, 1982) (fig. 35) and *Sen nen kizami no hidokei: Magino mura monogatari* (The sundial carved by a thousand years of notches: The Magino Village story, 1987). The first formal relation between the anti-airport movement and Ogawa's film movement, therefore is the ability to organize collectively, to build a collective outside dominant forms (political parties or unions for the farmers and film companies for Ogawa). This is a new type of collective, established spontaneously and unconventionally. In short, it is an amateur collective.

This discussion of utopian political action and utopian cultural practice requires further theorization. To argue that utopian politics and culture are wrapped up inside their form is not to suggest that a certain form will always be utopian. In other words, the utopian is always historical, and thus it is always mutating into something else in relation to its historical context. Osanai and Tanizaki attempted to produce the individual amateur actor who

35. Promotional flyer for Ogawa Shinsuke's
Nippon koku: Furuyashiki-mura (A Japanese
village: Furuyashiki-mura), 1982.

would come into being when placed in opposition to a professional actor, just
as the amateurs of the rice riots came into being when placed in opposition
to elected political representatives, factory bosses, and individual landlords.
The "amateur" in Hani's and Ogawa's films refers to the group or collective.
What emerges is a social actor, a sort of social amateur, in which the collective organizes to bring about social change. Unlike the amateur of the
1920s, when actors fought for their individual rights by criticizing the public
sphere, the amateur of the 1960s relates to a new possibility of the collective.
For Hani and Ogawa, however, the collective amateur actor came into being
in opposition to governmental officialdom—that is, government officials as a
collective who stood in for something that exceeded their individual selves.

But, of course, the invocation of the collective as the new agent also had
its problems. For all of Ogawa's desire for inclusivity, his collective veered
dangerously close to nativist discourses, and even *nihonjinron* (Japanese essentialist discourse). By celebrating ritual (without interrogating the oppres-
sions built into it) and by promoting historical return as a way to criticize
the present juggernaut of instrumental modernization, Ogawa's group found
itself on the conservative end of the postwar leftist movements. For example,
in many works by New Wave filmmakers, such as Oshima's *Seishun zan-
koku monogatari* (The cruel story of youth, 1960) and Imamura's *Nippon
konchugi* (The insect woman, 1963), the background of fictional scenes contain documentary footage of Zengakuren marches. Here, the professional
actor, the protagonist of the dramatic film, is juxtaposed with the amateur

152   The Flash of Capital

as group. These films were criticizing the treatment of the individual that the new group formations tended to marginalize. It was precisely this failure to deal properly with difference within the identity of the group (in terms of women—as Barbara Hammer's documentary about Ogawa [*Devotion*, 2000] so powerfully exposes—as well as ethnicity, and class), that the refigured trope of the social amateur concealed. Finally, if the backlash to the new individualism of the 1920s was the fascism of the collective during the 1930s and '40s, then the backlash to the new collectivism of the 1960s was an apolitical consumerism of the 1970s and '80s that acquiesced to the so-called economic miracle.

Second Interlude: The Structure–Agent Problematic Revisited

On the republication and new translation in Japan of Marx's *The 18th Brumaire of Louis Bonaparte*, Karatani Kojin made a provocative argument about the essence of fascism.[51] Karatani detected a formal repetition of fascism (something that the 1990s shares with the 1930s) that is linked to a breakdown in representation (politically and economically). For Karatani, fascisms do not betray similar content (the events will indeed be different), they betray similar forms: "Structural isomorphism" in the form of what Karatani calls "Bonapartism."[52]

In capitalist society, "Bonapartism" refers to a regime in which the rule of a single individual emerges to represent all groups and classes. But, of course, this type of representation is functionally impossible within the capitalist system, a system in which the different classes necessarily require representatives who will work for their particular interests, which, in turn, are necessarily at odds with the interests of other classes. But even this type of parliamentary representation cannot ideally work, for if the working class is properly represented, then the system itself (one that must offer a structural privilege to those who own the means of production) would be undone and thus unable to reproduce itself. When an undoing of this sort threatens the system, yet the ruling class can no longer maintain its rule by parliamentary and constitutional means and the working class is not able to affirm its own hegemony, a crisis erupts, and parliamentary representation gives itself away as fraudulent. It is precisely at crisis moments such as this that Bonapartism surfaces as an imaginary solution to this breakdown of representation.

In Europe (1848) and Japan (1927), the onset of universal suffrage drove the collapse. Under universal suffrage, the relation between the representative and represented is arbitrary. Representation is estranged; it does not contain an essential connection. The represented and representative "may be as far apart as heaven from earth."[53] This can also be said for the capitalist economy. The relation between money and the commodity is arbitrary, meaning that there is no essential relation between five hundred yen and a bowl of *soba*. But that fact must be in a constant state of repression. When crisis hits, however, the repressed returns, and the relation between money and commodity is revealed as arbitrary; money is then hoarded in order to manage the new unstable system of value. It is precisely in moments of crisis that this arbitrariness of the representational system is revealed and the situation is primed for Bonapartism. Karatani presents the example of Japanese peasants of the 1930s who revered the emperor as their master: "This perverted representation occurs *not by a mythos* descended from ancient times, as advocated by some cultural anthropologists, but by *a lack immanent in the modern* system of representation."[54] He concludes, "We should not forget that the advent of the system of representation elected by universal suffrage preceded the occasion of Emperor fascism, and not vice-versa."[55] In other words the emperor emerged as a very modern imaginary solution to an equally modern crisis in the representational system.

As for the capitalist system, the crisis of representation appears as financial panic. The French bourgeoisie, for example, embraced Bonaparte after the panic of 1851. A crisis in the economy had been brought about by the falling rate of profit, which then had to be managed by colonial policies. It was at this crisis point (in the middle of the nineteenth century) that Louis Bonaparte emerged to square the circle (to be a protectionist and free-trader, a nationalist and internationalist); it was also at such a crisis point that Hitler and Hirohito emerged in the 1930s. After setting up this structural repetition, Karatani then delivers the terrifying force of his argument: that the current crises in both the nation-state (the parliamentary system of representation) and the capitalist system (which can no longer be managed by national economies) augurs Bonapartism in the years to come.

What I want to add to this argument is that along with the dystopian moments of Bonapartism come utopian ones—indeed, it is impossible to have one without the other. This utopian dimension is not simply imaginary—

that is, it is not always reactionary, always recuperating the existing system and thus always standing in the way of significant social change. Moreover, this genuinely utopian dimension is itself formally repeated throughout modern history. It is the other side of what Karatani is arguing: It is a utopianism that emerges not merely as a way to manage the current crisis but also as a genuinely revolutionary possibility to transform the system itself. What must be stressed, however, is that this is no mere coexistence of the fascist and utopian dimensions of social life, so that the optimist chooses the utopian one and the pessimist the fascist one. Rather, the two dimensions work simultaneously, in dynamic relation, so that each supplements the force and possibility of the other. In short, every moment of fascism necessarily presupposes a simultaneous moment of utopian transcendence.

In what have been identified as the first two moments of the amateur in Japanese film, the category has been examined in terms of political agency and in terms of moments of structural change within capitalism. The first invocation of the amateur, as individual, relates to the formation of the capitalist system, and the second invocation, as collective, relates to the system's monopoly restructurings, including colonial expansion, corporate consolidation, and a heightened discourse of nationalism. It is the amateur that contains the fascist and utopian dimensions at the same time. Now the task is to examine the role of the film and political actor in relation to the most recent capitalist transformations, ones that have brought a critical decline in decision-making power by the nation-state and a concomitant rise in power by the transnational corporation. In other words, in what ways (if any) is the category of the amateur being invoked today, and what are its possibilities and limitations in generating significant social change?

The Global Amateur   We are now clear on what Bonapartism will look like during a crisis of representation. What, then, might its content look like in the age of globalization? That is difficult to say, but it does seem that the Bonaparte figure will not be tied to a nation-state, as past such figures have. As the decision-making power of national politicians (representatives) declines in the face of the rising power of transnational executives, the possibility will emerge for a transnational Bonaparte. This is a figure who will be able to appeal to the working class of various nations as well as to the transnational managerial class. Because of a heightened state of celebratory global discourse and refunctionalized national ideologies, a transnational Bonaparte will not present the same threat as did an older national politician crossing borders to "save" a suffering people (the imperial paradigm). Rather, the new Bonaparte may very well appear to short-circuit the usual pork-barrel politics of a national situation. Perhaps the recent crisis in Japan, in which everyone laments a lack of leadership—or, at least, of leaders who are bought and sold to such a degree that it seems systemically impossible to advance policies of any significance—is a sign of things to come.

All of this might be easier to recognize when one looks at the global economy. What are The North American Free Trade Agreement (NAFTA), the Asian-Pacific Economic Forum (APEC), the World Bank, the WTO, and G-8 if not responses to the new demands of capitalism, demands that cannot be managed by national politicians who must tolerate, however begrudgingly, the needs of local constituencies, not to mention the welfare state. This "de facto world government" is simply more effective at managing the world economy.[56] When the IMF grants loans to Mexico, Indonesia, or Russia, the funds' economists come off as heroes. How far away is Japan or even the United States from the moment in which local citizens will entrust—indeed, eagerly hope for and solicit—a representative from a transnational corporation to come and work for their particular interests? This political and economic breakdown in representation is what defines the current historical moment. But if a Bonaparte figure might emerge to manage the crisis of representation and crank the nation-state–based world system up to one of full global integration, then what are the possibilities and limitations for a world historical actor who might transform the system completely? Can there be an actor (or actors) who will not merely recuperate the crisis but exploit its revolutionary potential to ignite full-scale structural change? In short, where does this leave the amateur?

In Japan, many have deemed certain single-issue politics, or what have been called the "new social movements," an invocation of the amateur. I am thinking about the environmental, homeless, comfort women, and antinuclear movements, the AIDS movement over the tainted-blood scandal, the call for compensation by Korean laborers whom Mitsubishi forcibly brought to Hiroshima during World War II, as well as various citizens' movements, such as the one in Zushi over the construction of U.S. military housing. I would not be the first to mention that even the Aum affair (the cult that

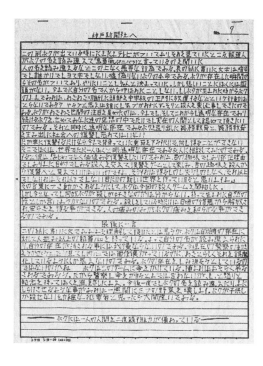

36. Letter written to the *Kobe Shinbun* newspaper by fourteen-year-old murderer.

spread poison in a Tokyo subway) has a relation to political agency. It is difficult to forget the Tokyo University graduate students who, when asked why they joined Aum, noted that with the de-Marxification of the universities and the decline of serious anticapitalist and anticonsumerist movements, Aum seemed the most reasonable substitute.[57]

And, of course, there is the killer of Hase Jun in Kobe, mentioned at the beginning of this chapter. In the letter sent to a Kobe newspaper a week after the murder, the killer explained that his actions were a response to the compulsory education system that had made him invisible, a non-subject with no nationality (*kanashii koto ni boku ni wa kokuseki ga nai*) (fig. 36). The killer's note, with its twenty-three uses of the word *boku* (a colloquial and male word for "I") and its mentioning that the killer killed to make his invisible self visible in the imagination of the nation, seems to be, in however abhorrent and distorted a way, an expression of desired political agency. I certainly do not want to equate the contemptible crimes of Aum and the Kobe killer with the important work being done by the new social movements. But at the same time, I do want to argue that all are symptoms of

Structure, Agent, Amateur 157

this new situation of global capitalism. It does not seem likely that the new amateurs will be individual psychotic killers who use the mass media to terrorize a country. At the same time, the new amateur—the new social actor who might be capable of bringing about significant historical change—most probably will not find its home in single-issue political groups, either.

Although such groups have taken some important steps toward political change, post-bubble cynicism and malaise seem to be at an all-time high. In the face of huge scandals, such as the ones beginning in 1997 involving cooperation by the Dai-Ichi Kangyo Bank and Nomura Security with *sokai-ya* (extortionist) racketeers, political pronouncements of reform seem to generate more scorn than support. For example, when former Prime Minister Hashimoto Ryutaro took responsibility for the financial meltdown in the summer of 1998 ("The crisis is due to my incompetence," Hashimoto is remembered for contritely remarking), most people recognized that a single individual could never possess the needed power to undo the entire financial system. It was a grand utopian gesture to pretend that a single individual (even the prime minister of the country with the world's second-largest economy) could change the course of the global economy. Most recognized that the gesture, though dramatic, had little to do with reality.

This paralysis can also be seen in contemporary Japanese film. To be sure, there are high points, such as the 1997 victories at Cannes by Imamura Shohei and Sento Naomi, and the 1999 Toronto Film Festival's granting of the spotlight director honor to Kurosawa Kiyoshi, as well as interesting developments in independent and experimental film production, most notably by Oki Hiroyuki. Yet most who live in Japan have little interest in domestic films, and the number of tickets sold and of theaters is at a disappointingly low level. (Theaters that specialize in independent film and canonical Japanese film are dying at a devastatingly high rate.) The point is that the skeptical response to contemporary political action and Japanese film that many of us are so used to talking ourselves into has less to do with the quality of individual politicians, activist movements, or films themselves than with the difficulties of making sense of, representing, and attempting to shape the rise of transnational corporatism. In other words, the rule of the nation-state— the force that Osanai, Tanizaki, and the Taisho democracy movements faced in the 1920s and Hani and Ogawa and the mass movements faced in the postwar period—is now weakened, and any attempt to place it back in the center of resistance will be ineffectual. It is for this reason that any hope for a new golden age in Japanese national cinema or mass political activism focusing solely on the Japanese state is anachronistic. I am not suggesting that there is any substitute for resistance as a coordinated mass-organizing process, or that film has lost the capacity to lodge effective attacks on societal contradictions. I am suggesting, instead, that the object of resistance has mutated in that it now includes the transnational corporation just as much as it does the nation-state. It is with this reality that any resistance or cultural worker must come to terms.

The present contradiction between the possibilities of an older national political actor or national film actor and the realities of transnational capitalism appears to have halted the reemergence of the amateur. But it is also out of this contradiction between the *national* and the *transnational* that I think the amateur will spring. How are national ideologies and identities refigured within the emerging space of transnationalism? At the present moment, there are no answers to this question, and this, I think, explains why a refigured category of the amateur—in film or politics—has yet to emerge. But as usual, cultural products, and the aesthetic in general, are good places to search for hints (tremblings, flashes) of what this amateur might look like. I will conclude this chapter by offering two examples.

One is a film by the young director Iwai Shunji titled, *Swallowtail Butterfly* (1996); the other is the later work of Ogawa Shinsuke, in particular his *Sundial Carved by a Thousand Years of Notches*. It is hard to think of two more radically different films. Iwai's film is a diasporic car crash of different languages and cultures turning on a community of foreigners (laborers, prostitutes, criminals) who are attempting to scrape together as many overvalued yen as possible. Ogawa's film, by contrast, is a three-and-a-half-hour paean to a small farming village in Yamagata Prefecture. These short descriptions suggest that *Swallowtail* speaks more significantly to the problems of global capitalism, while *The Sundial Carved by a Thousand Years of Notches* is a nationalistic fetishization of village life that must betray equally parochial impulses. But there is a reversal when we move from the level of content to that of form, for it is precisely on the formal level that the values of the two films invert. It turns out that Iwai's film is the more parochial and gratuitous, and Ogawa's is the more suggestive—the one that flashes what we might take as a new form of acting in the decades to come.

37. Iwai Shunji's *Swallowtail Butterfly*.
Pony Canyon, 1996.

Swallowtail Butterfly opens with grainy black-and-white footage of industrial Tokyo. With different-size English text keyed on top of the newsreel-style images (also titled in Japanese), a young woman's voice reads the following in highly accented English:

> Once upon a time, when the yen was the most powerful force in the world, the city overflowed with immigrants like a gold-rush boomtown. They came in search of yen, snatching up yen, and the immigrants called the city Yen Town. But the Japanese hated that name, so they referred to those Yen thieves as Yentowns. It's a bit puzzling, but Yen Town meant both the city and the outcasts. If you worked hard, earned a pocket full of yen, and then returned home, you could become a rich man. It sounds like a fairytale, but it was a paradise of yen, Yen Town. And this is the story of Yentowns in Yen Town. [fig. 37]

This is Ageha's voice. Ageha's mother, originally from Shanghai, worked as a prostitute in Tokyo for several years but had recently died. Alone and barely able to speak Chinese anymore, Ageha is taken in by Gliko (played by the pop-music sensation Chara), another prostitute, who is originally from Shanghai. Chinese, Taiwanese, African Americans, Filipinos, Moroccans, and others are all working hard, scheming, and looking to get rich, if not merely to survive. When it begins to rain, old umbrellas are quickly collected and brought to Tokyo to sell. Or someone shoots out a car tire from a distance and is then kind enough to change it (for a reasonable fee) for the thankful and mildly suspicious driver. At one point, a gangster roughs up Gliko, a fight breaks out, and the gangster is punched straight out of a second-story window. When the body is buried, a cassette tape of Frank Sinatra singing "My Way" is discovered, but the tape also contains a magnetic code that produces perfect counterfeit yen notes. After striking it rich, the group heads to Tokyo, where the members open a club in which Gliko is featured as the lead singer of a band called Yen Town (made up, of course, of Caucasians who grew up in Japan and speak only Japanese). The band is wildly successful, but it only causes grief for Gliko, who is forced to pretend that she is Japanese (and not a prostitute) so the band can be marketed. The Chinese mafia wants the cassette tape; an investigative reporter wants to expose Gliko's past; and the evil music-company executives want to split up the group by sending Gliko's boyfriend to jail on trumped-up immigration charges. Stylized violence, drug use, and chaos ensue. After returning to Yen Town, Ageha, disgusted at what the yen has produced, tosses the remaining suitcases of cash into a fire and gives the cassette tape away. The text read at the beginning of the film is repeated (this time over black-and-white images of a more contemporary, skyscraper-laden Tokyo), and the community is restored.

Iwai is one of the rising stars of the Japanese film world. He started out making music videos and short films and won awards in Europe before he directed his first feature film, *Love Letter*, in 1995.[58] In *Swallowtail*, Iwai brings out every trick of the trade: jump-cut editing, freeze-frames, hand-held camera, sepia lighting. When a swallowtail butterfly (like Gliko's) is being tattooed on Ageha's chest, the spinning camera and hand-painted frames become nothing less than oppressive. These gratuitous aesthetic gestures, together with a cloying soundtrack, make it difficult to think through (at any time during the two-and-a-half hour film) the issues of foreign labor and the effects of Japan's bubble economy. The language stew is certainly fascinating, as native Chinese speakers speak English, Japanese natives speak Chinese, and native English speakers speak Japanese. But somehow, like the expedient and expendable formal devices, the linguistic vicissitudes do not disorient; they just distract. Still, the film was wildly successful not only with Japanese youth, but with youth throughout Asia. It was this success that has earned Iwai the moniker "*Asian*" star.

Essentially, Iwai ends up aestheticizing away *Swallowtail*'s content so that the formal techniques consume the film. In some respect, this formalism was part of an older avant-gardist project (in both Japan and the West). But in the postmodern (or late-capitalist) moment, these strategies are refunctionalized because of what I will call a *dialectical inversion of the mod-*

ernist paradigm. Part of the New Wave project was to draw attention to the processes by which film is made, to draw attention to aesthetic strategies to foreground the fact that film is something that is shaped by its material conditions, something that is meticulously organized around aesthetic choices. By disrupting spectatorship with jump-cuts and still shots, with whimsical camera angles and disjunctive soundtracks (or whatever would disrupt the dominant cinematic grammar of the time), Oshima, Imamura, Suzuki, Shinoda, and others hoped to activate spectatorship. With this image pedagogy, the filmmakers ultimately wanted to elicit sensitivity to that dimension of everyday life that goes unseen—the totality. The totality is the abstract. The "social structure," "capitalism," and "Japan" are abstractions that can be grasped only in their separate parts. To accept that capitalism is a system that contains an inherent logic demands something on the order of a leap of faith—a leap that can abstract a totality out of its fragmented expressions (such as money, commodities, labor, technology). Radical theory, radical culture, and radical politics always depart from the desire to express something that cannot be seen—that which structures the dominant and the marginal and has been naturalized to such a degree that the very capacity to produce (or even think) an alternative is nearly annihilated. For the New Wave filmmakers, then, if a viewer could understand the making of the film—the parts of the film that are not plot, dialogue, or decor (the seen) but the narrative structure, composition, editing, acting style (the unseen)—then they might be able to transfer this way of seeing to society at large and ultimately break through the suffocating structure of modern Japanese society.

An ambitious project, indeed. And, of course, many in the New Wave did not live up to these grand ideals. But the point is that what, at an earlier moment (the 1960s), functioned to prod a spectator out of the autonomy of the film and into an expanded and politicized critical space has transformed. One very obvious example is the mobile or "shaky" camera: so unmistakably identified with the unprofessional spirit of the avant-garde in the late 1950s early '60s, the shaky camera has become thoroughly commodified in any number of music videos and television quiz and cop shows crowding the air waves today.[59] A new historical moment and different reception habits have transformed its meanings and effects. Instead of prodding Japanese spectators to see how their fetishization of foreigners (the darker, poorer, and more abused the better, but always physically attractive) reinforces the investment

38. Promotional flyer for Ogawa Shinsuke's
*Sen nen kizami no hidokei: Magino mura
monogatari* (The sundial carved by a thousand
years of notches: The story of Magino Village).

in the Japanese–non-Japanese binary, Iwai's *Swallowtail Butterfly* only lulls
its audience into admiring the freakish editing and curious camera work of
a cinematic *wunderkind*.

Ogawa's *Sundial Carved by a Thousand Years of Notches* comes in at
three hours and forty-two minutes. It is a huge film about small things: rice
farming, village history and mythology, storytelling, and the art of making
film (fig. 38). In the early 1970s, just as the student movement and the anti-
airport movement in Sanrizuka were declining, a group of farmers in Yamagata Prefecture contacted Ogawa and invited him to live in their village.
They admired his films but felt that he did not understand what drove the
farmers to such desperate acts of resistance. In 1973, Ogawa and his crew
moved into an old house and embarked on a long-term commitment to learn
about rice farming. *The Sundial Carved by a Thousand Years of Notches* is
the fourteen-year culmination of that project.

The film is organized around the seasonal struggle to grow rice. Of course,
because Ogawa and his crew had practically no experience cultivating rice,
they had to come at it scientifically—that is, from a direction that differed
from the villagers' experiential and folk knowledges. But Ogawa exploits his
strengths as he intricately incorporates the filming process into the learning process. For example, there are time-lapsed closeup shots of blooming
rice plants as well as storyboard-like charts on how to conquer the low yield
of paddies infected by contaminated groundwater. All of the protagonists
are set up: wind, snow, water, and land. Interrupting the scientific discourse

are five stories about myth and history. One story is of the thousand-year-old legend of how water came to the village, while another is a reenactment of the discovery of a *dosojin*, a traveler's guardian deity shaped like a huge penis. After thirty or forty more minutes on rice cultivation, the film tells the story of Yoki and his sister Non-naka (played by the famous *butoh* dancer Hijikata Tatsumi and "pink" (soft pornography) actress Miyashita Junko, respectively). Womanizing and gambling reduced Yoki to begging, and Ogawa depicts his life in a full dramatic episode. It is here that the film shifts from a documentary mode to a fictional one. But the transition is not quite so clean, for Ogawa's films are always about complicating the boundary between fiction and documentary.

It is now well known that the word for "documentary film" (*kiroku eiga*) was not extensively used in Japan until after World War II. Before that, "culture film" (bunka eiga) or "PR film" (*pr eiga*) were common. One defining quality of Japanese film is that almost all the significant directors have made both documentary and feature films. And in some way, this accounts for why Japanese documentaries must be recognized as some of the most extraordinary films in the history of filmmaking. Of course, when the first films were made of the Japanese theater in the 1890s, no one was concerned with whether they should be called documentaries (of the actors' performing) or dramatic films (of the play's narrative). But postwar Japanese film critics do seem to debate the matter, breathing life back into the dead horse of whether the Lumière brothers (documentary) or Méliès (fiction) had more influence over the origins of Japanese cinema. The experiment of blending amateur and professional actors is what is most interesting about Ogawa's film. In the penultimate episode, for example, a rebellion that broke out in the village more than 250 years ago is reenacted. Ogawa films an inquiry into the cause of the rebellion, with the samurai interrogators played by professional actors and the peasants played by the villagers themselves. This is no longer the Sanrizuka's peasants acting in front of Ogawa's camera during the anti-airport movement; now the farmers have become film actors in a film that stands somewhere amid community theater, television drama, historical documentary, experimental film, and bad home movie. The amateur actors are endearing in their stiff but impassioned style (fig. 39).

No doubt, there is a romanticization of the farmer in Ogawa's film, not to mention in his whole oeuvre. Moreover, sentiments that are unquestion-

164 The Flash of Capital

39. Ogawa Shinsuke's *The Sundial Carved by a Thousand Years of Notches;* the villagers (amateur actors) pose.

ably nationalistic come through. But if the peasants of the rice riots of the 1920s and '30s revered the emperor as father and master, and if the farmers of the anti-airport movement emerged as a collective precisely because of their anti-emperor stance (thus opening the space in which to emerge as an inclusive group in an attempt to represent themselves), then what can be made of the farmers of Magino village in the 1980s and '90s? One reason the farmers invited Ogawa to live in their village was that the village itself was in a state of collapse. Few young people would stay, and the older folk were dying off. Yamagata Prefecture rarely had the opportunity to get first-run movies, and there was no way to compete with the seductiveness of urban culture. But the farmers recognized that the battle was not merely between the city and the country. Things had transformed so that the battle could no longer be waged against this or that national policy, because a global culture industry had emerged that was everywhere and nowhere at once. A global situation would take global measures, so, urged on by Ogawa's vision, the farmers—in cooperation with other towns and cities in Yamagata Prefecture—created an international film festival: the Yamagata International

Documentary Film Festival. In an article about the festival, Ogawa explains that part of its driving force was to attract an international audience to hear about the village's problems and, ultimately, to start an international movement that would seriously study and resist the more destructive effects of capitalist development.[60]

The biennial festival, which attracts more than 300 hundred applicants from more than 50 nations, is one of the more encouraging events to hit the film world in some time. In an industry that is split between a highly corporatized Hollywood dimension (which, of course, is global) and an increasingly corporatized independent film dimension (which for many of its hopeful practitioners is only a short step to Hollywood), the space to produce and find an audience for overtly politicized and experimental documentary film has practically disappeared. Oddly enough, what appears to be one of the most parochial and nationalist groups, the Japanese farmers, has produced an international movement that is a great deal more substantial than the "internationalization" (kokusai-ka) program forwarded by the Japanese government since the mid-1980s. Kokusai-ka is an attempt to open Japan to the rest of the world; for the average Japanese to feel more comfortable around and better understand the Other. Unfortunately, the program ultimately has become no more than an excuse to expand global business networks and spend lavishly on local communities that would benefit much more from general infrastructural upkeep than from underused international convention centers. Finally, internationalization has a suspicious tendency to include only the wealthy industrialized nations.[61]

Notwithstanding his glamorous, young, and poor international community, which recognizes how money jeopardizes the utopia of its situation, Iwai, like his sponsors (Fuji Television) celebrates consumer culture and transnational corporatism. What Ogawa's *Sundial Carved by a Thousand Years of Notches* (and the Yamagata Documentary Film Festival that it inspired) suggests is that new transnational networks must be built, no matter how unprofessional and utopian, in order to wrest at least some of the power away from the core of brokers whose monopoly on world power grows increasingly consolidated by the day. As the nation-state weakens and transnational identities strengthen, will it take amateur groups such as the ones in Magino to resist the tempting and historically repetitive discourse of a transnational Bonaparte?

v. pornography

Totality, Reality Culture, Films of History

The Problematic of Pornography   Despite the colossal force of the pornography industry in Japan, accounting for more than 2.2 trillion yen (22.3 billion dollars) in annual sales, there is no debate over the issue like the vehement one in the United States over the past thirty years.[1] Initially framed around First Amendment rights, the U.S. debate in the 1970s squared off feminists against American Civil Liberties Union lawyers and other anticensorship advocates. The first group, best represented by Andrea Dworkin and Catharine MacKinnon, argued for the causal relation between pornography and sexual violence,[2] whereas the second group, while admitting a personal distaste for the stuff, nevertheless supported the pornographer's freedom of expression. Over the past fifteen years, however, the terrain has shifted, with the most ardent debate now between so-called pro-porn and anti-porn feminists. Dworkin and MacKinnon still spearhead the anti-pornography squad and still argue that images of violence against women tacitly sanction rape by desensitizing men to sexual violence. In short, for MacKinnon and Dworkin, all pornography is misogynous. There is no shortage of social-scientific studies from which they can choose to corroborate their position. Pro-porn feminists, mostly situated in academe and best represented by Linda Williams, Constance Penley, and Laura Kipnis, argue that pornography is a legitimate object of scholarship that unsettles social conventions and exposes bourgeois pretenses.[3] As Kipnis writes about pornography, "Like your boorish cousin, its greatest pleasure is to locate each and every one of society's taboos, prohibitions, and proprieties and systematically transgress them, one by one."[4]

It is difficult to speculate on why such debates over pornography do not exist in Japan. Certainly the different histories of feminism and constitutional legal studies are significant. So, too, might be the different histories of violence and sexuality, not to mention different material and discursive boundaries of the public and private spheres. Moreover, different histories of shame and repression can be added to this list. But the issue to be pursued here is epistemological, one that has to do with a different dominant view of society—a different way of making sense of everyday life, a different ideological impulse. At the risk of overgeneralizing, let us consider the following claim: The totality of society—that is, the abstract system in which the various concrete parts dynamically relate (in however open, contingent and overdetermined a way)—is more readily sensed in Japan than in the West. It is for this reason that many are quick to grasp the crucial sociological point that everything is connected to everything else and to go after the pornography industry is at once to go after the heart of the Japanese capitalist system itself.

The obvious comparison here is to the yakuza. Most are aware that, in Japanese society as it is now configured, the yakuza cannot simply be eliminated, for it serves crucial functions that contribute to the maintenance of Japanese society. The police, business executives, and politicians, not to mention critics and scholars, depend on the yakuza. A recent example was the 1997 arrest of the extortionist Koike Ryuichi for bribing executives of the country's leading security firms. Koike was part of a *sokai-ya* racket in which the companies paid off the extortionists to "keep the peace" and forestall any disruption at the annual stockholder meetings. But when the police arrested Koike, everything began to unravel. From the Big Four security firms (Nomura, Yamaichi, Nikko, Daiwa) to banks (Dai Ichi Kangyo) to corporations (Mitsubishi, Toshiba), all were implicated.[5] There were ritual suicides and instances of finger-pointing, but most realized that to expose one facet of the system (Koike and the sokai-ya scams) meant to pull the rug out from under the system itself.

Or we can take the education system. Most agree that the costs are exorbitant and the pressures unbearable. From elementary school on, most students enroll in costly cram schools (*juku, yobiko*) to help prepare for the next set of entrance examinations. Thoroughly corporatized, the cram-school industry works closely with the publishing industry, for which education preparatory materials make up a substantial market. Thus, even small-scale educational changes, such as in the curriculum, become almost impossible to execute. Changing the curriculum might jeopardize a student's ability to pass an examination, and could jeopardize the publishing company's capacity to generate profit. Teachers, parents, and students almost certainly acquiesce in such an integrated network of obstacles. I am suggesting a different relation to the social totality, an epistemological dominant that is markedly different from the positivism and nominalism that dominates late capitalist North America. In fact, I will go so far as to argue that this Japanese totalizing impulse is a prescient and informed view of how things work. What needs to be stressed is that this is not one more attempt to essentialize "the Japanese" or to construct a false homogeneity on top of all the others that have accompanied the history of Western Orientalism and Japanese self-Orientalism.[6] Rather, I want to stress that this totalizing impulse is of a thoroughly historical nature.

If there is indeed a penchant to recognize the connectedness of social life in postwar Japan, it comes from the historical context of Japanese modernity and the history of the modern world system. No doubt it is connected to the defeat in World War II, Japan's role in the Cold War, and the fact that many of today's elite in Japan were yesterday's radicals. Here one might want to recall the *Zengakuren* members who attribute their success as corporate managers to the lessons they learned while reading Marx's *Capital*. By stressing that capitalism is a historical system operating under a certain logic, Marx's work—alongside its more revolutionary possibilities—offered the most realistic and least romantic model for how to manage successfully (indeed, profitably) the mode of production. That is, although Marx's project was certainly to inspire and effect proletarian revolution, at bottom Marxism was, and still is, about the analysis of capitalism as a dynamic totality—a totality in which one cannot think about money without simultaneously thinking about labor, and one cannot think about thought itself without simultaneously thinking about the material conditions of existence. In short, a Marxist theory of capitalism will be just as useful to the radical as it is to the corporate manager.

The most famous example of this comes from the eminent Marxist economist Uno Kozo, who taught at the University of Tokyo from 1947 to 1977. Most Ministry of Finance bureaucrats today, a majority of whom graduated from the University of Tokyo, studied under Uno and were intimately familiar with his theories. Uno's most important idea stresses that the theoretical and practical operations of capitalism must be studied separately, and that one of Marx's errors when writing *Capital* was to combine journalism with pure theory.[7] In contrast to Marx's, Uno's Marxism divides into three registers: pure theory, middle-range structural analysis, and day-to-day historical studies. For his own part, Uno dedicated himself to working through the categories of pure theory, such as value, the commodity, and crisis.[8] By the middle of the 1960s, it is said, more than 60 percent of Japanese economists fashioned themselves Unoists. Unlike Marx, Uno never staked out an ethical position about capitalism (in which the collectivity of the proletariat is privileged over the collectivity of the bourgeoisie), and Uno's followers were just as readily found on the right as on the left. What united them was a way of understanding capitalism as a historical system that operates under a certain logic that affects all of social life. To underscore what is being suggested here, this propensity to sense the totality does not always lead to a more radical politics. This, however, challenges some of the most famous positions regarding totality and politics—in particular, that of the most significant Western thinker of totality, Georg Lukács.

For example, in the essay "The Marxism of Rosa Luxemburg," Lukács explains that what sets Marx apart from bourgeois thought is not the "primacy of economic motives in historical explanation" but "the point of view of totality."[9] Lukács continues, "The category of totality, the all-pervasive supremacy of the whole over the parts is the essence of the method which Marx took over from Hegel and brilliantly transformed into the foundations of a wholly new science."[10] Lukács feared that the division of labor, the separation of the worker from the means of production, and the atomization of society wrought by endless production would seep into the very consciousness of those living under the capitalist mode of production and make it nearly impossible to attain the point of view of totality. David Ricardo may have understood that labor is the content of a commodity's value,[11] and Adam Smith may have understood the harmful effects of the division of labor,[12] but neither of them adequately asked why these forms arose in the first place and why they are able to reproduce themselves. To pose the famous "why" question, to move from description to explanation, can be done only when the isolated facts of social life are seen "as aspects of the historical process and integrate[d] in a totality."[13] It is this totalizing imperative, for Lukács, that gives Marxism its revolutionary edge.

But is not this totalizing imperative, this bent to sense the connection between even the most isolated attempt to change educational curricula and the totality of Japanese society, precisely the type of sensibility that many have possessed in postwar Japan? Of course, there are always exceptions— for example, other categories of difference within the nation, such as ethnicity, gender, and class, that complicate this sensibility, not to mention recent globalization processes that seem to restructure this totalizing impulse from day to day. But how else can one explain the ubiquity of complaints coming from workers, students, executives, scholars, and even government officials, complaints that are invariably punctuated by the now prophetic refrain, "*Shikata ga nai*" (nothing can be done)—a mantra on the order of a postwar national anthem. Of course, we hear similar complaints in the United States and Canada, but they are usually linked to fierce criticism of an individual politician, party, or policy; the institution itself—indeed, the system itself—remains unscathed and thus legitimated. More often than not, this conception of the totality in Japan seems to persuade against even attempting the most trivial reform. Whenever a national event erupts, such as when the fourteen-year-old boy killed eleven-year-old Hase Jun in Kobe and blamed the compulsory education system for the act, a national conversation does begin, but it quickly fades out—within months, if not weeks. Unlike that in the United States, Japan's dominant ideology can be characterized as realistic, not cynical; practical, not idealistic. One cannot be cynical or idealistic unless one believes that the system can perform better than it does. But when the system is understood for what it is—a system fundamentally structured in dominance that cannot be made benign no matter how inventive the reforms—then one must accept that the negative must always exist alongside the positive: rich with poor, crime with uprightness, pornography with mainstream film and television. The dominant ideology in the United States is that things will be better once crime, pornography, and government corruption are extinguished. No one in the United States, save a few marginalized dissidents, argue that there might be a dialectical relation between the punishment industry and the booming economy (Angela Davis), or that the corruption in Washington, D.C., is in fact what makes the system work so well (Noam Chomsky).[14] But it is precisely this relation that seems to be grasped, for better or worse, in Japan.

This might seem quite a distance away from the problem of pornography, but the risk in this chapter is to argue that it is not. The absence of a similar debate over pornography in Japan is due partly to this totalizing impulse, to the general view, however unconscious, that the pornographic is intricately connected to the non-pornographic. But if the pornography debate is not ensconced in its private history, and if the totalizing impulse has generated a paucity of focused discussion about pornography in Japan, then this leads to the following question: How has the issue of pornography been, and how is it being, critically engaged vis-à-vis the totality? Before attempting to answer this question, I will first develop this notion of pornography's shifting position in the totality, its dialectical relation to all that it is not—to the non-pornographic. To begin with the most obvious dependence between the pornographic and the non-pornographic, we must turn to the film industry itself. It is well known that the major Japanese film corporations have been in decline since the early 1970s. And since the mid-1980s, when the videocassette player became a common household appliance, the number of theaters has dramatically declined. In the meantime, the video-rental industry has boomed. Just about every town (and village) in Japan has one—if not two or three—video store. Until the early 1990s, these stores were privately owned, with no "chain" outlets, as is commonly the case in the United States.[15]

The average Japanese video store is about 1,000 square feet. The inventory is divided among Hollywood film, Japanese animation, Japanese feature films, and adult video (with an assortment of video games and compact disc rentals). For the most part, Hollywood films dominate. One is more likely to find Alfred Hitchcock's *North By Northwest* than Mizoguchi's *Ugetsu monogatari*. Even the most rural video store might contain a copy of *Intolerance* or *The General*. The following statistics, collected in 1996 at People Video in Tokyo, should be representative of most stores in the country: People Video stocks 10,000 videos, with adult video making up nearly half this number (with no gay pornography). Each day, customers rent approximately 330 videos, 140 of which are adult videos. The average rental period is two nights and three days for a fee of 300 yen (2.5 dollars) (with slightly higher rates for newly released films). Each month, the shop rents approximately 9,000 films. Men make up more than three-quarters of the customer base and close to 100 percent of adult video renters.[16] During interviews with the manager of People Video and the managers of two other local video shops within a quarter-mile radius, each explained that, without the adult video business, the shops would not be able to stay in business. Arai Taro of People Video put it as follows: "Sometimes, but very rarely, a person complains about the large inventory of [adult video] copies and the huge amount of floor space they take up. When this happens, I simply explain that, without this element of the business, they would not have the chance to rent the mainstream videos they want."[17]

In the recent book *Nihon eiga ha, ima* (Japanese film today), Sano Shinichi dedicates an engaging chapter to the fifty-year history of Japanese pornographic film and video.[18] The industry emerged in the late 1940s and boomed in the early 1950s. First there was blue film, a rag-tag operation of amateurs and misfits that produced twenty-minute shorts. Blue film was followed by pink film, which produced soft-porn sponsored by the major film companies to offset the loss of revenue from declining ticket sales brought about by the popularity of television.[19] Once video technology hit a critical mass, and smaller theaters were gasping to pay the inflated real-estate prices brought on by the bubble economy, pink stepped aside for adult video.[20] During adult video's debut in 1983, the market was marginal; by 1991, however, more than 3,600 films were being released a year, and more than 250 female stars were making their debuts.[21] When this enormous output is compared with the combined output of the big three film corporations (Shochiku, Toei, Toho), which at their height in 1960 produced 545 feature-length films, the difference is staggering. Sano's blue–pink–adult trajectory offers a good start at historicizing the links among the three dominant moments of pornography. But what such a linear study forgoes is the lateral move, the move that positions pornography in synchronic relation to other forms existing at the same moment.

Pornography is interesting and significant not for what it is, not as a discrete object of study, but for how it exceeds itself (and for how its meanings and effects transform from one historical moment to another). Pornography's most critical social function is to legitimate that which it is not—the "non-pornographic." As the logic goes: If that is pornographic and socially improper, then this must be proper and sanctioned. The non-pornographic (from high culture to mass culture) attains its identity, its legitimacy, by virtue of its dialectical relation to what it is not; indeed, the non-pornographic desperately depends on its Other, on pornography. But this is not to suggest that the two categories are stable. Rather, the relation between the pornographic and the non-pornographic—not to mention the very categories themselves—are historical and in an endless state of transformation. In fact, to preview the argument to be made in the conclusion of this chapter, the boundary separating the pornographic and the non-pornographic seems to have mutated once again in late capitalist Japan (a mutation in which the boundary separating the two terms is becoming more and more blurred). Thus, to study pornography in this way is to engage the most pressing social issues and transformations of modern Japanese society. Indeed, one of the more fascinating historical documents to emerge from Japan in the past ten years is a film series titled *Fuzoku kogata eiga*.[22] This series, subtitled *A History of Blue Film in Japan*, includes more than four hours of clips from various blue films and is accompanied by an overnarration explaining each film's context. Of course, the films do not comment on the war, the economy, foreign affairs, or other issues of high seriousness. But how much can be gleaned from watching newsreels that do directly engage these issues? Indeed, what is most interesting when watching historical newsreels today is not so much the content being expressed as how that content is expressed— the way the narrative is structured, the framing, and the use of explanatory devices such as overnarration and titles. Thus, tracking the clips of various pornographic films with an eye to how they are made, who is watching them, and how they are transforming over time could provide insight into mainstream culture and ideology on an order more profound than that revealed when focusing solely on the mainstream. Again, this returns us to the issue of form as the crucible of meaning. For it is form that jumps the space between the pornographic and the non-pornographic.

It is precisely an examination of the formal relation between the pornographic and the non-pornographic that has produced some of the most important films of postwar Japan. In this chapter, I examine three such films. These are films that turn on the problematic of pornography and end up as some of the most significant historical documents of the modern period. But these are not films that are commonly called historical films (films that take place in distant pasts — say, a film during the Heian period); nor are they films about history (such as *The History of Blue Film in Japan*, in which past films are analyzed from the perspective of the present). Rather, they fall into a third category and concept of film that I will call films *of* history. Films of history work through *on their formal level* (not necessarily in their narrative content) the most crucial events of their own historical moment before there is a common language to speak about these events. This is to say that a debate about pornography has indeed existed in Japan over the past thirty years, but it has taken place on the level of cinematic form. This has occurred not because of some essential Japanese modesty about discussing such issues, or because of some inherent brilliance at subtlety and indirection. Rather, it has occurred because the totality that needs to be engaged when examining pornography is something that is inaccessible, it is something that — although sensed — cannot be directly represented by everyday discourse. Instead, the totality is best flashed by the aesthetic itself — the aesthetic as symptom for something that, although operative and alive, is unrepresentable. The first film on the list, made in 1966 by Imamura Shohei, is *Jinruigaku nyumon* (The pornographers: An introduction to anthropology); the second, made in 1976 by Oshima Nagisa, is *Ai no koriida* (The bullfight of love, or, as it is better known in the West, *In the Realm of the Senses*); and the third, made in 1987 by Hara Kazuo (and discussed in chapter three), is *Yukiyukite shingun* (The Emperor's Naked Army Marches On). Following the readings of these films, I will link them to a more recent film by Isaka Satoshi, titled *Focus* (1996) — a film that develops the connection between pornography and the growing mainstream genre of what I will call "reality culture."

Imamura's mid-1960s' *The Pornographers* anticipates a moment in which planeloads of Japanese businessmen will be heading to Thailand and the

Philippines on group sex tours; in which the U.S. pornography industry will be vigorously exported abroad; in which the Japanese pornography industry will transform from a random array of social outcasts (blue films) to a thoroughly corporatized operation (adult video); and in which prostitution rings will begin traveling the globe, following the path of transnational business executives. The film draws attention to the way in which the pornographic figure is contained in the content not only of the blue films that the characters make, but also in the feature film that Imamura makes. And, more important, we get a glimpse of how the category of pornography is transforming at a particular historical moment so that it will no longer be contained only in low-budget porn films; it will now find a home in mainstream images, as well.

If Imamura anticipates the transformation of the pornographic figure, then Oshima's now famous *In the Realm of the Senses* (1976) sits dead-center in it. For instance, if we compare Oshima's work with *The Pornographers*, we see that *Senses* is not *about* pornography; it *is* a pornographic film.[23] Through the critical distance one gets to his film, Imamura draws attention to how the process of producing and consuming pornography is integrally tied to producing and consuming images in general. Oshima's film, released ten years after *The Pornographers* and financed, produced, and distributed by international interests, by contrast, collapsed this critical distance and quite remarkably, and happily, became what Imamura anticipated: the transnational pornographic commodity par excellence. Even though the two films are different on the level of narrative content, they become similar in their critical meanings when we account for the third moment of Japanese film and capitalism: Both attempt to expose and intervene in the corporatization of pornography in Japan, and both attempt to reveal that the commodification of sex is no longer neatly contained within that thing called pornography. That category has been blown apart so that it now spreads over what is generally considered the non-pornographic (or general mass-culture artifacts). In short, both directors, in ways that coordinate with their different historical situations, reveal the political stakes involved in such a rigid distinction between the pornographic and non-pornographic—that is, both directors flash the totality of Japanese society through their respective formal inventions.

Just as Oshima's film seems to fulfill Imamura's prophecy, Hara Kazuo's *The Emperor's Naked Army Marches On* seems to fulfill Oshima's. As mentioned earlier, Hara follows a former World War II Japanese soldier (Okuzaki Kenzo) around on his mission to locate and murder the officers of his military regiment. By actively narrating Okuzaki's story, Hara not only interprets Okuzaki's actions; he changes them, as well. And something about this new form of documentary seems to share something with the most recent boom in adult video, films that I call *dokyuporuno* (Docupornography). This new wave of adult video, which foregrounds the nonfictional search of a man looking for sex, now accounts for more than 75 percent of the market and mirrors any number of reality culture shows that have burst on the scene of Japanese and global popular culture in recent years.

Reality culture comprises real-time reportage, quiz shows, cop shows, certain types of pornography, amateur video, snuff films, surveillance films, docu-dramas, live Webcams, and more. It is a form in which an event is not just recorded; it is simultaneously produced in order to service (and construct) a growing market of viewers who want to experience these so-called real events. Reality culture cranks up to a new dimension the very old logic that an event exists not as something discrete but as something that exceeds itself, something that is produced by the very dynamic among representer, represented, and spectator. Reality culture marks a heightened challenge to truth claims, a rise in fakery, a suspicion of ever properly catching and representing reality, a new relationship to (and conception of) the real, and, most specifically, a prodigious leap in representational technology. As in the "Happenings" of the 1960s, the allure of reality culture is that events occur unpredictably. But unlike the Happenings, reality culture attempts to commodify and reproduce these seemingly unreproducible events. The danger, of course, is that once a proven market for such "real" events emerges, the events must then be produced at all costs. It is not difficult to imagine the dystopian dimension to all of this, such as the production (however indirectly) of crime and murder. At the same time, reality culture offers a utopian dimension; it marks a desire for openness, for a spontaneous eruption of the unexpected, the accident, the unpredictable, the messianic, the apocalyptic, the Houdini act that performs the impossible escape no matter how utopian or dystopian it might be. I view the current boom in reality culture (in production and consumption) as expressing the social dreams and nightmares of the current post-miracle moment in Japan and the world. Or to put this in the form of a question: Might the desire to watch two hours of a bank's surveillance tape, with the hope of possibly catching the split-second moment of the bank robbery, be symptomatic of political fantasies and fears?

Immediately after *Focus* premiered at the 1996 Tokyo International Film Festival, Isaka was asked questions that shot straight to the heart of this emerging phenomenon. *Focus* is about the eagerness and bad faith of a television director who is making a documentary about a twenty-something *otaku* (passionate, obsessive) who is obsessed with audio surveillance technology. Although the sweet and bumbling otaku played spot-on by the rising star Asano Tadanobu only likes to eavesdrop on cell-phone conversations and the girl across the way, the television director wants to incorporate the overheard information into his piece, especially after he overhears two yakuza exchanging information about a gun transfer. The finished television documentary doubtless will appear unpredictably to have encountered the spellbinding and violent events that follow (a murder, high-speed chase, and rape, and the death of the young eavesdropper), whereas the director himself (together with an all-too-agreeable cameraman and mildly suspicious production assistant) will have directly provoked the events. At one point in *Focus*, a pornographic film is made so it can be used later in a possible blackmail scheme (more on this later).

Isaka's film came on the heels of the Tokyo Broadcasting Systems (TBS) scandal in which television executives allowed higher-ups in Aum Shinrikyo to view footage of an interview with the anti-Aum lawyer Sakamoto Tsutsumi. In return, TBS gained greater access to Aum (including an interview with its leader, Asahara Shoko, in Germany), and Aum received assurances that the interview would not be aired. Sakamoto, his wife, and the couple's one-year-old son were subsequently murdered by Aum members. Questions about news gathering and journalistic ethics circulated wildly— particularly about journalists' complicity with the very events they are representing. The TBS debacle, combined with the not-so-faded memory of the 1992 faked Nihon Hoso Kyokai (NHK; Japan Broadcasting Corporation) documentary about a near-death experience in the Himalayas, was at the center of the post-screening discussion.[24] Isaka was asked how he could pretend that his own film was morally superior to such television programs, or even pornographic videos. To attract us to his film, is Isaka not employing the same strategies as the very television programs and pornography he is condemning? Similar questions followed: Could Isaka's critique of the television and pornography industries be lodged against his own film, and if so, would this delegitimate the critique? Is *Focus* about an obsessed TV director on a campaign to make it in the industry at all costs, or is it about an obsessed industry that leaves no room for individual agency and rigor? How does one criticize anything when the elements of criticism (namely, representation) have been called into question so radically? Isaka ducked and parried; he doubtless expected more sympathy. Hesitant silence prevailed.

The trajectory of the pornographic figure is traced not by searching over time for images of naked bodies, sex, or direct bodily exploitation; it is traced by searching for shared meanings and effects that persist from one historical moment to another. Of course, all of this depends on a more mutable conceptualization of pornography (one that is less tied to content than to how the body is represented in the frame, one that is concerned with the way film and images relate to libidinal and psychic desire, to temporality, and to the way in which spectacular content fetishizes social relations of power). When a television reporter shoves a microphone in the face of someone sobbing over the death of a loved one, or when the images of a city being carpet-bombed are transmitted over the television, we might call this pornographic. The conceptualization of pornography to be produced in the pages that follow forces us to take this response deadly seriously and question what is at stake when pornography no longer refers only to those so-called dirty films in the back of the video store.

Introduction to the Pornographic The central character in *The Pornographers* is Ogata, who lives in Osaka with Haru and her two children from a former marriage, Koichi and Keiko. Haru's husband has been dead for a while, and she believes that his spirit is upset because of her infidelity. Ogata and two partners (Kabo and Banteki) make and distribute low-budget porn movies for a growing and profitable market, notwithstanding the constant worries about police interference and about the encroaching yakuza. Incest is everywhere. Koichi needs "spiritual" help from his mother in order to pass the university entrance exams; Ogata desires Keiko; flashbacks reveal that both Ogata and Haru were molested by their own parents; and during a porn shoot, one learns that the actors are a father and his mentally disabled daughter. Ogata wants to take care of the family and believes that, by selling pornography, he can pay the exorbitant and corrupt education fees for

40. Imamura Shohei's *The Pornographers*. Imamura Productions, 1966.

both children and provide an antidote for a society that has become hypercompetitive, so that "men can't even get an erection after the age of fifty." (Haru, in fact, tells her friends that Ogata sells medical instruments.) After Haru becomes ill and dies, Ogata becomes even more disturbed by the societal destruction wrought by industrialization and the sexual symptoms that it brings. But then, as if jolted by the dialectic itself, he sees the utopian possibilities of machines ("They don't talk back") and decides to build a sex doll that will eliminate the need for pornography and prostitution by properly managing human desire. Living alone in a houseboat under the beauty shop that Keiko has inherited from her mother, Ogata becomes more and more obsessed with his project, until the film finally ends with the houseboat's line breaking away from the pier. Ogata, the boat, and the doll float toward the open sea.

The film opens at a train station, where Ogata meets Banteki, Kabo, and two amateur actors before going to a secluded outdoor location to shoot an eight-millimeter porn movie. The cameras begin rolling; then there is a jump-cut to a small screening room, where the three partners are presumably watching the film that we just saw them shooting. The film is titled *The Pornographers*—the film that we have already been watching for a few minutes. With the sound of the projector as a background, the film credits roll as images of the three men watching the film are reflected on the screen. In this film-inside-a-film scene, we (the viewers) are watching them (the actors) watch the film that they have just shot (fig. 40). But soon, a strange fish appears on the screen (their screen); then a bridge behind Ogata's home appears before the film-inside-the-film expands to take over the entire shot, and the sound of the projector stops. During the last scene, as Ogata's small houseboat is floating into the sea, the projector sound returns, and the screen becomes smaller as we find ourselves back in the screening room. "You understand this man, don't you Ogata?" asks Banteki. "No, I don't," Ogata responds. "I wonder if he will die?" asks Kabo. "Who cares; let's get on to the next one," is the response.

On its edges, then, *The Pornographers* is portrayed as a feature film while its body is portrayed as just another porn flick. First we are watching Imamura's feature film; then we are watching the porn film; then we finish by watching the feature film again. Or to put this another way, and to preview why I think this film is profound, we are watching both at the same time. Imamura draws attention to how the pornographic element is contained not only in the content of the blue films that Ogata makes, but also in Ogata and Haru's everyday life and in the feature film called *The Pornographers*. The pornographic (as in commercial pornography) is the commodification of human bodies in which labor and exploitation is hidden. On a stylistic level, pornography is marked not so much by nakedness and sexual intercourse among the actors as by the absolute centrality of the body—to the marginalization of everything else—in the frame. We can see this same aesthetic (which I call the "pornographic aesthetic") emerging in television dramas of the times, as well as in advertisements, in which consumer goods are absolutely central in the composition. Pornography, moreover, is the commodity par excellence: The production processes and everyday lives of those who produce it are fetishized, or fantasized away, by those who consume it. On a material level, commercial pornography is *generally* about sex, the wanton destruction of women's bodies, and commodity exchange; on an ideological level, it is about the management of human desire and the promise of revealing that which cannot be revealed. But the logic of the promise forbids its fulfillment, and the case of pornography is no different. The seduction of pornography lies in the expectation of seeing something that in reality is impossible to see (such as commercial pornography without the exploitation of women or commodity production without the exploitation of labor). The more pornography is censored and designated as immoral, the more attractive and promising its promise becomes. As we will see in Oshima's *In the Realm of the Senses*, it is precisely the role of censorship and the nearly complete occupation of commodification by the mid-1970s that heightened the film's pornographic dimension.

But when Imamura made his film in the mid-1960s, the spectacle of pornography, in which its commodification had reached the point of total occupation of social life, was not yet possible because the technology and means of mass-producing it were not yet developed. Demand for Ogata's films far exceeds supply, and he and his partners can only make a few copies at a time. Although they dream of building their own laboratory in order to produce an unlimited number of duplicates, the capital needed for such a startup is so enormous that only the yakuza and big business can succeed. At the end of *The Pornographers*, when Ogata has been living and building the doll in the houseboat for more than five years, a man named Furukawa comes from Kyoei Industries to offer Ogata a proposition to join his firm.[25] Furukawa wants to export the doll to the South Pole and later to the moon and to Mars. Furukawa explains that his company's engineers have been trying to build a doll but, unlike Ogata, they just do not have the touch. As we hear jet planes flying overhead, Ogata looks into the sky; expressing disgust at Furukawa, he mumbles, "Idiots like you could never understand." Furukawa wants to open markets and envisions the doll as the ideal commodity. Ogata, by the end of the film, wants to move beyond the commodification of sex and desire by way of the commodity.

The body of the film contains an abundance of difficult code. There are many flashbacks for which Imamura does not offer viewers the usual cinematic preparation in order to make sense of them. Instead, Imamura demands that the viewers actively interpret the temporality of each scene. In one scene, for example, Ogata and Keiko, both about ten years younger, are shown walking through a cemetery, Keiko runs into the street and is hit by a car. Here, as in the way history really functions, the past is not neatly separated from the present; it shoots right through it in unexpected and untimely ways. One way Imamura draws attention to his codes is by employing still shots that last for more than three seconds. For example, during fantastic representations of Haru's hallucinations and other moments of heightened action, the stills seem to give the viewer time to catch his or her breath and make sense of what is going on in the narrative. There is even a subtle allusion to the role of early Japanese cinema: When Ogata shows some of his blue films to a group of businessmen, he plays the role of a benshi and comments on the images as they are being projected. "This is the best position" and "You can tell by the size of this one that he is obviously an American," Ogata overnarrates.

Imamura's codes are an attempt to lead a viewer back and forth from the individual to the social and from the present to the past to cultivate a critical distance on the meaning of contemporary Japanese society. On this level, *The Pornographers* distinguishes itself most from the pornographic genre, as it self-consciously draws attention to its own voyeuristic desires while de-emphasizing—to that of the larger societal operations—the individual bodies of the characters. Contrary to the narrative structure of most melodrama, moreover, in which the social contradictions of the collective are mapped onto the life of a single character, then falsely reconciled, Imamura's film maps the individual contradictions onto the structure of society and hints that, to manage the problems of the individual, we must at the same time manage the problems of the collective. In *The Insect Woman* which was made only three years before *The Pornographers,* Imamura follows the life of a single character, Tome, from her poor, rural family life in the Tohoku region before the Pacific war; to her success, then demise, as a madam in Tokyo during the immediate postwar period; then back to her hometown in the early 1960s. The film ends with the utopian gesture of Tome joining her daughter in the country as they embark on a life at a collective farm as one of the few ways to resist urban destruction and consumerism. Although *The Pornographers* has no such idealistic ending, as Ogata is heading toward a sure death and companies like Kyoei Industries toward sure expansion, we can locate a utopian dimension in the form of the film itself.

This is the utopia of criticism, of being able to take a complicated and thoroughly sophisticated situation—one that appears to have no logic and to consist of parts that act autonomously, with no relation to the whole—and organize it in a way that can (however impossibly) flash the dialectic of cause and effect. It is demanding to watch an Imamura film. We need to cultivate a way of seeing and thinking that makes historical connections, that decodes, that can travel freely between the worlds that are on and off the screen. It is this type of difficult hermeneutic work that Imamura asks us to bring to our analysis of society, for without it we will never be in a position to properly transform society. To understand this formal utopian dimension better, Imamura's films need to be viewed in the context of political activism in the 1950s and '60s, such as the student movement that, by 1960, comprised more than 1 million students, and the rapid growth experienced by the Japanese economy during the 1960s.

The *Zengakuren* was founded in 1948 on a rather moderate democratic platform that had more to do with local university issues, such as that at Ibaraki University over autonomy and student control of dormitories, than with leading a world revolution. The U.S.–Japan Security Treaty, which was the center of intense political struggles at its ratification in 1960 and 1970, mobilized the students to think more about national and global issues by revealing the nature of U.S. imperialism and Japan's complicity. After aligning with the Japanese Communist Party (JCP) in 1958, most of the student factions who viewed the JCP as too moderate made decisive breaks away from its domination.[26]

The struggles at Waseda and Tokyo universities, in which courses were canceled and students barricaded themselves in university buildings, are symptomatic of hundreds of other demonstrations and sit-ins. The movement began to weaken, however, after the ratification of the U.S.–Japan Security Treaty in 1960 and the economy heated up to remarkable degrees. Live broadcasts of the Olympic Games in Tokyo in 1964 also marked the growing significance of television, as more than 16 million Japanese homes owned at least one set. Public broadcasting, represented by NHK, and commercial television began in 1953. As a new medium, television experienced a "golden age" between 1953 and 1965, filled with great experimentation by many young directors and scriptwriters who felt constrained by the strict hierarchies of advancement and staid aesthetic approaches of the film corporations. In 1958, film-ticket sales surpassed 1 billion yen (2.77 million dollars), and over 7,000 theaters were operating throughout the country; by 1965, ticket sales had dropped about 300 percent, and the number of theaters was down to about 4,700.[27] The film corporations, reacting to this severe decline in their market, dumped large amounts of capital into the television industry. This trend, along with the realization by political leaders of television's mass-marketing potential, rid the new medium of its radical possibilities, as regulations were enforced that canceled rebroadcasts of many politically engaged programs. Imamura made *The Pornographers*, then, after the heat of the social movement began to cool and as the embers of the Japanese economy were burning hot. The film corresponded to these times by (1) inhabiting the utopian notion of distance and criticism that earlier was part of a healthy resistance; (2) pointing to a present moment in which those on the left, especially the increasingly dispersed and fratricidal students, were losing popular

41. Imamura Shohei's *The Pornogra-phers*. Imamura Productions, 1966.

support; and (3) foreboding a time in which criticism would, like no other time in history, run the serious risk of becoming just so much grist for the commodity mill. In this way we can understand *The Pornographers* as supporting the ideals of the students in their desire to change society from the ground up while, at the same time, criticizing the student movement for not being properly self-critical of its own volunteerism and lack of coordination. Imamura negotiates this difficulty of theory and practice both by creating a work that is a fierce criticism of industrial society and by acknowledging his own film's function as just another spectacular commodity—as just another pornographic film.

Imamura seems to turn this narrative trick in order to suggest that feature films and pornographic films might soon be indistinguishable. This prediction is echoed throughout the film's compositional level in the way he organizes the mise-en-scène. For example, he used Cinemascope for the first time (and expertly), and almost every shot is taken through windows, *shoji*, fish tanks, metal bars, or slightly opened doors (fig. 41). This causes much of each frame to be occupied by "obstructions," leaving only a marginal portion for what might be called "active content." But just as the complexity of Imamura's narrative can at one and the same time suggest what might be considered its Other (a porn narrative), so, too, can the complexity of his compositions suggest a pornographic composition.

But what is a pornographic composition? Recall the shot in the screening room when the frame inside the frame expands to take over the entire shot (when the porn film takes over the feature film). What is happening is that the frame is pushing out, crowding out, snuffing out significant relational elements of the shot (for example, the doubleness of the actors looking at themselves). It is precisely this transformation (when the active content monopolizes the absolute centrality of the frame, to the marginalization of everything else) that puts us dead-center in the pornographic aesthetic. For Imamura, when the body, mug shot, consumer good, or other active content occupies the center of the frame, it crowds out its relations—relations among elements in the mise-en-scène, relations to history, and social relations of power.

In 1966, *The Pornographers* anticipated this pornographic aesthetic as one that would dominate in the decades to come. Imamura suggested, however, that this aesthetic would no longer be found only in porn films; it would ooze into mainstream cultural artifacts, as well—into the domain commonly called popular culture, which includes feature film, television, urban signage, and advertising. He negotiated this emerging situation by creating a feature film that was a blue film and a blue film that was a feature film—a film that became precisely what it criticized and thus a criticism that became the film itself. *The Pornographers* is a film of history, a film that represents a transformation before it has happened; a film that finds a language for something before a language has been assigned; a film that flashes the totality of modern Japanese society in a way that is unavailable to other forms of discourse.

In the Realm of the Pornographic
Imamura might wink at us when he calls his film pornographic. Oshima, by contrast, might shoot back a contemptuous look were his *In the Realm of the Senses* called anything but pornographic. More than twenty-five years have passed since the premiere of Oshima's *Senses*—the so-called high-art pornographic film that captured the interest and desire of critics and viewers from Paris and New York to Tokyo. The critical conversation spawned by the film, regarding questions of film theory, feminism, fascism, psychoanalysis, censorship, violence, sexuality, and pornography, peaked in the 1980s as Oshima's name became as widely known in the West as Kurosawa's and Ozu's.

Senses is the story of Sada, a former prostitute, who starts working in the house owned by Kichi. When Kichi sees Sada for the first time, she is raising a knife to threaten another serving girl during a scuffle in the kitchen. Kichi is immediately attracted to Sada. After Kichi suggests that Sada should be holding something other than a knife, the mutual obsession that drives the film is unleashed. Shot episodically, with sex organizing each scene, the film achieves an increasing degree of sadomasochism, with the deadly object of desire an almost constant state of arousal. After moving to an inn, where Sada and Kichi will be uninterrupted (especially by Kichi's bothersome wife: "My wife is just a household decoration"), Sada begins to strangle Kichi to heighten their passion: "When I choke you, I can feel it move." Finally, willed or unwilled by Kichi, Sada manages to murder Kichi with the cords of her kimono before slicing off his penis with a nearby carving knife. After writing in blood on Kichi's left thigh and on the sheet, "Sada and Kichi; two alone," Sada places the penis and testicles in a *furoshiki* (a cloth for wrapping gifts) and walks the streets of Tokyo for three days before she is arrested.

Oshima's film is a retelling of Ishida Kichizo and Abe Sada's relationship, which gained national attention in 1936 following publicity about the castration. By committing her act of violence on May 18, 1936, Sada was following on the heels of a national act of violence that had served to consolidate Japanese militarism. On February 26, of that year, a group of young military officers attempted a coup d'état to remove the despots surrounding the throne and bring about national reconstruction (a Showa Restoration). About 1,500 troops surrounded government headquarters while a cabal, using guerrilla tactics, attempted to assassinate a number of top national officials, including the prime minister, key cabinet ministers, and members of the imperial court bureaucracy. The coup was immediately squashed and subsequently used as an excuse by the government to restore discipline and consolidate its power in order to pursue a full-scale military campaign. Using the February 26 incident as a fulcrum, the government had increased military spending to 46 percent of the GNP by the end of the year, and many viewed the failed coup as the last chance to reverse the ensuing course of fascism. The relation between the February 26 incident and Sada's act on May 18 is made quite evident in Sekine Hiroshi's 1971 poem "Abe Sada," which contains verbatim accounts of much of Sada's vivid confessional statement. The poem begins:

the conclusion of the 2/26 incident
was the war
but my incident, in the same year
is still not concluded.[28]

Sada was released, with many other political prisoners, at the beginning of the U.S. occupation, after serving only eight years in prison. The question of what it means that Sada walked free alongside thousands of political activists is certainly interesting, for now it is important to note that after the May 18 incident, Sada acquired the status of folk heroine and has often been constructed as an important figure of protest.

The relationship between sex and fascism is one that Wilhelm Reich wrote about in his 1933 work *The Mass Psychology of Fascism*.[29] While trying to understand why "the majority of those who are hungry don't steal and why the majority of those who are exploited don't strike," Reich studied the psychological structure of the masses and its relation to the economic base. Unsatisfied with the vulgar Marxist notion that the economic base one-dimensionally determines the ideological superstructure, Reich sought to nuance the prevailing Marxism in order to explain why people would act contrary to their material interests. Like other Western Marxists, Reich considered the dialectical effect that the ideological superstructure had on the economic base. This move allowed Reich to construct a sex–economic sociology that combined the work of Marx and Freud in order to ask the central question of his book: "For what sociological reasons is sexuality suppressed by the society and repressed by the individual?"[30] Of course, one answer lies in the material profit that can be gained by a ruling minority, an answer that served as Reich's thesis in his attempt to explain the rise of fascism. We see this sublimation of the libido at work in Japan precisely at the time that Sada and Kichi meet. With militarism on the rise, a resurgence of Confucian ethics was taking place, symbolized by the distribution to millions of people of the *Kokutai hongi* (The chronicles of national polity), which stressed, in mystical prose, the ideals of patriotism and filial piety. Yet, unlike Sekine's poem, which foregrounds the historical and places Sada's act in direct relation to Japanese militarism, Oshima's gestures are not concrete and are much more meaningful.

Oshima's direct gestures to the political are sparse and take place only "outside": when a group of children tease a derelict by poking his genitals with the staff of the wartime hinomaru (Japanese flag); in a background scene of flying kites, indicating the National Boys' Day Celebration; when we see Kichi walking in the opposite direction of a military parade; and when we hear the crucial voiceover (Oshima's actual voice) at the end of the film,

". . . this happened in 1936." Before commenting on these "outside" scenes and accounting for why they are integral to how *Senses* functioned in Japan at the time of its 1976 release, I will first examine the critical reception of the film, beginning with the conversation that erupted in Western film journals. I will begin with non-Japanese analyses not only because Oshima produced the film primarily for Western viewers and critics (its financing was French, and it was initially released abroad), but also because the Japanese conversation about the film was almost entirely consumed by questions of censorship. (This emphasis, as will be shown later, is crucial to my reading of the type of cultural work *Senses* performs in Japan.)

In the 1977 edition of *Wide Angle*, Steven Heath began the conversation about *Senses* by examining the portrayal of the look.[31] Arguing that all cinema is driven by voyeurism, Heath demonstrated that, in *Senses*, Oshima radically questions and exposes how both looks and images are related to the sexual. The first scene after the credits is a tight closeup of Sada lying on a futon, staring off in front of the frame at the spectator. This implicates the spectator, involving her or him in the network of looks that will ensue. We see Sada and another serving girl looking through the open space of a shoji at Kichi and his wife making love. In a later scene, we see Kichi looking in a mirror that reflects Sada looking at him. At stake is the fact that it is always women doing the looking: "Thus with a play on 'looking at looking,' is set up a constant figure for the film: the sexual is seen and seen seeing; when Kichi and Sada make love, the look is passed elsewhere, to geishas, servants, always women."[32] This troubling of the look, according to Heath, disrupts classic cinema's narrative of the woman's body as an object of male desire and control. For Heath, then, Oshima's question is one posed to the institution of cinema itself, a question that is similar to those that other avant-garde filmmakers have asked.

Ten years after publishing Heath's significant article, *Wide Angle* dedicated an entire issue (fall 1987) to the work of Oshima.[33] In "Oshima: The Avant-Garde Artist Without an Avant-Garde Style," Peter Lehman challenged Heath's notion that the structure of the look creates a serious disruption of the visible in the classical cinema.[34] Lehman argued, instead, that *Senses* fulfills the more important function of foregrounding the role of women's desire and pleasure. The insistent look of the female and Sada's control and dominance by the second half of the film, however, presents a paradox for Lehman: "It overthrows the usual phallic representation of the male in order to present a literal body, mercifully freed from its usual symbolic function, but then it constructs a narrative about female desire which can only be fulfilled by the penis."[35] Lehman is right to point out that Sada's sexual desire is totally focused on Kichi's penis, therefore undermining the film's attack on the symbolic by placing *Senses* back in the phallocentric order.

Maureen Turim, in "Signs of Sexuality in Oshima's Tales of Passion," goes even further by focusing not on the portrayal of the look, as Heath does, but on the portrayal of the object of the look—the representation of sex and violence. Turim locates the narrative of the film in its series of role reversals. First, after the scuffle in the kitchen, in which we are given a vital glimpse of Sada's inclination toward aggression and violence, Kichi firmly grabs Sada's chin and forces her to meet his look. The relationship is initiated by an act of male desire and dominance that is reinforced by the first sexual encounters in which Sada is passive. By the middle of the film, however, Sada has become the aggressive female whose constant demand for sexual arousal, combined with her violent behavior (threatening Kichi with a pair of scissors, making love with a knife in her mouth), positions her as the traditional male. Turim, like Lehman, warns that this reversal, which culminates in the final castration scene, should not be seen as an affirmation of women's sexuality. Heath's, Lehman's, and Turim's readings are rich, close analyses that do much to explain why, as Turim puts it, the film is "at once so terrifying and fascinating."[36] Yet what seems to be underdeveloped in all three readings is how *Senses* functions within its historical context of production and circulation in both the West and Japan. It is at this point that Oshima's gestures to the "outside" are crucial. Unlike these critical readings, in which the focus is on the "inside" both physically (the rooms where Sada and Kichi make love) and psychologically (inside the heads of the characters and of Oshima), my move is to emphasize the film's relation to the social collective. How can the question of what makes *Senses* so terrifying and fascinating be addressed without inquiring into the Japan of 1976? That is, what does *Senses* mean in relation to questions of history, economic development, and nationalism in postwar Japan?[37] How did this film figure in Japan? How did it anticipate the historical transformation to globalization (that by 1976 has already turned the corner)? And how did it refer to what I have called the pornographic aesthetic? To pursue these questions, we must first examine the issue of censorship, which is central to the film and its Japanese reception.

Outside the Realm of the Pornographic

I really want to see it.
You can't see it unless you go to France?
When will we be able to see it in Japan?
I guess we won't be able to see the vital parts of it in Japan.
Can some special arrangement be made so we can see it?
Please let us see it.[38]

So went a conversation that Oshima narrated to his wife about the ban on showing *Senses* in its entirety in Japan. (Until the mid-1990s, Article 175 of the Japanese Penal Code prohibited the exposure of genitalia and pubic hair in cultural artifacts.) This restriction forced Oshima, who shot the film in Japan, to rush the dailies to France for editing. The film did play in Japan during its release, however, with scenes showing the genitalia "clouded" by government censors (a sort of technological figleaf and a law that, ironically, was inspired by the Americans during the U.S. occupation). In addition, a book containing the script and stills of the film was distributed throughout the country and sold wildly. Ironically, it was the book that came under attack by the censors and brought Oshima to court in February 1978 to give widely publicized testimony defending the book and film. At one point in his speech, Oshima noted that one out of every four Japanese who traveled to France—about 70,000 or 80,000—had seen *Senses*.[39] For Oshima, showing something that is forbidden (or merely giving the pretense of doing so) is precisely what pornography is. In other words, the essence of pornography is that it makes people think that they will be shown something, "it makes them think there is something there."[40] *Senses*, according to Oshima's definition of pornography, becomes the perfect pornographic film in Japan precisely because it cannot be seen there: "Its existence is pornographic—regardless of its content."[41]

If one pushes Oshima's definition of pornography further, one can see that it is the images of everyday consumer society (the ones about which Imamura had warned only ten years earlier)—such as television, advertising, urban signage, and so on—that had become pornographic by the mid-1970s.

As Oshima reminds us about his film, "Once it is seen [uncensored], *Senses* is no longer pornographic."[42] *Senses* loses its pornographic attraction when it is uncensored, yet it is precisely those seemingly benign consumer images that do the most significant pornographic work: They offer a promise that you can enjoy the products without being implicated in their relations of production. Here, pornography is opposed to everyday consumer images, which attain their legitimacy, their sanction, by *not* being pornography. Yet, as in any supplementary relationship, the existence of these images depends on pornography for its positive valence.

It is precisely to this new way of posing the problem of pornography, by which the categories are inverted, that *Senses* draws our attention. It must be stressed, however, that I am not suggesting pornography's inherent radicalness.[43] Rather, I am arguing for the radicalness of Oshima's film precisely because he is not a pornographic filmmaker and because he does not enter *Senses* into the pornographic economy. What is most important about the film is that Oshima coordinates it with a historical moment in which the circulation of the image, just like the circulation of commodities, is penetrating the globe as it has at no other time in history. Oshima had the film financed by Anatole Dauman, an independent producer who worked on films by, among others, Jean-Luc Godard, Alain Resnais, and Chris Marker. Only with the flexibility provided by Dauman, and with the confidence that *Senses* would find markets abroad, did Oshima decide to make the film and thereby challenges Japan's censorship laws. Given the global business environment, with its new methods of flexible production and circulation, it is no coincidence that Oshima's strategy is similar to the methods employed by a growing number of corporations that change identities and addresses to suit their needs, raise capital from any possible source, and circumvent national regulations by whatever means necessary.

Senses desperately wants to be pornography, just as it desperately wants to question what pornography is and how the pornographic functions. There are no codes to be interpreted in *Senses*, no critical faculties to be honed; instead, the film fills the gap between what it is about and what it is. It is pornography as well as a feature film; but it is also a feature film as well as a documentary. Discussions of *Senses* in Japan have seldom turned on the narrative of sexuality and fascism that took place in the 1930s; they have almost always been consumed with questions about how the actors and Oshima managed to make the film in 1976. Thus, *Senses* documents what it was like for a famous director to shoot a porn film. Most Japanese knew while viewing the film that Matsuda Eiko, who played Sada, was celebrated for being a "Pink Queen" of Japan, and that the actor who played Kichi, Fuji Tatsuya, was a famous mainstream actor with a "normal" family life. Oshima commented on the importance of having the well-known Fuji in the film: "It is significant because the taboos surrounding sexual intercourse that derive from the sacralization of the monogamy system were thereby broken."[44] Fuji's role in the film takes the spectator outside the narrative and into issues regarding how having sex on the set might affect his family life or his later career. Indeed, Fuji and Matsuda are "really doing it," and just as we will see with Hara's filming of Okuzaki in *Naked Army*, we are forced to look at these images and think about what it means to be filming them.

But the most important link between *Senses* and *Naked Army* has to do with spectacle. Oshima knows in advance that his film will be controversial and a cause for debate in Japan (as well as in the United States, where it was banned at the 1976 New York Film Festival). *Senses* does not become a spectacle only because of its ensuing controversy; it is openly produced as a spectacle at a time in Japanese history in which the total occupation of the commodity has finally arrived and the political struggles of the 1960s and the fascism of the 1930s are quickly being forgotten. This is where those subtle "outside" scenes that gesture to the politics of the 1930s, such as Kichi walking in the opposite direction of the military parade, take on heightened significance. No matter how total the commodity becomes, and no matter how successfully we are disciplined to stare into the eye of the spectacle, history remains and can never be totally obliterated. But what the censors managed to do with their "clouds" was direct attention to the sexual, thus diverting attention from the historical that Oshima wanted to sneak in.

This leads, finally, to the link between this issue of censorship and Imamura's *The Pornographers*—in particular, to the pornographic aesthetic that monopolizes the mise-en-scène with bodies. The censor's markings in so many of the shots in *Senses* serve to direct attention to what is behind them; thus, the relations *inside the frame* are essentially cut out (such as the exquisite juxtaposition of color and the meticulous compositions that de-center Sada and Kichi's sex by foregrounding a knife, food, or the ubiquitous voyeur) (fig. 42). Perhaps even more important, the relations *outside the frame* are cut

42. Oshima Nagisa's *In the Realm of the Senses*, with censors' mosaic. Oshima Productions, 1976.

out, as well (such as fascism in the 1930s and the important economic transformations occurring in the 1970s). What the censors attempted to cover in 1976, therefore, were (1) the inability to come to terms with the earlier period of Japanese colonialism; (2) the inability to challenge the reconsolidation of power that emerged only a few years after the U.S. occupation and that remains to the present; and (3) the logic of capitalism that now recuperates the past in the form of spectacle in order to manage its own contradictions.

Oshima knew that *Senses* would begin a debate about censorship in Japan, and he correctly anticipated the moment in which the censorship laws would be reformed and the film would be shown uncensored. In 1996, the ban was finally lifted, and *Senses*, on its twenty-year anniversary, was screened unclouded. After an uncensored screening in Kyoto, a man rose from the audience to make a comment: He had viewed *Senses* for the first time in 1976, and he remembered it as much more erotic and sexual.[45] The reason for this, no doubt, is that the censored and uncensored versions are really two different films, and the uncensored version can never fulfill the expectations that the censored version produced. After the man's comment, which was met by similar comments and confessions, the discussion turned to Japanese fascism during the 1930s, then to the state of Japanese film (and society in general) in the 1990s. What emerged when the censorship was finally lifted was not the sexual, but the historical. What was unspeakable at the time of Imamura's and Oshima's films in the 1960s and '70s had, by the second half of the 1990s, found its voice.

Indeed, there does seem to be a recent easing of the self-disciplined ban to speak about history and past events of Japanese modernity. Conversations about school textbooks and the comfort-women issue stand as two examples. But in this moment, as this history is being addressed (however

194   The Flash of Capital

negligibly) and as *Senses* is being screened uncut, drawing attention back to the historical and away from the sexual, a different history, globalization, is being repressed. So I will now turn to another film of history—a film that flashes the totality of this emerging history: Hara Kazuo's *The Emperor's Naked Army Marches On.*

Toward the Accident: Transformative Narration, Reality Culture, DocuPornography

As we recall from chapter 3, *Naked Army* narrates Okuzaki Kenzo's relentless search to find the truth about a murder that was committed in New Guinea on August 23, 1945. The film opens with Okuzaki raising the garage door of his used-battery shop in an early morning in Kobe. Covering the garage and the building immediately above it, in various colors and sizes, are painted sentences by political positions and moral injunctions. ("We must be able to respect every person's life equally," reads the first sentence.) In larger letters than the rest is written, "The Death Penalty for Former Prime Minister Tanaka." After we see Okuzaki raise the shutter, the first two titles are presented: Okuzaki Kenzo, age sixty-two, then Okuzaki Shizumi (his wife), age sixty-four. Then there is a jump-cut to a procession of cars, with Okuzaki's truck, equipped with loudspeaker and banners of text, leading the way to a wedding. Okuzaki is chosen as the go-between (*baishyaku-nin*) for a marriage of two acquaintances who have "fought the establishment." With him as the official go-between, Okuzaki gives the required speech at the reception, in which, after briefly introducing the bride and groom, he introduces himself: "I am the Okuzaki Kenzo who killed a real-estate broker, fired a pachinko pellet at Emperor Hirohito outside the Imperial Palace, and distributed pornographic handbills of the emperor outside department stores in the Ginza, Shibuya, and Shinjuku."[46]

One of the most striking scenes in the film comes when Okuzaki attacks former Sergeant Yamada for refusing to apologize for his actions during and after the war. Okuzaki blames Yamada's illness and his recent need for bone-marrow surgery on his refusal to repent for the crimes he committed during the war. "It is divine provenance (*tenbatsu*) that you should be ill," Okuzaki says, with satisfaction, while rebuking Yamada. Pathetically weak, with drops of mucus running out of his nose and with blankets covering his frail body, Yamada refuses to say the right things. Okuzaki then unexpectedly jumps him, pins him to the ground, and beats him with his fist. This is the scene for which Hara has received the most criticism of his own role as provocateur, and by questioning it I intend to open the discussion of documentary and its connection to the most recent transformations in pornography.

Several contributors to the collection of essays *Gunron, Yukiyukite shingun* (The emperor's naked army marches on: Opinions) comment on the implications of this scene.[47] For example, the literary critic Kuroko Kazuo is so taken with Okuzaki's power and ability to guide the film that he asks, "I am thoroughly confused as to who is making this film: Is it Okuzaki Kenzo or is it Hara Kazuo?"[48] *Naked Army*'s ambiguous method of drawing attention to who is speaking and in control confounds Kuroko to the point that he begins (however naively) to wonder whether the film is a documentary or, in his words, a "drama." Later in the same piece, after commenting on Okuzaki's constant awareness of his position as the main character, Kuroko wonders whether Okuzaki, even during the fight scene with Yamada, is not always in complete control of the film's aesthetic choices. He writes, "I am not able to satisfactorily sense the director's subjectivity; instead, from beginning to end I am overwhelmed by Okuzaki's performance and control."[49]

In his own article in the collection, Hara also focuses on this controversial scene. Hara begins by explaining that, immediately following a private screening of *Naked Army*, a friend inquired about the technique of performing the roles of both camera operator and director: "Didn't this method limit the way you could deal with the fight scene [between Okuzaki and Yamada], since on the one hand you wanted to let the camera continue rolling, while on the other hand you wanted to stop the violence?"[50] In thinking about this question, Hara returned to one of his earlier films, *Goku shiteki erosu-renka 1974* (Very private eros: Love song 1974). In that film, Hara—from behind his camera—follows his former lover to Okinawa in order to come to terms with his jealousy regarding her desire to separate from him. After returning to Tokyo, Hara films the former lover in a cramped Tokyo apartment giving birth—by herself—to a baby she intentionally conceived with a U.S. military serviceman. Hara explains that the nature of that film forced him to draw attention to the apparatus of the camera and how it structured his position vis-à-vis his former lover. The act of filming and the act of being filmed (*toru watakushi to, torareru watakushi to*) cannot be separated for Hara. "The camera is like a double-edged sword [*moroha no tsurugi*], and when holding it I am simultaneously shooting (or cutting) the person in front of it as well as myself," Hara writes.[51] He goes on to explain that there was no choice but to take on the roles of both camera operator and director. Given the nature of his films, in which he is quite aware of his own role as a character—as a former lover in *Eros* and as provocateur in *Naked Army*—to take the risk of being on the other side of the camera is the only way to take responsibility for the changes the narration might cause. Hara is aware that the process of making a film changes the film itself. He is also acutely aware of how the spectatorial desire to see what he is filming (a murder in *Naked Army*, a live self-birthing in *Eros*, a man with cerebral palsy interrogating onlookers on a crowded Tokyo street in *Sayonara CP*, a man's death in *Zenshin shosetsu-ka*) inspires the filmmaking process that then transforms the very event itself.

Thus, *Naked Army* foregrounds the role of film as being not only interpretive but also transformative, a function that I will call "transformative narration."[52] One could say that *Naked Army* reveals how spectacle is produced during a transnational moment. "The spectacle is the moment when the commodity has attained the total occupation of social life. Not only is the relation to the commodity visible but it is all one sees: the world one sees is its world," writes Guy Debord.[53] Like money, the spectacle in global capitalism becomes the general equivalent "for what the entire society can be and can do."[54] Hara confronts head-on the problem of how to produce anything within this new situation—how to represent the spectacle of Okuzaki vis-à-vis the spectacle of filmmaking; how to escape the spectacle by means of the spectacle. Like all commodities, film, in order to persist, must not only continually find and record new markets (or spectacles); it must also actively produce these markets, these spectacles. This is not to go so far as to say that film and video producers create wars in order to film them, but it should not prevent us from recognizing that there is more than a mere one-dimensional movement from the event to the representation.

Just as a commodity not only meets needs but also participates in the creation of such needs, so, too, do film and television participate in the creation of their object of study. This nonlinear temporality of the event and the representation, in which the two moments dynamically relate so that one does not necessarily come before the other, is always at work. But I do want to historicize this category of transformative narration and suggest that a qualitative difference exists in the way it operates and functions in the age of global capitalism. Hara's nonfiction film form and overt gestures to transformative narration are exactly where many films of the 1960s and 1970s, including Imamura's *The Pornographers* and Oshima's *In The Realm of the Senses,* were heading. But certain conditions had to come into being first. The socioeconomic situation had to shift and information and telecommunication technology had to arrive to allow the country—and world—to be wired with real-time video in schools, banks, and city streets; with live feeds from the nose of missiles and the sleeves of soldiers; and with countless camcorders locked on record mode and other surveillance devices. The possibility had to exist for a type of global accident (as Paul Virilio calls it) in which an event could occur simultaneously in different places, such as a cyber-virus or the so-called Year 2000 (Y2K) problem. Only after these factors become thinkable as dystopia for some—and utopia for others—could a form such as reality culture thrive.[55]

Hara is a self-labeled guerrilla filmmaker who scoffs at what he calls the bourgeois notion of privacy.[56] As we have learned, Hara is very much an actor in his films, as he can often be heard asking questions and provoking situations. In a certain way, Hara represents the leftist version of the emerging phenomenon of reality culture.[57] At the heart of reality culture is the possibility that the unexpected can occur and hijack the show from its usual course (which, of course, is about anticipating the hijack in the first place). For example, in the television show *Ikebukuro: 24 Hours,* cops are shown walking down a street and suddenly spotting adolescents buying amphetamines. The chase begins. The cameraman and commentator follow close behind. Of course, the viewer also is there. No doubt, the viewer realizes that the show is not live, but being live is not the point. Rather, the point is to open the possibility to catch something real and accidental. Although such a show is similar to a traditional news broadcast, the difference lies in the idea that one is supposed to be catching sight of a spontaneous act. For the regular news, the spectacle occurs, then the network sends a crew to conduct the banal job of recording it. In this type of reality culture, by contrast, the crew is already recording the banality of everyday life when the spectacle interrupts—or, at least, that is how both forms sell themselves.

Another example can be seen in recent quiz programs. One show in Japan's Kansai region turns on the classic theme of performing a task in a limited timeframe. In one episode, a four-year-old child stands on a stage in front of a crowded studio audience. Behind the child is a larger clock that ticks down thirty seconds. The child's mother is spotted in the audience. A person dressed as a ninja then appears and pretends to attack the child's mother. The challenge is to see whether the child will start crying before the thirty-second time limit expires. After showing this segment, the network was overwhelmed with complaints and soon cut it from the program. For many, this "game" went over the top, spawning a brief debate about child psychology and trauma. The power of the show lies in the fact that the viewer is enthralled by what might happen. We hold our breath waiting to see whether the child will turn to hysterics. It is spellbinding. The moment of truth is also the moment of a certain utopia, however cruel, because the moment comes off as truly unpredictable. It is an event that presents to the viewer a temporary interruption of everyday life's seeming progression, from present that becomes future; from past that was present. The instant of unpredictability is a mix of past–present–future; it contains all three moments in a single instant.

This moment of chance, of open possibility, of a breaking point is precisely what Hara wants to exploit in his experimental documentaries. It is a move from suspense to surprise.[58] His film is double-sided: It is real and virtual at the same time.[59] What it might become and what it is are not cordoned off from each other but entangled at the same instant so that cause-and-effect explanations are shattered. It is not simply that Okuzaki's desire to murder causes our fascination; nor is it simply that our fascination causes Okuzaki's desire to kill. Rather, there is an interrelation between the real and the virtual; the past, present, and future; the image and the thing; the event and the representation. And with the technology enabled by global capitalism, this interrelation has been cranked up to a hitherto impossible dimension. Catching this moment of possibility, for Hara, is a thoroughly political act. He wants to enter this moment to flash the openness of the Japanese social totality, to break through the limitations of contemporary Japanese society.

But just as Hara recognizes that this moment of unpredictability is politically ripe, so, too, does he seem to recognize its dystopian dimension. An aesthetic such as reality culture is mesmerizing and just another strategy to keep people glued to their television sets and to reproduce the structure that Hara wants to dismantle. The narrative conventions of television, broadcast news, variety shows, and quiz shows are in crisis; their appeal has weakened. At crisis moments such as this, there is always a qualitative leap in formal strategies. The move from black-and-white to color television and from the sedate and serious reporting of the news to a more stimulated and irreverent style are examples of this attempt at recuperation. Reality culture is just such an attempt to recuperate the current cultural crisis. And the most profound expression of reality culture can be seen in the recent mutation in the adult-video industry—that is, in adult-video documentary, or Docupornography. Approximately seventy-five percent of current adult-video films in Japan are documentary-style—that is, their narratives are not couched in fiction (if we are still to invest these terms with their traditional meanings). They are films in which a man—presumably the filmmaker—walks the streets searching for women. Unlike the earlier modes of adult video and the dominant type in the West, in which there is, however flimsy, a narrative fiction on which to hang the sex, this new genre of Japanese adult video is the nonfictional account of a man asking for sex. Many women shy away, but there are regularly some (however fabricated) who respond. For the viewer, the setup of the sex is just as important as the sex itself, and it is just as erotic. It is the idea of the amateur, the person that anyone, no matter how shy or socially inept, could have. The more ordinary, the more erotic. One of these films opens in an airplane over the Pacific with a man explaining that he is going to South America and the United States to find women to be in his film. He arrives first in São Paulo and encounters a nineteen-year-old mark. They go to a park to talk about life in Brazil and Japan in broken Japanese, Spanish, English, and Portuguese. At one point, the man asks the girl why she wants to be in the film. She candidly refers to her poverty and how desperately she needs the money. She adds, "The money I will make from working in this one film is more than I earn in a month working as a maid." She finishes by saying "Japan is a rich country, and this might lead to more opportunities in the future." Throughout the conversation, the man is nodding in agreement tinged with sympathy.

The two proceed to an apartment, where the soon-to-be sex partner cooks dinner as the conversation about Brazil and Japan continues. After eating dinner and washing the dishes, they move to a bedroom, where the man sets a camera on a tripod before the two have automatic and stereotypical sex. Next the man is off to Los Angeles, where he loiters around the University of California, Los Angeles, campus asking women who happen to pass by to show him their underwear. His English is barely comprehensible, and the

43. Isaka Satoshi's *Focus.* Seiyo
Productions, 1977.

women seem confused at first; then they turn hostile and warn him to get lost or else. This is not Tokyo. Neither is it as fortuitous as the São Paolo segment. The man finds one woman who is intrigued and who follows him back to a house he is temporarily renting in the Hollywood hills. When he asks her how much she wants to take off her clothes, she becomes terrified and quickly leaves. Contritely bowing to the camera as if apologizing to the viewers for his ineptitude, the man promises one final escapade. After some cagey bargaining by an interested woman, the film ends with an extended sex scene back at the house.

When we move to Isaka Satoshi's 1996 *Focus,* its similarities to and differences from Hara's films and this new genre of Japanese pornography become quite stunning. But before discussing these connections we must first compare *Focus* with Imamura's *The Pornographers,* for, like Imamura, Isaka also employs a film-within-a-film narrative. But instead of stressing the relation between the 35 millimeter and eight millimeter formats (feature film and blue film, respectively), Isaka stresses the relation between 35 millimeter and video (feature film and television, respectively). *Focus* begins with a carefully composed scene of a Sony videocamera. The shots linger and eroticize the camera, not unlike the way in which a film might enticingly introduce its main actor. Delicately moving around the videocamera, the film camera then zooms in on the video's viewfinder until we see through it and focus on the dubious TV director (Iwai) interacting with Kanemura, the young eavesdropper (fig. 43). The video frame is then inside the feature-film frame, and we see both at the same time. Soon the film's main title appears, and, not unlike in *The Pornographers,* the title is for both the video inside the film and the film itself. The rest of the film is then represented as shot through

Totality, Reality, History   **201**

the videocamera, complete with the harder video image and all of the requisite lights indicating low battery, record mode, and so forth on the sides of the frame. After Kanemura is shot dead at the end of the film, the battery apparently goes dead, and an abrupt cut to black signals the film/video's end.

The decision to remain in video for the whole film and not to return to the feature-film frame is significant because it marks the coming into being of the precise situation Imamura predicted. The critical distance at the center of Imamura's 1966 film, which allows him to wink at us as he calls his high-modernist film pornographic, is collapsed under this transformed situation thirty-five years later. Isaka's film is not a clever film about reality culture; it is, as his critics noted after the film's premier, reality culture itself.

Halfway through *Focus*, the young eavesdropper Kanemura, the director, the camera operator, and the production assistant park on a dark side street to look at a gun they have just found. The director wants to film Kanemura as he views the gun for the first time. Disappointed with Kanemura's rather un-dramatic reaction, the director shoots the scene twice more, until Kanemura can properly act excited. But at some point, a pair of curious skateboarders approach the car and are madly impressed that an actual television show is being produced. They are agog and disruptive, and the director orders them to get lost. A fight ensues, and Kanemura ends up shooting the two boys with the gun. Flustered and no longer content with taking direction from the di-rector, Kanemura turns the tables and takes the three hostage. Once they re-turn to his apartment, Kanemura gives the directions (for how they will deal with the murders and for what and how everything will be filmed). Kane-mura forces the director and the female production assistant to have sex in front of the camera so that the pornographic footage can be used to guaran-tee the film crew's silence. After the scene, Kanemura, rather disgusted at the reality of porn, turns to the cameraman and asks why adult video is so popular. "Because people want to see," the cameraman quickly responds as if answering the question about the reality culture documentary that they have been making all along.

In *The Pornographers*, Imamura anticipated the corporatization of the pornography industry and exposed the vulnerability to this trend of his own film practice. In *Senses*, Oshima anticipated how the censorship of his film would draw attention away from significant past and present historical de-tails. And Hara's *Naked Army* anticipated this new type of pornographic aesthetic in which the viewer watches an event unfold in a presumably spontaneous and unpremeditated way. But what Imamura, Oshima, and Hara were flashing for us is that this new type of reality documentary, reality culture, and DocuPornography is not limited to experimental film, shoddy news and quiz shows, or adult video. Rather, they argue through the very form of their films that the pornographic impulse of reality culture is shaping all culture. All three directors highlight the desire for openness and for a spontaneous eruption of the unexpected, but they do so by stressing its simultaneous utopian and dystopian dimensions. This prescient insight is precisely why I label these films "films of history"—films that search for an aesthetic language to flash the most crucial social transformations of contemporary Japan.

The pornographic–non-pornographic binary may no longer be as functional as it once was—in fact, the pornographic may be evenly spread throughout contemporary Japanese culture. What, then, might this mean for politics and political resistance? It is here that a return to the issue of totality is in order. If there is a penchant in Japan to sense the totality, then it is a totality that is closed, one that is thoroughly predictable and capable of being overturned only in one fell swoop. It is a sensibility, however accurate, that militates against reformism and cultivates acquiescence in the current situation. In the United States, and to a lesser extent in Canada, the general refusal (inability) to grasp the totality, to follow the threads (however frayed) that tie the system together, produces a political consciousness that is confined within the latest political issue, military strike, or scandal. The structural dynamic is very rarely grasped. But what this allows is a belief in reformism, a belief that this or that reform might make things right. If the United States is reformist with no sense of the totality, then Japan is totalizing with no sense of reform. What both dominant ideologies share, however, is an aversion to significant social change. The formal experiments of the films mentioned here attempt to thread this needle, to recognize the connectedness of all things without allowing this recognition to stand in the way of attempts to change society (no matter how reformist this impulse might be). They anticipate the current cultural moment in Japan—to split it open in the face of so much reality culture that has had to be invented in order to suture it.

VI. rereading

Canon, Body, Geopolitics

When Manny Farber's *Negative Space* was republished in 1998, the renowned film critic answered questions from a small bookstore audience.[1] In the pages of the journals the *Nation* and *Artforum* during the 1950s and '60s, Farber often extolled the work of Godard, Fassbinder, and Fuller. Farber wrote full-throatedly, coining phrases and cracking open clichés. His lateral criticism and go-for-broke style is entirely lost on today's popular critics; he would perform on the level of his termite sentences precisely what he was celebrating or berating in the films themselves.[2] Halfway through the casual bookstore discussion, the infamous question came: "Why haven't you ever made film?" Farber breezily ignored the question and went on to the next one. He then hesitated and, in what surely seemed a concession, explained himself. He said he always received that question and always disregarded it in the same cutting way. At bottom, Farber explained, the question is a blind-side slap at criticism. It assumes that criticism itself is not an art; that it does not require the same creativity, attention to detail, dramatic impulse, and courage. The question, for Farber, is symptomatic of one of the great assumptions about criticism: that the critic—first and foremost—serves the artist and the artwork (or in its more dramatic form that the critic is parasitical to the artist and the artwork). For Farber the most appropriate way to respect an artist and to comment on the meaning of his or her work is to generate your own ideas and inspirations from it. This chapter stresses why seemingly luxurious readings, ones that refuse to be hemmed in by the text or the author/director, ones that push the text into places it never intended to go, are legitimate and desirable. For without rethinking what criticism is and does, without venturing off the beaten track of criticism, without questioning the ideological effects of reading that critics and spectators produce, we smother the gift of art—the gift that flashes a path to the impossible.

It is in service to this gift that I will now reread some of the most famous works in the canon of Japanese cinema. Mizoguchi, Kinugasa Teinosuke, Ozu, Kurosawa, Tsukamoto Shinya, Oshii Mamoru—the names are familiar. Attached to each canonical name is perhaps a more familiar tag: "Painterly Composition," "Avant-Garde," "Formal Precision," "Humanism," "Cyberpunk," "Anime." These taglines are not wrong; indeed, persuasive arguments are made for why they fit. Instead of working through how such tags emerged (say, such tired ones as Ozu is the most Japanese filmmaker and Kurosawa is the most Western), the task is to perform alternative readings of six of these directors' most canonical films. They are read as both great works of the creative imagination and products of the three sociological problems identified throughout this work: colonialism, the Cold War, and globalization. Kinugasa's *Page of Madness*, Mizoguchi's *Sisters of the Gion*, Ozu's *Late Spring*, Kurosawa's *Rashomon*, Tsukamoto's *Tetsuo*, and Ishii's *Ghost in the Shell* make up the list; the last two films are included because of their canonical status in the cyberpunk and animation genres, respectively. First, however, I will discuss the stakes of reading by turning to two recent attempts that connect to the methods I employ in this chapter and throughout the book.

Reading Exercises In "Death, Empire and the Search for History in Natsume Soseki's *Kokoro*," Jim Fujii examines the canonization of modern Japanese literature's most popular work. *Kokoro* is invariably read as the great prose narrative of man's loneliness in the modern world. Taking place at the transition from the Meiji to the Taisho period (1912), the work narrates the relationship between a university student (the "I" for the first two parts of the shosetsu) and a middle-aged man (sensei) who meet one day on Kamakura beach. Following the Meiji emperor's death and the ritual suicide (*junshi*) by General Nogi, Sensei kills himself after writing an extended suicide note to the student. *Kokoro* is presented in three sections. The first two are narrated by the student, and the third consists solely of the suicide note. Fujii marvels at how the very context that gave rise to *Kokoro* in the first place— modernity and territorial expansion—is obscured by Soseki and consistently absent from the more than three hundred Japanese studies of the shosetsu, an absence that is even more remarkable given that *Kokoro*'s serialization (110 installments in the *Asahi* newspaper from April 20 to August 11, 1914) shared space with news articles that referred directly to Japanese foreign policy. Yet it is precisely this absence, according to Fujii, that serves as a requirement for *Kokoro*'s canonization.

There are two things at work in Fujii's provocative reading that need to be distinguished. First, there is Soseki and the text itself, which, Fujii argues, "refuses or is unable to address the imperialist dimensions of Japanese modernity"; and second, there are the countless critical readings over the next eighty-five years that reperform this refusal or inability.[3] But "refusal" and "inability" are two very different motivations that, first, turn on the knotty category of artistic agency and self-consciousness; and second, require historicization. For example, what for Soseki might be an inability resulting from certain discursive limits in 1914 might very well be a refusal for a critic writing four or five decades later.[4] But Soseki's inability or refusal to confront colonialism directly is offset for Fujii by the narrative strategies of *Kokoro*, a certain "ambivalence" and "indeterminacy" on the formal level that does indeed gesture to modernity's colonial logic. For instance, the shosetsu opens with the student spying sensei for the first time as he swims with a conspicuous Westerner. If not for the Westerner, the student would not have noticed sensei; their relationship would not have formed; and *Kokoro* would not have been written. But the indispensable foreigner is then mysteriously cut out of the shosetsu and never mentioned again. This absence is repeated in the relationship between the student and sensei, which is based on a similar absence of knowledge as to why sensei lives as he does (dispassionately and distantly). For Fujii, *Kokoro*'s greatness is marked by these formal strategies combined with how the work exists ambivalently between high and low literature and how it negotiates an uneasy relationship with the generic dominance of *shizenshugi* (naturalism).

What cannot be represented directly on the level of *Kokoro*'s narrative content is flashed on the level of literary form—for example, sensei accounting for his own psychic state by acknowledging not only his shame toward K (a close friend who had committed suicide partly as a result of Sensei's behavior) but also his contradictory feelings about Japan's colonial presence in Taiwan and Korea. Or to put it another way: What is refused and cannot be expressed on the level of content turns into—for some writers—a desire and ability to express such an impossibility on the aesthetic level. Edward Said makes a similar argument in *Culture and Imperialism* while reading Joseph Conrad's *Heart of Darkness.* Said writes, "For if we cannot truly understand someone else's experience [in this case, that of the African natives] and if we must therefore depend upon the assertive authority of the sort of power that Kurtz wields as a white man in the jungle or that Marlow, another white man, wields as narrator, there is no use looking for other, non-imperialist alternatives; the system has simply eliminated them and made them unthinkable."[5] Despite this inability to think an alternative to imperialism, an alternative to a world carved up into spheres of Western domination, Said argues, Conrad nevertheless desires to break out of this worldview through formal devices: "Conrad's self-consciously circular narrative forms draw attention to themselves as artificial constructions, encouraging us to sense the potential of a reality that seemed inaccessible to imperialism, just beyond its control, and that only well after Conrad's death in 1924 acquired a substantial presence."[6]

Of course, the great difference between *Kokoro* and *Heart of Darkness* is that *Kokoro* takes place in the metropolis and *Heart* in the colonies.[7] But the brilliance of Said's *Culture and Imperialism* is that it reads the canonical literature of the metropolis in the same way—the way in which Jane Austen's *Mansfield Park,* for example, is opened up to questions that exceed the private, domestic issues and unworldliness of the novel's content. Although Austen's work is not a novel about colonialism, like Conrad's, it is most certainly a novel of colonialism, like Soseki's, and warrants such a reading—a reading that connects its stylistics, narrative choices, and assumptions about time and space with the conceptual space of empire.[8] This argument is not unlike Toni Morrison's notion of Africanism, in which even American literature that does not reference African Americans or slavery is still imbued with the African presence and crucial in forming the way whites see themselves and their world.[9] This brings us to the issue of reading itself and to the legitimacy of, and stakes in, allegorizing culture to that which exceeds the confines of the text.[10]

We can already hear the complaints. Doesn't Fujii grant too much importance to the Westerner? Or, why does Said need to push *Mansfield Park* to the other side of the earth? The standard critique of such allegorical readings is that they shortchange the aesthetic; they shoot to soon to the sociopolitical level, thus attending insufficiently to the text itself. They erase the author and the labor involved in producing culture. But in the cases of Fujii and Said, this critique falls flat, given the remarkable detail and sophisticated literary analysis both writers employ. The text is not merely a pretext; it is the indispensable key to rethinking colonialism, and vice versa. In fact, their allegorical methods demand the same formalist attention that is usually reserved for the complainants themselves.[11] The next critique is then wheeled out: Don't they afford too much authorial intention to trivial textual details? For example, how does Fujii know that Soseki's use of the Westerner is a gesture to Japan's colonial project? How does Said know that Conrad's circular narrative is an attempt to overcome his limitations and blindspots to imperialism? In short, where's the proof? It is here that the debate splits into two possible directions. One direction leads toward biography and an appeal to the author's word regarding his or her intentions. This is the moment in which the critic is exposed as a fraud (when Woody Allen's dream about Marshall McLuhan's proving once and for all that the inflated professor is flat wrong comes true), or the critic is revealed as an expert (when he or she raises up the golden ticket, the authentic document attained by the critic's exclusive archival access).[12] The other direction leads toward an alternative theory of reading, one that questions the authority given to the author and text and shifts the focus to the ideological effects of reading itself, to the various forms of reading—including, of course, a self-reflection on the very form used to produce such a critique in the first place. As usual, the directions overlap, but if both Said and Fujii seem to lean toward the latter direction, it is because both have a larger project in mind. For instance, Said wants to stress that an older colonial imagination is still with us today and how this shapes (and is shaped by) dominant readings of any number of contemporary issues, from the Middle East to the most banal views of everyday life.

Reading is a practice. It is not simply about the final argument but about the very process by which the final argument is produced. When we read (a film, a newspaper, ourselves) we exercise our critical faculties, which means that we build intellectual muscle that serves our conceptual needs. The fact that the current state of the world—what just about everyone calls global-ization—seems so hard to get our minds around, and why the most popular stories used to describe it (the congratulatory myth of progress, the apolo-getic myth of a nostalgic past) are so unsatisfying, has less to do with intel-lectual flabbiness than with obstructing muscular habits that dominate our ways of reading. I am arguing for a different exercise regime of critical ac-tivity, one that makes different connections (however adventurous they may seem), one that takes a film and a historical problem and produces their re-lation (however tenuous it seems). For me, this is what it means to theorize. Rather than plug in so much theoretical jargon (so many words and names that stand in for thinking), to theorize means to produce the relation be-tween two seemingly disparate, isolated, and unrelated elements, then to support rigorously how such a relation works and what such a method opens for intellectual and political life in general. Such readings can not only culti-vate the conceptual skills to produce more satisfying ways of understanding modern Japanese history; they can also cultivate the skills needed to nar-rate (and intervene with) more satisfyingly the present world system. This, at least, is the hope of the following six readings.

Kinugasa's Bodies   Readings of Kinugasa's *Page of Madness* (1926) invariably stress the film's surrealism, the dreamlike representation of the sick wife's psychosis. This is a film, as the readings go, that represents subjectivity from the inside out.[13] The diseased interiority of the patient is expressed in terms of cinematic strategies: breakneck montage, crimping, overlays, spinning camera movement, and a certain expressionistic acting that is even more radical given that the film was one of the first to use women to act female roles. Recognized as the first avant-garde masterpiece in Japan, *Page of Mad-ness* exceeds many of the coterminous cinematic experiments of Germany and France.[14] But I will read *Page of Madness* in terms of the representation not of the mind or interiority but of the body—the diseased body, the languid body, the dancing body, the female body.[15] Then I will make the move to the national body and show what this rethinking of the disavowed body (and elevated mind and spirit) will open up for thinking through the problem of colonialism and Japanese modernity in general.[16]

Page of Madness was believed to have been destroyed until Kinugasa himself discovered a print in an old rice barrel in 1970. Known as a famous onnagata star throughout the 1910s, Kinugasa was impressed by the new modernist currents emerging in the early 1920s (especially around the literary work of Yokomitsu Riichi and what became known as the *shinkankaku-ha* [new sensationalist school]). After severing his affiliation with a Kansai actors' association in 1922, Kinugasa focused on directing film—film that would match the intensity and theoretical depth of the literary experiments. Although an onnagata himself, his first order of business was to terminate the role and invite female actors into the film world.

Yokomitsu catapulted onto the literary scene in 1923 with the publication of two short stories, "Hae" (The fly) and "Nichirin" (The sun). In 1925, Kinugasa experimented with transforming these new literary strategies into cinema by adapting "Nichirin" to the screen. Kinugasa asked Yokomitsu to write the script for his next project; Yokomitsu refused but urged Kinugasa to consider Kawabata Yasunari.[17] Kawabata had earned notoriety for his first published story, "Shokonsai ikkei" (A view of the Yasukuni festival), in 1921, a work that shared many of the new sensationalist's formal strategies, such as a folding together of dream and reality and fragmented and cut-up narratives that attempted to express the sensation rather than the nominal surface of the object in question. Kawabata wrote the script for *Page of Madness* in the same year that he wrote *The Izu Dancer*. *Page of Madness* (or *The Crazy Page*, as it is also known) unfolds and refolds (shreds and scatters) the story of a man who does odd jobs at a hospital for the psychotic. The man's wife is one of the hospital's patients (inmates); her mental illness came about partly from watching her child drown (although it is not clear how long after that trauma she was institutionalized). Appalled by his wife's treatment and distrustful of modern psychiatric science, the forlorn man plots a feeble and failed escape.

To focus on *Page of Madness*'s surrealism is to reproduce a number of

44. Kinugasa Teinosuke's *Page of Madness*. Kinugasa Productions, 1926.

assumptions regarding the subject and subject formation. The first assumption is that the body is a product of the interior state. The sick in the mental hospital are physically ill and ugly, listlessly strewn on the floor or staring off vacantly into space. Or they are frantic and feral, pounding violently on walls and shaking prison-like bars. Sexually wild or dumbly docile, their manic physical states are read as effects of their psychological illnesses. In this reading, we have the original trauma producing psychological damage, which then produces physical damage, only to be exacerbated by corrupt state doctors and gratuitous scientific experimentation. Indeed, this is similar to a dominant view of Japanese foreign policy at the time: the original trauma (modernity) produced psychological damage (ultra-nationalist ideology), which then produced physical damage (aggression and imperialism abroad), only to be exacerbated by corrupt state officials and gratuitous scientific experimentation. The grotesque national body is an effect of a sick interiority; the body is constituted through projection as the limit of subjectivity—the "inside" (however abnormal) is privileged.

Kinugasa's film can also be read as disrupting this inside-out view. The emphasis on, and strategies for, shooting the body suggest what might be called an outside-in view in which the psychic is an effect of the body and its inscription by sociocultural practices and institutions.[18] The film is fraught with medium closeups of faces and bodies, not the subjective view of the sick but the detached view of Kinugasa's camera (fig. 44). The languid body is juxtaposed to the dancing and festive body throughout the film. About midway through *Page of Madness*, the husband, staring out a hospital window, notices a parade. The marching musicians and banners trigger a memory (or fantasy) of him at a festival. The atmosphere is raucous, with bands of people yelling, eating, and laughing. The husband acquires a lottery ticket and wins

Canon, Body, Geopolitics   211

45. Kinugasa Teinosuke's *Page of Madness*. Kinugasa Productions, 1926.

the grand prize. By this time, he is howling with delight as those around him physically display their pleasure. The festival is frenzied and precarious (unhierarchical and classless)—it mocks the dogmatism and conventional decorum of everyday life, not to mention the rules and regulations of the mental hospital. From the unrefined dancing to the boisterous laughter, the festival body is free to travel the edge of alterity.

Then there is the dancing of the female patients. After the opening montage sequence, the scene dissolves to a set with a huge spinning ball in front of a costumed woman. The woman is dancing in a modern style, indifferent to structure and stylized precision. The shot is then overlayed with a female patient dancing in her cell. From the festival to the hospital, from the dance stage to the cell, the extended and undisciplined body is being institutionalized just as much as the sick mind. At one point, as a female patient is dancing in her cell, a crowd of male patients come and watch, fighting for position (fig. 45). This long scene undoes the rule of the hospital, as a rebellious and sexual energy is unleashed. What is important here is the representation of sexual difference. For the female patient, it is the desire to dance (a corporeal memory) that, in however distorted a form, persists from her previous life outside the hospital, while for the men, all that persists is a reactionary and violent libidinal response.[19] This is an uneven gendered response to modernity, one that becomes much more apparent when represented by the relatively egoless mentally ill patients. The coming of modernity might very well present all new structural possibilities and limitations for subject formation (that is, modernity produces different forms of making sense of the world vis-à-vis different cultural, political, and economic practices), but different subjects live through these possibilities and limitations in quite different ways. Moreover, residual subjectivities (such as pre-Meiji ones) persist and are crucial in producing such difference. This uneven way in which historical transformation plays itself out in and on the bodies and subjectivities of characters will be developed later, especially when we reach the contemporary moment of how globalization processes and new technology enter the body (and how this is lived differently by male and female characters) in films such as *Tetsuo* and *Ghost in the Shell*. Moreover, the female body as the crucial figure in all six films analyzed in this chapter will be examined again in the Epilogue, in which I will return to the work of Haneda Sumiko and how her representations of the female body relate to the six male directors studied in this chapter. But first, to return to Kinugasa's film, at a moment in which this complex dialectic of subject formation is being ignored, *Page of Madness* reemphasizes it, and it does so not only within the confined space of the mental hospital but also within the larger space of the Japanese film industry.

For example, female actors performing female roles, as mentioned earlier, is not the only issue. One can also examine how this film relates to the benshi system. By 1926, the year in which the film was made, the benshi system had come under siege. New licensing practices and regulations were being prescribed, and Japanese film seemed to be heading in two directions: (1) toward the new talkie as modeled on classical Hollywood cinema (continuity editing, centering of plot and dialogue, and, in Japan's case [as discussed in chapter 4], an emphasis on "faithfully" adapting *jun-bungaku* [pure literature]); or (2) a reactionary defense of the benshi system that had more to do with anti-Westernism for the purpose of defending the vocational positions of the benshi than with experimenting with their great possibilities. *Page of Madness* breaks a new path. First, it is a criticism of the benshi system insofar as its very aesthetic strategies close off the possibility for a benshi to participate properly. In other words, the speed of the film, its nonlinear narrative, and the sheer complexity of the plot make providing real-time commentary nearly impossible. Second, it is far away from the classical Hollywood cinematic strategies that will soon be employed throughout the film industry. Third, although it does gesture to both German Expressionism and French Impressionism, it does so in a way that is not uncritical—as seen, for example, in the film's searing criticism of Western medicine and psychiatry. However much the film might be understood as thoroughly dystopian on the level of narrative content (the wife cannot conceptualize what the very idea of escape means, and by the film's last shot, the husband is mopping the hospital floors, reinforcing the very institution he wants to destroy), on the level of film form *Page of Madness* is one of the more utopian works of the late Taisho and early Showa moment. By cracking open (in terms of film art and the Japanese film industry) new possibilities in the face of impossibility, *Page of Madness* rehearses in an aesthetic register a solution to the historical problem of colonialism.

This takes us to how the film can be placed in relation to the philosophical and geopolitical trends of the late Taisho and early Showa moment. As the Western colonial powers returned to their Asian markets following World War I, Japan's first great economic miracle (which was based on entrance into these very markets) came to a sudden halt. Old vulnerabilities and fears of Western influence and power returned with a vengeance. Although the underlying impulse of the Meiji Restoration was to build a strong modern state in order to fend off the encroaching West, it was always assumed that, when the country was properly modernized, a return to a Japanese "essence" (and the expulsion of the no-longer-useful West) would occur. Kindled by an intellectual genre praising Japan's uniqueness and premodern tradition, this nativist return was in full force by the mid-1920s. There are, for example, Watsuji Tetsuro's "Studies in the History of Japanese Spirit" (Nihon seishin-shi kenkyu, 1926), Naito Torajiro's "Studies on the Cultural History of Japan" (Nihon bunkashi kenkyu, 1924), Abe Jiro's "Studies in Arts and Crafts of the Tokugawa Period" (Tokugawa jidai ni okeru geijutsu no kenkyu, 1928) and Kuki Shuzo's "The Structure of Tokugawa Aesthetic Style" (Ii no kozo, 1929). At bottom, these works invoked a unique Japanese interiority (spirit) in need of reawakening in order to ward off the polluting effects of Western materialism.[20]

We can now return to the two dominant readings of the film. The first, which emphasizes the film's surrealism and powerful portrayal of the sick wife's subjectivity, is a statement about Japan's militarist project—a bad interiority produces a violent exteriority. But Japan's militarist project was not only about bad seeds that bloomed violently; it was just as profoundly about an exteriority (world system) that shaped a violent interiority (a bloomed world system that planted the seeds of Japanese colonialism). It is this second reading that I will highlight here, one that places the trauma of modernity in relation to an exteriority (the world system) that produces an ultra-nationalist interiority. At stake here is how the war and Japanese modern history is narrated. When the first line of analysis is stressed, the narrative of Japanese modernity remains within the borders of the four islands and of the Fifteen Year War (1931–45). When the second line of analysis is stressed, the narrative of Japanese modernity exceeds these limited geographical and historical borders and becomes inextricably linked to the world and to a stretch of time that began well before the Manchurian Incident. In short, this second reading, this rereading of *Page of Madness*, stresses how the war and the Japanese colonial project are linked to the very logic of modernization itself.

Mizoguchi and Colonialism Kinugasa went on to marry the main actress (Yamada Isuzu) in the next film on our list, Mizoguchi Kenji's *Sisters of the Gion* (Gion no shimai), made in 1936. The film tells the story of Omocha and Umekichi, two sisters working in the gay quarter of Kyoto. The younger sister, Omocha, possesses a modern education and a feminist sensibility that expresses itself as a radical critique of men and the geisha system. Because men treat us like toys, Omocha reasons, they deserve to be deceived. Umekichi, the older sister, understands quite well what Omocha is saying but still believes that she has an obligation to the patrons in her life. Furusawa is one of these patrons, but, having gone bankrupt, he is now hanging on with Umekichi and Omocha. Omocha plots to send Furusawa away and persuades Umekichi to take on a wealthier patron, a shifty curio dealer named Jurakudo. Omocha convinces a young kimono salesman, Kimura, to embezzle expensive silk so that Umekichi can properly court Jurakudo. After Kimura's boss, Kudo, discovers the theft, he angrily engages Kimura and then Omocha. Omocha sweetens up to Kudo, and, in one of four breathless seduction scenes, softens Kudo and becomes his mistress. The duty-bound Umekichi still wants to be with Furusawa, and, after she uncovers Omocha's plot to keep them apart, she leaves her house and moves in with Furusawa. Kimura, the young kimono salesman, is angry not only at Omocha for her deception but also at his boss for his duplicity and decides to take revenge on Omocha. He hires a taxi and has the driver pick up Omocha at her house; Omocha is under the impression that Kudo has sent for her. Driving down the nighttime streets of Kyoto, Omocha realizes that Kimura is in the taxi and intends to get even. The film then cuts to Umekichi and Furusawa being told that Omocha has been terribly injured—she has jumped out (or, it is unclear, has been thrown out) of a moving taxi. Umekichi goes to the hospital to see Omocha, who is bandaged and weak but even more emphatic about the mendacity of men and the corruption of society. Umekichi listens half-heartedly, as she has just learned that Furusawa has left her to return to his wife in the country and a start-up rayon business.

Four interrelated systems are at work in the film: (1) the gender system; (2) the socioeconomic system of Japan; (3) the cinematic system; and (4) the geopolitical system of imperial capitalism. The gender system is most apparent and links up with Mizoguchi's reputation as a filmmaker who takes on women's issues. From the very first time we meet Umekichi and Omocha, we hear them discussing the state of women. Omocha recognizes that the system is structured by dominance, therefore rendering it foolish to trust any man or feel guilty about the misfortunes that might beset them. Umekichi stresses that she is not dumb to the oppression women face and seems perturbed by Omocha's condescension; Omocha fires back, "Then why don't you act like you understand?" This oppressive structure is not limited to the sisters; it also affects the higher-class wives of Furusawa and Kudo. They are betrayed just as readily as their female servants. The plot is a prison. Omocha's modern solution to her situation nearly results in her death; Umekichi's traditional solution is equally disastrous. The other women are deceived left and right. We are locked in defeat.

The socioeconomic system is also hard to miss. Furusawa has built his wealth in the cotton business, the industry at the forefront of Japan's first economic miracle, which lasted from the Meiji period to its decline in the early 1930s. By the end of the film, Furusawa has returned to his wife and to a new rayon business, an industry that signals the move to heavy industry and, ultimately, to Japan's war effort. Another industry is also booming at the time: traditional Japanese artifacts. Bidders try frantically to buy up Furusawa's belongings, and Jurakudo's dubious curio business (selling real and imitation Japanese antiques) is flourishing. This is not a coincidence, given the return of Japanese nativism at the time. The film offers no alternative to the economic transformations and to the consolidation of Japan's war machine, just as it offers no alternative to Omocha's and Umekichi's fates. Yet it is this unstoppable linear drive of the plot, this one-way street to misery and destruction, that makes the breathtaking formal experiments within the cinematic system remarkable.

46. Mizoguchi Kenji's *Gion no shimai*
(Sisters of the Gion). Daiichi eiga, 1936.

The film opens with one of the most memorable scenes in narrative cinema: an auction in which Furusawa's possessions are being sold to a party of eager bidders. For more than a minute, the camera horizontally tracks the auction, from left to right and from room to room, always remaining on the same vertical axis. First we are in a space behind the auctioneer, where two workers are handling pieces that have just been on the block; then the shot slides into the main room, where the auctioneer is spinning a silver vase and describing the next item up for bid, a family altar (figs. 46 and 47). At the same even pace, the shot moves to the seated bidders excitedly waving their fans, then it moves to another room, where two more workers are clearing away boxes. The shot is then cross-dissolved with another that moves forward into a room where Furusawa and his assistant, Sadakichi, are seated. This is the signature one-shot, one-scene technique for which Mizoguchi is famous. Without a single cut, Mizoguchi was able to edit the film in dramatic fashion. The camera moves to follow not a center (such as Furusawa or the auctioneer), but the relations among the various elements of the shot. If the brilliance of film is that it can flash not what it directly represents but the relation—the absence, the abstraction, the unseen—that connects two separate things, then we need to ask what relation Mizoguchi might be attempting to flash and how he is able to do it so successfully. To engage these questions properly, however, we need to historicize Mizoguchi's strategies in relation to the emergence of sound film, the decline of the benshi, and the dominant cinematic grammar of the day.

Of course, one-shot, one-scene filmmaking was nothing new by the 1930s. In fact, the very first films were precisely this. Recall that one of the arguments to displace the benshi was that they impeded the progress of filmmaking: The art of editing was slowed as the benshi served to drive the drama

47. Mizoguchi Kenji's *Sisters of the Gion.* Daiichi eiga, 1936.

of the narrative; the benshi thus edited from outside the text itself. In the 1920s, more editing emerged to preempt the benshi, leading to the talkie, which snuffed out the last bit of energy of the benshi system. But the talkie presented new technical difficulties for linking image and sound.[21] This reversed the trend of heavier editing, producing longer takes with fewer cuts to soften the aural transitions. The task then was to return to more editing, and by the time Mizoguchi made *Sisters of the Gion*, sound technology, heavy editing, and the centering of the plot had become dominant. Just as the shorter take came back into vogue, Mizoguchi moved to the longer take and his signature one-shot, one-scene strategy.

The auction scene decenters the individuals and draws attention to the connections among them and the structures in which they live. This is why the film is so far removed from what is generally called melodrama. Melodrama maps social and structural contradictions onto the bodies of individual characters, then resolves those contradictions through personal tragedy or triumph. *Sisters of the Gion* does the opposite. It maps individual characters onto the structures of society and resolves those contradictions through formal experiments. This first tracking shot introduces the star of Mizoguchi's film—structure itself. At a moment (1936) in which geopolitics is being melodramatized so that the West stands in for evil and Japan for good, a foregrounding of structure reveals a logic that exceeds these cartoons of the nation. It reveals the imperialist logic of capitalism, a logic that requires territorial expansion to manage internal crisis.

By "imperialism" I mean the economic and cultural system of external investment that depends on the control and penetration of markets, raw materials, and subjectivities. Although imperialism is used in several contexts, it implies, at bottom, a relation of structural domination and suppression—often violent—of the heterogeneity of the subjects in question. But this domination and suppression is reserved not for those subjects in the colonies; imperialism also suppresses groups within the imperializing nation itself. In his classic text *Imperialism* (1911), J. A. Hobson puts it this way: "Irrational from the standpoint of the whole nation, [imperialism] is rational enough from the standpoint of certain classes in the nation."[22] Although a myth exists that colonialism benefits the metropole as a whole, the reality is that only certain groups benefit. For all of Hobson's simplicities, his most brilliant and enduring observation lies in reframing the problem of imperialism to question the unity of the nation and the workings of the world system.[23] Only by rethinking the frame in which such relations work does Hobson open a wholly alternative way to analyze imperialism.

Despite Mizoguchi's inability to articulate an alternative to imperialism and nationalism (such as a critique of nationalism as a political discourse, as ultra-nationalism, or as a critique of nationalism as a conceptual discourse, such as the nation as the primary and autonomous unit of analysis), he—like Soseki and Conrad—nevertheless desires to break out of this worldview through formal devices. Mizoguchi's one-shot, one-scene forms draw attention to themselves as artificial constructions, encouraging us to sense the potential of a reality that seemed inaccessible to imperialism and nationalism. Mizoguchi's breathtaking camera movement (which is cranked up to an even greater level of proficiency in *Story of the Last Chrysanthemum* [1939]) is read here as an attempt to resolve the antinomy of colonialism.

The non-tracking compositions of *Sisters of the Gion* exemplify this even more. Mizoguchi frames the shots, which usually take place in the sisters' home, so that the dialogue and the characters' bodies do not dominate. The shots are loaded with information, and, with the long takes and the methodical way in which the seduction scenes occur, it becomes hard not to focus on the system itself. There are four seduction scenes: Omocha's seduction of Kimura so he will give her expensive material for a kimono, which lasts more than three minutes (fig. 48); Omocha's seduction of Jurakudo so he will become Umekichi's patron, which lasts about four minutes (fig. 49); Omocha's seduction of Furusawa so he will leave Umekichi, which lasts about three minutes (fig. 50); and Omocha's seduction of Kudo, Kimura's boss, so he will become her patron, which lasts about eight minutes (fig. 51). Two devices link these four scenes together: (1) Mizoguchi's decision to film each

48 and 49. Mizoguchi Kenji's *Sisters of the Gion*. Daiichi eiga, 1936.

shot in deep focus so that equal attention is drawn to the props, the architectural structure of the rooms themselves, and the characters (effectively decentering the individual actors); and (2) Omocha's negotiation of the space that connects and separates her from her victim.

Take, for example, the scene in which Omocha seduces Furusawa. Furusawa has become too comfortable in the sisters' home, and Umekichi is so dedicated to him that she is sacrificing any chance to obtain a more secure patron. Omocha enters the room and pours Furusawa four quick cups of sake. Before he knows what has hit him, Omocha is escorting him out the door. Mizoguchi films the six-mat room through opened *fusuma* (sliding doors). On the right side of the frame, in front of the fusuma, stands a conspicuous flower. In the left-center is the low table where Furusawa and Omocha sit. And in the back of the frame is the *genkan* (entrance to the home). From the moment Omocha enters through the genkan to the moment Furusawa hurries back to grab one last cigarette before Omocha hands him his hat and shoves him off, the camera never moves. This creates an effect in which all points in the room are active; everything has meaning, and everything means in relation to everything else. Again, there is an emphasis on relations—not by camera movement, as in the auction scene, but by frame composition. Indeed, the shots figure Mizoguchi's desire (however unconscious) to make meaning relationally within an overall system. They are an aesthetic experiment or even solution to the political-economic problem thrown before the nation—colonialism.

One more seduction scene, the most extraordinary by far, requires mention: when Omocha (played by Yamada Isuzu) seduces the spectator when introduced at the beginning of the film. Omocha has just woken up to find

50 and 51. Mizoguchi Kenji's *Sisters of the Gion.* Daiichi eiga, 1936.

Furusawa and Umekichi chatting in the main room. Dressed in a slip and stretching her slim arms to cover her mouth during a luxurious yawn, Omocha sleepily lumbers through the room, creating a stark contrast to the stiff figures of Umekichi and Furusawa (fig. 52). After circling within the frame, Omocha winds up at the washbasin and brushes her teeth. As Umekichi explains that she has invited Furusawa to live with her and Omocha, Omocha punctuates her silent disapproval by vigorously rinsing her mouth. Only after Furusawa leaves to run errands does Omocha deliver the full force of her irritation. It is hard to think of another woman's performance before 1936 that matches the teasing intensity of Yamada's firecracker acting. It is true that, by the time Mizoguchi made *Sisters,* the modern-girl phenomenon in which young women sported a new attitude toward their bodies and toward men and society in general was already cooling (as a return to more traditional gender roles was coordinated with heightened nationalist discourse). Yet in the film world, women's film acting was only beginning to bloom (due primarily to the prohibitive presence of the onnagata during the first twenty years). Yamada's character practically jumps out of the film, from the way she gulps down a quart of milk to the way she seizes a cigarette from Kimura's hand and takes a short and knowing drag. It is certainly not wrong to read this exceptional performance as offsetting her sister's stiffness and traditional impulses and as a reference to the modern girl. However, I will read it in terms of Mizoguchi's aesthetic system and my earlier point about structure and acting.

In tweaking the system itself, with the tracking shots and decentered compositions, a new form of acting emerges. As I mentioned in chapter 4, "acting" and "agency" are always meant in relation to a given structure.

52. Mizoguchi Kenji's *Sisters of the Gion*. Daiichi eiga, 1936.

Actors shape structures just as much as structures shape actors. Yet there is a crucial historical component to this axiom. That is to say that certain historical moments produce more agency and possibilities for acting. (On top of all this, the very category of agency, and the modern subject on which it is based, is historical.) By opening the possibility for such an astounding performance by Yamada while, at the same time, decentering cinematically (in terms of both narrative and composition) the individual characters in the film, Mizoguchi's *Sisters of the Gion* brilliantly foregrounds the structure–agent problematic as it existed in the mid-1930s.

Ozu's Time   Ozu Yasujiro is well known for his aesthetic system: very little camera movement, precision acting, dissolveless cuts and cutaways, low camera angles, frontal shots, methodical pace, and thematic and formal links that are seen not just in each film but in all of his films. Whenever another filmmaker employs a long take with no camera movement or shoots in slow black-and-white, the inevitable moniker "Ozu-like" is wheeled out as a decisive signifier, one that turns out to declare less about the film in question than about the critic's presumed acumen. Take, for example, the work of the filmmaker Hou Hsiao-hsien from Taiwan. After being hounded by critics who claimed he had been originally influenced by Ozu, Hou said that he had not watched his first Ozu film until later in his career. Then, in a great cinematic tease, Hou incorporated into his 1995 film *Good Men, Good Women* a scene from Ozu's 1949 *Late Spring*.

Good Men, Good Women kaleidoscopes Taiwan's past and present by twisting the mid-1990s moment of social malaise into Taiwan's war against the Japanese until 1945; the White Terror after 1949 (an era from 1949–1987 of harsh political repression under Kuomintang rule, during which martial law was enforced and many people—especially intellectuals and the cultural elite—were persecuted); and the economic miracle of the 1980s. In the film, actors in a contemporary film troupe are performing the roles of (and merging with) resistance heroes and heroines from the 1940s, in particular Chiang Bi-yu, a member of the anti-Japanese resistance in China and a left-wing activist in Taiwan in the late 1940s, and her husband, Chung Hao-tung, who was executed in the anticommunist terror of the early 1950s. In a small Taipei flat (in the 1990s temporal line of Hou's film), a television is playing *Late Spring*. The scene shows Hara Setsuko's character, Noriko, riding her bicycle along Kamakura beach with a friend. The scene is one of *Late Spring*'s brightest moments, coming before the viewer learns that Noriko's friend (who is also her father's faithful assistant) is engaged to marry someone else and that Noriko would rather live with her aging father (and willfully break tradition) than get married.

No doubt, there are similarities between these two great filmmakers: a penchant for the banal and the long take and for narratives that patiently and circularly accumulate emotional intensity, as opposed to narratives that are set in logical motion by front-loading the very first scene. Still, Hou's and Ozu's films are as far apart as the fifty years that separate them. Hou vigorously integrates four temporal lines that shoot through one another like a palimpsest, while Ozu's film plods along like the local trains his characters inevitably ride. As two perceptive critics, Abé Markus Nornes and Yeh Yueh-yu, acutely point out, the formal differences between the two directors, such as the method of shot transition and camera angle and the use of cinematic space, are significant.[24] What can we make, then, of Hou's decision to quote Ozu in *Good Men, Good Women?*

I choose to read this in relation to one of the more subtle but crucial similarities between Hou and Ozu: Both of their films were produced by the same company, Shochiku. Ozu made almost all of his fifty-three feature films, from 1927 to 1962, with Shochiku, and Hou's three most recent films (*Flowers of Shanghai* [1998], *Goodbye South, Goodbye* [1996], and *Good Men, Good Women*) were jointly produced by Shochiku. But the Shochiku of the late 1940s and the Shochiku of the late 1990s are two very different companies—or, rather, the national and global situation within which Shochiku existed in the late 1940s and in the late 1990s are quite different.

The two brothers at the helm of Shochiku, who started out with a stake in the theater industry, had recognized the enormous potential of film by the late 1910s. After accumulating talent from the theater and literary worlds, as well as from Hollywood, Shochiku built a studio in Kamata, Tokyo, and committed to making only modern, new-style films. In an attempt to consolidate its power in the late 1910s and 1920s, Shochiku purchased smaller film companies and built flamboyant theaters in many of Japan's leading cities. Shochiku's most significant move came in 1936, when it built a new studio in Ofuna, Kanagawa Prefecture, to replace its studio in Kamata. To mention the Ofuna studio is at once to mention some of the masterpieces of Japanese film history, from Shimizu Hiroshi's *Kaze no naka no kodomotachi* (Children in the wind) to Ozu's *Late Spring*. In May 2000, Shochiku sold its Ofuna studio to Kamakura Women's College for 10.8 billion yen (117 million dollars).[25] Without a single hit since the last installment of Yamada Yoji's *Otoko wa tsurai yo* (It's hard to be a man) in 1996, Shochiku had been hurting for years. In 1998, the company's president, Okuyama Toru, and his son Kazuyoshi were overthrown in an attempt to restructure and streamline the company. In December of the same year, Kamakura Cinema World (the film theme park located on the Ofuna lot) was closed after only three dismal years of existence.

Many of the New Wave filmmakers broke with Shochiku in the early 1960s, and since then, few have looked to the celebrated company for quality. Yet by catering to popular tastes and seizing the distribution of film via a system of block-booking, in which a movie distributor must continually provide new movies to affiliated movie houses where only the company's films are shown, Shochiku had continued to rank as one of the more stable entertainment companies in Japan. With the emergence of video in the 1980s, the prominence of television, the trend of television companies breaking into film production, and new entertainment media such as the Internet, Shochiku found itself in the red for most of the 1990s. Although the company produced seventeen movies in 1999, its annual revenues from distributing the films totaled only 3.1 billion yen (26 million dollars), less than one-fifth of the 16 billion yen (177 million dollars) that the U.S. film *Titanic* grossed.[26] This poor performance and new business environment forced Shochiku, along with the other big film companies, to abolish block-booking and focus on horizontal integration with other producers and distributors.[27]

Of course, the large U.S. film companies made this move from vertical integration, with studios acquiring theater chains, to horizontal integration much earlier, starting in the 1950s, after the Hollywood studio system disintegrated. But back in the late 1930s, the big five U.S. film corporations employed their own type of block-booking, owning or controlling about 80 percent of metropolitan first-run theaters.[28] The big five rationalized their operations, formed departments headed by professional managers, Taylorized the division of labor, and, not unlike in a Ford Motor Company factory, excelled at assembly-line production. The undoing of the studio system began in the 1940s as producers, directors, writers, and actors grew less enamored with the paternal hand of the studio heads, and as antitrust laws increasingly were enforced. In the 1948 "Paramount decision," for example, the Supreme Court called for the divorce of production and exhibition of films and for the elimination of unfair booking practices.[29]

By the 1960s, the studios were no longer self-contained factories of production; they were simply financing and distribution companies, places where independent producers would go with prefabricated packages. These producers would effectively outsource all of the tasks (director, actor, production assistance, and so on) of a potential film—not unlike the approach Ford began taking at about the same time. Although Hollywood was no longer composed of tightly knit and loyal studio-system teams, filmmaking was still an American industry. This would change in the 1980s. Global consumer markets made even more accessible by the standardized videocassette recorder and a new discourse of globalization following the end of the Cold War changed the criteria for a successful project. Now critical and financial failures at home could recoup their losses in new markets abroad, and other films were being tailored for these new markets from the very outset.[30] Using global production markets, such as Vancouver and Toronto—not to mention location shooting in Third World countries—became an essential way to cut costs. At the same time, the major companies themselves were changing hands. In 1985, 20th Century Fox was purchased by Rupert Murdoch's Australian publishing conglomerate, and Japan's Sony and Matsushita acquired Columbia Pictures and MCA in 1989 and 1990, respectively.[31] Unlike Sony and Matsushita, the Japanese film corporations (Shochiku, Toho, Toei, Daiei) failed to adjust to this more flexible world system. They paid the price.

By the mid-1990s, Shochiku no doubt recognized the great potential of

Asian markets for Japanese popular culture. Japanese music, manga, anime, fashion, and food has captured the attention of youths from Hong Kong to Taiwan, a phenomenon that is lost on many who expect popular culture to flow in only one direction—from the United States to the rest of the world.[32] Unable to fill its theaters and finally recognizing its business model as defunct, Shochiku closed the doors of its last theater in 1999 and committed to a path of downsizing, streamlining, and moving laterally, as the Hollywood studios had begun to do several decades earlier. What is the cost of all this? Some people formed a "Save Shochiku" association in the belief that, more damaging than the elimination of one hundred and fifty jobs, losing Shochiku would harm the Japanese film industry itself. But anyone who has followed Japanese film over the past twenty years knows that the most interesting films—documentary and feature—have been produced independently, outside the four main studios.

This short industrial history is all preparation for reading Hou's inclusion of Ozu's *Late Spring* clip as a marker of difference rather than similarity. The two filmmakers differ in relation to their very different moments of production. No matter how much emphasis each director places on formal precision, in the seemingly ahistorical qualities of a shot's duration or stillness, these formal strategies necessarily gesture to the historical issues and debates that were occurring while the film was being made. Hou's film is about the most recent colonization of Taiwan, not by Japan or China, but by the forces of globalization. These forces have brought greater wage inequality over the past fifteen years than Taiwan has seen at any time in the past one hundred years and a situation in which the total gross domestic product of Taiwan lags well behind the economic clout of the world's leading corporations.[33] Promoting export-oriented industrialization, an undervalued currency, and dirt-cheap labor throughout the 1980s, Taiwan, by the time of Hou's film in the mid-1990s, was suffering the consequences, such as inadequate public-welfare services and an environmental nightmare in which most of the country's rivers and streams had become seriously polluted with untreated sewage, pesticide, and fertilizer runoffs. The reference to Shochiku is a brilliant way to stress that *Good Men, Good Women* is not simply a film about history (about the successive bouts of past colonization in modern Taiwanese history) but a film of history (of the present processes of globalization).

But if all this can be said about Hou's film, then what about Ozu's *Late Spring?* It, too, can be located in relation to its specific moment of production—in particular, a moment in which Japan (and the U.S. occupation) was retreating from the original ideals of demilitarization and democratization; a vigorous debate about subjectivity (the active dimension of human agents) had called all parties to the matter, from literary critics and philosophers to social scientists and psychoanalysts; Japan's postwar reconstruction project had taken off; and the Cold War was heating up, with the Korean peninsula about to erupt. This claim, however, brings us into conflict with a popular strand of Ozu criticism. For although Ozu is recognized as a filmmaker of Japan's modernity (because he attends to changes in the city and the family, for example), he is regularly believed to exist outside any specific historical problem, in a total aesthetic system that attains meaning in relation to its own modifications (such as the move to the talkie or to color). We confuse the plots and characters of his films: Was it in *Early Autumn* or *Late Spring* that Chishu Ryu peeled the apple in teary-eyed solitude? The many characters and plots seem to meld into one system. Or perhaps there is the Early Ozu (silent and prewar films) and the Late Ozu (talkies and postwar films).[34] Still, like no other Japanese director, Ozu is pulled out of history and pushed into the ahistorical and transcendental realm of Zen or Japanese aesthetics or an essentialized Japanese identity. But what is opened when *Late Spring* is read not in relation to a larger Ozuian text or even to the more general problem of Japanese modernity, but to the specific sociohistorical problem of the late 1940s—namely, the paradox of the individual and the "reverse-course" policies at the dawn of the Cold War?

Late Spring centers on the relationship between a father, Somiya, and daughter, Noriko. The film takes place less than five years after the dropping of the atomic bombs, and the two live in relative comfort and perfect rhythm in Kamakura, the famous tourist and temple town about an hour south of Tokyo. Somiya, a widower, teaches at a Tokyo university, and Noriko, while taking care of Somiya and the house, is recovering from wartime famine and forced labor. Because Noriko is in her late twenties, both Somiya and a niggling aunt want her to marry. They persuade Noriko that Somiya will take another wife, thus dispelling Noriko's grounds for not marrying (to take care of her father). Noriko is furious not only about her father's desire to remarry (which we learn later is nothing but a ruse) but, more intensely, at the prospect of leaving her father and current lifestyle. Noriko finally submits as the film ends on the day of her marriage and as Somiya returns to an empty house and deep sadness.

Noriko is an ambiguous character. Is she traditional because of her filial piety, her distaste for remarriage (her uncle Onodera has recently remarried, and Noriko calls him filthy [fuketsu]), and her incredulity toward divorce (her friend Aya believes that bad husbands should be overcome like so many outs in a baseball game)? Or is Noriko progressive because of her desire not to marry and break tradition? Can Noriko be considered a feminist because of her wish to follow her own desire and buck the patriarchically inscribed institution of modern marriage? This is not clear, and the brilliance of Ozu's Late Spring—in its narrative development, temporal strategies, and controlled acting—is to push this ambiguity, to inhabit this in-betweenness for the entire length of the film.

Late Spring is produced at a crucial juncture of postwar Japan—the moment of the reverse-course. The Japanese media invented this term to refer to the Americans' (and Japanese collaborators') dramatic departure from many of the ideals proclaimed at the beginning of the U.S. occupation in 1945.[35] From a new antagonism with organized labor to brutal "red purges," from the open support of former wartime leaders to economic decisions based on old zaibatsu lines, the decision makers of postwar Japan betrayed their earlier promises one by one. All of this was done in the name of protecting Asia and the world from communism. If the ideals of "individual freedom," "democracy," "freedom," and the other slogans touted by the Potsdam Declaration and Douglas MacArthur's officials had held any hope, they were running on empty by the time Ozu finished Late Spring.

Ozu directly engages this situation. Take, for example, a scene early in the film in which Somiya, at home with his assistant Hattori, is struggling to finish an academic article. Hattori is scanning a reference guide for information about Fredrick List, a noted German economist who became a naturalized American citizen after being exiled for his radical views on trade and tariffs. Somiya warns not to confuse List with Franz Liszt, the Hungarian composer. But when Hattori gives List's date of birth and death, he mistakenly gives the information for Liszt, an error that goes unnoticed by Somiya (and presumably by Ozu himself) and one that speaks to the complacent nature of Somiya's scholarship. It is clear that Somiya is merely meeting a bureau-

53. Ozu Yasujiro's *Late Spring.*
Shochiku, 1949.

cratic deadline set by the university press. This is underscored when Noriko berates Somiya for wanting to play mah-jongg with friends instead of finishing the article. At any rate, Somiya explains that List was a self-made man who loathed bureaucracy, qualities that Somiya admires. But then an employee of the state-owned electric company abruptly enters the home and interrupts their conversation. After checking the house's electrical meter, the employee once again interrupts the conversation about List by explaining that Somiya is three kilowatts over the allotment. However much Somiya might share List's disdain of huge bureaucracies and the danger that they might suppress individual will (as during the war), the overriding bureaucracies have returned and still interrupt his everyday life.

After Noriko begrudgingly accepts the marriage proposal, she travels to Kyoto with Somiya one last time before moving out of the house. It is a pleasant trip, but on the final evening, right before going asleep, Noriko makes one last plea to stay with her father. Somiya explains that only through marriage is human life and its history carried on. Noriko must live apart from him and start her own life. But Somiya's logic is not as self-evident as it appears, and both he and Noriko seem to express this doubt. Surely, the human species will continue if Noriko does not marry. Surely, history will carry on despite Noriko's decision not to reproduce. The isolation, loneliness, and sourness with which the film ends urges us to speculate on other possibilities. What if Noriko had remained with her father? What type of life could she have lived? *Late Spring* opens the possibility to take these alternatives seriously, virtual worlds within the worlds already chosen.

One way it does this is by extensively spacing the delivery of information. Take, for example, the remarkable scene at the noh theater (fig. 53). As Noriko and Somiya are enjoying the performance, Somiya spots in the audi-

54. Ozu Yasujiro's *Late Spring.*
Shochiku, 1949.

ence the woman he supposedly will wed. Noriko first notices Somiya offer a nod of recognition, then she follows with a nod herself. Noriko is angry and refuses to look or talk to her father for some time after. This whole scene, moving back and forth between long takes of the noh performance and Noriko and Somiya, lasts about seven minutes. As in noh itself, time is slowed down so that it bends and forks and opens new ways to exist within it.

Or there is the train ride from Kamakura to Tokyo. The first shot is from outside the train itself, with the camera placed alongside one of the cars and aimed down the tracks (fig. 54). This is followed by a shot of a crowded car in which both Somiya and Noriko are standing. The next shot is outside from another angle, followed by another internal shot of Somiya sitting and Noriko standing. Finally, as the train approaches Tokyo Station, and as the throng of passengers has thinned, both Somiya and Noriko are sitting. Nothing happens inside this stretched time. Or everything can happen.

Perhaps the greatest example of this spacing of time is the scene in which Somiya learns that Hattori plans to marry and is therefore no longer a prospect for Noriko. I cannot think of a more perfect scene in all of cinema. Somiya has resolved to ask Noriko about marriage, and about Hattori in particular. The six-minute scene begins with a low angle, medium shot of a narrow corridor in the house. Noriko walks into the shot to grab some towels to be folded in the main room. The next shot is outside the house as Somiya walks toward the camera, then takes a right turn into the house. Noriko greets him, takes his hat and attaché case, and reminds him of an upcoming P.E.N. Club meeting. With both Somiya and Noriko in the frame, Noriko delivers the news: Hattori had come by earlier in the afternoon and they had gone bicycling together along the ocean. Before Noriko finishes her sentence, there is a cut to a medium closeup of Somiya expressing sur-

55. Ozu Yasujiro's *Late Spring.*
Shochiku, 1949.

prise. Noriko continues to express how pleasant the day was, and Somiya becomes even more energized, practically bouncing up and down. After Noriko leaves the room to prepare dinner, Somiya is wound up with expectation and throws his jacket and shirt on the tatami. Walking past Noriko to the washbasin, Somiya asks whether Hattori had come to see him. Not particularly, Noriko replies, and by this time Somiya is fully animated by his good fortune. After they sit down to eat, Somiya takes his time before pushing further. As the shot cuts to a frontal closeup of Somiya, he asks Noriko what she thinks of Hattori. With a frontal reverse shot, Noriko explains that he is quite nice and even her type. Somiya, about to burst, cannot contain himself. To the question of whether Hattori would make a good husband, Noriko once again amazes her father by answering with an unreserved yes. Somiya, now smiling ear to ear, delivers his idea of an arranged marriage between Noriko and Hattori. Almost choking on her food, Noriko coughs up a joyless laugh at the proposal. After composing herself, Noriko explains that Hattori is already engaged to marry another woman. Somiya is stunned (so, indeed, is the audience, as we are also hearing this information for the first time). The accumulation of energy over the past five and a half minutes has been snuffed out, like a sudden blackout or stalled car (fig. 55). After repeating the disconcerting news over and over in his subtle but broken way (*soo ka . . . ah soo ka . . . soo kai*), Somiya eats the rest of his rice in deflated silence.

There is a representation of time in these three scenes that is quite extraordinary, one that works differently from time as it is represented by the modern clock. In fact, the following shot in each of the three scenes just discussed (the noh theater, train ride, and Somiya and Noriko's conversation about Hattori) is of a clock: two of the prominent clock atop one of Tokyo's

56 and 57. Ozu Yasujiro's *Late Spring*. Shochiku, 1949.

landmark buildings, and the other of a wall clock inside Aya's home (figs. 56 and 57).[36] The modern clock is an instrument that measures the passage of time, the linear movement from the present to the future present. Clocks and the influence of clock time also influence the way people think and live, the way in which people mediate themselves to the world. Modern clock time obeys a logic that is reactionary; each tick of the clock reacts to the one before it. Indeed, this clock time is what has most influenced the way time is represented in cinema.

One of the most interesting meditations on time and the cinema (as well as on Ozu's temporal strategies) can be found in Deleuze's two cinema books *Cinema 1: The Movement-Image* and *Cinema 2: The Time-Image* (1983 and 1985, respectively). Departing from Henri-Louis Bergson's *Matter and Memory*, Deleuze examines the two great logics of cinema: the movement image, which presupposes an action that prompts a reaction (a sensory-motor image); and the time image, in which actions "float" in situations rather than bring these situations to conclusion.[37] For Deleuze, the movement image relates in principle to pre-World War II cinema, the cinema of Griffith, Eisenstein, and Chaplin, but most specifically to classical Hollywood cinema. The movement image produces a rational interval, the cut that serves to end one shot and begin the next (such as the cut from a terrified boy to a dangerous bear). With the time image (as in De Sica, Rossellini, Resnais, Ozu), linking occurs through "irrational" divisions. The interval is autonomous, no longer forming the ending of one and the beginning of another segment. The movement image is an indirect representation of time. It constitutes time in its empirical form, the succession of instants of time. The time image is a direct representation of time. It is a crystal that is double-sided,

58 and 59. Ozu Yasujiro's *Late Spring*. Shochiku, 1949.

mutual, both actual and virtual in perpetual exchange—not actual that becomes virtual, but actual and virtual at the same time so that the two are indiscernible.

A perfect example of a time image for Deleuze is the cutaway to a vase in *Late Spring*. Somiya and Noriko, having spent a full day in Kyoto, are lying on their futons. After the lights have been turned off, Noriko apologizes to Somiya for calling Onodera unclean after taking a second wife. Noriko is about to apologize to her father for feeling the same way toward him when she realizes that Somiya is sleeping. Half-smiling, Noriko stares up to the ceiling (fig. 58). The camera then cuts away to a vase that is situated in the room (fig. 59). After five seconds, it cuts back to Noriko, who is now close-mouthed and on the verge of tears (fig. 60). This is followed by another shot of the vase, this time lasting about ten seconds. For Deleuze, the vase is time, time itself, "a direct time-image, which gives what changes the unchanging form in which the change is produced."[38]

Time is an abstraction; it is a totality that cannot be narrated except in its separate moments. It is like history in this sense, something that necessarily exceeds its representations, its narrations. "It is a matter of something too powerful, or too unjust, but sometimes also too beautiful, and henceforth outstrips our sensory-motor capacities."[39] These totalities (time, history) are composed of elements that are constantly mutating, elements that exist in dynamic relation with one another and are therefore at regular risk of being neglected. What the still shots of the vase—as well as the still shots of the clocks—flash is the absent presence of these totalities, the relations external to their terms. To fight to represent and see these relations, is to fight to see the structuring forms and the ineffable logics of our lives.

60. Ozu Yasujiro's *Late Spring.*
Shochiku, 1949.

The transformation from the movement image to the time image is not a progression but a mutation. Deleuze writes:

> The rise of situations to which one can no longer react, of environments with which there are now only chance relations, of empty or disconnected any-space-whatevers replacing qualified extended space. It is here that situations no longer extend into action or reaction in accordance with the requirements of the movement-image. These pure optical and sound situations, in which the character does not know how to respond, abandoned spaces in which he ceases to experience and to act so that he enters into flight, goes on a trip, comes and goes, vaguely indifferent to what happens to him, undecided as to what must be done. But he has gained in an ability to see what he has lost in action or reaction: he SEES so that the viewer's problem becomes "What is there to see in the image?" (and not now "What are we going to see in the next image?").[40]

These new situations and environments in which the time image emerges are the crisis of both the action image and the American dream. It is no coincidence that the great experiments with the modern cinema follow the social, economic, political, and moral crises that came with World War II and its consequences. Filmmakers are theorists who theorize with images. The postwar moment produced a situation in which new theories, new ways of seeing the world, were required. For Deleuze, the filmmakers of the immediate postwar period who produced the time image were doing the work of philosophy with images before philosophers could do it with concepts.[41]

Ozu, of course, was producing these time images before the crisis of the war (and on the other side of the world). Indeed, his silent films might provide even better examples of the time image than his talkies. For this reason, Deleuze explains that Ozu "invents" and "anticipates" the time image, which reaches the Italian, French, German, and American avant-garde in the three decades after the war. Still, Deleuze never accounts for Ozu's anticipatory function, just as he does not account for possible differences in the time image when produced out of different aesthetic and philosophical traditions, such as those of Japan. Ozu is one of only a few non-Western filmmakers (along with Mizoguchi and Kurosawa) whom Deleuze examines, so this difference does seem noteworthy and to warrant consideration. Are the meanings and effects of the time image similar in different situations? It is true that by the time Ozu began to make film, classical Hollywood codes had become dominant in Japan. Still, this difference deserves distinction.

I insist on reading Ozu's *Late Spring* more in relation to the late 1940s than in relation to his oeuvre. John Dower points out that, in 1948, a majority of Japanese still responded affirmatively when asked whether they believed their country was heading in a good direction, but by 1949 the majority response was negative.[42] The betrayal and opportunism were clear to see. The particular requirements of the moment took precedence over the larger principles insisted on immediately following the war. The time images of the vase and the clocks are read here as a way of coming to terms with a world in which various needs and desires were interpreted as symptoms of something larger, as something that, in however distorted or unknowable a form, exceeded immediate demands. To be attentive, weary, and respectful of this "something larger"; to act as if it has rules and a logic, even though these rules and logic may be continually broken and may never be "verified"; to act as if our individual lives have meaning because of it and give meaning to it— this is how a cutaway to a clock quietly implores us not to recoil into an exclusive and hazardous particularism. This is also how a seemingly apolitical film quietly implores us to read it allegorically.

Through his formal experiments, Ozu engages the most profound political problems of the day and produces a way of seeing that cannot be produced in other realms. One character in *Late Spring*, however, seems to see this quite clearly: Somiya's housekeeper. While Somiya and Noriko are away, Hattori visits their house. After greeting the housekeeper, Hattori leaves his wedding photograph. The housekeeper looks attentively at the traditional photograph, then invites her friend, a similarly classed worker, to take a look (fig. 61). "It's amazing how much it looks like Mr. Hattori,

61. Ozu Yasujiro's *Late Spring.*
Shochiku, 1949.

exactly," the housekeeper exclaims in her marked working-class speech. But what is so surprising? The technology of photography? Or is Ozu performing an argument about his own use of still shots? Could it be that, in his still shots, Ozu desires not to reproduce the object in near-perfect verisimilitude but—within the temporality of cinema—to represent something that is unrepresentable, to flash a path to the impossible? Now we must situate Ozu's impulse in relation to the great social problematic of those years.

The Shutaisei Debate and Kurosawa's *Rashomon*   The chief intellectual debate in the immediate postwar era turned on the issue of subjectivity (shutaisei), or the degree to which active human agents shape themselves and their social environment. If Japan was to generate radical reform or revolution following the war, if it was to live up to the ideals of the Potsdam Declaration, a theory of the subject was essential. The debate turned on the individual, for many concluded that one way to explain what had gone wrong over the past fifteen years had to do with the lack of a proper philosophical conceptualization of the individual and of a proper, politically felt experience of the individual. To prevent such a historical repetition from occurring, the individual, the subject, would need to be fleshed out. The question became, "What type of an I can I be/become." For literary critics such as Honda Shugo, the problem centered on the subjectivity of authors and their literary forms of expression; for philosophers such as Umemoto Katsumi, the problem centered on how to theorize individual agency and freedom without ignoring the structuring force of historical processes; and for political scientists such as Maruyama Masao, the problem centered on the subject of history in relation to the nation-state and Japanese modernity.

In *Revolution and Subjectivity in Postwar Japan* (1996), J. Victor Kosch-mann describes how, immediately following the war, the *Kindai Bungaku* (modern literature) writers responded to the persisting assumption of the pre-war proletarian literary movement that the author's subjectivity must be suppressed in order to represent objectively the interconnectedness of every-day life. Only a sharp scientific eye could properly narrate the usually unseen social relations of modern life. Yet the Kindai Bungaku writers challenged the assumptions that an unmediated representation of the everyday is pos-sible and that culture must follow politics. For these writers (who included Haniya Yutaka, Ara Masato, and Odagiri Hideo), their own subjectivity had to be cultivated by giving freer rein to literary expression. Even though the content of their writing was not necessarily about social relations and jus-tice, the form of focusing on their own subjectivity would have crucial politi-cal effects for readers. But this priority on the artist's desire to express his or her autonomous view of the world (his or her own petit bourgeois status) put these writers at odds with the Communist Party's view that the artist should serve the party and working class. The Kindai Bungaku writers countered: How can citizens cultivate self-expression and a revolutionary conscious-ness while being directed by a heavy-handed party apparatus? The backlash was severe, as critics—Nakano Shigeharu foremost among them—charged the group with a depoliticized formalism that elevated the bourgeois indi-vidual by downplaying the very real historical obstacles of capitalist produc-tion.[43]

But this debate over subjectivity exceeded those intellectuals who en-gaged it head-on. It is true that no filmmakers engaged it as such (al-though the film critic Tsumura Hideo was an important participant in the overcoming-modernity debate of the 1940s).[44] I will read Ozu's and Kuro-sawa's films as carving out positions within this debate. It is difficult not to think of *Rashomon* as a film of history, a film of 1950. Indeed, it is about sub-jectivity and representation. Remember where Kurosawa's content comes from: It is taken from two Akutagawa Ryunosuke short stories, "Yabu no naka" (In a grove) and "Rashomon" (1917 and 1919, respectively). Akutagawa's "Rashomon" takes place in the twelfth century during wholesale destruc-tion. Rashomon refers to the main gate that marks the entrance to the capi-tal region, Heian-kyo (modern-day Kyoto). The gate is half-destroyed, and under it a discharged servant shelters himself from the pouring rain. Spying a woman cutting the hair off corpses and appalled by this behavior, he admonishes her. The woman explains that she does this only to get by during such exacting times. He strikes her, steals her last possessions, and justifies his actions by using her defense: that he is only getting by during such exacting times. "In a Grove" more closely resembles Kurosawa's film. A woodcutter, in a police courtyard, describes what he knows about a recent rape and murder. Other characters—the bandit who allegedly committed the crime; a woman who has been raped and her dead husband, whose story is represented by a medium; a traveling priest; a policeman; and an old woman— represent the same event, but differently, from their own perspectives. The story abruptly ends with the last representation, and Akutagawa gives no hint as to how to think about the accounts. Kurosawa not only combines these two stories but adds the character of the commoner, who provokes the priest and woodcutter to tell the story in the first place, and a crucial final scene, in which the woodcutter decides to care for a crying baby found abandoned near the gate.

When asked what *Rashomon* was about, Kurosawa said rape and a death, nothing more. This is important: A woman is raped, and a man dies. Truth exists: There was a rape. Kurosawa does not want to erase this fact. The film is less interesting when studied in terms of how truth is relative, or how truth does not exist. It is more interesting when studied in terms of how individuals come to terms with truth and how they represent it. We are always mediated to this truth by such things as language, gender, ego, and social position. No one is lying; everyone is telling the truth. The bandit tells the truth from his position, the woodcutter from his, the husband from his, and so on. One recurring theme in all of Kurosawa's films is that, when individuals talk about themselves, they invariably exaggerate. For instance, when the bandit describes the event, he comes off as a skilled swordsman; the husband commits suicide (which would be the most dignified way for him to die), and even the woodcutter describes the event so that the bandit steals the dagger (thus exonerating himself of any guilt). According to Kurosawa, we always describe events so that we come off in the best light.

But there is a problem here, and Kurosawa recognized it. What do we do in the face of a reality in which our actions are always determined and particularistic? A woodcutter must always act like a woodcutter; a bandit like a bandit; a woman like a woman; and so forth. What about the individual? What about the agency of the individual subject over and above the social structures that they themselves have constructed? What about difference within the identity of such rigid categories? Not only does this connect to philosophical and political controversies over representation, namely the relation between representor, represented, and the event, or on a more immediate level how to represent the event of World War II (as an act of Japanese aggression toward its Asian neighbors or as an act of liberation from the colonizing West) precisely at the time when Japanese interest groups from both sides of the political spectrum are beginning to appropriate the meaning of the war and the dropping of the atomic bombs in order to advance their particular ideological positions, but this also puts us dead-center in the shutaisei debate.[45] To negotiate this problem on the narrative level, Kurosawa came up with the scene in which the woodcutter steps out of his programming and acts freely by choosing to care for the abandoned baby. Japanese critics panned the scene, saying it was a gesture to Christian charity. But Kurosawa felt trapped. He needed this act of nonconformity, of hope, of self-determination in order to move beyond the determining function of history.

It is on the formal level, however, that Kurosawa's engagement with the shutaisei debate can be most interestingly read. Kurosawa produces different cinematic languages to represent *Rashomon*'s different characters. For example, the two fight scenes between the bandit (Tajomaru) and the husband, employ radically different cinematic languages. Tajomaru describes the first representation, while the woodcutter describes the second. In his representation, Tajomaru, who possesses a language with which to articulate the details of sword fighting, lasts two minutes and comprises twenty-five cuts (each shot therefore lasting less than five seconds). These quick cuts, punctuated by stylistic music, are fluid and practiced (fig. 62). The camera navigates the landscape, cutting angles and parrying strikes as expertly as Tajomaru battles. Yet when the woodcutter represents the same fight scene, it is entirely different—not in the events but in the language chosen to describe what has happened. For this representation, Kurosawa chooses a cinematic language that is clumsy and gritty, shaky and unsure of itself (fig. 63). This scene lasts for more than six minutes and comprises only twenty cuts (with an average shot lasting eighteen seconds). Tajomaru and the husband are flailing about, rolling around on the ground, and desperately throwing dirt at each other. There is no music; only the grunts and groans of the two fighters

62 and 63. Kurosawa Akira's *Rashomon*. Daiei, 1950.

accompany the agonizingly long takes. Because the woodcutter would not have the language with which to describe a sword fight, Kurosawa attempts to match this by constructing an inept and ungainly representation.

Yet when the woodcutter describes his daily walk through the forest before discovering the dead body, the cinematic language is as authoritative and poised as ever. Here I refer to the famous forest scenes for which Kurosawa has received so much attention and praise. The shadows cast by the intense sun shining through the tall trees, the din of running water, and the remarkable combination of dollying the camera in one direction while panning in the other represented motion like no other film at the time. The subtle language of the forest is surely one that the woodcutter can deftly describe (fig. 64).

When the narrative reaches the representation by the husband (via the medium), the style once again changes. The scene begins with the husband tied up after being forced to watch Tajomaru rape his wife (Masago). As he watches Masago beg Tajomaru to take her with him (since she and her husband have been so humiliated), the husband betrays his aesthetic/*bushido* sensibility by confessing how beautiful she looks—more so than at any time since he has known her. Revolted at the wife's disloyal plea, Tajomaru throws Masago to the ground and asks the husband how she should be punished. She manages to escape, and as Tajomaru chases after her, the husband is left alone. The long shot of the husband sitting cross-legged in the distance is not unlike a landscape painting—asymmetrical and full of negative space, the open space surrounding the solid forms (fig. 65). After Tajomaru returns and explains that Masago has managed to escape, he frees the husband and flees. Alone and distraught, the husband is represented in

64 and 65. Kurosawa Akira's *Rashomon*. Daiei, 1950.

a medium-long shot walking toward the camera. He then stoically turns from the camera and commits suicide by thrusting the dagger into his chest. Kurosawa matches the mise-en-scène, medium-long shots replete with aesthetic aplomb and refined melancholy, to the bushido sensibility of the husband.

When it comes time for Masago's representation, however, Kurosawa chooses a language more closely related to melodrama. Closeups and medium closeups dominate (fig. 66). Following the rape, Masago (played by Kyo Machiko) looks into her husband's eyes, but instead of seeing pity or compassion, she sees only cold hatred. She demands to be killed, but he refuses. Hysterical and delirious, she picks up a dagger to do the job herself but faints. She wakes only to find the dagger in her husband's chest. Unlike the other representations, Masago's focus is more on psychology and emotion, and the closeups that crowd out the landscape differ quite dramatically from the elegant long shots and graceful compositions described by the husband, the forceful and violent quick shots described by Tajomaru, and the enchanting and effortless ballet shots of the forest described by the woodcutter.

Then there is Kurosawa's cinematic language. Kurosawa was born in 1910 at the end of the Meiji period. His father came from a samurai family in the north, and his mother from a wealthy Kansai merchant family. In the Kurosawa home, a strict samurai ethic was enforced that, together with living in modernized Tokyo and watching his older brother Heigo (an out-of-work benshi) commit suicide, led to Kurosawa's spiky view of the world. On the one hand, he relentlessly criticized Japanese society, a society that can produce such injustice and inequality while appealing to such noble principles. On the other hand, Kurosawa criticized and lampooned any coordinated so-

66. Kurosawa Akira's *Rashomon*. Daiei, 1950.

cial movement or collective action, the only way to change the very society
that he condemned. We see this unresolved tension in much of his work, and
I think it is what ultimately produces the inventive force that pressurizes
his films.

What finally emerges is Kurosawa himself—Kurosawa the risk-taker,
Kurosawa the free agent. Situated within shutaisei discourse, Kurosawa
leans toward those who de-emphasize historical limits and stress the possibilities, however unreachable and exaggerated, of the subject. Whereas Ozu
seemed to place his hope in the supplementary logic of any structure—that
any structure is necessarily transformable because by its very logic it is open
(as surplus and as replacement)—Kurosawa places his hope in the extraordinary individual who can exceed structural limits by sheer willpower and
earnestness.

A World in Which Japan No Longer Exists: Cyborg Dreams and Global Capitalism

Tsukamoto Shinya's 1989 *Tetsuo* and Oshii Mamoru's 1995 *Ghost in the
Shell* are clearly about the body and subjectivity. *Tetsuo*'s main character
metamorphosizes into a metalicized scrap heap, while *Ghost*'s Motoko loses
her body altogether. The question of the immediate postwar moment (as exemplified in the shutaisei debate) was, "What type of I can I be?"; the question
forty-five years later is, "What is an I, and how might I exceed this category?"
But at the moment in which the problem of the subject, of the "I," can be
radically questioned by so many cyberpunks and animators (not to mention
so many social and cultural theorists), another problem emerges that has yet
to find an appropriate language: the problem of globalization, the problem of
a globalized system in which nations are steadily losing their sovereignty. I

67 and 68. Tsukamoto Shinya's *Tetsuo*. Kaijyu Theater, 1988.

read *Tetsuo* and *Ghost in the Shell* less as narrating the breakup of the subject and more as allegorizing the breakup of the nation. In short, the "I" is to the "cyborg" as the "nation" is to the "global"—the latter categories destabilize the former.

This analogy requires development. Let us begin with the first two terms —"I" and "cyborg"—by recounting how they are employed in the two films. Tsukamoto's *Tetsuo* is a sixty-seven-minute, monochromatic car crash of steel rods, flaming metal scales, occupied bodies, prosthetic phallic drills, hard wires, and urban pixilation. Every corner of every frame is stuffed full of metal; the junkyard and the junkman are one. Within months of its release, the film became legendary in the cyberpunk canon, and Tsukamoto's international fame was assured. At bottom, *Tetsuo* is a revenge film. A metal fetishist shoves a ten-inch corrugated rod into his thigh and, after detecting living metal cells in the wound, runs hysterically down a Tokyo street before being struck by a car. The salaryman driving the car dumps the injured body but gets infected (as part of the fetishist's revenge plot). What starts as a small metal pimple on the salaryman's cheek progressively occupies more of his body, until he and the metal fetishist merge.

In the deserted factory where the film opens, the fetishist is enclosed by mountains not only of scrap metal but also of paper cutouts of professional runners (figs. 67 and 68). The runners (all men of color) are in mid-stride, their perfect bodies competing in the oldest sport. After the rod enters the fetishist's thigh, the paper cutouts sizzle and burn away into nothingness. We have entered the world of the new body. In fact, at the moment of the car crash, Tsukamoto pans across a chain-link fence that reads "New World." As the salaryman and his lover dispose of the body, there is a cutaway to televisual

Canon, Body, Geopolitics   **243**

images of them having desperate, stand-up, outdoor sex. The whole experience has cranked up desire to a qualitatively different level. Indeed, in one sequence, the metamorphasizing salaryman is entered from behind by his girlfriend with a snake-like prosthetic phallis. He then grows an industrial-size electric drill from his groin, and, after blazing a hole up through the *kotatsu* (low table), chases his lover in an uncontrollable fit. After the fetishist and salaryman merge (however sexually), they (it) triumphantly resolve(s) to "rust the world."

Tetsuo's low-tech, stop-action film (a cartoon with humans) no doubt expresses an intense fear of technology and viral contagions, of sexualized women and urban isolation—not to mention of what all of this might mean for desire and the individual subject at the moment in which biotechnology is no longer the stuff of science fiction but of the present. (*Tetsuo*, we must remember, takes place in the present.) The "I" has been invaded and has lost control of itself as presently configured; only a new cyborgian body (whether it is still gendered is not clear) that "rusts" the old world and builds the new one offers any chance of survival. Yet the film is already dated, for its wires and steely spaces, jagged edges and industrial beats do not come close to the pacific-blue cyberspatial flows, wireless and bodyless, that dominate the present Internet imagination. Indeed, there is not a single computer in all of *Tetsuo*.

The excruciating pain and pleasure of *Tetsuo*'s metamorphoses (the sting of being born again and not dying) is absent from Oshii's *Ghost in the Shell*. Sex, desire, and the body have been radically transformed. We are in the near future (2029), and the planet, although still tenuously organized around nation-states, is connected by a web of information. Kusanagi Motoko is a special agent working for Section 9, an antiterrorist outfit of the Ministry of Internal Affairs. All but two members of Section 9 are cyborgs, assemblages of manufactured bodies (what makes up the shell) and their still human souls, or ghosts. Motoko, whose entire body has been provided by a corporation and is serviced by the government, is beginning to question the authenticity of her ghost. Is she an "I"? And how would she ever know whether her answer is indeed hers or supplied by someone else? In the film, Motoko is on the case to track down the "Puppet Master," a bodyless secret agent that lives in the information web and can hack not only into top-secret corporate and governmental data but—more alarmingly—into anyone's ghost, as well. It is learned, however, that the Puppet Master is in fact a secret project (Project 2501) created by Section 6 of the Ministry of Foreign Affairs as the perfect international espionage weapon. All is undone, however, when Project 2501 concludes that it is itself a life form and devises a strategy to free itself from its creators, apply for political asylum, and reproduce. With a new body, Project 2501 is now on the run, as both ministries fight over jurisdiction. For Major Kusanagi (Motoko), the issue is "personal": She wants to find Project 2501 in order to learn more about herself and manage these doubts about her own identity. When they finally meet, Project 2501 explains that its own perfection (a system with no variability) creates its own extinction. It wants to reproduce and proposes a merging with Motoko that would produce the needed differentiation. Motoko accepts and, after merging with Project 2501, is reborn with the body of a junior-high-school girl.

Inspired by Masamune Shiro's manga, *Ghost in the Shell* is a combination of single-cell and computer-generated animation. The film is more cinematic (in terms of mise-en-scène, narrative development, and editing) than most animation. It is also an introductory lesson in philosophy for its huge number of teenage and twenty-something viewers worldwide. For those of us who teach in North American universities, and especially who teach courses that are at all connected to Japan, we know that the demographics of our students have changed dramatically over the past years. Students were primarily attracted to the arts and Eastern religion in the 1960s and '70s; in the 1980s, they were chasing the overvalued yen; and today, they are consumed by (and consumers of) Japanese popular culture—namely manga and anime. The majority of these students seem to have no trouble questioning their own subjectivity and understanding themselves as cyborgs. Unlike many students in other courses, they do not, when intellectually pushed, return nervously to notions of bourgeois individualism in which everything—from poverty and crime to disease—is explained away by brandishing the autonomy and will (or lack thereof) of the individual subject. In fact, the challenge in these courses is usually to urge the students to think through how a watered-down notion of themselves as cyborgs might itself be one of the great ideologies of postmodernity, depoliticizing students to the extent that all that is left to do is consume so much cyberpunk paraphernalia.

Yet this questioning of identity and their eagerness to discuss issues of hybridity, multiple subjectivities, liminality, difference, and simulation rarely exceeds the territory of the individual subject, rarely moves to the question of national or global subjectivity. By national subjectivity I mean not understanding ourselves as national subjects—surely, there is no dearth of debate on this topic—but understanding how modern discourses have granted subjectivity to the nation, so that the nation is the agent through which self, other, and world are known.

In their book *Empire* (2000), Michael Hardt and Antonio Negri point to how much work under the rubric of postcolonial studies resorts to an older language of the nation and modern sovereignty, one that remains fixed on attacking an older form of power and one that views liberation only in terms of that older terrain.[46] To speak of Homi Bhabha's politics of hybridity (the subversion of power structures organized on binary logic) is still to speak of a form of domination based on modern sovereignty, a perspective that is primarily concerned with colonial sovereignty and not receptive to the new forms of rule that have emerged over the past thirty years. This is not so much an attack on contemporary postcolonial and postmodern work as it is a historicization that reads these intellectual currents as symptoms of a rupture in the tradition of modern sovereignty. But a new global order has emerged, a new global sovereignty. This new form of rule is what Hardt and Negri call "Empire." The term is not a synonym for imperialism or colonialism; it is "a new inscription of authority and a new design of the production of norms and legal instruments of coercion that guarantee contracts and resolve conflicts."[47] Relying on a new global monetary system, new global policing and military forms, and a new flexible and global network of communications, Empire has become the political subject that regulates the global market and global circuits of production.

The planet is organized differently under Empire. Unlike under European and Japanese imperialism, nation-states do not extend sovereignty beyond their borders; rather, Empire is itinerant, not bound to older configurations of linear time and space. It is "a decentered and deterritorializing apparatus of rule that progressively incorporates the entire global realm within its open expanding frontiers."[48] Despite *Empire*'s Western-centeredness and its choice not to engage with globalization discourse (academic and journalistic), *Empire* is one of the more ambitious and productive conceptualizations of globalization to date. It produces the concept of globalization and its entire set of requisite juridical, philosophical, cultural, economic, corporeal, and social categories. On top of all this, it offers a project for change—not a concrete blueprint for progressive change, but one that flashes its theoretical possibility, one that, first and foremost, must resist nostalgia for the nation-state. However much the nation-state appears to be (or actually is) a progressive force against the forces of globalization (as argued persuasively by a range of thinkers, including Paik Nak Chung, Geeta Kapur, and Nestor Garcia Canclini), once entrenched, its progressive dimension expires.[49] Globalization, rather, must be confronted in its globality; otherwise, it is destined to run safely ahead of its sentence. New global subjects, new global movements, and new global resistances must form to challenge the new global order.

We now know that a teleological conception of capitalism—one that is based on the nation-state—misses the mark. The United States, whose economic hegemony following World War II seemed unshakable, was a model of what appeared to be the success of Fordism. Fordism, which turns on mass-production and the consumption of homogenous goods, was remarkable because workers would be paid enough money to purchase the goods they produced. With the workers playing an integral part not only in production but also in consumption, many radical thinkers (Herbert Marcuse, for instance) lost faith in the workers' ability to instigate revolution on the factory floor. This produced a paradox: Technology and automation produced the potential for qualitative change in advanced industrial society, while the existence of these forces froze this potential by buying off the worker on the level of need and desire.

Looking back at the intellectual work of the 1950s and '60s, it seems clear that much of it misread the path of capitalism. By the early 1970s, marked by the oil shocks that set off quakes around the capitalist world, the rigidity of Fordism could no longer contain the inherent contradictions of capitalism. The capitalist system could recuperate itself only by radically changing its mode of organization—hence, the shift from Fordism to post-Fordism, or globalization. Ultimately, this new flexibility has not only provided the license for corporations to have much greater mobility, the ability to move from site to site searching for cheap and controllable labor; it has also meant the weakening of the power of the nation-state and the great increase of power for transnational corporations. These corporations serve the interests not of any one nation or state but of its own class of executives, politicians, journalists, artists, and academics, who affiliate first and foremost with one another, regardless of nationality, race, ethnicity, or gender. The international division of wealth between the world's rich and the world's poor is growing greater and greater: The gap in per capita income between the industrial and developing worlds tripled from 1960 to 1993, and the wealth of the world's 475 billionaires is greater than the combined incomes of the poorest half of humanity. At the same time, this new form of capitalism is permeating, however unevenly, the most remote of areas.[50]

This new form of capitalism no longer seems bent on "bourgeousifying" the proletariat, giving them enough income to satisfy their needs. In fact, it seems clear that what is happening is a reproletarianization of the international working class, a class that now far exceeds the factory itself and includes those working in the service economy of the first world just as much as it does those toiling in the factories of transnational capital—not to mention the growing number of impoverished who are marginalized from the very process of transnationalization itself.[51] As the culture industry consolidates and is exported around the world, and with the continued weakening of traditional labor unions and the ineffective growth of international ones, how can one express this reality and formulate a program of organization and resistance?

In one form or another—among philosophers and militants, filmmakers and cyberpunks—a search is under way for a new language and means of intervention, a common language whose grammar articulates the relation between the new flexibility of the world system and the hard fact that more than 36 million Africans are infected with HIV; a grammar that moves fluently from the local corruption of politicians in a Japanese village to the fact that one in every five children in the world lives in poverty. No one working in the intellectual or artistic realms today can turn away from the macrological facts of our current historical moment. Take, for example, Jacques Derrida, certainly one of the world's greatest living philosophers, and *Specters of Marx* (1994), in which he lists ten plagues of the new world order, including unemployment, homelessness, contradictions of the free market, foreign debt, the arms industry, and interethnic wars. Derrida warns that these empirical facts cannot be forgotten at a time that so many are celebrating the triumph of liberal democracy and the capitalist market. Derrida writes, "Let us never neglect this obvious macroscopic fact, made up of innumerable singular sites of suffering: no degree of progress allows one to ignore that never before, in absolute figures, never have so many men, women, and children been subjugated, starved or exterminated on the earth."[52]

The appeal to a "macroscopic fact" is not what we expect from a thinker such as Derrida. Yet as more years pass since that fateful year 1968, as the conservatism of the American school of Deconstruction becomes more apparent, and as a facile Francis Fukuyama becomes the philosopher-king of our post-Cold War CNN moment, Derrida realizes that we must, in the name of "justice" and "responsibility," affirm that which is unaffirmable, conceptualize that which is unconceptualizable, and hope for the possibility of that which is impossible. In other words, we must think our way out of the "end of history" rhetoric, which in the end is nothing but the reactionary rejection of, or the inability to think, a radically different alternative to the here and now.[53] To do this, Derrida argues for the concept of spectrality. The specter is neither presence nor the positivistic facts of everyday life; it is a trembling, reminding us that we cannot give up thinking and working toward the hope of an alternative way to organize our lives. Throughout this work, I have heard the rattling of this specter in the cinematic experiments of Japanese film history. When the specter rattles in *Tetsuo* and *Ghost in the Shell*, it rattles for the global, for Empire, for something beyond the assemblage of nations.

But before returning to the two films, I will first return to Japan, for never has the time been more dire for a discourse that exceeds the nation than in contemporary Japan. Ever since the bursting of the bubble in the early 1990s, a neo-nationalist sentiment has grown. Two examples—former Prime Minister Mori Yoshiro's comment that Japan is "a divine country with an emperor at its center" and Tokyo Governor Ishihara Shintaro's derogatory reference to foreigners in Japan as "people from third countries" (*sankoku-jin*)—show that the return to neo-nationalist sentiments in the face of globalization is ripe.[54] There is also growth in organizations, with names such as Diet Members League for a Bright Japan and Society for the Making of New School Textbooks in History, that attempt to reverse the recent strides made by various victims groups, such as those advocating compensation for comfort women and Koreans who were forcibly brought to Hiroshima and Nagasaki during World War II.[55] I read *Tetsuo*'s and *Ghost in the Shell*'s focus on the breakup of the individual as a desire to express the breakup of the nation, a desire that still cannot be conceptualized. If we think about the salary-man's body in *Tetsuo* or Motoko's body in *Ghost* as representing the national body, then we can understand the cyberpunk genre as symptomatic of a greater desire to map the global system. The problematic of the "I" and its instability, the realization that we are irrevocably cyborgian and that this is nothing to regret, prefigures the problematic of the "nation" and its instability. These films express the desire to speak about (to see . . . alas—to act on) something that at this point can only be felt: a world in which "Japan" no longer exists.

For example, we have *Tetsuo*'s gesture to viral infection, to body- and life-transforming contagions, at a moment in which AIDS is just beginning to register in Japan. The year *Tetsuo* was released, 1989, was also the year in which what became known as the tainted-blood scandal swelled. The government admitted that although it knew about the risks of unheated blood products in 1983, it waited until 1985 to approve the process of heating blood. Moreover, by 1983, officials of the U.S. Centers for Disease Control and Prevention had warned Japanese officials about the dangers of hemophiliacs' contracting HIV through blood products. More than 40 percent of Japan's hemophiliac community contracted HIV, and many died. The fear of HIV and AIDS in Japan is also the fear of a government that prioritizes collusive ties among public regulators, the pharmaceutical industry, and the medical establishment over the general welfare of the populace. To speak of a body infected with AIDS in Japan is at once to speak of the national body infected with a diseased state. But the same is also true on the larger, global scale.

In 2000, AIDS killed more than 3 million people worldwide—more than ten times the number who died in armed conflict. AIDS is now the single leading cause of death in Africa, and HIV-infection rates are soaring in parts of Asia and Eastern Europe. In Botswana, Zimbabwe, and South Africa, one-half of all fifteen-year-olds will likely die of AIDS. Thirteen million sub-Saharan African children have now lost one or both of their parents to AIDS, and the number is expected to reach 40 million by the end of the decade.[56] Eleven percent of the adult population of the Ivory Coasts is believed to carry HIV.[57] With an estimated half-million Chinese infected, and with the rate growing at more than 30 percent a year, China could very well be the next great epicenter of the disease.[58] Or take Cambodia, where today 3 percent of the adult population is infected, and some predict that, in the next few years, more people could die of AIDS than died at the hands of the Khmer Rouge. This global AIDS pandemic is not only the most perfect metaphor for globalization; it is globalization.

Money, goods, people, information, and disease travel more flexibly and at speeds hitherto unimaginable. Despite the integration of the planet, the sub-Saharan African HIV population is left to die (costs of anti-retroviral drugs far exceed the annual incomes of the infected), while in the First World infection rates have leveled off, and survival rates have increased. The global AIDS pandemic is not only about uneducated Africans who primitively ascribe their illnesses to local mythology; nor is it only about unscrupulous African officials who refuse to spend money on anti-retroviral medicine. It is also, and more profoundly, about the transformations in the world system: transnational institutions (pharmaceutical corporations and the WTO) that are not at liberty to suspend the logic of competition and profit; new global flows in the sex industry; new labor flows that are mobile and gendered; and a post-Cold War, postcolonial, and post-Fordist world order in which the political motivation for supporting the South has ended.

We must remember that in the days of decolonization, in the 1950s and '60s, public health was a priority in most African nations, and infant-mortality and life-expectancy rates improved dramatically. After these countries experienced economic crisis in the 1980s, health-care budgets were slashed, and the World Bank and IMF imposed austerity measures known as Structural Adjustment Programs (SAPs). These programs, imposed on more than seventy developing countries, were the fulcrums on which globalization turned. The SAPs were designed to promote exports made cheap by currency devaluation and to reduce "inefficient" government spending to allow nations to earn enough foreign exchange to pay back their loans. But the benefits from the new programs were never properly distributed to nations as a whole. The measures also created conditions conducive to the spread of HIV by displacing young women and children from rural villages to cities, where they resorted to commercial sex work, and by displacing packs of men to urban areas, where they were more likely to engage in unsafe sexual practices. As health-care spending dropped, AIDS education and treatment programs evaporated, and the conditions for an AIDS crisis were optimized. The HIV and AIDS crisis is as much a symptom of globalization as it is of immune deficiency.[59]

69. Tsukamoto Shinya's *Tetsuo*. Kaijyu Theater, 1988.

Tetsuo and *Ghost in the Shell* allegorize all of this. The films stress how individual and biological events are simultaneously social and political events. They call on us to make the impossible connections, to tease the red thread that weaves the social text. They flash for us what Bill Haver calls the "Real of AIDS," the unthinkable multiplicity that is AIDS, the specter that exceeds the dominant discourses that render the event routine and neatly ensconce it within a localized AIDS industry (composed of pharmaceutical and health-care companies and government regulatory and social-service agencies).[60] Yet these films do this at a historical moment in which the social and political events are difficult to articulate. In the late 1980s, when *Tetsuo* was produced (before the bursting of the Japanese bubble), it was much more challenging to make the connections for two reasons: First, because globalization as a discourse had yet to pervade the culture; and second, because of sharp self-censorship that permeated the nation. The most spectacular analogy to this self-censorship is the orchestrated silence around Emperor Hirohito's duodenal cancer at the end of 1988.[61] Indeed, Hirohito's body was in crisis and had been transformed, but no one spoke about it. Why such a stunning silence? Perhaps because, if revealed, it might flash the dishonorable link between Hirohito and the multitudes of others who die of cancer (Japanese and non-Japanese); reveal the disquieting continuity of the emperor system both before and after the war; highlight the privileged Japanese state and the multitude of Japanese who do not share in the spoils of the economic miracle; and drive home the fact that Japan exists in constitutive relation to the world. Tsukamoto relinks the chain; he literally bites it and drags it across his teeth for the world to see (fig. 69).

Ghost, made after the economic crisis and in animated form (although

70 and 71. Oshii Mamoru's *Ghost in the Shell.* Bandai Visual, 1995.

the manga by Masamune that inspired it had been serialized much earlier),
is more direct about the connections. The film opens with the following
statement: "In the near future, corporate networks reach out to the stars,
electrons and stars flow throughout the universe. The advance of comput-
erization, however, has not yet wiped out nations and ethnic groups." Why
not? Surely the nation as a provider of infrastructure and social services has
been wiped out. In *Ghost,* the trash is not picked up; shootouts occur in
public markets, discounting the safety of the people; and ecological disasters
abound. Perhaps it is the nation as a functional idea or ideology that is yet to
be wiped out. Although political economy exceeds the nation, culture and
ideology are still deeply rooted in it. This uneven development is pressed
throughout the work but most acutely in the narrative line of subjectivity:
The characters have exceeded the human subject in terms of the technology
of the body, while culture and ideology is still deeply rooted in it. This is illus-
trated in two extraordinary scenes, both relating to Motoko and gender. In
the first, she refers to menstruation, and in the second, Bateau recoils when
he glimpses her naked body.

When Motoko communicates telepathically with others in Section 9, her
colleagues comment on the static interference in her brain. "It must be
that time of the month," she hurls back. In this asexual world of information flows and computer-generated bodies—of the end of time, space, and
the body as once configured—the menstrual flow presumably has stopped,
as well. Indeed, it has stopped. But like a phantom limb, its memory, its
feeling, remains. The same goes for Bateau's sexual attraction to Motoko's
body. Motoko has been scuba diving, a dangerous act for a cyborg, because
if her automated "floaters" fail she will surely drown. Bateau asks Motoko

why she risks so much. "Wouldn't you come in and save me?" she sarcastically snaps back. Clearly upset, Bateau turns to voice his disapproval, only accidentally to see Motoko stripping off her wet suit (fig. 70). Ashamed and self/cyborgconscious, Bateau quickly darts his glance away and scowls in silence (fig. 71). Again, a residual human form persists in its present cyborgian self; the technology of the body has developed more quickly than the ideology of the body. Whereas Motoko understands this, as demonstrated by her irony and cyborg-effacement regarding the human menstrual cycle, Bateau does not. He remains humiliated and concealing about his human desire. It is Motoko's recognition that the past lives in the present and the present shapes the future that positions her as the utopian figure in the film, the one who will risk opening herself up (quite literally) to the future. When Bateau asks what she feels when floating in the ocean, Motoko responds, "I feel fear, loneliness, darkness, and perhaps even hope." "Hope?" Bateau shoots back. "Yes, when I float to the surface and see my reflection, I feel I can change into something else." Is this desire to exceed herself, to transform into something else, not also the hope of the nation?

epilogue

In the face of chapter 6's three different historical contexts—colonialism, Cold War, globalization—a crucial continuity remains: the body, and the female body in particular. There is the wife's sick and institutionally committed body in *Page of Madness*; Omocha's injured and hospitalized body in *Sisters of the Gion*; Noriko's child-rearing body as the mandatory machine of the nation in *Late Spring*; Masago's raped body in *Rashomon*; the girlfriend's sexually threatening and domineering body in *Tetsuo*; and Motoko's exploding body in *Ghost in the Shell*. These six canonical films engage the dominant sociohistorical problem of their moment vis-à-vis an appropriation of the female body.

This gender distinction is particularly interesting when considered in relation to the gendering of time during the construction of the nation-state. Anne McClintock argues that the temporal anomaly within nationalism (between nostalgia for the past and a desire to move away from the past) is "typically resolved by figuring the contradiction in the representation of time as a natural division of gender." McClintock adds, "Women are represented as the atavistic and authentic body of national tradition (inert, backward-looking, and natural), embodying nationalism's conservative principle of continuity. Men, by contrast, represent the progressive agent of national modernity (forward-thrusting, potent, and historic), embodying nationalism's progressive, or revolutionary, principle of discontinuity. Nationalism's anomalous relation to time is thus managed as a natural relation to gender."[1]

Each of the six films submits in some way to this gender distinction—even *Tetsuo* and *Ghost in the Shell.* In *Tetsuo,* the salaryman's male body represents the progressive principle of discontinuity (that which breaks into the "new world"), while in *Ghost* it is the female ghost and shell as formerly configured that must be overcome in order to provide the quantum leap into the new world. But how might this gendering relate to the fact that all of these films were made by men, a question that not only provides a path into the issue of gender and film but also shoots straight to the center of the theoretical problems concerning directorial agency and the auteur?

To mention the category "Women and Film in Japan" is almost always to mention those male directors who most interestingly employ women in their films, such as Mizoguchi, Naruse, and Imamura. But to mention the category "Women and Literature in Japan" is almost always to mention the most famous female writers of Japanese literary history, such as Murasaki Shikibu, Higuchi Ichiyo, and Miyamoto Yuriko. The obvious explanation for this is that so few women have made film in Japan. It takes a great deal more capital to participate in the film industry, mainstream or independent, than it does to write a prose narrative. Add to that gender biases against women in the larger collectives required by the filmmaking process, and it is clear why the history of women as writers is more developed. No one disputes these facts, but they still fail to account fully for why female directors have been consistently written out of Japanese film history and criticism. Another explanation is that one of the most important directors in Japan—Haneda Sumiko, who is a woman—makes documentary films, a parallel cinematic form and industry that never attains the same level of attention as feature film. Haneda has dedicated almost fifty years to rethinking how to represent the body, male and female. She is the director who made

72. Haneda Sumiko.

the eight-hour film about the kabuki actor Kataoka Nizaemon discussed in
chapter 1 (fig. 72).

Born in Manchuria, Haneda joined Iwanami Productions in 1950, where
she stayed for almost twenty years—much longer than the rest of her cohort,
such as Hani Susumu, Ogawa Shinsuke, Kuroki Kazuo, Higashi Yoichi, and
Tsuchimoto Noriake. Haneda then went on to make independent documentary films, including *Usuzumi no sakura* (The cherry tree with grey blossoms, 1976), a gorgeously haunting representation of a famous cherry tree's
seasonal transformations in Gifu Prefecture, punctuated by the coming-of-
age changes of a teenage girl; *Hayachine no fu* (Ode to Mount Hayachine,
1982), a meditative and non-nostalgic look at the persistence of ritual dance
culture (*Kagura*) in villages coming to terms with modernization; *AKIKO:
Aru dansa no shozo* (Akiko: Portrait of a dancer, 1985), a radiant glance at
the modernist dance legend Kanda Akiko as she prepares her troupe for a
performance entitled "Mary Magdalen"; *Chihosei rojin no sekai* (How to
care for the senile, 1986), an unorthodox examination of geriatrics and elder-
care services, with special attention to issues of dementia; *Kabuki Yakusha: Kataoka Nizaemon* (Kabuki actor: Kataoka Nizaemon, 1992–94), the
long-form documentary mentioned earlier that examines both the daily-life
banalities of Kataoka Nizaemon together with the spectacular performances
and ceremonies expected of one of the country's most important cultural
icons; and *Onnatachi no shogen* (Proof of women, 1996), a sharp archeologi-
cal examination of gender relations focusing on the troubles faced by a num-

ber of older women during their earlier and present participation in Japan's labor movement. Haneda, who has directed more than forty-five films and assisted on scores more, deserves the same status as any other director in the canon of Japanese film history. At the same time, her struggles as one of only a handful of women in the industry raises her significance to near-heroic proportions.

This leads to the issue of directorial agency and how it relates to the concepts of problem cinema and films of history. "Problem cinema" refers to how film comes to terms with the most profound social problems of its age. Colonialism, the postwar struggle between the individual and the collective, and the contradiction between the national and the transnational have been the organizing problems of this analysis—problems that have been thrown before film. I use the literal meaning "problem" (*proballein*) as something that is "thrown before" and thus must be scaled, penetrated, circumnavigated, destroyed, denied, or simply neglected, to stress that film cannot help but exceed itself. Film cannot help but be about what it is not immediately about. The other side of this is that the analysis of film cannot help but exceed itself; it cannot help but be about something other than film. I have located Japanese film's gesture to the "outside" not in its content but in its form. *What* films are about (a medieval war, a samurai battle, a modern tryst) seems less significant than *how* films are about (narrative structure, mode of production, editing, composition, acting). But this does not imply that form is simply the opposite of narrative content. Rather, film form, as discussed here, is not unlike other totalities, such as time and history. It is that abstraction produced by the relations of the film's various elements (elements that range from the stylistic to the content-based). It is that something that cannot be pinpointed by an examination of any concrete element; rather, it is precisely that which exceeds the elements but is nothing without them. Film form as relation necessitates an integration of the spectator, and thus the spectatorial context, into its meaning. To mention film form, therefore, is at once to mention not only the crash of stylistic and narrative elements, but also the crash of these elements into history.

If all films are problem cinema—that is, if all films are symptoms of the most profound problems of their own historical moment—then are not all films also what I have called films of history, films that seem actively to intervene with the historical problem at hand? I will answer "no" to this

73. Promotional flyer for Haneda Sumiko's
Proof of Women.

question. Not all films take the same risks. The language of risk invests new
agency in filmmakers and raises difficult questions of cultural theory; without such a language, however, all film would flatten as so many equivalent
symptoms. Indeed, some filmmakers take more risks than others. They risk
speaking a language for which there is no established grammar. They risk
representing the unrepresentable. They risk coordinating their work with
the most pressing social problems of their historical moment. They risk
taking the temperature of the age, then making film that is a bit too hot or a
bit too cold for our comfortable habits. They attempt to intervene with the
world and provoke the viewer to do the same.

This distinction came home to me while interviewing Haneda in Tokyo.
The director, who was just finishing her film about women and the labor
movement, explained that she would not have made the film if she had
not discovered that many of the women involved were dying year by year.
She put aside other projects—projects in which she had more interest at the
time—to make *Proof of Women* (fig. 73). In addition, in the year in which
Haneda made the film, the Japanese economy suffered a swift downturn,
and much of the progress women workers had made was reversed. Throughout the late 1980s and early 1990s, the number of female managers hired by
large corporations gradually increased; yet when new downsizings occurred,
in the mid- to late 1990s, these female hires were dismissed first, and new
female college graduates were once again overlooked. An intervention on
Haneda's part was required.

74. Promotional flyer for Haneda Sumiko's *AKIKO*.

75. Promotional flyer for Haneda Sumiko's *How to Care for the Senile*.

Proof of Women discloses the contradictions of the labor movement: how issues of gender can be heavy-handedly deferred to seemingly more immediate concerns. The women in the film often speak about the reproduction of unequal power relations within the labor movement itself. Haneda focuses her camera on the aging bodies of these women. There are long takes of eighty-year-old women canvassing streets with political leaflets, and luxurious closeups of the old cohort discussing the past. The female body here does not allegorize anything; it is not appropriated in order to rethink labor history or present the women's movement. Instead, the representation is about the women themselves—women who are in front of the camera and who are the film. Haneda used a similar approach in shooting the dancer Kanda Akiko, who studied with Martha Graham. In *AKIKO*, the most spectacular scenes are those not of the performances but of Akiko smoking cigarettes at her modest kitchen table while assessing the last rehearsal (fig. 74). Referring to herself in the third person (*Akiko ha ne . . .*) and repeatedly emphasizing that dance is her life, Akiko is represented in terms not of spectacle or crisis but in her everyday survival and being.

Haneda also shoots the everydayness of the patients suffering from senile dementia in *How to Care for the Senile* (fig. 75). Reflecting on this film, Haneda writes, "In regard to the senile, people pay attention to their extraordinary behavior. It is true that we can observe extraordinary symptoms and abnormal manners among those with senile dementia; however, as I got to know those people, I found out that they are very serious about their conditions, and they are trying to live life as fully as they can. . . . In the small world of the senile care hospital, I could face that they were devoting their lives to survival."[2] In the face of crisis, of "extraordinary symptoms" and "abnormal matters," Haneda is interested in the everydayness of the patients. In one scene in which an old woman wants to leave the hospital to visit an imaginary friend, the staff decides to let her go (accompanied by a staff member). The woman eventually returns to the center in a state devoid of disappointment or rejection. Haneda is impressed that the doctors do not resist the patients' impossible desires. Despite the deterioration of the patients' mental states, their emotional states and reactions function unchanged, and it is to these sound states that the hospital staff dedicate most of their care. This is not crisis-driven medical attention. Nor is this crisis-driven cinema. Haneda does not use the hospital to examine the crisis in elder health care in Japan. Rather, the film discloses how crisis is built into everyday life and therefore opens a form of representation that exposes the ideological work produced by such binaries as health and illness, normal and abnormal, and soundness and crisis.

Is Haneda able to do this because she makes documentary film? Because she is a woman? Yes and no. Yes, documentary film lends itself to non–crisis-driven cinema primarily because of relatively different viewer expectations and industrial demands. Yes, Haneda remains in the documentary field primarily because there is much more room for a woman to maneuver there than in the feature-film industry. But at the same time, no, because feature film is just as capable of producing non–crisis-driven narratives. And no, because Haneda's directorial choices cannot be reduced to her gender. Directorship is a site of negotiation in which Haneda (or her gender) does not disappear from the mix. Nor does she (or it) serve as a golden ticket to all meaning and interpretation. Here, a privileging of the conscious auteur (as individual director, collective, or critical construct) can exist together with a de-emphasizing of the director as just another term in the process of spectating. This desire to have it both ways—to square the circle of the structuralist/auteur debate—opens the possibility for both concepts, problem cinema and films of history, to work together, without one precluding the other.

I have made more than a few methodological leaps in my own work. Disparate categories such as money and perception, historiography and capitalist development, film adaptation and nationalist discourse, film acting and social agency, and pornography and mainstream culture, routinely have been pushed into the same idea. The very form of placing these categories in relation to each other is essential to the arguments made. Wrapped up in this work's form are the very arguments made on the level of each chapter's content. And as in the films made at the present moment, the problem of globalization, between the national and transnational, stands before my work. Indeed, business executives and political elites are not the only ones compelled to rethink their projects in the face of globalization. The transformation of the university, academic disciplines, nation-state, and world system demands a rethinking of intellectual work. But for all that has been written here about culture and capital, about the film aesthetic and the geopolitical, there still does not seem to be an effective language with which to express the transformations occurring at the present moment. The languages of film studies, with its psychoanalytic, semiotic, and close-analysis traditions, and of Japanese studies, with its anthropological, Orientalist, and insular traditions, seem to fall short in getting at what is at stake at the current moment. The search for a different language—one that can attend to the particularities of Japan and Japanese cinema while remaining sensitive to how these categories exceed themselves at every turn—has been at the heart of this study.

notes

INTRODUCTION

1   For example, Iijima Tadashi, *Shin eigaron* (New film theory) (Tokyo: Seito Shorin, 1936) and *Eiga bunka no kenkyu* (Film culture research) (Tokyo: Shinchosha, 1939); Iwasaki Akira, *Eiga no riron* (Film theory) (Tokyo: Iwanami Shoten, 1956); Imamura Taihei, *Eiga to bunka* (Film and culture) (Tokyo: Yumani Shobo, 1991) and *Eiga geijutsu no keishiki* (Forms of film art) (Tokyo: Yumani Shobo, 1991).

2   Economic Stabilization Board, "Taiheiyo senso ni yoru waga kuni no higai sogo hoko-kusho" (Comprehensive report on damages to Japan from the Pacific War), April 1949, as cited in Tsuru Shigeto, *Japan's Capitalism* (Cambridge: Cambridge University Press, 1993), 8.

3   On the transnational capitalist class, see Leslie Sklair, *The Sociology of the Global System* (Baltimore, Md.: Johns Hopkins University Press, 1991), 117.

4   See chapter 3 of this volume.

5   Sklair seems to overstate the case by arguing that the cultural-ideological sphere (in

this case, the global ideology of consumerism as replacing national ideologies) will be moving at the same speed as the political-economic sphere.

6 The emerging influence of citizens' groups led to the enactment of the Nonprofit Organization Law (NPO) in December 1998. Nearly 1,000 groups received official NPO status during the following year. Although these groups focus on a range of activities, their common thread is to protect and enhance public interest. For example, leading up to the winter 1999 WTO conference in Seattle, a few groups (calling for a rethinking of free trade) energetically questioned and challenged government officials. Another citizens' group in Sendai protested a 15 million yen (166 thousand dollars) lecture fee paid to the British politician Margaret Thatcher.

7 I want to emphasize a distinction between a contradiction and an antinomy, a distinction that is most interestingly noted by Fredric Jameson and one that I work through in more detail in chapter 2. Jameson argues that a contradiction can be resolved through praxis, whereas an antinomy is a conceptual paradox, an unthinkability that requires textual engagement to dispel its "intolerable closure" (Fredric Jameson, *The Political Unconscious: Narrative as a Socially Symbolic Act* [Ithaca, N.Y.: Cornell University Press, 1981], 82–83). See also p. 270 n. 2.

8 It is important to note at the outset that by film form I do not simply mean the opposite of narrative content. Rather (and as will be performed in the following chapters and returned to in the epilogue), I mean an abstraction that is the totality of relations among the various elements of the film (stylistic and content), the film's historical moment and place of production, and spectatorial perception practices. See also the epilogue, p. 258.

9 I thank one of this manuscript's anonymous readers for suggesting that this point be stressed.

CHAPTER 1: RELATION: FILM, CAPITAL, TRANSFORMATION

1 Adapted from a noh version, *Momijigari* takes place on a clear autumn day as Taira no Koremochi sets off to hunt deer on Mount Togakushi. When offered sake by a noblewoman who is resting under a tree, Koremochi accepts, then dozes off into a powerful dream. In the dream, a mountain goat explains that the noblewoman is in fact a demon and that he must care for his life. On waking, Koremochi slays the demon.

2 *Jijiyo Shincho*, January 9, 1901 (Meiji 33), as quoted in Tanaka Junichiro, *Nihon eiga hattatsu-shi: Dai ichi kan* (Tokyo: Chuo Koron, 1957), 72.

3 For more information about the Lumière brothers' screenings in Japan, see Koga Futoshi, ed., *Hikaru no tanjyo: Ryumieru!* (Tokyo: Asahi Shinbun-sha, 1995), 67–77; and Yoshida Yoshishige, Yamaguchi Masao, and Kinoshita Naoyuki's *Eiga denrai* (The prehistory of film) (Tokyo: Iwanami Shoten, 1995).

4 Rey Chow, *Primitive Passions: Visuality, Sexuality, Ethnography, and Contemporary Chinese Cinema* (New York: Columbia University Press, 1995). Chow describes the

Chinese writer Lu Xun's first film experience. While studying medicine in Japan during the Russo-Japanese War, Lu Xun was shown images of a Chinese man being publicly executed for being a Russian spy. Going against the traditional view that the intense content of this filmic experience inspired Lu Xun to give up medicine and turn to literature, Chow reinterprets this story as one about modernist shock and how self-consciousness is linked to the position of being a spectator. Chow writes, "To put it simply, Lu Xun discovers what it means to 'be Chinese' in the modern world by watching film. Because it is grounded in an apprehension of the aggressiveness of the technological medium of visuality, self-consciousness henceforth could not be separated from a certain violence that splits the self, in the very moment it becomes 'conscious,' into seeing and the seen": ibid., 9.

5 Tanaka, *A History of Development of Japanese Film*, 73.

6 This relation between forms of exchange and forms of thought is inspired by Alfred Sohn-Rethel's very suggestive book *Intellectual and Manual Labour: A Critique of Epistemology* (London: Macmillan, 1978). This thesis, in which the daily act of exchange inscribes itself into our conceptual categories, will be invoked in the final section of this chapter. The most recent incorporation of Sohn-Rethel's work is in Slavoj Žižek's equally suggestive *The Sublime Object of Ideology* (London: Verso, 1989). Žižek seizes on Sohn-Rethel's notion of "practical solipsism," in which each time we engage in an exchange we necessarily misrecognize the situation as one between two individuals instead of one that ricochets throughout the social totality. This allows Žižek to link the Freudian symptom with the Marxian one, and thus offer a theory of ideology that is less about "false consciousness" than about "a social reality whose very existence implies the non-knowledge of its participants as to its essence": Žižek, *Sublime Object*, 16–21.

7 Monma Kishi, "Kabuki to eiga" (Kabuki and film), in *Kabuki Yakusha: Kataoka Nizaemon*, ed. Monma Kishi (Tokyo: Box Office, 1995), 2–4.

8 Three works that draw relations between the structure of a film and the structure of the film experience are Vivian Sobchack, *The Address of the Eye: A Phenomenology of Film Experience* (Princeton, N.J.: Princeton University Press, 1992); Gilles Deleuze, *Cinema I: The Movement Image*, trans. Hugh Tomlinson and Barbara Habberjam (Minneapolis: University of Minnesota Press, 1986), and *Cinema II: The Time Image*, trans. Hugh Tomlinson and Robert Galeta (Minneapolis: University of Minnesota Press, 1989). Sobchack writes, "The spectator and the film together uniquely negotiate and constitute the significance of visual and visible existence": Sobchack, *Address*, 260–61.

9 Aum was a cult that practiced a scaled-down form of Indian Buddhism in Japan. Led by Asahara Shoko, Aum had come under suspicion for criminal activities even before the poison attack.

10 I do not mean to suggest that this dominance of the visual and its effects is limited to contemporary popular culture, such as advertisements, television, and other forms.

Literature and theater, two traditional artistic bastions, are not sheltered from the effects and displacements of technologized visuality.

11 Jameson puts it this way: "Human time, individual time, is out of sync with socio-economic time, with the rhythms or cycles the—so-called Kondratief waves—of the mode of production itself, with its brief windows of opportunity that open into collective praxis, and its incomprehensible inhuman periods of fatality and insurmountable misery": Fredric Jameson, "Actually Existing Marxism," in *Polygraph 6/7* (Durham, N.C.: Duke University Press, 1993), 172. And Deleuze puts it this way: "The sensory-motor break makes man a seer who finds himself struck by something intolerable in the world, and confronted by something unthinkable in thought": Deleuze, *Cinema 2*, 169.

12 Kawabata Yasunari, *Asakusa kurenaiden* (The Asakusa crimson gang) Kawabata Yasunari Zenshu, vol. 2 (Tokyo: Shinchosha, 1981).

13 J. A. Hobson puts it this way: "Thus we reach the conclusion that Imperialism is the endeavour of the great controllers of industry to broaden the channel for the flow of their surplus wealth by seeking foreign markets and foreign investments to take off the goods and capital they cannot sell or use at home": J. A. Hobson, *Imperialism: A Study* (Ann Arbor: University of Michigan Press, 1965), 85.

14 Part of this Ur-history can be detected in the merchant ideology that was firmly in place before 1868. Tetsuo Najita explains how this pre-logic of capitalism was being constructed intellectually in the famous merchant academies of Osaka: see Tetsuo Najita, *Visions of Virtue in Tokugawa Japan* (Chicago: University of Chicago Press, 1987).

15 From 1885 to 1911, the length of government-operated railways increased from 212 miles to 4,775 miles; the number of post offices increased from about 5,000 to 7,000; and the number of telegraph offices increased from 50 to 4,500: Yoshihara Kunio, *Japanese Economic Development* (Oxford: Oxford University Press, 1994), 5–6.

16 During the period 1914–18, a surplus of 1.475 million yen (737.5 thousand dollars) was recorded in the trade account, and from 1915 to 1920, a surplus of 2.07 million yen (1.05 million dollars) was recorded in the invisible account: ibid., 10–11.

17 Nakamura Takafusa, *Showa keizaishi* (A history of Showa economics) (Tokyo: Iwanami Shoten, 1986), 27.

18 See the list of films compiled by Koga Futoshi in *Hikaru no tanjyo*, 51–107.

19 Hasumi Shigehiko, "Gaburieru bairu to eiga no rekishi" (Gabriel Veyre and the history of film) in *Hikaru no tanjyo*, 20–26.

20 Komatsu Hiroshi, "Shinematogurahu to nihon ni okeru shokieiga seisaku" (The cinematograph and the first films in Japan) in *Hikaru no tanjyo*, 40–45.

21 A benshi is a commentator who, facing the audience below and to the left of the screen, performed the roles of the characters on-screen, provided context for the film, explained about production processes, and gave political commentary. The importation

of the first successful talkie in Japan, Joseph von Sternberg's *Morocco* (1931), put most of the benshi out of work.

22 "Genbun itchi" refers to a new, more "ordinary" writing style that deemphasized the direct, figural, and visual meaning of Chinese ideograms by emphasizing the more concrete qualities of phonetic sound.

23 The benshi system underwent a significant change after the Japanese Ministry of Education issued new regulations in the mid-1930s. I expand on this aspect of the benshi system in chapter 3.

24 It was also at this time that Kamei Fumio was admonished for *Shanghai* (1938) and *Tatakau heitai* (Fighting soldiers, 1939), two mildly critical documentaries about the Japanese army in Shanghai that contains an audio track (of the renowned benshi Matsuda Shunsui) that synthesizes some progressive elements of the benshi system with elements from the newly emerging talkie.

25 Of course, Ozu had made some of his great films before the mid-1930s, and Ito Daisuke made his best films in the 1920s.

26 In a general sense, this is represented by the so-called revisionist school of thinkers who argue that the nature of Japanese capitalism is different from that of Western capitalism and therefore demands an institutional and cultural approach. See, for example, the work of Chalmers Johnson (*MITI and the Japanese Miracle* [Stanford, Calif.: Stanford University Press, 1982]); James Fallows (*More Like Us* [Boston: Houghton Mifflin Company, 1989]); Karel VanWolferen (*The Enigma of Japanese Power* [London: Macmillan, 1989]); and Clyde Prestowitz (*Trading Places* [Tokyo: Charles E. Tuttle Company, 1988]).

27 Here one can cite thinkers ranging from Sakakibara Eisuke and Imai Kenichi to a number of Western journalists, such as Eamonn Fingleton.

28 Nagasu Kazuji, *Kokusai jidai no nihon keizai* (Japanese capitalism in the age of internationalism) (Tokyo: Kawade Shobo, 1973). I was reminded of this phrasing by Tessa Morris-Suzuki's *A History of Japanese Economic Thought* (London: Routledge, 1989), 86.

29 Here I have in mind Joseph Anderson's "Second and Third Thoughts about the Japanese Film," in Donald Richie and Joseph Anderson, *The Japanese Film* (Princeton, N.J.: Princeton University Press, 1959), 439–56.

30 Kurosawa himself is the most emphatic thinker to argue this point, as can be seen in his *Something Like an Autobiography* (New York: Vintage, 1983). See Eric Cazdyn, "Cult of Kurosawa's Westernness," in *Ribbon of Dreams: Great Directors Series*, dir. John Menier, University of California, San Diego, Television (1995) (hereafter UCSD TV).

31 Long waves or periodic crises have been a rich object of study in the field of political economy. From Engels and Luxemburg to the Russian Nikolai Kondratiev and Joseph Shumpeter, from Uno Kozo and Ito Makoto to the French Regulationists, the issue has been under constant debate. Moreover, this debate has not been confined to the Marx-

ist economic tradition. Strong Keynesian links with new work are being produced by the Social Structure Accumulation group in the United States and many others.

32 Robert Wade and Frank Veneroso have argued that the crises in South Korea, Indonesia, and Thailand have more to do with record-level bank lending by Japanese and Western banks in combination with constant pressure to deregulate by the IMF and the World Bank. In other words, the crises have been generated more by the needs of the world system than by disconnected mistakes made by inexperienced and greedy businessmen; Robert Wade and Frank Veneroso, "The Asian Crisis: The High Debt Model Versus the Wall Street–Treasury–IMF Complex." *New Left Review* 228 (1998): 3–23.

33 This is expressed in mass layoffs, offshore outsourcing, trade disputes, and the global chase by transnational corporations after cheap labor.

34 John Belton, *Widescreen Cinema* (Cambridge, Mass.: Harvard University Press, 1992).

35 Oshima Nagisa, *Cinema, Censorship, and the State* (Cambridge, Mass.: MIT Press, 1992), 9–10.

36 I take this phrasing from Meagan Morris's introduction to Paul Willeman, *Looks and Frictions: Essays in Cultural Studies and Film Studies*, (Bloomington: Indiana University Press, 1994). Morris writes: "This is a way of displacing the 'the subject,' 'the gaze' and 'the text' as privileged terms of analysis by asking a different questions about historical experience in cinema": ibid., 19.

37 Roman Jakobson lucidly works through these ambiguities in "On Realism in Art," in *Language in Literature,* ed. Krystyna Pomorska and Stephen Rudy (Cambridge, Mass.: Harvard University Press, 1987), 19–27. Jakobson presents a number of examples of how realism is used in painting and literature to bring "the extreme relativity of the concept of 'realism' into sharp relief." From understandings that emphasize the producer's notion of reality to ones that emphasize the perceiver, and from tendencies that attempt to deform the given artistic norms to approximate reality to the "consistent motivation and justification of poetic constructions" as realism, Jakobson stresses the importance of distinguishing the various meanings of realism in order to avoid confusion and naivete.

38 Karatani Kojin, *Nihon kindai bungaku no kigan* (Origins of modern Japanese literature), trans. Brett deBarry (Durham, N.C.: Duke University Press, 1993), 51.

39 Ibid., 56.

40 This is how Ueno Toshiya, by referring to the 1930s philosopher Nakai Masakazu and his work *Bigaku nyumon* (An introduction to aesthetics), Nakai Masakazu Zenshu, vol. 2 (Tokyo: Bijutsu shuppan-sha, 1967), 313–55, differentiates the role that film played at the turn of the twentieth century: "Nakai terms the shock generated by these new technologies and media 'beauty of the machine.' Just as we can be deeply impressed by a natural landscape, we experience similar emotions when faced with human constructions, or the dynamic movement of machines. Nevertheless, this emotion differs qualitatively from the one generated by traditional arts such as painting

or sculpture, which are essentially 'hand-produced.' This . . . is because things and in-struments designed and made by humans have not necessarily been produced with the original intention of providing an aesthetic enjoyment": Ueno Toshiya, "Eiga no hajimari, eiga no soto" (The beginnings of cinema, the outside of cinema), in 7 *Trans-figurations in Electronic Shadows*, published in coordination with the Yamagata International Documentary Film Festival (1995), 16–17.

41 "The transaction of trade through money, he [Kusama] further reasoned, was not merely a 'physical' exchange but an emotive and 'ethical' one as well because the consistent content of money made 'trust' between men based on a nonarbitrary, fair, and objective norm possible": Najita, *Visions of Virtue*, 235.

42 This section on the relation between money and perception was inspired by a talk delivered by Fredric Jameson at the University of California, San Diego (UCSD): Fredric Jameson, "Culture and Finance Capital," public lecture, UCSD, May 1997, published as Fredric Jameson, "Culture and Finance Capital," *Critical Inquiry* 24 (fall 1997): 246–65. I also take inspiration from Deleuze's two cinema books—*Cinema 1* and *Cinema 2*—which stress that film itself is an image of thought.

43 Sohn-Rethel, *Intellectual and Manual Labour*, 20.

44 Uno Kozo, *Keizai genron* (Principles of economics) (Tokyo: Iwanami Shoten, 1967), 42.

45 Ibid., 43–44.

46 Uno uses the term "*undoutai no shutai*" (the subject of movement) at the end of a footnote, after explaining the elements of money: see ibid., 40.

47 Donald Richie, *Japanese Cinema: An Introduction* (Hong Kong: Oxford University Press, 1990), 2.

48 Doug Henwood, *Wall Street: How It Works and for Whom* (London: Verso, 1997), 10.

49 Yamada Atsushi, "Advances in Technology Call for New Measures to Stabilize Markets," *Asahi Shinbun*, August 20, 1998. Available from: http://www.asahi.com.

50 Henwood, *Wall Street*, 45. In 1977, foreign-currency reserves amounted to more than fourteen days' worth of the amount spent on foreign-currency transactions; by 1998, the transactions themselves ($1.3 trillion) were greater than the reserves ($1.25 trillion): ibid.

51 Paul Krugman, "Are Currency Crises Self-fulfilling?" *NBER* [National Bureau of Economic Research] *Macroeconomics Annual*, 1996.

52 Jameson, "Culture and Finance Capital," 259–60.

CHAPTER 2: HISTORIOGRAPHY: NATION, NARRATIVE, CAPITAL

1 Iwasaki Akira, *Eiga to shihon-shugi* (Film and capitalism) (Tokyo: Sekai-sha, 1931); *Nihon eiga-shi* (Japanese film history), film, produced by Shinko Film Corporation and Ministry of Foreign Affairs (1941); Tanaka Junichiro, *Nihon eiga hattatsu-shi* (A history of the developments of Japanese film), 5 vols. (Tokyo: Chuo Koron-sha, 1957); Donald Richie and Joseph Anderson, *The Japanese Film* (Princeton, N.J.: Princeton University

Press, 1959); Oshima Nagisa, dir., *Nihon eiga hyaku-nen* (One hundred years of Japanese cinema) film, produced by British Film Institute (1995); and Sato Tadao, *Nihon eiga-shi* (A history of Japanese film), 4 vols. (Tokyo: Iwanami Shoten, 1995).

2   Jameson, *The Political Unconscious*, 82–83. Jameson also explains ("Of Islands and Trenches: Neutralization and the Production of Utopian Discourse," in *The Ideologies of Theory, Volume 2: The Syntax of History* [Minneapolis: University of Minnesota Press, 1977] 75–101) that he prefers the word "antinomy" to "contradiction" because it confronts some of the attacks on a linear and continuous historiography (coming particularly from Michel Foucault's *Archeology of Knowledge*, trans. A. M. Sheridan Smith [New York: Pantheon, 1972]). This attack argues that a theory studying the "resolution" of contradictions fails to appreciate that a given *episteme* cannot be modified or resolved; it can only be replaced by a totally different episteme, one that is structured with different logical possibilities. Jameson responds by writing: "Such antinomies cannot be solved or resolved in their own terms; rather, they are violently restructured by an infrastructural praxis, which, rendering the older oppositions meaningless, now lays the preconditions for some new conceptual system or ideology which has no *immediate* link with the preceding one": Jameson, "Of Islands and Trenches," 90. This struggle of trying to be attentive to synchronic breaks in history while not forfeiting the explanatory power of a diachronic analysis goes straight to the heart of my inquiry.

3   Jameson, *The Political Unconscious*, 82–83.

4   Iwasaki, *Film Theory*.

5   After Kurosawa Akira won the Golden Lion at the 1951 Venice Film Festival and an Academy Award for Best Foreign Picture in 1952, Japanese film offered a new utopia for many Western critics and filmmakers. See my "Cult of Kurosawa's Westernness," in the *Ribbon of Dreams* Great Directors Series made for UCSD television. Here I argue that *Rashomon* won the 1951 Golden Lion (and Japanese film in general won the hearts of Westerners) less for being a superb film (which it is) than because at that particular moment, for important geopolitical reasons, the West was ready to discover a Japanese filmmaker: Cazdyn, *Ribbon of Dreams*, UCSD TV.

6   Iwasaki Akira, *Eiga geijutsu-shi* (*A History of Film Art*) (Tokyo: Sekai-sha, 1930). The first two chapters of *A History of Film Art*, written in 1927, are near-poetic glosses of Hollywood film life in the 1920s. Chapter 1, "A History of Film Art," is composed of disconnected sections with such headings as "California Rhapsody" and "Scenario Writer." But, as Iwasaki explains in the book's preface, the last chapter, "On Montage," should be read first because it was the work of the Russian filmmakers that he considered to be most important to introduce to a Japanese audience.

7   Iwasaki, *Film and Capitalism*, 1.

8   *Nihon eiga-shi: Dai Ichi Bu/Dai Ni Bu* (Japan film history: Parts 1 and 2), Dai Nihon Eiga Kyokai, benshi Matsuda Shunsui (1941). For a very brief mention of the film, see *Kinema Jumpo* 44 (November 11, 1940) and *Nihon eiga nenkan* (Japan film handbook)

(Tokyo: Daido-sha, 1975), 5: 701. I viewed this film at the National Film Center in Tokyo on May 16 and June 5, 1997.

9   For a brief introduction to the Film Law in English, see Darrell Williams Davis, *Picturing Japaneseness: Monumental Style, National Identity, Japanese Film* (New York: Columbia University Press, 1996), 64–69. For an introduction in Japanese, see Sato, *A History of Japanese Film*, 2:21–37, in which Sato writes about the law and about a number of films that were made under it.

10 *Kanto taishi taika jikkyo* (The real conditions of the great Kanto earthquake), film, photographer Shirai Shigeru, produced by Ministry of Education, Social Education Department (September 1, 1923). The film depicts nothing about other great horrors of the quake, such as the persecution of Koreans and the hoarding of food and money.

11 Shinko was a subsidiary of Shochiku, which helped produce the film.

12 See Masao Miyoshi, *Off Center: Power and Culture Relations Between Japan and the United States* (Cambridge, Mass.: Harvard University Press, 1991), 17.

13 Ibid., 18.

14 Iwasaki, *Film and Capitalism*, 5–6.

15 Walter Benjamin, "Theses on the Philosophy of History," in *Illuminations*, trans. Harry Zohn (New York: Schocken Books, 1968), 253–64.

16 Harry D. Harootunian, "The Benjamin Effect: Modernism, Repetition, and the Path to Different Cultural Imaginaries," in *Walter Benjamin and the Demands of History*, ed. Michael P. Steinberg (Ithaca, N.Y.: Cornell University Press, 1996), 62–87.

17 Susan Buck-Morss, *The Dialectics of Seeing: Walter Benjamin and the Arcades Project* (Cambridge, Mass.: MIT Press, 1991), 67.

18 Ibid., 67–68.

19 Kamei Fumio, *Tatakau eiga: Dokyumentarisuto no showa-shi* (Fighting film: A documentarist's history of the Showa era) (Tokyo: Iwanami Shincho, 1989), 18.

20 Ibid., 8.

21 The person who made the suggestion was Matsuda Shunsui, who was the most famous benshi of the day and was featured in the *Japanese Film History* (1941).

22 Kamei, *Fighting Film*, 60–61.

23 Sergei Eisenstein, *Film Form: Essays in Film Theory* (New York: Harcourt, Brace, and World, 1949), 28–32.

24 Not only is this evident in the passage that I quoted earlier, but Kamei devoted an entire film to one of the most renowned haiku artists, Kobayashi Issa (*Kobayashi Issa*, 1941).

25 I purposely use this phrase to stress the relations between the methodological emphases of Benjamin, Kamei, and Eisenstein and those formulated by Marx in *Grundrisse*. Marx writes that thought is most critical when it rises from the abstract to the concrete: Karl Marx, *Grundrisse* (London: Penguin Books, 1973), 101.

26 Compare this with the following comments by Jean-Pierre Gorin: "The only thing I

can say is a political film which disconnects the normal links of reality, which suddenly breaks the world apart gives you space where suddenly you can think and breathe and deal with the elements": Gorin, as quoted in Martin Walsh, "Godard and Me: Jean-Pierre Gorin Talks," *Take One* 5 (1985): 14–17. Gorin, who made nine films with Jean-Luc Godard between 1968 and 1972, is known for attempting to work out a dialectical filmmaking that turns on the problem of temporality.

27 Sato Tadao, "Nihon Eiga no seiritsushita shidai," (The Formation of Japanese cinema) in *Nihon eiga no tanjyo* (The birth of Japanese cinema), vol. 1, ed. Imamura Shohei (Tokyo: Iwanami Shoten, 1985), 215.

28 Noel Burch, *To the Distant Observer: Form and Meaning in the Japanese Cinema* (Berkeley: University of California Press, 1979), 11.

29 Richie and Anderson, *The Japanese Film*, 17.

30 This issue of a diachronic history, and the related term of a synchronic history, is one that brings with it a whole host of philosophical problems, such as identity and difference; continuity and discontinuity; subject and object; representation; totality; and, of course, historiography, the issue under consideration here. At this point, however, I am not arguing for one over the other—for synchronic over diachronic, for example. Instead, I am arguing that a chronological history employs a diachronic method, but one that, in the most general sense, is unconscious of the very problematic of diachrony-synchrony. The consciousness of this problematic, regardless of which term is privileged, is significant in shaping the type of history that will be written. For more on the problem of historiography, see the section called "Continuity, Discontinuity, Crisis" in chapter 1.

31 Tanaka, *A History of the Development of Japanese Film*, 1.

32 When the work was originally published, the individual volumes were not subtitled. The following subtitles were added later: Volume 1: "*The Period of the Moving Picture*"; Volume 2, "*From the Silent Film to the Talkie*"; Volume 3, "*Post War Film Liberation*"; Volume 4, "*The Golden Age*" (1945–63); and Volume 5, "*The Arrival of the Image Age*" (to 1975).

33 Richie and Anderson, *The Japanese Film*, 35.

34 Ibid., 126.

35 Gregory Barrett has translated various essays by Sato Tadao. They are compiled in *Currents in Japanese Cinema* (Tokyo: Kodansha, 1982). This work is too short, however, and it is not comprehensive, as is Richie and Anderson's. Therefore, it does not qualify here as a chronological history. Also, new translations are being prepared all the time, such as recent articles by Iwamoto Kenji and Komatsu Hiroshi. See, for instance, Komatsu Hiroshi, "Some Characteristics of Japanese Cinema Before World War I," trans. Linda C. Ehrlich and Yuko Okutsu, and Iwamoto Kenji, "Sound in the Early Japanese Talkies," trans. Lisa Spalding, both in *Reframing Japanese Cinema: Authorship, Genre, History*, ed. Arthur Nolletti, Jr., and David Desser (Bloomington: Indiana

University Press, 1992). I must also mention recent transformations in this situation brought about by the emergence of scholars who can research in the Japanese language and remain sensitive to issues in film studies and writing history in general.

36 Richie and Anderson, *The Japanese Film*, 182.

37 Ibid., 385.

38 Ibid., 390.

39 Tanaka, *A History of Development in Japanese Film* 2:406–08. It might also be useful to note that Tanaka contributed to Prokino's journals.

40 Some Prokino filmmakers worked outside of the Communist Party, and several more established filmmakers of the day—Mizoguchi, for example—contributed to the group's activities.

41 Richie and Anderson, *The Japanese Film*, 60.

42 I wonder how the terrain of Japanese film criticism in the United States and Europe would have changed if the decisive text had been written by someone who was, say, not as enamored of Kurosawa's impressive corpus of films and inspired, rather than embarrassed, by the risks taken by directors such as Kamei and Imai. Would other paths have been carved so that the English book on Japanese film would look considerably different—with, for example, other directors being stressed and other problematics being engaged? Or would the absence have seriously set back the progress of English research on Japanese film work, leaving even more of a dearth of criticism than we see today? Or perhaps Richie and Anderson's negligent critical asides do not make the slightest difference when compared with the function their work serves as the field's premier reference guide in English.

43 Karatani Kojin, *Origins of Modern Japanese Literature* (Tokyo: Kodansha, 1980).

44 Richie and Anderson, *The Japanese Film*, 5.

45 Ibid., 388.

46 Ibid., 380.

47 Tsuji Kyohei, *Eiga no tosho* (Tokyo: Yoshikaze Press, 1989).

48 David Desser, *Eros Plus Massacre: An Introduction to the Japanese New Wave Cinema* (Bloomington: Indiana University Press, 1988); Davis, *Picturing Japaneseness.*

49 Iwamoto Kenji, ed., *Nihon eiga to modanizumu: 1920–1930* (Japanese film and modernism: 1920–1930) (Tokyo: Riburo Poto, 1991); Komatsu Hiroshi, *Kigen no eiga* (Cinema of origins) (Tokyo: Seidosha, 1991).

50 Davis, *Picturing Japaneseness*, 26.

51 Desser, *Eros Plus Massacre*, 15.

52 Audie Boch, *Japanese Film Directors* (New York: Kodansha International, 1978).

53 Desser, *Eros Plus Massacre*, 16.

54 Ibid.

55 Mitsuhiro Yoshimoto "Logic of Sentiment: The Postwar Japanese Cinema and the Question of Modernity" (Ph.D. diss., University of California, San Diego, 1993), 180.

56 Desser, *Eros Plus Massacre*, 20.

57 One question that I have not yet engaged is whether the stages of writing Japanese film history might be different in Japanese and English. This presents a very complicated problem of deciding which histories should be considered part of the English or Japanese group. For example, Richie and Anderson would seem to fall into the Japanese group, whereas Desser, who rarely uses Japanese sources and who does not seem influenced by Japanese historiography, would fall into the English group. Then there are the cases of Sato and Iwasaki, who read English and were familiar with the English literature on Japanese film. For these reasons, I have decided to lump the histories together with the hope that these problems will be engaged as they emerge.

58 Oshima Nagisa, *Sengo 50 nen, Eiga 100 nen* (Fifty years after the war, One hundred years of film) (Tokyo: Fubai-sha, 1995), 8.

59 The expository mode is one of four modes that Bill Nichols marks off in his important work *Representing Reality: Issues and Concepts in Documentary* (Minneapolis: University of Minnesota Press, 1991), 32–38, although it should be noted that Oshima's film does integrate other modes. For example, by commenting about his own films in the first person, he troubles the "voice-of-god" quality that such documentaries usually affect.

60 For example, Scorsese shoots himself sitting in a chair, relaxed and in conversation with the viewer, whereas Wenders's narration takes place in a famous movie house, where most of Germany's leading filmmakers are chatting about the images on the screen and their own careers.

61 Oshima, *Fifty Years*, 8.

62 On this transition, see David Harvey, *The Condition of Postmodernity* (Cambridge: Blackwell, 1989), and Ernest Mandel, *Late Capitalism* (London: Verso, 1978). For analyses of the Japanese situation, see the works listed in note 63.

63 Ito Makoto, *Keizai riron to gendai shihon-shugi* (Economic theory and contemporary capitalism) (Tokyo: Iwanami Shoten, 1987); idem, *Sekai keizai no naka no nihon* (Japan in the global economy) (Tokyo: Shakai Hyoronsha, 1988); idem, *Seikai keizai no tenkan wo kangaeru* (Thinking about transformations in the global economy) (Tokyo: Jiji Tsushin-sha, 1993); and idem, *Nihon shihon-shugi no kiro* (The fork in the road of Japanese capitalism) (Tokyo: Aoki Shoten, 1995).

64 Ito, *Fork in the Road*, 181–218.

65 Oshima, *Fifty Years*, 124.

66 Miyoshi, *Off Center*, 187.

67 This translates as, "And you, and you, and you, and you. . . ."

68 Oshima has stated his dislike for this term numerous times, most recently in *100 Years of Japanese Cinema* itself and in an article he wrote in 1960 titled, "In Protest Against the Massacre of Night and Fog in Japan." Oshima Nagisa, *Cinema, Censor-*

ship, and the State, ed. Annette Michelson, trans. Dawn Lawson (Cambridge, Mass.: MIT Press, 1992).

69 This is taken from Gregory Barrett's "An Interpretive Biography" at the end of his translation of Sato, *Currents in Japanese Cinema,* 263.

70 The four volumes are organized as follows: Volume 1 begins with a long preface titled "Standards of Japanese Film," in which such topics as film music, narratives, acting, genres, foreign-film influence, and the contributions of women are examined. Following this, the chronology begins with the first three chapters, titled, "Beginnings: 1896–1923," "The Establishment of the Silent Cinema: 1924–1934," and "The End of Silence, The Beginning of the Talkie: 1931–1940," respectively. Volume 2 continues this line, with its first chapter titled, "Films Under War: 1937–1945," then a chapter titled, "Films of Japanese Colonialism and Occupation," followed by "The [Japanese] Film World Under the Occupation: 1945–1949" and a chapter on the golden age of the 1950s. Volume 3 begins with a chapter on the crises and transformations of the 1960s, followed by a chapter on the diversity of the 1970s and a chapter titled, "The End of the Studio Age and the Search for the New: The 1980s." This ends the chronology proper, as volume 4 includes only one chapter, titled, "From a Different Direction," in which Sato deals in detail with questions of genre and topics such as the emperor, the police, the Japanese Communist Party, sex, and the representation of Japanese cities. The work concludes with more than 200 pages of chronological tables and an extended index.

71 Sato, *A History of Japanese Film,* 2:109–57.

72 Ibid., vol. 4 sec. V.

CHAPTER 3: ADAPTATION: ORIGIN, NATION, AESTHETIC

1 Kawabata Yasunari's *Izu no odoriko* (The Izu dancer) has been adapted as *Izu no odoriko,* dir. Gosho Heinosuke (1933); *Izu no odoriko,* dir. Nomura Yoshitaro (1954); *Izu no odoriko,* dir. Kawakami Jiro (1960); *Izu no odoriko,* dir. Onchi Hisashi (1967); *Izu no odoriko,* dir. Nishikawa Katsumi (1974). Tanizaki Junichiro's *Shunkinsho* (A portrait of Shunkin) has been adapted as *O-koto to saske* dir. Shimazu Yasujiro (1933); *Shunkin monogatari,* dir. Ito Daisuke (1954); *Sanka,* dir. Shindo Kaneto (1972); *Shunkinsho,* dir. Nishikawa Katsumi (1976). Tanizaki Junichiro's *Chijin no ai* (A fool's love) has been adapted as *Chijin no ai,* dir. Kimura Y. (1945); *Chijin no ai,* dir. Kimura Y. (1960); *Chijin no ai,* dir. Masumura Yasuzo (1967); *Naomi,* dir. Takabayashi Yojiro (1970). Mishima Yukio's *Kinkakuji* (The temple of the golden pavilion) has been adapted as *Enjo,* dir. Ichikawa Kon (1958); *Kinkakuji,* dir. Takahashi Youichi (1976). Natsume Soseki's *Kokoro* has been adapted as *Natsume Soseki no Kokoro,* dir. Ichikawa Kon (1955); *Kokoro,* dir. Shindo Kaneto (1973). Natsume Soseki's *Wagahai ha neko de aru* (I am a cat) has been adapted as *Wagahai ha neko de aru,* dir. Ichikawa Kon (1975). Terayama Shuji's *Sho wo suteyo machi e deyou* (Throw out your books, Storm the streets!) has been

adapted as *Sho wo suteyo machi e deyo*, dir. Terayama Shuji (1971). Nosaka Akiyuki's *Jinruigaku nyumon* (The pornographers, or An introduction to anthropology) has been adapted as *Jinruigaku nyumon*, dir. Imamura Shohei (1966). Oe Kenzaburo's *Shiku* (The catch) has been adapted as *The Catch*, dir. Oshima Nagisa (1959).

2   Of course, Western film is also replete with cinematic adaptations of literature. For instance, Morris Beja reported in 1979 that, since the inception of the Academy Awards in 1927–28, "more than three-fourths of the awards for 'best picture' have gone to adaptations": Morris Beja, *Film and Literature* (New York: Longman, 1979), as quoted in Brian McFarlane, *Novel to Film: An Introduction to the Theory of Adaptation* (Oxford: Clarendon Press, 1996), 8.

3   Nishikawa Tatsuki, *Izu no odoriko monogatari* (The story of *The Izu Dancer*) (Tokyo: Firumu Aato, 1994); and Chiba Nobuo, *Eiga to Tanizaki* (Film and Tanizaki) (Tokyo: Seiabou, 1989). I insist on calling the Japanese prose narrative by its Japanese name, *shosetsu*. Although shosetsu has become synonymous with "the Japanese novel," I find it useful to retain the Japanese term in order to stress the specificities of its own historical coming into being. Of course, there are similarities in the rise of the novel form and the rise of the shosetsu, especially in relation to the first stages of capitalist development that emerge in Japan and many Western countries (albeit at different moments). For more on the differences between the shosetsu and the novel, see Masao Miyoshi, "Against the Native Grain: The Japanese Novel and the 'Postmodern' West" and "The 'Great Divide' Once Again: Problematics of the Novel," in *Off Center*, 37–61.

4   For instance, by focusing on the crucial scene in *The Izu Dancer* in which Watakushi unwittingly spies the Izu dancer's immature naked body and thus is no longer sexually intimidated by her and finally able to fall in love, questions can be engaged regarding transformations in (1) technology (What are the possibilities and limitations of working out this scene in the silent film and the talkie, or in black and white and color?); (2) censorship (What could be shown and when?); and (3) issues of the fetish (How does the meaning of Watakushi's fetishization of the dancer's beautifully made-up hair—and the spectator's own investment in Watakushi's fetish—transform so that, in certain films, the scene stands for issues of class difference but in another for city and country differences, and in still another to the fetishized difference of burakumin and non-burakumin Japanese?).

5   In 1923, Japan produced 4,686 films, and the West produced 9,896, whereas in 1924, Japanese production grew to 9,379 films, and Western production dropped to 7,636; *Kinema Jumpo* (April 1, 1930), 166.

6   Several different modes of adaptation experiments had been made before this time, but no dominant form emerged with any historical significance (at least, in the way I argue the "fidelity" mode emerges in the 1930s).

7   Teshigahara Hiroshi, dir., *Antonio Gaudi*, film 72 min, 1984. Distributed by Kino International, New York.

8   George Bluestone, *Novels into Film* (Berkeley: University of California Press, 1957), 63.

9   Jean Mitry, "Remarks on the Problem of Cinematic Adaptation," *Bulletin of the Midwest Modern Language Association*, vol. 10 (1971), 1–9.

10 As quoted in Benjamin Rifkin, *Semiotics of Narration in Film and Prose Fiction* (New York: P. Lang, 1994), 9.

11 Jameson, *The Political Unconscious*, 40. Jameson redefines transcoding as "the invention of a set of terms, the strategic choice of a particular code or language, such that the same terminology can be used to analyze and articulate two quite distinct types of objects or 'texts,' or two very different structural levels of reality."

12 Tanizaki Junichiro, "Genji monogatari no gendai goyaku ni tsuite," *Chuo Koron* (1938), in *Tanizaki Junichiro Zenshu*, 30 vols. (Tokyo: Chuo Koron-sha, 1982–83).

13 Jameson, *Postmodernism, or The Cultural Logic of Late Capitalism* (Durham, N.C.: Duke University Press, 1991), 6.

14 Walter Benjamin, "The Task of the Translator: An Introduction to the Translation of Baudelaire's *Tableaux Parisiens*," in *Illuminations*, ed. Hannah Arendt (New York: Schocken Books, 1968), 69–82. The Japanese translation is by Kawamura Jiro, in *Bodoreru: Buaruta benyamin chosakushyu* 6 (Tokyo: Chuo Koron, 1975), 262–88.

15 As Derrida writes in his comments on Benjamin's preface, "The promise is not nothing, it is not simply marked by what it lacks to be fulfilled. As a promise, translation is already an event, and the decisive signature of a contract. Whether or not it be honored does not prevent the commitment from taking place and from bequeathing its record. A translation that manages, that manages to promise reconciliation, to talk about it, to desire it or make it desirable — such a translation is a rare and notable event": Jacques Derrida, "Des Tours de Babel," in *Difference in Translation*, ed. Joseph F. Graham (Ithaca, N.Y.: Cornell University Press, 1985), 191.

16 Tanizaki, *Tanizaki Junichiro Zenshu*, 21:326–27.

17 Of course, at first glance this text seems diametrically opposed to Benjamin's preface. Tanizaki mentions the importance of producing a literary (*bungakuteki*) translation, which is the last way someone might describe the Holderlin translation of Sophocles that Benjamin brandishes as translation par excellence. Tanizaki's reference to the receiver also goes against Benjamin's insistence that "no poem is intended for the reader, no picture for the beholder, no symphony for the listener": Benjamin, "The Task of the Translator," 74. But we must not be weighed down by Benjamin's tone. Remember what the underlying polemic is: to de-emphasize meaning and work toward "the intention underlying each language as a whole — an intention, however, which no single language can attain by itself but which is realized only by the totality of their intentions supplementing each other: pure language."

18 Of course, this is not a very realistic assumption for those who are not trained in more than their native language. In Benjamin's Germany, it may very well have been the case that anybody who picked up a German translation of Sophocles would have been able to read the original Greek. One might remember that Benjamin retains the actual Greek word for "in the beginning was the word" in his preface instead of translating it into German.

19 Miyoshi writes, "It might be necessary finally to be satisfied with Tanizaki having written so few pieces in any way supportive of the war, rather than to be repelled by these few words of collaborative evidence": Miyoshi, *Off Center*, 139. Miyoshi also points out that *In Praise of Shadows* should not be dismissed simply as an essentialist document by a writer embarrassed with his own past adulation of the West and now enchanted by his own traditions: "One does need to recall, however, that this was written in the middle of gradually heightening nationalism and chauvinism. A few years, later *In Praise of Shadows* would have been at least frowned upon, if not outright censored. In that sense, perverse as it is, Tanizaki's aesthetic manifesto could be appreciated for refusing to surrender to the growing fanatic self-congratulation and for inserting a moment of self-mockery": ibid., 142.

20 Tanizaki, *Tanizaki Junichiro Zenshu*, 27:192.

21 Benjamin, "The Task of the Translator," 81.

22 When commenting on his first translation in the preface to his second translation, "Genji monogatari shinyaku yo" (Preface to the new translation of *The Tale of Genji*) (1951, in *Tanizaki Junichiro Zenshu*, 23:252), Tanizaki writes that he was dissatisfied while rereading his first translation, and changes needed to be made. Tanizaki mentions that, although he could be quite "fluid" (*ryurei*) in the first translation, he had to sacrifice "clarity" and "conciseness" (*kanketsu*). In the second translation, Tanizaki explains that he would abandon the principles that had guided his first translation by being more colloquial and less formal; the only way to do this would be to pass over the first translation and base the new translation solely on the original text: Tanizaki, *Tanizaki Junichiro Zenshu*, 23:254.

23 Derrida writes, "Between the transcendental law (as Benjamin repeats it) and the actual law as it is formulated so laboriously and at times so crudely in treatises on copyright for author and for works, the analogy can be followed quite far, for example in that which concerns the notion of derivation and the translations of translations: these are always derived from the original and not from previous translations": Derrida, "Des Tours de Babel," 199.

24 Komatsu, "Characteristics of Japanese Cinema," 240. See also Yoshida Chieo, *Mo hitotsu no eiga-shi: Katsuben no jidai* (Another film history: The age of the silent film interpreter) (Tokyo: Jiji Tsushin-sha, 1978).

25 A. A. Gerow, "The Benshi's New Face: Defining Cinema in Taisho Japan," *Iconics* 3 (1994): 73.

26 Takeda Kokatsu, "*Setsumeisha no shimei*," *katsudo kurabu* 4, no. 12 (1921): 96. Writing in 1921, Takeda lobbied for the role of the benshi to be limited to that of translators (*honyakusha*) and restricted to providing uninspired translations of foreign-language films.

27 E. J. Hobsbawm, *Nations and Nationalism Since 1780: Programme, Myth, Reality* (Cambridge: Cambridge University Press, 1990), 132.

28 Tanizaki Junichiro, "Eiga e no kanso—Shunkinsho Eiga-ka ni saishite," in *Tanizaki Junichiro Zenshu*, 21:317–21. It was originally published in *Sande haru no eigago* (April 1935).

29 Idem, "Eiga no tekunikku," in *Tanizaki Junichiro Zenshu*, 28:113–20; originally published in *Shakai kokka* (October 1923). Idem, "Karigari hakushi wo miru, Tanizaki," in *Tanizaki Junichiro Zenshu*, 28:107–12; originally published in *Katsudo Zashi* (September 1923).

30 Idem, "Katsudo shashin no genzai to shorai," in *Tanizaki Junichiro Zenshu*, 28:13–21; originally published in *Shin-Shosetsu* (October 1918). Tanizaki, along with Kurihara Thomas, were recruited by the Yokohama startup film company Taikatsu in 1920. On Tanizaki's films and work at Taikatsu, see Chiba, *Eiga to Tanizaki*, esp. 7–22.

31 The shosetsu appears in *Tanizaki Junichiro Zenshu*, 1:67. I am referring to this edition unless otherwise noted.

32 Tanizaki Junichiro, "Watashi no mita osaka oyobi osaka-jin," in *Tanizaki Junichiro Zenshu*, 20:347–97.

33 Tanizaki, "Eiga e no kansou," 21:321.

34 Inoue Mitsuaki, *Nihon eiga koryuki no sakuhin mokuroku* (A film-by-film record of the periodic rise in Japanese cinema) (Tokyo: Fukui Shokai, 1988).

35 David Bordwell and Christen Thompson, *Film Art: An Introduction* (New York: McGraw-Hill, 1997), 108.

36 Tanizaki, "Eiga e no kanso," 21:317 (emphasis added).

37 Ibid., 21:317–18.

38 The characters for *Sanka* mean "song of praise." But this song of praise, as I will argue, is not necessarily one for Sasuke and Shunkin; rather, it is Shindo's song for Tanizaki.

39 Almost inexplicably, these blood scenes seem to comment on the seduction of storytelling and the ceaseless back-and-forth movement between losing ourselves in the content of a story (legend, ideology, etc.) and regaining our critical attention to the means of representation. Shindo's only explanation of the scene comes in the enigmatic line, "The author's drops of blood relate to him eating the lives of Shunkin and Sasuke": as quoted in Matsumoto Kenichi, "Kindai shugiteki meishi no kansei: Shindo Kaneto *Sanka* to Tanizaki Junichiro *Shunkinsho* no kiretsu" (The pitfalls of modernist transparency: The gap separating Shindo Kaneto's *Sanka* and Tanizaki Junichiro's *Shunkinsho*), *Eiga hihyo* 1 (1973): 37. Indeed, it is this image of consuming past narratives for present sustenance that seems consistent with the argument being made here.

40 For this quotation, I have used Howard Hibbett's translation in *Seven Japanese Tales* (New York: Vintage International, 1996), 44.

41 Matsumoto, "Eiga hihyo, kindai shugiteki meishi no kansei," 32–40.

42 Ibid., 38.

43 Ibid.

44 Matsumoto predictably refers to Tanizaki's *Inei Raisan* (In praise of shadows) to dramatize Shindo's misrepresentations: Tanizaki Junichiro, *In Praise of Shadows*, trans. Thomas J. Harper and Edward G. Seidensticker (New Haven, Conn.: Leete's Island Books, 1977).

45 Mori Yuki, *Ichikawa Kon no eigatachi* (The films of Ichikawa Kon) (Tokyo: Waize Publishing, 2000).

46 Joan Mellen, *Voices from the Japanese Cinema* (New York: Liveright, 1975), 124–25. See also idem, *The Waves at Genji's Door: Japan Through Its Cinema* (New York: Pantheon Books, 1976), 194.

47 Shindo has actively participated in leftist political movements since the 1950s. Known for living an extremely modest lifestyle with Otowa (before her death in 1995), Shindo is a prolific writer and public speaker and has a dedicated following among Socialist Party and Communist Party members.

48 The unevenness of cultural-ideological and political-economic developments will be a crucial topic of discussion in chapter six.

49 Hara writes about his views on documentary filmmaking and Japanese society in *Fumikoeru kyamera: Waga hoho, akushon dokyumentari* (The intrusive camera: My method of action documentary) (Tokyo: Firumu Aato-sha, 1995). See also idem, *Dokyumento, Yukiyukite shingun* (Tokyo: Shisso Production, 1994).

50 Tanaka Kakue became prime minister in 1972. He was forced to resign in 1974, however, due to his role in the Lockheed scandal in which bribes were accepted in exchange for pressure placed on All-Nippon Airways to make certain aircraft purchases.

51 Hara writes about the film in *Zenshin shosetsu-ka: Mo hitotsu no Inoue Mitsuharu* (A dedicated life: Another Inoue Mitsuharu) (Tokyo: Kinema Junpo-sha, 1994). See also idem, *Fumikoeru kyamera*, part 6.

52 Edogawa Rampo, *Japanese Tales of Mystery and Imagination*, trans. James B. Harris (Tokyo: Charles E. Tuttle, 1956), 154.

53 On detective fiction, and on Manuel Vásquez Montalbán in particular, see Mari Paz Balibrea Enriquez, *En La Tierra baldia: Manuel Vázquez, Montalbán y la izquierda Española en la postmodernidad* (In the wasteland: Manuel Vásquez Montalbán and the question of Spanish postmodernism) (Madrid: El Viejo Topo, 1999).

54 Rampo, *Japanese Tales*, xi.

CHAPTER 4: ACTING: STRUCTURE, AGENT, AMATEUR

1 Various passages and words in the killer's letter were said to resemble those by the famous "Zodiac" killer in San Francisco in the late 1960s. There were also sharp similarities to a number of U.S. horror films, such as *Scream 2* (a VHS copy of which the killer was said to own).

2 This discontent was particularly directed against the Japanese education system. In a letter sent to the local *Kobe Shinbun* on June 6, 1997, the killer attacked the "compulsory education system that has produced me." Carefully drawn with a ruler in block characters to disguise the killer's identity, the letter was then printed throughout Japan in various newspapers. In fact, the whole event turned into a national frenzy. Daytime talk shows were consumed with the issue, and images of chaperoned children, frightened and confused, filled the airwaves.

3 The moral debate over cultural imitation seems to take a different form in Japan from that in the United States. In Japan, the tendency is initially to dismiss the imitative behavior (one hooked to social influences) and immediately ascribe it to an individualist cause.

4 This discussion took place, among other places, in an April 21, 1921, article by Osanai: Osanai Kaoru, "Shingeki haiyuu toshite no kabuki yakusha," (Kabuki actor as the new theater actor) in *Osanai Kaoru Zenshu*, vol. 6 (Kyoto: Rinkawa Shincho, 1975), 265–71.

5 On Tanizaki's film connection, see Tanizaki "Eiga no tekunikku," 28:113–20; idem, "Karigari hakushi wo miru," 28:107–12; and idem, "Katsudo shashin no genzai shorai," 28:13–21.

6 This was relayed by Kataoka Nizaemon during a talk he gave following *Kabuki Yakusha: Kataoka Nizaemon* (Kabuki Actor: Kataoka Nizaemon, 1992–94), Haneda's film about him. It is also documented in the pamphlet published by Nakano BOX for the theater's screening of all six parts of the film: see Monma, "Kabuki and film," 34.

7 Sato, *Japanese Film History*, 1:179.

8 *Osanai Kaoru Zenshu*, 5:186–94.

9 Osanai writes about the influence he received from Stanislavsky in "Sutanisurasuki no Kozo," in *Osanai Kaoru Zenshu*, 5:174. On Meyerhold, see "Meieruhorido no kiseki," in *Osanai Kaoru Zenshu*, 5:186–94.

10 Sato, *Japanese Film History*, 180.

11 Ibid., 179.

12 There is a wealthy man and his carefree daughter; a farmer living nearby with his household; the grown son of the farmer who, after leaving for Kyoto against his father's wishes to become a professional violinist is on his way home with wife and child; and two recently released prisoners who are also on the road.

13 "Constantly wavering between the cross-diegetic cutting of *Intolerance* and the homogeneous system of *Birth of a Nation, Souls on the Road*, through a varied and quite subtly gradual use of rhymes and other correspondences, sets up a system whose

sophistication remotely anticipates that of *Strike* or *October. Souls on the Road* is, moreover, an excellent illustration of the inadequacy of the classical distinction between 'alternate montage' and 'parallel montage,' since it partakes of both: at one level, the film is composed of two 'separate' diegeses. Yet these nonetheless communicate with each other through peripheral characters and two chance meetings on the road, one near the beginning of the film and other near the end": Noel Burch, *To the Distant Observer*, 104.

14 It should be noted that *Intolerance* did not come to Japan until 1919 (three years after its initial U.S. release) and *Broken Blossoms*, also delayed three years, was released in Japan in 1922.

15 Sergei Eisenstein, "Dickens, Griffith, and the Film Today," in *Film Form: Essays in Film Theory*, trans. Jay Leyda (New York: Harcourt, Brace and World, 1949), 238. Of course, Eisenstein had a fundamental critique of Griffith's films—most notably, regarding Griffith's undialectical way of juxtaposing good and evil.

16 Idem, "The Cinematographic Principle and the Ideogram," in *Film Form*, 28–44.

17 Ibid., 44.

18 Ibid.

19 Ibid.

20 Viktor Shklovsky, *Art as Technique: The Philosophy of Literary Form*, 3rd rev. ed. (Berkeley: University of California Press, 1973), 293–304.

21 The print of *Amateur Club* is no longer in existence. What remains is the script and other sources about the film. In particular, see Chiba, *Film and Tanizaki*, 33–36, 62–69, and Tanizaki, "Kurihara Tomasu shi no koto," in *Tanizaki Junichiro Zenshu*, 21:192–95.

22 Inomata Katsuhito and Tayama Rikiyo, *Nihon Eiga Haiyu Zenshu* (Collection of Japanese Film Actors) (Tokyo: Kyouyou Bunko, 1977), 228–229.

23 Sato, *Japanese Film History*, 1:179, and Inomata, *Nihon Eiga Haiyu Zenshu*, 228–29.

24 Hane Mikiso, *Modern Japan* (Boulder, Colo.: Westview Press, 1986), 196.

25 Harry D. Harootunian, *Toward Restoration: The Growth of Political Consciousness in Tokugawa Japan* (Berkeley: University of California Press, 1970). The quote comes from the new preface, titled "The Space of Restoration" in the 1991 edition.

26 Idem, "The Space of Restoration," in *Toward Restoration*, xviii.

27 For example, the idea of "mean" shifts from a noun to a verb or from an objective identity outside the knowing self to a quality dependent on human knowledge and action. There is also the example of how the character for independent authority, *ken*, emerged in many new words, such as *kenri* (rights), *jinken* (individual rights), *minken* (people's rights), *shuken* (sovereignty), *kokken* (national sovereignty), and *kenryoku* (political power): Tetsuo Najita, "Japan's Industrial Revolution," in *Japan in the World*, ed. Masao Miyoshi and Harry D. Harootunian (Durham, N.C.: Duke University Press, 1993), 13–30.

28 It should be remembered that the view of the benshi had changed substantially from the 1920s to the early 1930s. At first the benshi were recognized as a progressive force; by the middle to late 1920s, however, their function had been streamlined by the Ministry of Education and thus for the most part played a reactionary role within the film world.

29 Yoshino Sazuko, *Minponshugi-ron* (Democracy theory) (Tokyo: Shinkigen-sha, 1948).

30 Sugimoto Susumu, *Nihon puroreteria eiga domei (Purokino) zenshi* (The collected history of the Japanese Proletarian Film League [Prokino]) (Tokyo: Aido Shupan, 1986). See also, "Documentarist of Japan No. 5: Prokino, Interview with Komori Shikuo and Noto Setsuo," *Documentary Box* 5 (September 8, 1994).

31 "Prokino Zenshi," *Documentary Box* interview, Yamagata Film catalogue.

32 For the most recent material to come out about the shutaisei debate in English, see J. Victor Koschman, *Revolution and Subjectivity in Postwar Japan* (Chicago: University of Chicago Press, 1996), and Miyoshi, "Who Decides, and Who Speaks? *Shutaisei* and the West in Postwar Japan," in *Off Center*, 97–125.

33 I borrowed this phrasing from Fredric Jameson, "Periodizing the 60s," in *The Ideologies of Theory: Essays 1971-1986, Volume 2: The Syntax of History* (Minneapolis: University of Minnesota Press, 1989), 179.

34 Karl Marx, *The 18th Brumaire of Louis Bonaparte* (New York: International Publishers, 1987), 15.

35 Iwanami Film Productions began in 1949 as the film wing of the famous publishing company. I am indebted to Haneda Sumiko for information regarding Hani's work (personal interview March, 1997). Haneda, who is still making film, was one of the production assistants on *Kyoshitsu no kodomotachi*. For more on Haneda, see the epilogue.

36 Hani writes about the making of the film in the first chapter of *Engi shinai shuyakutachi: Kiroku eiga sakusha no manako kara* (Characters who don't act: From the perspective of a documentary film maker) (Tokyo: Chuo Koron, 1959).

37 Ibid., 16–18. See also Kawanobori Naokichi, *Dokyumentari Seishin Nitsuite: Kyoshitsu no kodomotachi no tojita mondai* (On the spirit of documentary: The problem of shooting *The Children of the Classroom*) *Kinema Jumpo*, no. 114 (1955).

38 Kamei writes about the production of the film in his *Fighting Film*, 20–34.

39 Hani, *Characters Who Don't Act*, 100.

40 For example, one of Hani's later films, *Buwana toshi no uta* (Buwanta Toshi, 1965) takes place near the border between Kenya and Tanzania. A Japanese researcher goes to East Africa to build houses but is left without his Japanese assistant. He resorts to asking the natives for their cooperation. At first he is insensitive to their work ethic and customs, but he then realizes how mutually dependent they are on each other. Besides Atsumi Kiyoshi (of *Tora-san* fame) and a few other Japanese actors, the actors were amateurs living in East Africa.

41 I must thank the tremendous generosity of Fuseya Hiro, the producer of most of

Ogawa's films. During 1996–97, I visited Fuseya about once a month. He lent me all of Ogawa's films and many others that were in Ogawa's personal collection. Fuseya is now among the most important producers of independent film in Japan. He had a hand in producing the work of Kawase (now Sento) Naomi, who won best new director at Cannes in 1996, and is instrumental in producing and distributing the work of filmmakers throughout Asia.

42　That is, these films were not only immensely popular among the farmers themselves as well as students and urban dwellers in Japan, but they also ignited the attention of New Wave filmmakers in Japan and Europe. According to Jean-Pierre Gorin, many involved in avant-garde filmmaking in Paris during the 1960s and 1970s were electrified when viewing Ogawa's films (private conversation).

43　Imamura Shohei and Oshima Nagisa have noted Ogawa's influence. In one film, in fact, Oshima travels to Ogawa's farm in Yamagata to interview him and his crew about his work and the state of filmmaking. Younger filmmakers, such as Suwa Nobuhiro (2 Duo, on which Tamura Masaki, the famous cameraman for most of the Sanrizuka films, also worked) and Sento Naomi (Suzaku), acknowledge a special debt to Ogawa.

44　As Ogawa's career progressed, he became more of an actor in his own films (by asking interviewees questions or entering the frame itself). This is most apparent in his two last films about farmers, farming, history, and historiography, Nippon-koku furu-yashiki mura (1982) and Sennen kizami no hidokei (1986). I examine the 1986 film later in this chapter. Ogawa also began to use more intertitles in his last Sanrizuka film, Sanrizuka: Satsuki no sora sato no kayoiji (1977).

45　The most thorough source in English about the anti-airport struggle is David E. Apter and Nagayo Sawa, Against the State: Politics and Social Protest in Japan (Cambridge, Mass.: Harvard University Press, 1984).

46　For example, Ueno Koshi argues this in an article in Eiga Shinbun, vol. 86 (April 1992), which is also excerpted as "Ogawa Shinsuke e no tabi" in the Yamagata International Film Festival official program (1993).

47　A sampling of Tamura's work includes Assassination of Ryoma (1974) by Kuroki Kazuo; A Farewell to the Land (1981), Himatsuri (1984), and Pao Janfu (1995) by Yanagimachi Mitsuo; and the recent 2 Duo, by Suwa Nobuhiro.

48　The controversy continues. For example, as recently as July 29, 1998, a time bomb, suspected to have been planted by an anti-airport guerrilla, exploded in the home of Harunari Makoto, a negotiator between the airport authorities and the protesters while he worked at the International Air Transport Division of the Civil Aviation Bureau: Asahi Shinbun (July 30, 1998). Available from http://www.asahi.com/paper/national.html.

49　Slavoj Žižek, The Sublime Object of Ideology (London: Verso, 1989), 40.

50　I will write more about this in the following section when commenting on Karatani Kojin's reworking of Marx's notion of Bonapartism.

51 I will quote from Kosaburo Kohso's English translation of Karatani Kojin's "Representation and Repetition: *The 18th Brumaire of Louis Bonaparte* Revisited," *Karatani Forum*. Available from http://www.karataniforum.org/represent.html.

52 Karatani writes, "When we say that the 1990s will be similar to the 1930s, it does not quite mean that the same event will repeat itself. Repetition occurs not in events themselves, but in the form immanent in them": ibid., 1.

53 Marx, *18th Brumaire*, 51.

54 Karatani, "Representation," 5.

55 Ibid., 5–6 (emphasis added).

56 This is Noam Chomsky's phrase in *Keeping the Rabble in Line: Interviews with David Barsamian* (Monroe, Maine: Common Courage Press, 1994), 48.

57 Nicholas Kristof of the *New York Times* reported on Sakamoto Shinnosuke, a University of Tokyo Ph.D. student who viewed Aum as essential to his late capitalist existence. Kristof writes: "As he sees it, the Aum form of Buddhism is replacing Marxism as the main rival ideology to capitalism. Mr. Sakamoto says that while capitalism celebrates greed, Buddhism emphasizes asceticism and restraint": *New York Times*, April 4, 1995, A6.

58 *Love Letter* was hugely successful and brought home for Iwai the Best Director and Best Picture awards from the Yokohama Film Festival and the Ministry of Education. His short film *Undo* (1994) won an award at the Berlin International Film Festival in 1995, and the following year Iwai took home the *Berliner Zeitung* Readers' Jury Prize Award for another short, *Picnic*.

59 "Ikebukoro ni ju yo ji kan" (Ikebukuro: 24 Hours) is an example. See chapter 5 for more on this program.

60 Ogawa writes: "The people themselves—and not officials or bureaucrats—try to be involved in the festival. This October [the first festival in 1989] the people will meet documentary filmmakers from all over the world and appreciate the films at the festival." Ogawa continues: "By the way, the city is surrounded by rice fields in every direction within ten minutes' drive from the center. This means that Yamagata is a typical Japanese agricultural district. But actually, highways are destroying these fields. The people who cultivate these fields are worried about their future—or about the future of Japanese agriculture. And the people who are involved in networking and organizing the festival all live in these areas—in the midst of the problems as well as taking part in the festival, they will try to invite the directors and guests from abroad to their villages and talk to them face to face" (Yamagata International Documentary Film Festival Program [1989]).

61 I write about kokusai-ka discourse and its meanings and effects in "Uses and Abuses of the Nation: Toward a Theory of the Transnational Cultural Exchange Industry," *Social Text* 44 (fall–winter 1995): 135–60.

1   Sano Shinichi, *Nihon eiga ha, ima—Sukuriin no uragawa kara no shogen* (Japan film today: Proof from behind the screen) (Tokyo: TBS Puritanika, 1996), 175–211. Compare this with estimated U.S. annual sales, which as of 1996 amounted to $11 billion: see Laura Kipnis, *Bound and Gagged* (New York: Grove Press, 1996), 161.

2   Dworkin and MacKinnon have written widely on pornography and abuse against women. See, for example, Andrea Dworkin, *Pornography: Men Possessing Women* (New York: Plume, 1989), and Catharine MacKinnon, "Pornography, Civil Rights and Speech," in *Feminism Unmodified: Discourses on Life and Law* (Cambridge, Mass.: Harvard University Press, 1987).

3   Linda Williams, *Hard Core: Power, Pleasure, and the "Frenzy of the Visible"* (Berkeley: University of California Press, 1989); Kipnis, *Bound and Gagged;* idem *Ecstasy Unlimited: On Sex, Capital, Gender, and Aesthetics* (Minneapolis: University of Minnesota Press, 1993); and Constance Penley, *The Future of an Illusion: Film, Feminism, Psychoanalysis,* Media and Society (Minneapolis: University of Minnesota Press, 1989).

4   Kipnis, *Bound and Gagged,* 164.

5   It has been reported that Koike received a total of 690 million yen (8.73 million dollars) from the Big Four security firms and considerably more from Dai Ichi Kangyo Bank: "Koike Admits Getting Payoffs From Big 4 Brokers, DKB," *Nikkei Net,* December 2, 1997.

6   I have written about both the Japanese education system and "self-Orientalism," a trend in which Japanese power-holders expediently employ Western discourses about Japan: see Cazdyn, "Uses and Abuses of the Nation" (1995): 135–60.

7   Uno Kozo, *Marukusu keizaigaku genriron no kenkyu* (Research on Marxist economic principles) (Tokyo: Iwanami Shoten, 1959).

8   Idem, *Keizai genron.*

9   Georg Lukács, *History and Class Consciousness: Studies in Marxist Dialectics,* trans. Rodney Livingstone (Cambridge, Mass.: MIT Press, 1968), 27. It is true that Lukács retreats from this position in the preface to the 1967 edition of *History and Class Consciousness.* There he admits that, by deemphasizing the economic categories, he undertheorized the importance of labor and praxis. Nevertheless, this does not reduce the importance of Lukács's privileging of the method of totality and its historical importance.

10   Ibid., 27.

11   Karl Marx, *Capital: A Critique of Political Economy,* vol. 1, trans. Ben Fowkes (New York: Vantage Books, 1977), 174.

12   Ibid., 483.

13   Lukács, *History and Class Consciousness,* 8.

14   Angela Davis, "Introduction," Black Women Writers and the High Art of Afro-American Letters Conference, University of California, San Diego, La Jolla, Calif.,

May 16, 1998. This is one of the constant themes of Chomsky's work. See, for example, Noam Chomsky, *Deterring Democracy* (New York: Verso, 1991).

15 Take, for example, the ubiquity of Blockbuster Video and Hollywood Video shops. In Japan, Tsutaya video (with headquarters in Ebisu) has chain stores throughout the country.

16 Arai Taro, interview, December 23, 1996.

17 Ibid.

18 Sano, *Japan Film Today.*

19 Nikkatsu's *Roman Poruno* (Romantic pornography) is the most famous example of Pink Film. Beginning in 1971, Nikkatsu had a tremendous seventeen-year run until its final film, *Rabugemu ha owaranai* (Endless love game) in 1988.

20 According to Sano, in 1977 only 10 percent of homes had videocassette players; in 1986, the percentage was 40 percent; in 1987, it was 50 percent; and by March 1995, more than 73 percent of homes had one: ibid., 202–203.

21 Ibid., 216–17.

22 *Fuzoku kogata eiga,* 4 vols. (English subtitle: "A short history of blue film in Japan") (Tokyo: Shikoku Takawa, 1994).

23 Oshima labels *Senses* pornographic not necessarily because of the sexual content but because of the Japanese censorship of the film that produced the desire in many Japanese to see it uncut. Since Oshima defines pornography as "that which cannot be seen," *Senses* became the quintessential pornographic film in Japan. I will develop this discussion later in this chapter.

24 *NHK supesharu: Oku himaraya kindan no okoku—Musutan* (NHK special—mustang: The forbidden kingdom deep in the Himalayas), NHK (Tokyo, 1992).

25 Although we never see the Chinese characters for *kyoei,* it might not be too much of a stretch to read *kyo* as representing the character for education and *ei* for that of film. This reading goes hand in hand with the argument that Imamura is implicating both the education and film industries in the ruin wrought by late capitalism.

26 The JCP pushed for a two-step revolution—first bourgeois, then proletarian. The anti-Yoyogi faction of the *Zengakuren,* named for the location of the JCP headquarters, called for a one-step revolution. The Zengakuren consisted of numerous factions, such as the pro-Communist Party *Minsei,* and a broad spectrum of non-Communist Party leftist groups, including Trotskyites, Maoists, structural reformists, revolutionary Marxists, and anarchists.

27 Sano, *Japan Film Today,* 13.

28 Sekine Hiroshi, "Abe Sada," trans. Christopher Drake, in *Contemporary Japanese Literature,* ed. Howard Hibbett (New York: Alfred A. Knopf, 1986), 319.

29 Wilhelm Reich, *The Mass Psychology of Fascism,* trans. Vincent R. Carfagno (New York: Noonday Press, 1946), 19.

30 Ibid., 28.

31 Steven Heath, "The Question of Oshima," *Wide Angle* 2, no. 1 (1977): 48–57.

32 Ibid., 51.

33 *Wide Angle* 9, no. 2 (1987).

34 Peter Lehman, "Oshima: The Avant-Garde Artist Without an Avant-Garde Style," *Wide Angle* 9, no. 2 (1987): 18–31.

35 Ibid., 22.

36 Maureen Turim, "Signs of Sexuality in Oshima's Tales of Passion," *Wide Angle* 9, no. 2 (1987): 32–46.

37 What about Europe and the United States at the time of *Senses'* release and the meaning the film has in terms of Western–Japanese relations or Orientalist constructions of Japan and Japanese history?

38 Oshima, *Cinema, Censorship, and the State*, 265.

39 Oshima, "Text of Plea," in *Cinema, Censorship, and the State*, 265.

40 Oshima, *Cinema, Censorship, and the State*, 253.

41 Ibid.

42 Ibid.

43 In fact, I want to take issue with Kipnis's thesis of the "transgressive" nature of pornography. No doubt, the type of pornography to which Kipnis regularly refers—S/M, fat, gay, etc.—does challenge mainstream ideologies about sexuality and the body. But surely the bulk of pornography is not of this sort. In fact, the bulk of pornography, in both the United States and Japan, is rather conventional and conservative. Although I admire Kipnis's project to read the class biases in anti-pornography groups and critics, I question the thesis that pornography necessarily challenges these biases. In fact, given the argument developed throughout this chapter, I argue that instead of challenging bourgeois categories, pornography functions to legitimate and reinforce them.

44 Oshima, *Cinema, Censorship, and the State*, 253.

45 This screening (part of a two-week retrospective on Oshima's work) was held at the Italian–Japanese Center in Kyoto in February 1996.

46 All quotes translated from the scenario are published in Hara, *Dokyumento*, 139–221.

47 Matsuda Masao and Takahashi Taketomo, eds., *Gunron yukiyukite shingun* (Tokyo: Togosha, 1988).

48 Kuroko Kazuo, "Nichijo o utsu shingun, Soshite hitotsu no wadakamari" (The divine army unsettles the everyday, yet an ambiguity remains), in Matsuda and Takahashi, *Gunron Yukiyukite Shingun*, 29.

49 Ibid., 30.

50 Hara Kazuo, "Sakusha no Hatsugen" (The director speaks), in Matsuda and Takahashi, *Gunron yukiyukite shingun*, 343.

51 Ibid., 347.

52 This is not unlike the term "transformative adaptation" (*eiga-ka*) that I employed in

chapter 3. Both terms suggest a dynamic relationship between the narrative and the act of representation.

53 Guy Deborg, *Society of the Spectacle* (Detroit: Black and Red, 1983), 38.

54 Ibid., 41.

55 On Virilio's notion of the general accident, see Paul Virilio, *Open Sky*, trans. Julie Rose (London: Verso, 1997), 69–86.

56 Hara writes about privacy in "Puraibashii no ryoiki ni fumikomu koto" (Breaking into the Realm of Privacy), in *Fumikoeru kyamera*, 8–16.

57 Bill Nichols writes about reality TV in "At the Limits of Reality (TV)," in *Blurred Boundaries: Questions of Meaning in Contemporary Culture* (Bloomington: Indiana University Press, 1994), 43–62. Nichols defines reality TV as that which "includes all those shows that present dangerous events, unusual situations, or actual police cases, often reenacting aspects of them and sometimes enlisting our assistance in apprehending criminals still at large": ibid., 45. Reality culture as a category encompasses more than Nichols's definition: It is a type of representation in which the event and the representation are mutually constitutive, so that the event is not only past when represented but contains in it a virtual image into which it can transform.

58 Virilio writes about this shift by quoting Alfred Hitchcock's statement, "Unlike cinema, with television there is no time for suspense; you can only have surprise." Virilio then explains that "this is the very definition of the paradoxical logic of the videoframe which privileges the accident, the surprise, over the durable substance of the message": Paul Virilio, *The Vision Machine* (Bloomington: Indiana University Press, 1994), 65.

59 In the last chapter of *Cinema 2: The Time-Image*, Deleuze calls this type of image a "crystal." He writes: "We are no longer in the situation of a relationship between the actual image and other virtual images, recollections, or dreams, which thus become actual in turn: this is still a mode of linkage. We are in the situation of an actual image and its own virtual image, to the extent that there is no longer any linkage of the real with the imaginary, but indiscernibility of the two, a perpetual exchange": Deleuze, *Cinema 2*, 273.

CHAPTER 6: REREADING: CANON, BODY, GEOPOLITICS

1 Manny Farber, *Negative Space: Manny Farber on the Movies* (New York: Da Capo Press, 1998 [1971]). Farber spoke in Del Mar, California.

2 Take this sentence on Kurosawa's *Ikiru:* "It sums up much of what a termite art aims at: buglike immersion in a small area without point or aim, and, overall, concentration on nailing down one moment without glamorizing it, but forgetting this accomplishment as soon as it has been passed; the feeling that all is expendable, that it can be chopped up and flung down in a different arrangement without ruin": ibid., 144.

3 James Fujii, *Complicit Fictions* (Berkeley: University of California Press, 1993), 128.

4 To complicate matters even more, perhaps we should change Fujii's "or" to an "and" and argue that the "refusal" and "inability" to acknowledge Japanese colonialism exist together—a condensation with Soseki leaning more toward inability and subsequent critics more toward refusal.

5 Edward Said, *Culture and Imperialism* (New York: Knopf, 1993), 24.

6 Ibid., 28–29.

7 This may also be the place to talk about some of the uncanny similarities. For example, both works are structured around the impossibility of expressing something, an impossibility that generates the four narratives themselves (Conrad's *Heart of Darkness*, Soseki's *Kokoro*, Marlowe's yarn [story] to those aboard the *Nellie*, and the student's narrative about his relationship with Sensei). Also, both works are structured around a lie to a female character that produces the very likely possibility of repetition. Until the cycle is broken—until Marlowe and the student disobey orders (from Kurtz and Sensei) and tell the "truth" to Ojosan and the girl ("my intentioned")—any chance of restructuring history is unlikely.

8 Said uses the term "contrapuntal" to describe his method of reading. "As we look back at the cultural archive, we begin to reread it not univocally but contrapuntally, with a simultaneous awareness both of the metropolitan history that is narrated and of those other histories against which (and together with which) the dominating discourse acts": Said, *Culture and Imperialism*, 51.

9 Toni Morrison, *Playing in the Dark: Whiteness and the Literary Imagination* (Cambridge, Mass.: Harvard University Press, 1992).

10 The canonical essays on this issue within Western literary theory are Roland Barthes, "The Death of the Author," in *Image, Music, Text*, ed. and trans. Stephen Heath (New York: Hill and Wang, 1977), 142–48; and Michel Foucault, "What Is an Author?" in *Language, Counter-Memory, Practice: Selected Essays and Interviews*, ed. Donald F. Bouchard, trans. Donald F. Bouchard and Sherry Simon (Ithaca, N.Y.: Cornell University Press, 1980), 113–38. See also Stanley Fish, *Is There a Text in This Class? The Authority of Interpretive Communities* (Cambridge, Mass.: Harvard University Press, 1980); Patrocinio P. Schwickart, "Reading Ourselves: Toward a Feminist Theory of Reading" in *Gender and Reading: Essays on Readers, Texts, and Contexts*, ed. Elizabeth A. Flynn and Patrochino Schwickart (Baltimore, Md.: Johns Hopkins University Press, 1986), 31–62.

11 I sympathize with such a critique, however, when it is lodged against a certain social scientific strand of cultural studies—one that is concerned solely with the materiality of the text (such as its publishing record, market, or technology) and inattentive to the text's formal aspects.

12 Of course, this is a reference to the classic scene in Allen's *Annie Hall* (1977).

13 For example, Sato Tadao situates Kinugasa's film in relation to trends in world cinema,

most notably Wiene's *The Cabinet of Dr. Caligari* (1919) and Eisenstein's *Battleship Potemkin.* Both films express the interior world (*naimen sekai*) of the characters.

14 Burch, *To the Distant Observer,* 126–36.

15 Richie and Anderson distinguish between impressionism and expressionism (naming Wiene's *Caligari* as expressionistic, or attempting to represent the subjectivity of the psychotic, and Kinugasa's *Page* as impressionistic, or not to be viewed through the insane but as the impression the insane made on Kinugasa).

16 Elizabeth Grosz, *Volatile Bodies: Toward a Corporeal Feminism* (Bloomington: Indiana University Press, 1994).

17 Sato, *Japanese Film History,* 1:265–67.

18 I take these phrases (inside-out and outside-in) from Grosz's *Volatile Bodies.*

19 In the last section of this chapter we will see a similar persistence of an uneven gendered relationship between two cyborgs in Oshii's *Ghost in the Shell.*

20 Tetsuo Najita and Harry D. Harootunian, "Japan's Revolt Against the West," in *Modern Japanese Thought,* ed. Bob Tadashi Wakabayashi (Cambridge: Cambridge University Press, 1998), 233–34. Najita and Harootunian explain that these works invoked ideals such as beauty, goodness, and truth as Japan's rock-bottom creative traits and are prime examples of how culture manifested the spiritual interiority of the subject.

21 In 1913, a number of experiments were conducted linking recorded commentary to the images. In the same year, the Nihon Kinetophone Company imported disk technology invented by Thomas Edison in the United States: Sato, *A History of Japanese Film,* 329–35.

22 Hobson, *Imperialism,* 47.

23 One of these simplicities is Hobson's reliance on an underconsumptionist model that does not consider other methods besides breaking open new markets to manage capitalist crisis. For more on this, see Anthony Brewer's *Marxist Theories of Imperialism: A Critical Survey* (London: Routledge and Kegan Paul, 1980), 73–87.

24 See Abé Markus Nornes and Yeh Yueh-yu's Internet-based book *City of Sadness.* Available from: http://cinemaspace.berkeley.edu/papers/cityofsadness/.

25 "Historic Studio Goes Down Fighting," *Daily Yomiuri,* May 18, 2000.

26 "Movie Industry May Have Happy Ending," *Daily Yomiuri,* March 25, 1999, Internet edition, available at http://yomiuri.co.jp.

27 Toho was the first of the big Japanese film companies to recognize this need. By scaling down production and purchasing films by other producers (in particular, those produced by film companies such as Fuji), Toho—unlike Shochiku and Toei—was able to generate a profit in 1999: ibid.

28 Thomas Schatz, "Hollywood: The Triumph of the Studio System," in *The Oxford History of World Cinema,* ed. Geoffrey Nowell-Smith (Oxford: Oxford University Press, 1997), 223.

29 Douglas Gomery, "Transformation of the Hollywood System," in *The Oxford History*

of World Cinema, 445. See also Thomas Schatz, *The Genius of the System: Hollywood Filmmaking in the Studio Era* (New York: Pantheon Books, 1988), 381–82, 404–407.

30   In the mid-1990s, only 20 percent of films earned back their investment at theaters in the United States, with the rest depending on worldwide audiences; Richard J. Barnet and John Cavanagh, *Global Dreams: Imperial Corporations and the New World Order* (New York: Simon and Schuster, 1994), 28.

31   On the globalization of Hollywood, see Tino Balio, "Adjusting to the New Global Economy: Hollywood in the 1990s," in *Film Policy: International, National and Regional Perspectives*, ed. Albert Moran (London: Routledge Press, 1996), 23–37.

32   On Japanese popular culture in Asia, see Leo Ching, "Imaginings in the Empires of the Sun: Japanese Mass Culture in Asia," in *Contemporary Japan and Popular Culture*, ed. John Treat (Honolulu: University of Hawaii Press, 1996).

33   Sarah Anderson and John Cavanagh, *Field Guide to the Global Economy* (New York: New Press, 2000), 52, 68.

34   David Bordwell, *Ozu and the Poetics of Cinema* (Princeton, N.J.: Princeton University Press, 1988).

35   John Dower, *Embracing Defeat: Japan in the Wake of World War II* (New York: W. W. Norton, 1999), 526–27.

36   Moreover, there are two moments in the film in which the clock's chimes are highlighted—one that sounds all twelve strokes at midnight.

37   Deleuze, *Cinema 2*, 5.

38   Ibid., 17.

39   Ibid., 18.

40   Ibid., 272.

41   Idem, *Cinema 1*, xi.

42   Dower, *Embracing Defeat*, 526.

43   Koschmann, *Revolution and Subjectivity*, 75–82. Also see Miriam Silverberg, *Changing Song: The Marxist Manifestos of Nakano Shigeharu* (Princeton, N.J.: Princeton University Press, 1990).

44   Thanks to Harry D. Harootunian for drawing my attention to Tsumura's participation.

45   Lisa Yoneyama pursues some of these issues in her *Hiroshima Traces: Time, Space, and the Dialectics of Memory* (Berkeley: University of California Press, 1999).

46   Michael Hardt and Antonio Negri, *Empire* (Cambridge, Mass.: Harvard University Press, 2000), 146.

47   Ibid., xx.

48   Ibid., xii.

49   For example, in arguing for the importance of the Korean National Literature Movement, Paik Nak-chung writes: "In view of the features of the present age [that is, the challenges of the global age following the collapse of Soviet Union], 'national literature' obviously leads one to an uncertain and even treacherous terrain, but a terrain away

from which no meaningful effort can be made in the endeavor to deal adequately with the problems of the age, and upon which for certain nations in a given conjuncture the main effort should be concentrated." See Paik Nak-chung, "Nations and Literatures in the Age of Globalization," in *The Cultures of Globalization*, ed. Masao Miyoshi and Fredric Jameson (Durham, N.C.: Duke University Press, 1998), 221. See also Geeta Kapur, "Globalization and Culture: Navigating the Void," in *The Cultures of Globalization*, 191–217; Nestor Garcia Canclini, *Hybrid Cultures: Strategies for Entering and Leaving Modernity*, trans. Christopher L. Chiappari and Silvia L. López (Minneapolis: University of Minnesota Press, 1995).

50 United Nations, *Human Development Report 1996* (New York: Oxford University Press, 1996), 2, as cited in Anderson and Cavanagh, *Field Guide*, 53.

51 Masao Miyoshi reminds us that, of the 5.5 billion people on Earth, fewer than 1 billion are elites in this age of transnational capital. "The rest," Miyoshi writes, "will live increasingly more delinked from the capital flow under brutal circumstances": Miyoshi, "Sites of Resistance in the Global Economy," *boundary 2* 22, no. 1 (spring 1995): 61–84.

52 Jacques Derrida, *Specters of Marx, the State of the Debt, the Work of Mourning, and the New International*, trans. Peggy Kamuf (New York: Routledge, 1994), 85.

53 "Us" for Derrida means scholars such as Horatio, who in *Hamlet* is urged to speak to the specter of Hamlet's father. "Thou art a scholar; speak to it, Horatio": ibid., 176.

54 Of course, this neo-nationalist repetition as a symptom of globalization is not unique to Japan. For instance, Pat Buchanan in the United States, Jorg Haider in Austria, and Stockwell Day in Canada spread much of the same discourse.

55 On the recent rise of these groups in relation to the comfort-women issue in particular, see Gavin McCormack, "Japan's Uncomfortable Past," in *History Today* 48, no. 5 (May 1998): 5–8.

56 Joint United Nations Program on HIV/AIDS (UNAIDS), "Factsheet," website. Available from: http://www.unaids.org/fact_sheets/index.html.

57 "AIDS Cuts Swath Through Africa's Teachers," *New York Times*, April 14, 2000, Internet edition, available at http://www.nytimes.com.

58 "Scientists Warn of Inaction as AIDS Spreads in China," *New York Times*, August 2, 2000, Internet edition, available at http://www.nytimes.com.

59 It is astonishing that, at the moment of such genocide, the United States is seriously considering a missile-defense project that will cost at least sixty times more than the amount granted for HIV/AIDS assistance in Africa. Following the summer 2000 AIDS/HIV conference in Durban, South Africa, the United States offered $1 billion in loans for AIDS/HIV assistance, whereas the proposed cost of a missile-defense program is estimated at $60 billion.

60 Bill Haver, *The Body of This Death: Historicity and Sociality in the Time of AIDS* (Stanford, Calif.: Stanford University Press, 1996). Haver writes: "The unthinkable has been rendered thinkable, the impossible possible, the extraordinary normative. And

this process, however inevitable and in fact necessary it may be, is nevertheless at the same time a forgetting of the Real of AIDS, an avoidance of the exigencies with which the force of that Real confronts us, a refusal to think the limits of what can be thought, a disavowal of historicity": ibid., 3.

61 I thank R. Bruce Marshall for reminding me of this connection.

EPILOGUE

1 Anne McClintock, "'No Longer a Future Heaven': Gender, Race, and Nationalism," in *Dangerous Liaisons: Gender, Nation, and Postcolonial Perspectives,* ed. Anne McClintock, Aamir Mufti, and Ella Shohat (Minneapolis: University of Minnesota Press, 1997), 92.

2 Haneda Sumiko, "On the Film *How to Care for the Senile,*" in *How to Care for the Senile,* ed. Okori Kojin (Tokyo: Equipe de Cinema 78, 1986), 8–9.

references

Anderson, Benedict. *Imagined Communities: Reflections on the Origin and Spread of Nationalism.* London: Verso, 1991.

Andrew, J. Dudley. *Concepts in Film Theory.* New York: Oxford University Press, 1984.

Balibrea Enriquez, Mari Paz. *En La Tierra baldia: Manuel Vázquez Montalbán y la izquierda Española en la postmodernidad.* Madrid: El Viejo Topo, 1999.

Barthes, Roland. "The Death of the Author." In *Image, Music, Text.* Ed. and trans. Stephen Heath. New York: Hill and Wang, 1977.

Benjamin, Walter. "The Task of the Translator." In *Illuminations.* Trans. Harry Zohn. New York: Schocken Books, 1968.

———. "Theses on the Philosophy of History." In *Illuminations.* Trans. Harry Zohn. New York: Schocken Books, 1968.

Brakhage, Stan. "In Defense of Amateur." In *Brakhage Scrapbook: Collected Writings, 1964-1980.* Ed. Robert A. Haller. New Paltz, N.Y.: Documentext, 1982.

Brewer, Anthony. *Marxist Theories of Imperialism: A Critical Survey*. London: Routledge, 1980.

Buck-Morss, Susan. *The Dialectics of Seeing: Walter Benjamin and the Arcades Project*. Cambridge, Mass.: MIT Press, 1991.

Burch, Noel. *To the Distant Observer: Form and Meaning in the Japanese Cinema*. Berkeley: University of California Press, 1979.

Canclini, Nestor Garcia. *Hybrid Cultures: Strategies for Entering and Leaving Modernity*. Trans. Christopher L. Chiappari and Silvia L. López. Minneapolis: University of Minnesota Press, 1995.

Cazdyn, Eric. "Uses and Abuses of the Nation: Toward a Theory of the Transnational Cultural Exchange Industry." *Social Text* 44 (fall–winter 1995): 135–60.

———, writer and presenter. "Cult of Kurosawa's Westernness." *Ribbon of Dreams: Great Directors Series*. UCSD TV, 1995.

Chatterjee, Partha. *Nationalist Thought and the Colonial World: A Derivative Discourse*. Minneapolis: University of Minnesota Press, 1986.

Chiba Nobuo. *Eiga to Tanizaki*. Tokyo: Seiabo, 1989.

Chomsky, Noam. *Deterring Democracy*. New York: Verso, 1991.

———. *Keeping the Rabble in Line: Interviews with David Barsamian*. Monroe, Maine: Common Courage Press, 1994.

Chow, Rey. *Primitive Passions: Visuality, Sexuality, Ethnography, and Contemporary Chinese Cinema*. New York: Columbia University Press, 1995.

Davis, William Darrell. *Picturing Japaneseness: Monumental Style, National Identity, Japanese Film*. New York: Columbia University Press, 1996.

Deborg, Guy. *Society of the Spectacle*. Detroit: Black and Red, 1983.

Deleuze, Gilles. *Cinema 1: The Movement-Image*. Trans. Hugh Tomlinson and Barbara Habberjam. Minneapolis: University of Minnesota Press, 1995.

———. *Cinema 2: The Time-Image*. Trans. Hugh Tomlinson and Robert Galeta. Minneapolis: University of Minnesota Press, 1995.

De Man, Paul. " 'Conclusions': Walter Benjamin's 'The Task of the Translator.' " In *Resistance to Theory*. Manchester: Manchester University Press, 1986.

Derrida, Jacques. "Des Tours de Babel." In *Difference in Translation*. Ed. Joseph F. Graham. Ithaca, N.Y.: Cornell University Press, 1985.

———. *Given Time: Counterfeit Money*. Trans. Peggy Kamuf. Chicago: University of Chicago Press, 1992.

———. *Specters of Marx: The State of the Debt, the Work of Mourning, and the New International*. Trans. Peggy Kamuf. New York: Routledge, 1994.

Desser, David. *Eros Plus Massacre: An Introduction to the Japanese New Wave Cinema*. Bloomington: Indiana University Press, 1989.

Desser, David, and Arthur Nolletti Jr. *Reframing Japanese Cinema: Authorship, Genre, History*. Bloomington: Indiana University Press, 1992.

Dienst, Richard. *Still Time in Real Time: Theory After Television.* Durham, N.C.: Duke University Press, 1994.

Dower, John. *Embracing Defeat: Japan in the Wake of World War II.* New York: W. W. Norton, 1999.

Dworkin, Andrea. *Pornography: Men Possessing Women.* New York: Plume, 1989.

Edogawa Rampo. *Japanese Tales of Mystery and Imagination.* Trans. James B. Harris. Tokyo: Charles E. Tuttle, 1956.

Eisenstein, Sergei. *Film Form: Essays in Film Theory.* Trans. Jay Leyda. New York: Harcourt, Brace, and World, 1949.

Erikawa Tadashi. *Ogawa Shinsuke wo kataru.* Tokyo: Firumu Aato-sha, 1992.

Fabian, Johannes. *Time and the Other: How Anthropology Makes Its Object.* New York: Columbia University Press, 1983.

Foucault, Michel. *The Archeology of Knowledge.* Trans. A. M. Sheridan Smith. New York: Pantheon Books, 1972.

Gerow, A. A. "The Benshi's New Face: Defining Cinema in Taisho Japan." *Iconics* 3 (1994).

Grosz, Elizabeth. *Volatile Bodies: Toward a Corporeal Feminism.* Bloomington: Indiana University Press, 1994.

Hane, Mikiso. *Modern Japan.* Boulder, Colo.: Westview Press, 1986.

Hani Susumu. *Engi shinai shuyakutachi: Kiroku eiga sakusha no manako kara.* Tokyo: Chuo Koronsha, 1959.

Hansen, Miriam. *Babel and Babylon: Spectatorship in American Silent Film.* Cambridge, Mass.: Harvard University Press, 1991.

Hara Kazuo. *Gunron Yukiyukite shingun.* Ed. Matsuda Masao and Takahashi Taketomo. Tokyo: Togosha, 1988.

———. *Dokyumento: Yukyukite shingun.* Tokyo: Kyoyo Bunko, 1994.

———. *Zenshin shosetsu-ka: Mo hitotsu no Inoue Mitsuhara.* Tokyo: Kinema Junposha, 1994.

———. *Fumikoeru kyamera: Waga hoho, akushyon dokyumentari.* Tokyo: Firumu Aatosha, 1995.

Hardt, Michael, and Antonio Negri. *Empire.* Cambridge, Mass.: Harvard University Press, 2000.

Harootunian, Harry D. *Toward Restoration: The Growth of Political Consciousness in Tokugawa Japan.* Berkeley: University of California Press, 1970.

———. "The Benjamin Effect: Modernism, Repetition, and the Path to Different Cultural Imaginaries." In *Walter Benjamin and the Demands of History.* Ed. Michael P. Steinberg. Ithaca, N.Y.: Cornell University Press, 1996.

Harvey, David. *The Condition of Postmodernity.* Cambridge: Blackwell, 1989.

Hasumi Shigehiko. "Gaburieru bairu to eiga no rekishi." In *Hikaru no tanjyo: Ryumieru!* Tokyo: Asahi shinbun, 1995.

Haver, Bill. *The Body of This Death: Historicity and Sociality in the Time of* AIDS. Stanford, Calif.: Stanford University Press, 1996.

Heath, Steven. "The Question Oshima." *Wide Angle: A Film Quarterly of Theory, Criticism, and Practice* 2, no. 1 (1977): 48–57.

Hobsbawm, E. J. *Nations and Nationalism Since 1780: Programme, Myth, Reality.* Cambridge: Cambridge University Press, 1990.

Hobson, J. A. *Imperialism: A Study.* Ann Arbor: University of Michigan Press, 1965.

Inomata Katsuhito and Tayama Rikiyo. *Nihon eiga haiyu zenshu.* Tokyo: Kyouyou Bunko, 1977.

Iijima Tadashi. *Shin eigaron.* Tokyo: Seito Shorin, 1936.

———. *Eiga bunka no kenkyu.* Tokyo: Shinchosha, 1939.

———. *Nihon eiga-shi.* Tokyo: Hakusuisha, 1955.

Iijima Tadashi, ed. *Eiga no mikata.* Tokyo: Kawade Shincho, 1956.

Imamura Taihei. *Eiga geijutsu no keishiki.* Tokyo: Yumani Shobo, 1991.

———. *Eiga to bunka.* Tokyo: Yumani Shobo, 1991.

———. *Nihon eiga no honshitsu.* Tokyo: Yumani Shobo, 1991.

Ishizuka Kozaburo, ed. *Besuto obu kinema jumpo: 1967–1993.* Tokyo: Kinema Jumpo-sha, 1994.

———. *Besuto obu kinema jumpo: 1950–1966.* Tokyo: Kinema Jumpo-sha, 1994.

Ito Makoto. *Keizai riron to gendai shihon-shugi.* Tokyo: Iwanami Shoten, 1987.

———. *Sekai keizai no naka no nihon.* Tokyo: Shakai Hyoronsha, 1988.

———. *The World Economic Crisis and Japanese Capitalism.* London: Macmillan, 1990.

———. *Seikai keizai no tenkan wo kangaeru.* Tokyo: Jiji Tsushinsha, 1993.

———. *Nihon shihon-shugi no kiro.* Tokyo: Aoki Shoten, 1995.

Iwamoto Kenji, ed. *Nihon eiga to modanizumu: 1920–1930.* Tokyo: Riburo Poto, 1991.

Iwasaki Akira. *Eiga geijyutsu-shi.* Tokyo: Sekai-sha, 1930.

———. *Eiga to shihon-shugi.* Tokyo: Sekai-sha, 1931.

———. *Eiga no riron.* Tokyo: Iwanami Shoten, 1956.

———. *Eiga ni miru sengo sesoshi.* Tokyo: Shin Nihon Shuppansha, 1973.

———. *Nihon eiga shishi.* Tokyo: Asahi Shinbun, 1977.

Jameson, Fredric. *The Political Unconscious: Narrative as a Socially Symbolic Act.* Ithaca, N.Y.: Cornell University Press, 1981.

———. "Of Islands and Trenches: Neutralization and the Production of Utopian Discourse." Pp. 75–101 in *The Ideologies of Theory: Essays 1971–1986, Volume 2: The Syntax of History.* Minneapolis: University of Minnesota Press, 1989.

———. "Periodizing the 60s." Pp. 178–208 in *The Ideologies of Theory: Essays 1971–1986, Volume 2: The Syntax of History.* Minneapolis: University of Minnesota Press, 1989.

———. *Postmodernism, Or The Cultural Logic of Late Capitalism.* Durham: Duke University Press, 1991.

———. "Actually Existing Marxism." *Polygraph* 6–7 (1993): 170–95.

———. "Culture and Finance Capital." *Critical Inquiry* 24 (fall 1997): 246–65.

Johnson, Chalmers. *MITI and the Japanese Miracle.* Stanford, Calif.: Stanford University Press, 1982.

Kamei Fumio. *Tatakau eiga: Dokyumentarisuto no showa.* Tokyo: Iwanami Shincho, 1989.

Karatani Kojin. *Marukusu Sono Kanosei no Chusei.* Tokyo: Kodansha, 1978.

———. *Nihon kindai bungaku no Kigen* (The origins of modern Japanese literature). Trans. Brett deBarry. Durham, N.C.: Duke University Press, 1993.

———. *Nihon kindai bungaku no kigen.* Tokyo: Kodansha, 1980.

Kawin, Bruce F. *Mindscreen: Bergman, Godard, and First-Person Film.* Princeton, N.J.: Princeton University Press, 1978.

Kawabata Yasunari. "Asakusa kuranaiden." Pp. 7–157 in *Kawabata Yasunari Zenshu,* vol. 2. Tokyo: Shinchosha, 1981.

Kipnis, Laura. *Ecstasy Unlimited: On Sex, Capital, Gender, and Aesthetics.* Minneapolis: University of Minnesota Press, 1993.

———. *Bound and Gagged.* New York: Grove Press, 1996.

Kittay, Jeffrey, and Wlad Godzich. *The Emergence of Prose: An Essay in Prosaics.* Minneapolis: University of Minnesota Press, 1987.

Koga Futoshi, ed. *Hikaru no tanjyo: Ryumieru!* Tokyo: Asahi Shinbun-sha, 1995.

Komatsu Hiroshi. *Kigen no eiga.* Tokyo: Seidosha, 1991.

———. "Some Characteristics of Japanese Cinema Before World War I." In *Reframing Japanese Cinema: Authorship, Genre, History.* Ed. Aurthur Noletti, Jr., and David Desser. Bloomington: Indiana University Press, 1992.

———. "Shinematogurahu to nihon ni okeru shokieiga seisaku." In *Hikaru no tanjyo: Ryumieru!* Tokyo: Asahi Shinbun-sha, 1995.

Koschman, J. Victor. *Revolution and Subjectivity in Postwar Japan.* Chicago: University of Chicago Press, 1996.

Kurosawa Akira. *Something Like an Autobiography.* New York: Vintage, 1983.

Lehman, Peter. "Oshima: The Avant-Garde Artist Without an Avant-Garde Style." *Wide Angle* 9, no. 2 (1987): 18–31.

Lukács, Georg. *History and Class Consciousness: Studies in Marxist Dialectics.* Trans. Rodney Livingstone. Cambridge, Mass.: MIT Press, 1968.

Marx, Karl. *Grundrisse.* Trans. Martin Nicolaus. London: Penguin Books, 1973.

———. *Capital: A Critique of Political Economy,* vol. 1. Trans. Ben Fowkes. New York: Vantage Books, 1977.

———. *The 18th Brumaire of Louis Bonaparte.* New York: International Publishers, 1987.

MacKinnon, Catherine A. "Pornography, Civil Rights and Speech." In *Feminism Unmodified: Discourses on Life and Law.* Cambridge, Mass.: Harvard University Press, 1987.

Mandel, Ernest. *Late Capitalism.* London: Verso, 1978.

Nagasu Kazuji. *Kokusai jidai no nihon keizai.* Tokyo: Kawade Shobo, 1965.

Nakai Masakazu. *Bigaku Nyumon*, 3 vols. Tokyo: Bijutsu shuppen-sha, 1967.

Nakamura Takafusa. *Showa keizaishi*. Tokyo: Iwanami Shoten, 1986.

Walsh, Martin. "Godard and Me: Jean-Pierre Gorin Talks." *Take One* 5 (1985).

McClintock, Anne. *Imperial Leather: Race, Gender, and Sexuality in the Colonial Contest*. London: Routledge, 1995.

Miyoshi, Masao. *Off Center: Power and Culture Relations Between Japan and the United States*. Cambridge, Mass.: Harvard University Press, 1991.

Miyoshi, Masao, and Harry D. Harootunian, eds. *Japan in the World*. Durham, N.C.: Duke University Press, 1993.

Morris-Suzuki, Tessa. *A History of Japanese Economic Thought*. London: Routledge, 1989.

Morrison, Toni. *Playing in the Dark: Whiteness and the Literary Imagination*. Cambridge, Mass.: Harvard University Press, 1992.

Najita, Tetsuo. *Visions of Virtue in Tokugawa Japan*. Chicago: University of Chicago Press, 1987.

———. "Japan's Industrial Revolution." In *Japan in the World*. Ed. Masao Miyoshi and Harry D. Harootunian. Durham, N.C.: Duke University Press, 1993.

Naremore, James. *Acting in the Cinema*. Berkeley: University of California Press, 1988.

Nichols, Bill. *Representing Reality: Issues and Concepts in Documentary*. Minneapolis: University of Minnesota Press, 1991.

———. *Blurred Boundaries: Questions of Meaning in Contemporary Culture*. Bloomington: Indiana University Press, 1994.

Ogawa Shinsuke. *Ogawa Shinsuke: Eiga wo toru*. Ed. Yamane Tadashi. Tokyo: Firumu Aato-sha, 1994.

Osanai Kaoru. "Shingeki haiyu toshite no kabuki yakusha." In *Osanai Kaoru Zenshu*, vol. 6. Kyoto: Rinkawa Shincho, 1975.

Oshima Nagisa. *Cinema, Censorship, and the State*. Ed. Annette Michelson. Trans. Dawn Lawson. Cambridge, Mass.: MIT Press, 1992.

———. *Sengo 50 nen, Eiga 100 nen*. Tokyo: Fubaisha, 1995.

Penley, Constance. *The Future of an Illusion: Film, Feminism, Psychoanalysis*. Minneapolis: University of Minnesota Press, 1989.

Perelman, Michael. *Marx's Crises Theory: Scarcity, Labor, and Finance*. New York: Praeger, 1987.

Reich, Wilhelm. *The Mass Psychology of Fascism*. Trans. Vincent R. Carfagno. New York: Noonday Press, 1946.

Richie, Donald, and Joseph Anderson. *The Japanese Film*. Princeton, N.J.: Princeton University Press, 1959.

Rifkin, Benjamin. *Semiotics of Narration in Film and Prose Fiction*. New York: P. Lang, 1994.

Said, Edward. *Culture and Imperialism*. New York: Knopf, 1993.

Sano Shinichi. *Nihon eiga ha, Ima—Sukuriin no urgawa kara no.* Tokyo: TBS Puritanika, 1996.

Sassen, Saskia. *Globalization and Its Discontents: Essays on the New Mobility of Power and Money.* New York: New Press, 1998.

Sato Tadao. *Currents in Japanese Cinema.* Trans. Gregory Barrett. Tokyo: Kodansha, 1982.

———. "Nihon eiga no seiritsushita shidai." In *Nihon eiga no tanjyo,* vol. 1. Ed. Iwamura Shohei et al. Tokyo: Iwanami Shoten, 1985.

———. *Nihon eiga shi.* 4 vols. Tokyo: Iwanami Shoten, 1995.

———. *Nihon eiga: 300.* Tokyo: Asahi Bunko, 1995.

Sawa Nagayo and David E. Apter. *Against the State: Politics and Social Protest in Japan.* Cambridge, Mass.: Harvard University Press, 1984.

Schatz, Thomas. *The Genius of the System: Hollywood Filmmaking in the Studio Era.* New York: Pantheon Books, 1988.

Schwickart, Patrocino P. "Reading Ourselves: Toward a Feminist Theory of Reading." In *Gender and Reading: Essays on Readers, Texts, and Contexts.* Ed. Elizabeth A. Flynn and Patrochino P. Schwickart. Baltimore, Md.: Johns Hopkins University Press, 1986.

Sekine Hiroshi. *Abe Sada.* Trans. Christopher Drake. In *Contemporary Japanese Literature.* Ed. Howard Hibbett. New York: Alfred A. Knopf, 1986.

Shell, Marc. *Money, Language, and Thought: Literary and Philosophical Economies from the Medieval to the Modern Era.* Berkeley: University of California Press, 1982.

Shizume Masanori and Fuihata Setsuo. *Uno Kozo no sekai: Marukusu riron no gendaiteki saisei.* Tokyo: Arinaga, 1983.

Silverberg, Miriam. *Changing Song: The Marxist Manifestos of Nakano Shigeharu.* Princeton, N.J.: Princeton University Press, 1990.

———. "The Modern Girl as Militant." In *Recreating Japanese Women, 1600–1945.* Ed. Gail Lee Bernstein. Berkeley: University of California Press, 1991.

Sohn-Rethel, Alfred. *Intellectual and Manual Labour: A Critique of Epistemology.* London: Macmillan, 1978.

Spivak, Gayatri Chakravorty. "Scattered Speculations on the Question of Value." In *In Other Worlds: Essays in Cultural Politics.* New York: Routledge, 1988.

———. "Limits and Openings of Marx and Derrida." In *Outside in the Teaching Machine.* New York: Routledge, 1993.

Stam, Robert. *Subversive Pleasures: Bakhtin, Cultural Criticism, and Film.* Baltimore, Md.: Johns Hopkins University Press, 1989.

Sugimoto Susumu. *Nihon puroreteria eiga domei (Purokino) zenshi.* Tokyo: Aido Shupan, 1986.

Suzuki Tadashi. *The Way of Acting: The Theatre Writings of Tadashi Suzuki.* Trans. J. Thomas Rimer. New York: Theater Communications Group, 1986.

Tanaka Junichiro. *Nihon eiga hattatsu-shi.* 4 vols. Tokyo: Chuo Koron, 1957.

Tanzaki Junichiro. *Tanizaki Junichiro Zenshu*. 30 vols. Tokyo: Chuo Koron-sha, 1982–83.

Tsuji Kyohei, ed. *Eiga no tosho*. Tokyo: Yoshikaze Press, 1989.

Turim, Maureen. "Signs of Sexuality in Oshima's Tales of Passion." *Wide Angle* 9, no. 2 (1987): 32–46.

Uno Kozo. *Marukusu keizaigaku genriron no kenkyu*. Tokyo: Iwanami Shoten, 1959.

———. *Keizai genron*. Tokyo: Iwanami Shoten, 1964.

Virilio, Paul. *Speed and Politics: An Essay on Dromology*. Trans. Mark Polizzoti. New York: Semiotext(e), 1986.

———. *War and Cinema: The Logistics of Perception*. Trans. Patrick Camiller. London: Verso, 1992.

———. *The Vision Machine*. Bloomington: Indiana University Press, 1994.

White, Hayden. "The Modernist Event." In *The Persistence of History: Cinema, Television, and the Modern Event*. Ed. Vivian Sobchack. New York: Routledge, 1996.

Willemen, Paul. "The National." In *Looks and Frictions: Essays in Cultural Studies and Film Theory*. Bloomington: Indiana University Press, 1994.

Williams, Linda. *Hard Core: Power, Pleasure, and the "Frenzy of the Visible."* Berkeley: University of California Press, 1989.

Yoneyama, Lisa. *Hiroshima Traces: Time, Space, and the Dialectics of Memory*. Berkeley: University of California Press, 1999.

Yoshida Chieo. *Mo hitotsu no eiga-shi: Katsuben no jidai*. Tokyo: Jiji Tsushin-sha, 1978.

Yoshihara Kunio. *Japanese Economic Development*. Oxford: Oxford University Press, 1994.

Yoshimoto, Mitsuhiro. "Logic of Sentiment: The Postwar Japanese Cinema and the Question of Modernity." Ph. D. diss., University of California, San Diego, 1993.

Yoshimoto Takaaki. *Jyokyo toshite no eizo: Kodo shinhonshugi shita no terebi*. Tokyo: Kawade Bunko, 1995.

Žižek, Slavoj. *The Sublime Object of Ideology*. London: Verso, 1989.

———. *Looking Awry: An Introduction to Jacques Lacan Through Popular Culture*. Cambridge, Mass.: MIT Press, 1993.

index

Eric Cazdyn is Assistant Professor of East
Asian Studies, Comparative Literature, and
Cinema Studies at the University of Toronto.

Library of Congress Cataloging-in-Publication Data
Cazdyn, Eric M.
The flash of capital : film and geopolitics in Japan /
by Eric Cazdyn.
p. cm. — (Asia-Pacific)
Includes bibliographical references and index.
ISBN 0-8223-2912-3 (alk. paper)
ISBN 0-8223-2939-5 (pbk. : alk. paper)
1. Motion pictures—Japan—History. 2. Motion
picture industry—Japan—History. 3. Motion picture
industry—Economic aspects—Japan. I. Title. II. Series.
PN1993.5.J3 C39- 2002- /791.43'0952—dc21   2002005423